A New History of British Documentary

A New History of British Documentary

James Chapman
University of Leicester, UK

First published 2015 by
PALGRAVE MACMILLAN

Palgrave Macmillan in the UK is an imprint of Macmillan Publishers Limited, registered in England, company number 785998, of Houndmills, Basingstoke, Hampshire RG21 6XS.

Palgrave Macmillan in the US is a division of St Martin's Press LLC, 175 Fifth Avenue, New York, NY 10010.

Palgrave Macmillan is the global academic imprint of the above companies and has companies and representatives throughout the world.

Palgrave® and Macmillan® are registered trademarks in the United States, the United Kingdom, Europe and other countries.

ISBN 978–0–230–39286–1

This book is printed on paper suitable for recycling and made from fully managed and sustained forest sources. Logging, pulping and manufacturing processes are expected to conform to the environmental regulations of the country of origin.

A catalogue record for this book is available from the British Library.

Library of Congress Cataloging-in-Publication Data
Chapman, James, 1968–
    A new history of British documentary / James Chapman.
        pages   cm
    Includes bibliographical references.
    ISBN 978–0–230–39286–1 (hardback)
    1. Documentary films—Great Britain—History and criticism.
    2. Documentary television programs—Great Britain—History and criticism. I. Title.
    PN1995.9.D6C4345 2015
    070.1′8—dc23   2014037997

In memory of Stuart Hall

Contents

Preface

Why do we need another history of British documentary? This is, after all, a subject on which there is already an extensive critical and historical literature: documentary can hardly claim to be a marginalized or neglected component of British cinema history (even if it continues to be a relatively marginal mode of film practice). In fact, the present book has been conceived to fill a gap in the existing historiography. It was while reviewing the extant literature on the British documentary movement of the 1930s for an undergraduate survey module on British cinema that I realized there was room for a new history of the film-making tradition that was once famously described as 'Britain's outstanding contribution to the film'. It struck me that there was a need for a book that offered more detail than the essay-length overviews in the standard text books on British cinema such as Charles Barr's *All Our Yesterdays* (1986) and Robert Murphy's *The British Cinema Book* (1997) but at the same time was broader in scope than research monographs such as Paul Swann's *The British Documentary Film Movement, 1926–1946* (1989) and Ian Aitken's *Film and Reform: John Grierson and the Documentary Film Movement* (1990). *A New History of British Documentary* is perhaps best described as a partially researched text book in the sense that it combines a synthesis of existing work on the subject with some original primary-source research.

So what is 'new' about *A New History of British Documentary*? This book differs from previous histories in three main ways. First it extends beyond the films produced under the aegis of the documentary 'movement' in the 1930s. All accounts of British documentary have to contend with the figure of John Grierson, who bestrides the subject like a colossus. Grierson is so widely regarded as the 'father' of British documentary that it seems redundant to attempt even to nuance let alone challenge this status. I do not deny Grierson's importance to the history of documentary film in Britain. But one of the things I want to show is that documentary did not begin and end with Grierson. Hence, Chapter 1 explores the history of pre-Griersonian documentary, while later chapters map the contours of documentary through the post-war decades when Grierson's presence, though still felt, was less central than it had been during the 1930s. The standard histories of British documentary have tended to see the period after the Second World War as a narrative of decline during which documentary lost something of its progressive social purpose. In contrast, I argue that documentary diversified into new forms and practices as it adapted to changing historical contexts.

The second 'new' feature of this book is that I have looked at both film and television documentary. Hitherto these have usually been treated separately and as being distinct from one another. This was brought home to me forcefully a few years ago when a research grant application by a colleague to examine the representation of the National Health Service in British film and television was turned down on the grounds 'that it was unusual for studies to look at both cinema and television, and as such the project was too broad'! This view reflects a wider intellectual division between the disciplines of film studies and television studies: the latter in particular often tends to see itself as a distinct subject in its own right with its own theoretical and methodological perspectives rather than as an offshoot of film studies. Yet this ignores the significant crossovers between cinema and television at both institutional and formal levels. For example, there is a historical lineage of documentary reconstructions extending from British Instructional Films in the 1920s (*Ypres*, *The Battles of the Coronel and Falkland Islands*) via the work of the GPO and Crown Film Units (*North Sea*, *Fires Were Started*) to television drama documentaries such as *Hillsborough* and *Bloody Sunday*.

The third defining feature of the book is that it is not a history of documentary *films* but a history of documentary *film* (and ditto television). It explores the history of documentary practice in the film and television industries but does not aim to cover every documentary of note. It is therefore a history sketched in broad strokes rather than through close analysis of individual texts. Of course the important films are discussed: it would be perverse to write a history of British documentary that did not include such landmarks as *Battle of the Somme*, *Drifters*, *The Song of Ceylon*, *Night Mail*, *Fires Were Started*, *Desert Victory*, *We Are the Lambeth Boys*, *Every Day Except Christmas*, *Cathy Come Home*, *The War Game*, *The World at War* and *Handsworth Songs*. However, it is necessary to range beyond the established canon if we are to arrive at a better understanding of the place of documentary in British film and television history. And this requires looking at documentary in the round rather than focusing just on its most lauded achievements. One of the consequences of this is that I have focused more on the modes and styles of documentary than on individual film-makers. In particular, readers may feel that Humphrey Jennings does not receive his fair due (so do I!) – though at least there is an extensive critical literature on Jennings to remedy this. But there are many other documentarists worthy of attention too. The work of post-war documentarists has yet to be afforded its place in the sun, and it is my contention that the films of Paul Dickson, Michael Grigsby and John Krish, to name just three, are as culturally and aesthetically interesting as those of the mainstays of the British documentary movement such as Paul Rotha, Basil Wright and Harry Watt. To this extent it is to be hoped that *A New History of British Documentary* will not be the last word on the subject.

Acknowledgements

This book could not have been written without access to primary source materials held in a range of archives and libraries. In no particular order I would like to record my thanks to the staff of the National Archives at Kew, the British Film Institute Library in London (especially Jonny Davies of the Special Collections Unit), the British Postal Museum and Archive, the BBC Written Archives Centre at Caversham, Reading, and the John Grierson Archive at the University of Stirling. Many colleagues have provided me either with specific references or with sage advice: particular thanks are due to Tony Aldgate, Scott Anthony, Guy Barefoot, Alan Burton, Mark Connelly, Krista Cowman, Jo Fox, Luke McKernan, Julian Petley and Peter Waymark. I am grateful to Patrick Russell for inviting me to contribute short essays to the BFI's DVD sets *Land of Promise* and *If War Should Come*, which reignited my interest in British documentary after several years of writing about secret agents and Time Lords.

The specific idea for this book emerged over a pasta lunch with Sally Dux at Sio Grilli on Goodge Street, where we struggled to find a suitable piece of critical writing on documentary to include in the student reading pack for our module on British cinema history. The existing options seemed either too brief or too detailed for teaching purposes. It was Sally who suggested I would have to write one myself! Felicity Plester at Palgrave Macmillan has been a supportive and patient commissioning editor. Last, though by no means least, it was while preparing this book that I met Llewella Burton, who has changed my life for the better in so many ways, not least by reminding me occasionally that there is more to life than 'The Book'!

A New History of British Documentary is dedicated to the late Professor Stuart Hall (1932–2014), who sadly passed away while I was writing it. There have been many tributes to Stuart Hall's immense contribution to British academia by friends and colleagues who knew him better than I. But the dedication seems appropriate for two reasons. One is his personal interest in documentary – an interest that culminated in John Akomfrah's brilliant tribute film *The Stuart Hall Project* that provides the conclusion to this book. The other is that he was a member of the interview panel that appointed me to my first academic post at The Open

University in 1996. I remember one of the questions he asked me concerned the trajectory of documentary from the Second World War to post-war television. I am not sure that he would have agreed with some of the arguments in this book – he would probably have regarded it as under-theorized – but I like to think that he would have appreciated the dedication.

Abbreviations

ACTT	Association of Cinema and Television Technicians
AFPU	Army Film and Photographic Unit
ATV	Associated Television
BBC	British Broadcasting Corporation
BBFC	British Board of Film Censors
BFI	British Film Institute
BIF	British International Films
BPMA	British Postal Museum and Archive
BTF	British Transport Films
CEA	Cinematograph Exhibitors' Association
COI	Central Office of Information
CUFA	Conservative and Unionist Film Association
EMB	Empire Marketing Board
GPO	General Post Office
HBO	Home Box Office
ICI	Imperial Chemical Industries
IWM	Imperial War Museum
MGM	Metro-Goldwyn-Mayer
MOI	Ministry of Information
NCB	National Coal Board
STV	Scottish Television
TNA	The National Archives

Introduction
Critical and Historical Perspectives on British Documentary

> There is no novelty today in the claim that documentary is the distinctively British contribution to cinema.
>
> Forsyth Hardy[1]

It has become commonplace to preface accounts of the British documentary film movement with a variation of the idea – most succinctly expressed in the 1947 Arts Enquiry survey *The Factual Film* – that 'documentary is Britain's outstanding contribution to the film'.[2] Indeed, as Forsyth Hardy's observation in the celebratory volume *Twenty Years of British Film*, also published in 1947, makes clear, the claim had by then already become something of a cliché. In his 1936 book *Documentary Film*, for example, the documentarist and critic Paul Rotha wrote that documentary was 'this country's most important contribution to the cinema as a whole'.[3] Of course it is only to be expected that documentary film-makers themselves would make such claims, but this view was also shared by the first historians of British cinema who placed documentary at the forefront of a critical project to create a distinctively national film culture. Consider, for example, Roger Manvell, writing during British cinema's 'golden age' of the Second World War: 'The story of British cinema, apart from documentary, has been a tragic one of opportunities squandered and pioneers unrecognised.'[4] Or Richard Griffith, who in his contribution to a new edition of Paul Rotha's seminal *The Film Till Now* in 1949, claimed that 'documentary was the most important, and almost the only, British contribution to world cinema until the war years. All that has since appeared and which has had any substance, has been guided by its example and nourished by its experience.'[5] So pervasive did this view become that even a commercial producer such as Michael Balcon – whose own influence on the history of British cinema should not be undervalued – nevertheless wrote in his memoir in 1969: 'The documentary movement, as symbolised by the Crown Film Unit, was in my view the greatest single influence on British film production and more than anything else helped to establish a national style.'[6]

The importance of documentary in British cinema has become so deep-rooted in the critical and historical discourses of that cinema that it has to be noted (and therefore by doing so reasserted) at the beginning of a project entitled *A New History of British Documentary* – if only as a preface to an interrogation of why this has become such a prevalent view. It should be pointed out that it is not only British critics who have championed British documentary. The influential postwar French film critic André Bazin, for example, who saw the Italian neo-realist cinema of the late 1940s as the apotheosis of the tendency towards realism in film aesthetics, also acknowledged the influence of the British documentary school: 'Already we were beginning to look toward England [sic] whose recent cinematic rebirth is likewise, in part, the fruit of realism: that of the school of documentarists who, before the war, had gone deeply into the resources offered by social and technical realities.'[7] While documentary was not a British invention – Robert Flaherty's *Nanook of the North* (1922), Walter Ruttmann's *Berlin: Symphony of a City* (1927) and Esfir Shub's *The Fall of the Romanov Dynasty* (1927) all preceded John Grierson's *Drifters* (1929), the film that is generally regarded as marking the starting point of the British documentary movement – it was in Britain that documentary first became institutionalized as a distinct mode of film practice. Ephraim Katz, for example, writes in *The Macmillan International Film Encyclopedia* that it 'was in England during the 30s that the documentary acquired the added dimension of social purpose'.[8] And the US film historians Kristin Thompson and David Bordwell make the point that it was in Britain that 'a major national filmmaking body' was established in the form of a government-sponsored production agency (the EMB Film Unit), while also highlighting that the critical preference for documentary 'focused a great deal of attention on this "realist" streak of British cinema, often to the exclusion of other, more entertainment-oriented filmmaking there'.[9]

The idea of documentary as a realist alternative to commercial entertainment cinema is a common one in film history. It can be traced to the origins of the documentary movement itself. In his 1932 article 'First Principles of Documentary' – the closest thing to a manifesto for the movement – John Grierson wrote: 'We believe that the cinema's capacity for getting around, for observing and selecting from life itself, can be exploited in a new and vital art form. The studio films largely ignore this possibility of opening up the screen on the real world.'[10] Grierson – widely regarded as the 'father' of the British documentary movement and certainly its most influential theorist – drew a distinction between documentary and other forms of non-fiction film such as newsreels and travelogues. In fact, the French term *documentaire* was originally applied to travelogues – a popular early film genre whose appeal arose from showing images of exotic places in the era before the emergence of mass tourism. Grierson, however, regarded travelogues as among the 'lower categories' of non-fiction film, while he dismissed the newsreels as 'just a speedy snip-snap of some utterly unimportant ceremony'.[11] He maintained that it was only when film amounted to more than a visual record of places or people that 'one begins to wander into the world of documentary proper, into the only world in which documentary can hope to achieve the ordinary virtues of an art. Here we pass from the plain (or fancy) descriptions of natural material, to arrangements, rear-rangements, and creative shapings of it'.[12] This seems to have been the origin of the term widely attributed to Grierson: 'the creative treatment of actuality'.[13]

So much ink has been spilled in defining and contesting the meaning of 'the creative treatment of actuality' that it becomes redundant to attempt to unpack the phrase any further. What has sometimes been overlooked, however, is that Grierson's idea of documentary film as being more than just a visual record was entirely consistent with the prevailing theories of film as an art form at the time. The formative tradition of film aesthetics – associated with early theorists such as the German Rudolf Arnheim and the Hungarian Béla Belâzs, and with the Soviet school of montage film-makers such as Sergei Eisenstein and Vsevolod Pudovkin – maintained that to be regarded as a creative art form, film must go beyond the photographic representation of external reality and explore the formal properties of the medium such as cinematography and editing. Arnheim, for example, argued that the historical development of film style was driven by the discovery of its expressive possibilities: 'What had hitherto been merely the urge to record certain actual events, now became the aim to represent objects by special means exclusive to film ... Art begins where mechanical reproduction leaves off, where the conditions of representation serve in some way to mould the object.'[14]

So how can we account for the importance attached to documentary in the critical and historical discourses of British cinema? There are several explanations, all to some extent rooted in ideological and aesthetic assumptions about what cinema is and should be. On one level the preference for documentary may be understood in the context of a wider critical preference in twentieth-century Britain for realism in the arts and in media as a whole that also extends to painting, photography, literature, theatre and television.[15] This preference may be seen as a legacy of the influential nineteenth-century art critic John Ruskin or (to stretch the point somewhat) as a throwback to the philosophical tradition of Plato that 'art imitates life'. In British film and television history, the dominant style has been what Andrew Higson has termed the 'documentary-realist tradition' – a mode of representation that also includes feature films such as *Love on the Dole* (1940), *Saturday Night and Sunday Morning* (1960) and other examples of British 'new wave' cinema, *Kes* (1969) and *My Beautiful Laundrette* (1985), television documentary dramas such as *Cathy Come Home* (1966) and *Boys from the Blackstuff* (1982), and even soap operas such as *Coronation Street* and *EastEnders*.[16]

Another reason for the special status of documentary is to be found in its credentials as a progressive element within film culture. This was part of the documentary project from the outset. Grierson believed that documentary was characterized by its 'progressive social intention' and represented 'a new idea for public education: its underlying concept that the world was in a phase of drastic change affecting every manner of thought and practice, and the public comprehension of the nature of that change vital'.[17] The British documentary film took shape within a discourse of public education and enlightenment that was very strongly influenced by Social Democratic ideals. While the Griersonian documentary idea was formed within the particular historical and ideological contexts of the interwar period, the idea that documentary is defined as much by its social purpose as by its content or form has continued to inform documentary theory and practice. John Caughie argues that the progressive impulse can be seen on television in documentary dramas such as *Cathy Come Home*: 'Documentary drama seems to me to have occupied a progressive role within television insofar as it has introduced into the discourses of television a repressed political, social discourse which may contribute to an audience's political formation, and may increase its scepticism of the other representations which television offers.'[18]

A further context for the critical prestige of documentary may be found in the nature of British film culture itself. For a long time British cinema was an unfashionable subject that did not inspire much critical attention. It seemed resistant to the dominant approaches to film analysis – *auteur* criticism and genre criticism – and was deemed, in Peter

Wollen's words, to be 'utterly amorphous, unclassified, unperceived'.[19] On the one hand British cinema was held to lack the psychological depth and formal innovation of European – especially French and Italian – cinema; but on the other hand it also lacked the zest and uninhibited popular appeal of American cinema, with its mythically rich genres such as the western and the musical. British cinema's critical status as betwixt and between was perhaps best summed up by Lindsay Anderson – himself a future documentary film-maker with the Free Cinema movement of the 1950s – when he observed that 'the British cinema seems to hover between the opposite poles of France and Hollywood. Our directors and producers never or rarely have the courage to tackle, in an adult manner, the completely adult subject: yet they lack the flair for popular showmanship that is characteristic of the American cinema.'[20]

This was the critical and intellectual context in which documentary was claimed as 'Britain's outstanding contribution to the film'. The documentary film represented one means through which British cinema could hold its own against the best of other European and world cinemas. The idea that documentary represents the 'national style' of British cinema positions it alongside other nationally specific movements such as German Expressionism, Soviet montage cinema, Italian neo-realism and the French *nouvelle vague*. In a seminal paper of 1969, for example, Alan Lovell responded to the claim that Britain had no tradition of art cinema to call its own by asserting the case for documentary:

> It seems to me that British documentary is our Art cinema, our equivalent of German Expressionism or French Surrealism. It is only because of the narrowly specific connotations that the term 'Art cinema' has come to have in this country in the past ten years or so that it isn't easy for us to see this ... From the Soviet silent cinema, through the British documentary movement to Italian Neo-realism, the question of documentary has been at the heart of discussion about the nature of cinema.[21]

Art cinema has conventionally been understood as an *auteur* cinema associated with highly individualistic directors such as Antonioni, Bergman, Buñuel, Fellini, Godard and Pasolini. In Britain it has been associated with directors such as Lindsay Anderson, Derek Jarman and Peter Greenaway whose work sits outside the commercial mainstream. Yet documentary also encourages formal innovation and positions itself as an alternative mode of film practice.

The fact that documentary has been so central to the critical and historical discourses of British cinema (and television) raises the legitimate question of whether there is really any need for another book on the subject. *A New History of British Documentary* arises from my conviction that the extant critical and historical literature is all to some degree inadequate. This may seem a contentious claim given that there have already been many critical studies of British documentary and several excellent monographs on the subject. However, much of the existing work has focused on the period between the late 1920s and the end of the Second World War, which is seen as marking the apotheosis of the British documentary movement. This rather narrow focus has tended to obscure the fact that there already existed a tradition of non-fiction film-making in Britain before the production of *Drifters* in 1929. It has also had the effect of privileging Grierson and his 'Documentary Boys', as they were known, at the expense of a later generation of film and television documentarists active after the Second World War whose work does not always fit easily into the Griersonian tradition. In fact the documentary sector of the British film industry expanded significantly in the post-war period and a much larger volume of documentary films was produced than during the 1930s. Yet these films – and the concurrent emergence of television documentary – have by and large been marginalized by the focus of most histories on the formative period of documentary in the 1930s. Another characteristic of the existing historiography is the emergence of a narrow canon of documentary films that recurs in all accounts: *Drifters, Industrial Britain, The Song of Ceylon, Coal Face, Housing Problems, Night Mail, North Sea* and *Spare Time*.

There have been several waves of criticism and scholarship focusing on the British documentary movement. The earliest histories of documentary were written by members of the movement itself – Paul Rotha's *Documentary Film* was the first in 1936 – and established a critical orthodoxy that remained largely unchallenged for several generations. The first point of critical mass came in the mid-1940s when the publication of *The Factual Film* and an anthology of Grierson's essays edited by his friend Forsyth Hardy (1946) offered the first historical perspectives on British documentary. *The Factual Film* was written by members of the documentary movement and was to all intents and purposes an official history. It was frankly propagandist in its intent: it lauded the achievements of the documentary movement during the Second World War and included a manifesto for its future direction, which included expanding the official apparatus for the production and distribution of documentary films developed during the war. *Grierson on Documentary* is valuable as the nearest thing to a book by Grierson himself: he was a prolific writer but most of his work appeared as essays and he never produced a book-length synthesis of his own thoughts on documentary. Hardy's volume demonstrates how Grierson's theory of documentary was never set in stone but developed over time, just as he believed that documentary itself should evolve as it adapted to changing ideological contexts. The second point of critical mass was in the 1970s – exemplified by Paul Rotha's *Documentary Diary* (1973), Hardy's biography of Grierson (1979) and by the interviews collected by Elizabeth Sussex in *The Rise and Fall of British Documentary* (1975) – which have the advantage of some historical distance but still present the history of the documentary movement in broadly (auto)biographical terms.[22]

The narrative that emerges from these accounts is consistent. It privileges Grierson's role as the intellectual driving force behind the emergence of the documentary movement in the 1930s and focuses on the small group of film-makers who clustered around Grierson first under the aegis of the Empire Marketing Board (EMB) and later at the General Post Office (GPO). The documentarists saw themselves as a separate group from the rest of the British film industry – including both the commercial feature film studios and the newsreels – and self-identified as a movement with common goals and a shared purpose. The overwhelming impression of the documentary movement is a sense of belonging to a progressive project for a socially purposeful cinema committed to the representation of real people and their lives. Many documentarists liked to cast themselves as amateurs learning the craft of film-making through a process of trial and error. Harry Watt, for example, who began his career at the EMB Film Unit in the early 1930s, characterized himself and his colleagues as 'just a bunch of enthusiastic kids, accepting the basic theme of the dignity of man from our brilliant but erratic boss, learning our job by trial and error, bubbling with ideas but making thousands of mistakes, cheerfully exploiting ourselves and each other in the absolute belief that what we did or were going to do was worthwhile'.[23]

The emergence of film studies as an academic discipline from the 1970s prompted a second wave of documentary criticism that adopted a more scholarly perspective – without, however, significantly challenging or extending the established canon. Alan Lovell and Jim Hillier's *Studies in Documentary* (1972) comprises three essays: on the documentary films of the 1930s, the films of Humphrey Jennings, and the Free Cinema movement of the 1950s. Lovell and Hillier explore the relationship between critical writing on documentary film and documentary practice: their analysis of films is largely from the perspective of film form and aesthetics. They conclude that: '[the] importance of the documentary movement lies, not in the quality of individual films, but in the impact it had in general on the British cinema'.[24] *Studies in Documentary* was written at a time when there was little academic interest in British cinema and it was concerned in part with the rehabilitation of 'the unknown cinema'. In contrast, Andrew Tudor in *Theories of Film* (1974) places Grierson's work in the context of the development of film theory, seeing it as a link between the formalism of Sergei Eisenstein and the realist aesthetics championed by André Bazin and Siegfried Kracauer. Tudor notes Grierson's 'practical social interest in film theory' in preference to purely aesthetic concerns, and explores the implications of this for understanding the medium as a whole. It is, as Tudor describes it, a 'context-dominant' film theory in so far as '*aesthetic* judgements about film are not simply conditioned by contextual assumptions about the social and psychological role of cinema, they are dominated' [*sic*].[25]

The idea of documentary as Britain's art cinema has also informed the evaluation of British documentary's one undisputed *auteur*. Lindsay Anderson once famously described Humphrey Jennings as 'the only real poet the British cinema has yet produced'.[26] It is an accolade that has been repeated in various forms in studies of the director and British documentary.[27] Yet in many respects Jennings is a problematic figure in British film history. He worked within the documentary movement but was hardly representative of it: indeed his 'poetic' style was regarded as an aberration from what documentary should be by some of the movement's purists. He was regarded as something of an aesthete and an intellectual – not a description that could be applied to many of his colleagues at the GPO and Crown Film Units – and dabbled in painting and poetry as well as film-making. And while he was interested in film as a form of social observation, exemplified by his association with Mass-Observation, Jennings also had an affinity with the Surrealist movement, which distanced him from the orthodox British realist discourse. Jennings's reputation rests on a relatively small body of films made during and immediately after the Second World War, though at least three of those – *Listen to Britain*, *Fires Were Started* and *A Diary for Timothy* – are often regarded as among the finest films of any type ever produced in Britain. These films – and others such as *Words for Battle*, *The Silent Village*, *The True Story of Lili Marlene* and his final film *Family Portrait* from 1950 – have been analysed in forensic detail for their complex formal properties and their imaginative meditations around the theme of British national identity. And Jennings, whom John Grierson once described rather grudgingly as 'a minor poet', has become one of the most admired of all British film-makers.[28]

A third wave of documentary scholarship since the late 1980s has moved beyond the tradition of aesthetic and formal criticism to examine the historical contexts of documentary film-making. The 'historical turn' in film studies that privileges primary sources and archival research has shed significant new light on the institutional and social conditions under which documentary films have been produced. Paul Swann's monograph *The British Documentary Film Movement, 1926–1946* (1989) is an institutional history of documentary that draws upon official records held by the Public Records Office (now known as the National Archives) to chronicle the relationship between the documentary movement and the state. Three points emerge from this research: the role (largely absent from previous accounts) of enlightened civil servants in the origins and early history of the documentary movement; the emergence of significant ideological differences within the movement by the mid-1930s; and the suggestion that for all the critical prestige attached to documentary, the films themselves were generally not widely distributed or even popular with audiences. Swann concludes that his book: 'is not intended to devalue the achievements of the British documentary movement in any way, but rather, not to succumb to the hyperbole often attached to statements made by members of the movement about the impact of their work or about the extent to which what they were doing ran counter to the dominant ideology of the time'.[29]

Ian Aitken has criticized Swann for laying too much emphasis on official records and suggests that his 'interpretation of the documentary film movement explains the evidence unsatisfactorily ... The inevitable consequence of his approach was to switch the focus of attention from the originators of the documentary movement, Grierson and the film-makers, to largely anonymous middle ranking government officials'.[30] Aitken's own monograph, *Film and Reform* (1990), also analyses primary sources but focuses instead on the materials held by the John Grierson Archive at the University of Stirling and explores both the intellectual and cultural contexts in which Grierson's theory of documentary was formed. In particular, Aitken examines the influence of Grierson's Scottish upbringing on his philosophical idealism and his academic studies in the United States in the 1920s, where he encountered the emerging subject of mass communications and was influenced by theorists such as Walter Lippmann. It is an important study, though Aitken has in turn been criticized for not distancing himself sufficiently from the Griersonian perspective.[31] And Aitken's conclusion 'that Grierson

and the documentary movement were a progressive and reformist phenomenon, in relation to the dominant Conservatism of the inter-war
period' ultimately endorses the orthodox view of the documentary
movement and its place in British film culture.[32]

Of course, documentary has not been without its detractors. One
of the first critics to react against the orthodoxy of the documentary
movement's significance in British cinema was – characteristically –
Raymond Durgnat. Durgnat pooh-poohed documentary's claims to represent a progressive realist aesthetic and dismissed the films of the
1930s as nothing more than 'romantic tone poems about the beauty
of work and industry, strenuously conformist to their "establishment"
sponsors (usually the GPO or the Empire Marketing Board)'. He was
dismissive of their social import and averred that 'it's for their purely
aesthetic qualities that only the very best documentaries will abide'.[33]
This marked the emergence of an ideological critique of documentary
that questioned the movement's progressive credentials. Stuart Hood,
for example, argued that Griersonian documentary was inhibited by its
institutional patronage and was therefore rather less progressive than
its advocates maintained. Hence even 'a beautiful and interesting film'
such as *The Song of Ceylon* nevertheless reveals its ideological limitations
as it 'totally avoids the question of colonial labour and the economic
exploitation of the colonies – which is not surprising, since it was
produced by the GPO Film Unit in conjunction with the Ceylon Tea
Propaganda Board'. *Housing Problems*, which exposed the conditions of
London's working-class slums, was similarly compromised as it 'was
made for the gas industry, which was concerned that the London City
Council was beginning to instal electric heating in council flats'.[34] And
Robert Colls and Philip Dodd have argued that a film such as *Housing
Problems* – generally cited as the foremost example of the progressive
social purpose of documentary in the 1930s – did not represent the
authentic 'voice' of its working-class subjects but rather was addressed
to the conscience of the middle classes: 'What the film shows is that
these people need our help and that we have nothing to fear if we provide them with better homes.'[35] In these assessments the documentary
movement is understood as a vehicle for the promotion of consensus
politics: its impulse was conservative in so far as – despite the left-wing
leanings of many documentarists themselves – the movement as a whole
was supportive of the social and political status quo.

A particular aspect of this critique was to see the documentarists
themselves as constrained by their own background and outlook. The
first generation of documentarists in the 1930s 'were overwhelmingly

middle-class and mostly graduates of Oxford or Cambridge'.[36] The same criticism has also been directed against the Free Cinema documentarists of the 1950s.[37] The fact that documentary has also been a largely male preserve has also opened up the movement to critique from a feminist perspective. Kathryn and Philip Dodd have argued that the documentary movement of the 1930s can be seen as an instrument for the promotion of a hegemonic construct of masculinity. In constructing heroic images of working-class manliness in films such as *Industrial Britain* and *Coal Face* the documentarists marginalized working-class women: even in those films where women have a 'voice' (such as *Housing Problems*) femininity was associated with the home rather than the workplace. The Dodds argue that the marginalization of women in documentary films 'was not just an unfortunate omission' but that it 'should be seen as an offensive against the feminization of Englishness in the 1930s, a process which was part of the crisis of dominant manly Englishness'.[38] One does not have to be a feminist to recognize that women are often a marginal presence in the documentary films of the 1930s, even though several women (for example Ruby Grierson and Evelyn Spice) directed documentaries. However, the argument that the films were a backlash against the 'feminization' of national identity seems flimsy in the extreme.

The reputation of documentary also suffered as historians of British cinema began to look anew at the commercial feature film – whose absence from early histories was largely a consequence of the prevailing legacy of documentary – and to explore its place in popular film culture. The emphasis here is not on the ideological limitations of documentary (real or perceived) but rather on its marginal status in the film industry as a whole. Jeffrey Richards and Anthony Aldgate have remarked upon the 'extravagant mythology [that] has grown up around the British documentary movement, which is often depicted, on the basis of a handful of genuinely moving films like *Housing Problems*, as the sole repository of realism in a predominantly conservative industry'. They point out that all the evidence suggests that the public preferred feature films over documentaries and conclude: 'The real value of the documentary movement of the 1930s was to act as a training ground for those directors who went into feature film-making during the war and brought a new patina of realism to fictional films. The idea that documentaries embodied a purer, higher truth is a dangerous fallacy.'[39]

The documentary movement's claim to represent the progressive or even radical wing of British film culture was also challenged by the historical rediscovery of other alternative and oppositional film-making practices that had long been overlooked by critics but which seemed in hindsight to demonstrate a more politically engaged outlook than the mainstream of the documentary movement. Bert Hogenkamp's book *Deadly Parallels* (1986) documents the history of political film-making in the 1930s by organizations such as the Progressive Film Institute and the Workers' Film and Photographic League, which aligned themselves with the organized labour movement rather than with the state or commercial sponsorship. Hogenkamp argues that these groups 'defined themselves not so much by their independence from commercial film production, distribution and exhibition, as rather by their dependence – voluntary, self-imposed – on the labour movement'.[40] While Hogenkamp's work is characterized by its reliance on archival and primary sources rather than by Marxist dogma, a more theorized perspective informs the collection *Traditions of Independence* (1980), in which Claire Johnston identifies these films as 'an area of social practice of cinema in the Thirties which has been repressed by orthodox film histories of the "documentary movement" of the period'.[41] A characteristic of the work reclaiming these marginalized ('repressed' is surely too strong a term) films is to relate them to contemporary oppositional film-making practices in the 1970s and 1980s, exemplified by groups such as Cinema Action, Amber Films and the Berwick Street Collective, which operated outside the institutional and economic structures of the British film industry. It is important to recognize the existence of a tradition of alternative documentary practice that in its political and formal articulations was indeed more radical than the mainstream of the documentary movement. At the same time, however, it must be noted that these films were even more marginal in British film culture than documentary: their exhibition was limited to film clubs and societies, and there is no evidence to suggest that they had any influence outside the labour movement.

The most sustained critique of the Griersonian documentary tradition has come from Brian Winston – a one-time television documentarist turned academic – whose book *Claiming the Real* (1995) is not so much a history of documentary theory and practice than an extended discursive rumination on the subject. Winston sets himself the task of 'trying to understand what the "First Principles of Documentary" actually were; where they came from; how they were legitimated; how these legitimations changed through time; and what, from time to time, their practical effects were, on the screen as well as politically and ethically'.[42] Winston is sympathetic towards the documentary project but finds that its achievements usually fall short of its ambitions. He is particularly critical of what he sees as documentary's early retreat from its original social purpose. He interrogates Grierson's mantra of 'the creative treatment of actuality' and concludes that it 'can now be seen as being at best naive and at worst a mark of duplicity'.[43] He argues that Grierson's claims for the social responsibility of documentary were merely 'rhetoric' and were 'largely negated by the artistic privileges implicitly and explicitly claimed by this "creative" person'.[44] He decries the trend towards aestheticization of subject matter and notes 'the social irrelevance of *Industrial Britain*'.[45] And he is scathing about Humphrey Jennings's *Spare Time*, which 'contains what are easily the movement's most alienated and alienating images of the working class in the pre-war period'.[46] It will be clear from these quotations that Winston is often highly opinionated in his views of the limitations of documentary: even so, it is an important book that, for all its flaws, cannot be ignored.[47]

While this work has challenged and qualified some of the claims made on behalf of documentary, it has not fundamentally undermined the position of documentary in British cinema history and film culture. Indeed, recent years have seen another wave of documentary scholarship – in part responding to some of the critiques – that has reasserted its importance. To some extent this renewed interest has been led by the release of DVDs of documentary films by the British Film Institute, including the British Transport Films Collection and the films of the National Coal Board as well as the familiar work of the GPO Film Unit and the independent documentary movement of the 1930s. Some of this work focuses again on the 1930s, though has generally been able to offer new perspectives. The inclusion of titles on Jennings's *Fires Were Started* (by Brian Winston) and the GPO Film Unit's *Night Mail* (by Scott Anthony) in the British Film Institute's 'Film Classics' series reinforces their place in the canon while exploring the reasons for their special status.[48] Anthony is also co-editor (with James G. Mansell) of the first – surprisingly so, given how central it was to the documentary movement – book-length study of the GPO Film Unit.[49] Other work, however, has contributed to a welcome opening up of the field of documentary scholarship. Alan Burton, for example, has explored the role of the Co-operative movement in non-theatrical film distribution during the interwar period: its sponsorship of documentary film provides an alternative to the more familiar models of state or corporate sponsorship for documentary.[50] Timothy Boon has documented the history of science documentary on film and television that extends the narrative of documentary practice beyond the end of the Second World War, and also argues for the importance of Paul Rotha,

whose role as both a documentary producer and theorist has sometimes been neglected in favour of Grierson.[51] The case for post-war
documentary film has been advanced by Patrick Russell and James Piers
Taylor's edited collection *Shadows of Progress* (2010) – and a DVD set of
the same title – which includes studies of hitherto neglected second-
generation documentarists including Peter Bradford, Guy Brenton, Paul
Dickson, Derek Knight, John Krish, Eric Marquis, Peter Pickering and
Derek Williams among others.[52] There have also been recently a number
of articles in academic journals – including the *Historical Journal of Film,
Radio and Television, Journal of British Cinema and Television* and *Twentieth
Century British History* – that all attest to the resurgence of critical interest in British documentary.[53] However, the expansion of documentary
scholarship has also provoked its own debates. Brian Winston, again,
questions the claims made for the importance of post-war documentary
and dismisses an entire field of documentary production – the world of
industry-sponsored film-making – on the grounds that it 'carried little
kudos'. Winston's problem is that post-war documentary had, in his eyes
at least, moved even further away from its social purpose that it could
barely be considered as belonging to the same tradition. 'The notion', he
declares, 'that this world offered in any meaningful way an alternative
career path to, say, television documentary or current affairs is, frankly,
risible'.[54]

Winston's disavowal of the post-war documentary film and his suggestion that the progressive impulse of documentary had by then
transferred to television reflects a generally held view. The emergence
of current-affairs television in the 1960s, exemplified by the likes of
Panorama and *World in Action* (where, incidentally, Winston began his
career), and the public debate generated by documentary dramas such
as *Cathy Come Home*, have been seen as marking the moment when television assumed the role of social responsibility that had for so long been
the preserve of documentary film. There is some debate as to whether
television documentary represents a continuation of the tradition of
documentary film or whether it should properly be seen as an entirely
new form in its own right. On the one hand, the formal and aesthetic
properties of television and the viewing context of television are different from film: hence this mandates different kinds of content and
a different relationship between text and spectator. The institutional
discourses of television assert its defining characteristics as being its liveness and immediacy. The popular idea of television as a 'window on the
world' implies a sense of detached observation rather than 'the creative
treatment of actuality'. John Ellis argues that television has 'developed a

distinct aesthetic form' that 'generates a kind of complicity with the TV viewer, a complicity that tends to produce the events represented as an "outside world" beyond the broadcast TV institution and the viewer's home alike'.[55]

On the other hand – and while not denying that film and television have very different institutional histories and aesthetic contexts – there is a case to be made for seeing television documentary as, if not a direct offspring of documentary film, then at least a relation of some sort. There are continuities and similarities on several levels. Most obviously there have been crossovers in personnel. Several key members of the documentary film movement, including Grierson and Rotha, worked in television during the 1950s, while television documentarists such as John Schlesinger and Ken Russell went the other way into the film industry. There are also parallels in form, especially in the prominence of the drama-documentary mode on television, which has often been seen as belonging to the same lineage as story-documentary films such as the GPO Film Unit's *North Sea* and *Men of the Lightship*. John Caugie, for example, reminds us that 'dramatic reconstructions of actuality have a history in cinema as old as cinema itself' and suggests that '[for] British television, the important cinematic antecedent could be found in the various ideologies and practices which were circulating in the documentary movement in the 1930s and 1940s'.[56] And on an institutional level there are broad parallels between the Griersonian ethos of documentary and the ideology of public service broadcasting as articulated by the first Director-General of the British Broadcasting Corporation, Sir John Reith. Higson identifies a direct continuity between documentary film and television: 'This gathering together of the documentary idea and the Reithian ethos of public service broadcasting (itself initially voiced in the same political-cultural climate as the documentary movement) continues the processes of post-war documentary-realist cinema: constructing a world of public affairs, while at the same time addressing the citizen – now the viewer at home – as separate from but influenced by that sphere.'[57]

The major theoretical debate around television documentary has focused on a specific form: the drama documentary. Here it is necessary to make some attempt at definition as the terms 'drama documentary' and 'documentary drama' – and other variations including 'dramatized documentary', 'dramadoc' and 'docudrama' – are often used interchangeably in critical discussion. Most television theorists now accept Derek Paget's distinction between 'drama documentary' (understood as a documentary that presents its material in a dramatic form, for example by using narrative storytelling and scripted dialogue) on the one hand, and 'documentary drama' (a drama shot in the style of a documentary, for example using location shooting and a hand-held camera) on the other.[58] In this schemata, television films such as *Hillsborough* and *Bloody Sunday* are drama documentaries (dramatic reconstructions of real events) whereas *Cathy Come Home* is a documentary drama (a fictional narrative presented in a documentary style). In practice, however, the distinction is often blurred and many drama documentaries/documentary dramas can themselves be seen as working through the tensions between their 'drama' and 'documentary' elements in various ways. Ellis suggests that one of the reasons these hybrid forms have become so associated with television is that the distinction between 'fact' and 'fiction' is more blurred in television than in film: hence 'the ease that TV has long since had of producing programmes that are ambiguous in their status: the documentary-drama, or the drama-documentary, forms that seem to have existed in the late 1950s at least on the BBC'.[59]

The blurring of fact and fiction in the documentary drama (or drama documentary) goes some way towards explaining the controversy that has often attended these forms. The BBC's *Cathy Come Home* became the focus of public debate not only for its exposé of an acute social problem (the shortage of suitable housing for those at the bottom of the social ladder) but also for its overlaying of a fictional story with factual documentary elements. And the reception of drama documentaries such as *Death of a Princess*, *Hillsborough* and *Bloody Sunday* has often been conditioned by similar debates. A cabinet minister – responding to the diplomatic storm between the United Kingdom and Saudi Arabia over Granada Television's *Death of a Princess* – even became involved in the drama-documentary debate, criticizing the 'formula of mixing fact and fiction ... [as] dangerous and misleading'.[60] It would seem that there is rather more at stake here than just the issue of factual accuracy. For some critics, the intrusion of dramatized or even fictional elements into documentary is inappropriate because it dilutes the factual content of the programme or the film: there is a sense that it is not really a 'true' documentary. However, the practice of dramatization in documentary was not a new innovation on television. It was already a familiar practice by the time of the First World War when camera operators 'reconstructed' certain sequences for the official film *Battle of the Somme* – another reason for seeing film and television documentary as parts of the same history.

A New History of British Documentary is an attempt to map the field of documentary production in Britain from the early history of cinema to the present day. It encompasses both film and television and, while the documentary movement of the 1930s is accorded its due, it is not unduly privileged. The scope of the project means that some topics have necessarily been elided. The aim is to provide a historical overview of documentary that combines its contexts – particularly institutional and ideological contexts – with an analysis of the formal and aesthetic practices of documentary. There is also some attempt to address the reception of documentary, though the fragmentary nature of primary sources makes this difficult. The methodology is empirical rather than theoretical: it is concerned with the nitty-gritty details of the production and consumption of documentary film and television rather than with the abstract philosophical notions of 'truth' that have preoccupied much documentary theorizing. The writing of most British documentary practitioners, it should be noted, has generally been more concerned with the practical issues affecting documentary: like any mode of film or television practice, the contexts of documentary need to be understood before any critique can be mounted of its perceived ideological or formal limitations. In other words it is unfair to criticize, say, *Shellarama* for its lack of social import when that was never the intention of the film in the first place. And no history of documentary film should ignore the issue of sponsorship: this was always one of the fundamental concerns of the documentary movement. In this way it should be possible to provide a balanced account of documentary's place in British cinema and television history that neither overstates its achievements nor underplays its importance.

1
Documentary Before Grierson

> My interest has always been to find anything new which
> has practical value, especially of an instructive character,
> develop and exploit [the] same for general use. I saw great
> instructive value in the motion picture as an educational
> factor... Throughout my entire connection with the motion
> picture industry I have specialized in educational subjects of
> science, travel and topical episodes, now referred to as 'docu-
> mentary' films.
>
> Charles Urban[1]

In most standard film histories the emergence of documentary is
generally understood as an international process in the 1920s when a
number of films across different national cinemas – including Robert
Flaherty's *Nanook of the North* (1922) in America, Alberto Cavalcanti's
Rien Que les Hueres (1926) in France, Walter Ruttmann's *Berlin: Symphony
of a City* (1927) in Germany, Dziga Vertov's *The Man With a Movie Camera* (1929) in the Soviet Union and John Grierson's *Drifters* (1929) in
Britain – gave rise to a new type of film that eschewed the melodramatic
antics of the fiction film in preference for social observation and authenticity in the representation of real people and locations.[2] The films cited
above all demonstrated, in different ways, Grierson's notion of documentary as 'the creative treatment of actuality'. Hence documentary
came to be seen as a progressive mode of film practice characterized by
aesthetic innovation and social purpose. However, as early film historian
Stephen Bottomore has pointed out, the association between documentary and progressive aesthetics has led to the eclipse of an older tradition
of non-fiction film in Britain and elsewhere: by 'implying that the documentary is art or it is nothing' the standard historiography posits 'that

18

no "real" documentaries were made before 1920'.[3] Since the late 1970s the critical 'rediscovery' of early cinema has seen the emergence of a revisionist historiography that has comprehensively redrawn the historical map of film production and exhibition during the medium's formative decades. Early cinema is no longer regarded as a primitive mode of film practice from which emerged – through a process of trial and error – the 'classical' cinema of Hollywood and other nations, but rather as a period of innovation and rapid transformation characterized by a wide and diverse range of film styles, genres and practices.[4] While the chief beneficiary of this historical revisionism has been the fiction film, the discovery of significant collections such as the films of Mitchell and Kenyon has also brought the non-fiction film into the spotlight.

Early British non-fiction film

It is important to understand the contexts of early film production and exhibition in order to appreciate the place of non-fiction film in the formative years of British cinema. For the first decade or so film production was something of a cottage industry. The pioneers of British film-making – including men such as R. W. Paul, James Williamson and Cecil Hepworth – saw themselves as businessmen rather than creative artists: their business was making and selling films to satisfy the public's interest in the new medium of moving pictures. Early cinema has been described as a 'cinema of attractions': its appeal was posited on 'an exciting spectacle – a unique event, whether fictional or documentary, that is of interest in itself'.[5] This is evident in the response to the first public screening in Britain by Birt Acres at the Royal Photographic Society on 14 January 1896, which included a one-shot film entitled *Rough Sea at Dover*. According to a review in *The Photogram*:

> The most successful effect, and one which called forth rounds of applause from the usually placid members of the 'Royal', was a reproduction of a number of breaking waves, which may be seen to roll in from the sea, curl over against a jetty, and break into clouds of snowy spray that seemed to start from the screen.[6]

As well as being a cottage industry, film was also very much a local enterprise. This was as true of exhibition as it was of production: until the establishment of permanent cinemas from around 1910, most film shows took place in fairgrounds and music halls or were held in rented spaces that functioned as temporary cinemas. The role of travelling

showmen in film exhibition during the Edwardian period has only
tardily been recognized but it was this practice that fuelled the market for films with a specifically local interest.[7] The largest collection of
non-fiction film in Britain before the First World War comprises over 800
titles by the Lancashire film-makers Sagar Mitchell and James Kenyon:
the majority of these were local subjects such as parades and sporting
events shot mostly across the north of England. The economic contexts of early cinema favoured local films: they were cheap to produce
and process, while exhibitors could hire cameras for the day to film
local items for their patrons. However, the tradition of local film-making
declined with the rise in the later 1900s of companies such as the British
Mutoscope and Biograph Company and the Warwick Trading Company,
which operated as producer-distributors on a national level.[8]

In Britain, as elsewhere, early film exhibition was notable for its diversity: a wide range of fiction and non-fiction films co-existed alongside
each other. Until the emergence of the long 'feature' film as the primary attraction in the 1910s – a process that coincided with and was
to some extent an outcome of the advent of purpose-built permanent
cinema sites – film shows would consist of a mixed programme of
shorter subjects that might include travelogues and 'topicals' (films of
newsworthy events) alongside story films and 'trick' films exploring the
medium's potential for artifice and illusion. The early cinematographers
often made films across different genres. Cecil Hepworth, for example, is
best known as the director of early story films such as *Alice in Wonderland*
(1903) and *Rescued by Rover* (1905) but he also shot many 'actualities',
including films of the Oxford and Cambridge Boat Race of 1898 and
the funeral of Queen Victoria in 1901. In his memoir, *Came the Dawn*,
Hepworth recalled that his camera caught the attention of the new king,
who 'halted the procession so that posterity might have the advantage
of the cinematograph record'.[9]

The idea of film as a record of contemporary events was prominent
in the discourses around early cinema. As early as 1898 the Polish cinematographer Boleslas Matuszewski had described film as 'a new source
of history' and had predicted that 'animated photography...will give
a direct view of the past': 'Perhaps the cinematograph does not give
history in its entirety, but at least what it does deliver is incontestable
and of absolute truth...One could say that animated photography has
a character of authenticity, accuracy and precision that belongs to it
alone.'[10] Matuszewski's claim for the 'absolute truth' of the filmic image
may now seem rather naive but it should be borne in mind that, like
other early cinematographers, he was seeking to legitimate the young

medium as being something more than a fairground attraction. In fact it is evident that by the turn of the century the first 'fakes' purporting to be actuality film had been made. Indeed Mitchell and Kenyon – now known for their extensive archive of genuine non-fiction subjects – were responsible for staging fiction films of scenes from the Boer War (*Winning the VC*, 1900) and the Boxer Rebellion in China (*Attack on a China Mission*, 1901). To be fair to early film-makers their intention was not necessarily to deceive, and such dramatic reconstructions were often acknowledged as such. R. W. Paul, for example, produced a series of topical films entitled *Reproductions of Incidents of the Boer War* and claimed in the sales catalogue that they had been 'arranged under the supervision of an experienced military officer from the front'.[11]

In the early days of film production and exhibition there was no distinction made between fiction and non-fiction film: all films were 'attractions' and were marketed as such. However, the growing popularity of story films from around 1905 saw some film-makers turn to non-fiction subjects as a conscious strategy of product differentiation. This was the aim of the Charles Urban Trading Company when it issued a series of films of the Russo-Japanese War in 1904–1905. Its sales catalogue declared:

> Every Russo-Japanese War picture listed by us is absolutely genuine and should not be confounded [*sic*] with the disgraceful series of fakes, eminating [*sic*] principally from French sources, which have, by their exhibition, misled the public and cast a doubt as to authenticity of the results obtained at great risk and expense by the conscientious Film Maker.[12]

Urban had sent cameraman Joseph Rosenthal to the Far East to cover the war, though most of the footage he obtained was of troop movements rather than actual combat. For all the hyperbole of its catalogue, the Urban Trading Company was not averse to perpetuating the same sort practices it accused others of: *The Bombardment of Port Arthur* (1905) was re-enacted at a British naval training base near Portsmouth.

It would be misleading to see early non-fiction film as a prototype of the documentary form that emerged later. Early topical films are perhaps better understood as precursors of the newsreels that began in France with *Pathé Journal* (shown in Britain as *Pathé Gazette*) in 1910. The prevalence of naval subjects – exemplified by films such as *The Launch of HMS 'Albion' at Blackwall* (1898) and *King Edward VII Launches HMS 'Dreadnought'* (1906) – suggests that such films may have been intended to impress the might of the Royal Navy upon audiences both at home and abroad. Another characteristic of early non-fiction film is its obsession with travel and, especially, with new forms of transport. The first batch of films offered by the Warwick Trading Company in 1898 included numerous examples of a genre known as 'phantom rides' – films shot from the front of a moving vehicle such as a train or a tram, which create an impression of movement. These films were often promoted on the basis of their pictorial qualities: the description of *View from an Engine Front – Entering Tavistock* (1898) points out that 'the picture includes viaducts and arches and numerous curves on the line besides the beautiful natural scenery inherent to this part of the country'.[13]

The most important figure in the history of early British non-fiction film was Charles Urban. Urban was an American-born salesman who had developed a projector known as the Bioscope, which reduced the distraction of the 'flicker' effect. Moving to Britain in 1897, Urban became manager the following year of the newly formed Warwick Trading Company, which specialized in topical and scientific films. Urban's commercial acumen turned around the fortunes of the company, which became the most successful producer-distributor of the early 1900s. It scored a particular success with its films of the Boer War, which were shown in Britain only three weeks after being shot in South Africa. In 1903 Urban left Warwick to set up his own business, the Charles Urban Trading Company, another successful enterprise that combined film production, distribution and equipment sales. While Urban produced some fiction subjects, such as Walter Booth's *The Airship Destroyer* (1909), a proto-science-fiction drama in the style of the acclaimed French pioneer Georges Méliès, he focused on the non-fiction film. It has been estimated that Urban was responsible for half of all non-fiction films produced in Britain between 1905 and 1910.[14] Urban's preference for non-fiction film ran against the trend towards story films that was emerging by this time: his success was due in large measure to astute marketing as well as the superior quality of his films.

Yet Urban was more than just a successful producer: he also developed an interest in the social utility of cinema. He was quick to spot the potential of film to serve the needs of education and preceded John Grierson as an advocate of a more socially purposeful cinema. As he declared in 1907:

I consider that the kinematograph business has arrived at its present stage principally through the catering for the entertainment and amusement of the public, and that while the 'amusement' branch of the business will constantly increase, the future mainstay of the business will be through the development of its most important fields, viz., the scientific, educational, and industrial branches, and in matters of State.[15]

The same year, Urban published a booklet entitled *The Cinematograph in Science, Education and Matters of State*, which argued that '[the] entertainer has hitherto monopolised the Cinematograph for exhibition purposes, but movement in more serious directions has become imperative'.[16] He recalled Matuszewski in acclaiming the 'accurate and truthful eye' of the cinematograph and in calling for 'motion pictures of current events...to be treasured as vital documents among the historical archives of our museums'.[17] In particular, Urban advocated the use of film by the military (recording tactics and manoeuvres) and in science and medicine (for example in recording surgical procedures for teaching students). And finally he also anticipated Grierson in recognizing the potential of showing films outside the usual exhibition spaces, arguing that 'the Cinematograph has to become, not – as some people imagine it – a showman's plaything, but a vital necessity for every barracks, ship, college, school, institute, hospital, laboratory, academy and museum; for every traveller, explorer and missionary'.[18]

What distinguished Urban from his contemporaries was his combination of business sense and his commitment to an idea of cinema as more than just an entertainment medium. This can be seen in his development (with cinematographer G. A. Smith) of an early colour process known as Kinemacolor. Kinemacolor produced 'a far greater sense of realism' than monochrome and therefore enhanced the pictorial naturalism of films.[19] At the same time, Kinemacolor could be marketed as an attraction in its own right that would draw patrons into film shows by offering something different from other films. Kinemacolor's potential for visual spectacle was demonstrated in its use for actuality subjects such as the unveiling of the Queen Victoria Memorial and the coronation of King George V (both 1911). *The Times* – which at this time condescended to review only the most important films – said of the former: 'Their [*sic*] advantage over the ordinary biograph pictures is patent, for the black-and-white effects of the latter cannot convey the sense of pomp and pageantry which rely for their very success upon a blaze of colours.'[20] Urban's greatest triumph was his Kinemacolor film *Coronation Durbar at Delhi* (1911) – a record of the spectacular ceremony anointing George V as Emperor of India – which was shown to much critical and popular acclaim at the Scala Theatre in London. Among the audiences were Paul Rotha (then aged five) and Ivor Montagu, who both recalled seeing the film at the Scala.[21]

To what extent can Urban be regarded as a precursor of the documentary movement? On the one hand Urban apparently saw himself in this tradition, evidenced by the comment in his memoirs that he specialized in what are 'now referred to as "documentary" films'. His writings indicate an interest in the educational potential of cinema and a sense that actuality subjects represented an alternative to the emergence of the story film. And some of his films, such as *A Day in the Life of a Coal Miner* (1910), produced by the Kineto Company, an Urban subsidiary, contain prototypical documentary elements. This film, shot at the Wigan Coal and Iron Company, is notable for its interest in the social lives of its subjects and its presentation of the physical condition of the workers who appear old beyond their years. As it was impossible at the time to film underground, some scenes were staged – a practice that the GPO Film Unit would later adopt for documentary films such as *Coal Face* and *Night Mail*. Patrick Russell contends that *A Day in the Life of a Coal Miner* is 'as close as any to being fully-fledged documentary before the fact'.[22] On the other hand Urban's biographer, Luke McKernan, cautions against adopting a teleological view of film history that identifies a direct lineage between early non-fiction film and documentary, arguing instead that 'documentary is accepted as a later development with pretensions to the interpretation of reality, whereas Urban's pretensions were limited to the exhibition of the uncomplicated evidence'.[23] And this was also the view of John Grierson, who drew a clear distinction between documentary and early actuality films, which he regarded as 'dim records ... of only the evanescent and the essentially unreal, reflecting hardly anything of the times they recorded'. Grierson did not mention Urban by name but he added in a dismissive aside: 'In curiosity one might wish to see again the Queen's Jubilees and the Delhi Durbars – with coloured coats that floated in air a full yard behind the line of march – the Kaiser at manoeuvres and the Czar at play.'[24] It is the prevalence of Grierson's idea of documentary in film history that is largely responsible for the marginalization of this earlier tradition of non-fiction film.

Mitchell and Kenyon: 'See yourself as others see you'

The example of Mitchell and Kenyon demonstrates how the map of early non-fiction film has been redrawn in recent years. In 1948 the pioneer British film historian Rachael Low wrote that the firm of Mitchell and Kenyon 'has left little trace. On the whole it is probably safe to say that although it made a solid contribution to the considerable British output of the time, it does not seem to have exerted any influence on the development of cinema technique'.[25] It was not until the discovery of 826 original negatives in the 1990s and their restoration by the National Film Archive that the full extent of Mitchell and Kenyon's non-fiction film-making activity was revealed.[26] Sagar Mitchell and James Kenyon exemplify the entrepreneurial nature of early film-making in Britain: their main business was in still photography but they diversified into cinematography in recognition of the demand for such films. Between 1898 and 1913 they shot hundreds of local actuality subjects across the north of England (the firm itself was based in Blackburn, Lancashire) with occasional excursions to Wales and Ireland. The films were mostly commissioned by exhibitors who wanted films reflecting the towns and areas in which they were shown. Hence the Mitchell and Kenyon collection provides a remarkable visual record of the social history of Edwardian Britain.

Low's premise that Mitchell and Kenyon made little contribution to the development of film technique is probably a fair one: the films themselves demonstrate little in the way of formal innovation and mostly consist of static takes with occasional panning movements (as the camera rotates on its axis to follow movement) and jump cuts (where the camera stopped turning and then restarted). Most of the films are short, between 50 and 100 feet in length, which at the upper end would equate to a running time of about a minute. It has been argued that early topicals such as these represent the purest form of non-fiction film. The intention of the film-makers was simply to record social reality rather than to impose an interpretation on it. Of course, even the simplest films are mediated to an extent: decisions have been made where to place the camera and how to edit shots into a sequence. Evidence of mediation can be seen in the films themselves: sometimes James Kenyon is present 'directing' the crowds around the camera operator. Leo Enticknap has argued that in their films of football matches, Mitchell and Kenyon developed techniques of camera movement and sequential cutting that represent 'a rudimentary version of "classical" continuity editing, which emerged in the late 1910s'.[27] Many of the Mitchell and Kenyon films, however, consist of a single take or just a few shots: they were content to let events unfold before the camera.

Mitchell and Kenyon advertised their films with the slogan 'See Yourself As Others See You': they were shot with the intention that their subjects should be both visible and able to recognize themselves on screen. A particularly notable feature of the films is the frequency with which the people being filmed look at the camera. This creates a sense of intimacy and recognition between the film's subjects and its spectators: the films therefore construct both their subjects and their audiences as part of the same community. This is particularly true of the so-called 'factory gate' films, which consist mostly of shots of workers leaving their place of work. It has been suggested that the association between documentary film and working-class subjects began with these films. Tom Gunning, for example, argues that they 'represent invaluable works of art as well as documents of history: an image of the working class as they move from the factory space into the space of their daily life'.[28] What evidence there is of the reception of the Mitchell and Kenyon films by contemporary audiences – mostly to be gleaned from reports of shows in the local press – suggests that they succeeded in holding the attention of viewers who were indeed fascinated to see themselves on the screen.

At a time when the formal distinction between documentary and newsreel had yet to be institutionalized, the Mitchell and Kenyon films can be seen to anticipate both modes. On the one hand the films of topical events are akin to the sort of items that would become a prominent feature of newsreels. Hence there are films of visiting dignatories (*Lord Roberts' Visit to Manchester*, 1901), royals (*Visit of HRH Princess Louise to Blackburn*, 1905) and military parades (*The Return of the Lancaster Volunteers*, 1901) as well as many dozens of football and rugby matches. The prominence of films of street processions in the collection – including schools, churches, temperance groups, friendly societies and trade unions – reveals the full extent of a culture that has now all but disappeared from mainland British towns: ironically it was the increasing popularity of cinema that contributed to the decline of this practice after the First World War.[29] The films of trade union marches such as *Bootle May Day Procession* (1903) and *Miners' Demonstration at Wakefield* (1908) inaugurated a genre that would extend to the workers' newsreels of the 1930s (which like the Mitchell and Kenyon films were shot mute): they document an arena of political activity that is represented in early non-fiction film but would disappear from national newsreels once the industry became institutionalized.

On the other hand the documentary impulse for social observation can be identified in films exploring the worlds of work and leisure. Paul Dave has argued that 'the films in the collection represent an inaugural moment in that extension of the coverage of the social, a moment which is so critical to the project of social realism'.[30] A feature of the

Mitchell and Kenyon films is the prominence of working-class subjects, particularly in the 'factory gate' films such as *The 'Hands' Leaving Work at North Street Mills, Chorley* (1900), *Alfred Butterworth & Sons, Glebe Mills* (1901) and *Pendlebury Colliery* (1901). These films offer more than just visual evidence of the material conditions of the industrial working classes in the Edwardian period: they also provide some insight into social relations. In particular, they challenge the orthodox view of the world of industrial production as an exclusively male preserve: it is not unusual to see women and children crossing over into the working spaces, for example in carrying food for their husbands and fathers. An insight into social relations and behaviour also emerges in films of the seaside: *Blackpool North Pier* (1903) and *Blackpool Victoria Pier* (1904), for instance, apparently show middle- and working-class people mingling on equal terms. This confirms the idea of the seaside resort as a place where different classes could enjoy themselves and share the same leisure spaces.[31] Overall, the impression of the Mitchell and Kenyon films is that contemporary social anxieties around 'the crowd' – the anonymous mass that emerged in the later nineteenth century through the historical processes of urbanization and industrialization – were misplaced: public gatherings, whether at football matches or factories, are notable for their general order and decorum.[32]

Mitchell and Kenyon were businessmen first and last: unlike Charles Urban they do not seem to have been interested in the artistic or educational possibilities of the medium. Yet in a sense this is the real value of their films: here there is no 'creative treatment of actuality' but simply an impulse to observe and record everyday life. The sheer extent of the collection has provided film historians with a much fuller picture of the style of early non-fiction film in Britain, which is best understood as a mode of film practice in its own right, with its own formal codes and conventions, rather than as a precursor of the documentary movement that would follow later.

Battle of the Somme (1916) and the origins of British documentary

It was during the First World War that the cinema came of age as a mass medium. The war impacted on cinema in several ways. On one level, wartime conditions enhanced the popular appeal of cinema as an entertainment medium: the massive demand for film is reflected in the rapid expansion of permanent cinemas in Britain from 1,600 in 1910 to 3,500 by 1915.[33] On another level, the disruption caused to European film industries during the war created the circumstances in which the United States would emerge as the dominant film-producing nation: the US film industry was quicker than its rivals to adopt mass-production methods and to institutionalize the narrative feature film, exemplified by super-productions such as D. W. Griffith's *The Birth of a Nation* (1915) and *Intolerance* (1916). American films were regarded by British critics and audiences as being technically superior to the domestic product: it was during the war that Hollywood began its colonization of British screens.

It was also during the war that – arguably, perhaps – the first true documentary films appeared. The context for this was the, admittedly somewhat tardy, recognition by the state of the value of film as a vehicle of propaganda. Official attitudes towards film were initially condescending or, at best, indifferent. A report for the War Cabinet averred that cinema was 'almost universally regarded as an instrument for the entertainment of the masses'.[34] In this respect it was the film trade itself that took the lead. The trade paper *The Bioscope* argued from early in the war that cinema could be more than just an entertainment medium:

> So wonderful are both the achievements and the possibilities of the cinematograph as a means of entertainment that one is sometimes apt to forget the extraordinary potency of this marvellous and many-sided instrument as a moulder of public thought and public opinion. Quite apart from its great educational value in more or less scholastic subjects, and apart even from its strong ethical influence, the cinematograph may nowadays exercise in social, political, and international questions, a power which is hardly inferior to that of the Press.[35]

No doubt the film trade's advocacy of the social and educational value of cinema arose to a considerable extent from its desire to legitimate itself as a responsible and patriotic business. But it also reflects a wider recognition that the growing popular appeal of cinema made it the perfect vehicle for the dissemination of propaganda – which all combatants recognized as a necessity for mobilizing public opinion during the first 'total war'. Charles Urban's visionary idea that cinema would serve 'matters of state' would be realized during the war.

Yet there was initially much official resistance to the adoption of film by the state. Lord Kitchener, the Secretary of State for War, was distrustful of the mass media and in September 1914 placed a blanket ban on all cameramen and newspaper correspondents at the front. One of the consequences of this decision was that most early British war films were fictional enactments that tended towards sensational melodrama rather than actuality films. The production of 'war dramas' soon came under criticism from exhibitors on the grounds that 'the public will, sooner or later, tire of the endless repetition of subjects dealing in a more or less theatrical manner with a war which has brought so great a sorrow into many thousands of lives'.[36] Instead, commercial producers such as the Gaumont Company turned to making what they termed 'war topicals' – albeit still involving dramatic reconstruction – and asserted that 'realism is the greatest factor making for the success of a War Topical'.[37] It was a full year before agreement was reached between the War Office and the film trade – under the auspices of a body called the British Topical Committee for War Films, chaired by the respected distributor William Jury – and not until November 1915 that cameramen were tardily allowed access to the Western Front. *The Bioscope* welcomed the first actuality films from the front:

> It has, we admit, taken a very long time to convince the Government and the Fourth Estate of the value of the cinematograph as the national historian, but now that approval is forthcoming and the work pronounced to be good, we can well afford to regard the time as well spent.[38]

This was the context in which *Battle of the Somme* (subtitled 'Official Pictures of the British Army in France') was produced. In fact, the first feature-length documentary of the war came about in a somewhat ad hoc fashion. In June 1916 two official cameramen, Geoffrey Malins and J. B. McDowell, were sent to film the British Fourth Army launching its offensive along the River Somme. They filmed the artillery bombardment and British troops being marched up through villages behind the lines. On the morning of 1 July, Malins filmed the explosion of a massive mine under the German strongpoint at Hawthorn Ridge, then followed the 1st Lancashire Fusiliers moving up through the assault trenches. He then joined his colleague McDowell at a dressing post where they filmed the wounded of both sides being treated. They also filmed captured German trenches and, finally, the survivors of the first assault coming out of the line to rest. At this point it does not seem that there was any intention to do more than to release the Somme footage as a short topical in much the same style as the 27 official films already issued during 1916. However, when the raw footage was shown to members of the Topical Committee in London on 12 July, they decided it was so good that it should be edited into a longer feature film. *Battle of the Somme* opened in 34 cinemas in London on 21 August and in other major cities a week later. It was an enormous popular and critical success, and remained on exhibition for well over a year.[39]

The contemporary reception of *Battle of the Somme* has been well documented.[40] There are reports of hundreds of thousands of people flocking to see it, with many audiences apparently regarding it as their patriotic duty to do so. The film received official endorsement when King George V saw it at Windsor and was quoted as saying: 'the public should see these pictures that they may have some idea of what the army is doing'.[41] The press notices were overwhelmingly enthusiastic. *The Times* saw it as nothing less than a legitimation of cinema: 'If anything were needed to justify the existence of the cinematograph, it is to be found in [this] wonderful series of films.'[42] (Most reviews describe *Battle of the Somme* as a series of films: the complete film consists of six parts but there is evidence that these may have been shown separately in some cinemas.) *The Manchester Guardian* found it 'the most remarkable photographic record of the war which has yet been obtained' and felt that 'it reveals war in its true aspect – as a grimly destructive and infernal thing'.[43] *The Bioscope* averred that 'no written description by an eyewitness ... no illustration by any artist ... no verbal description by the most interested participator in the event, could hope to convey to the man at home the reality of modern warfare with the force and conviction shown in this marvellous series of pictures'.[44] The most eloquent testimony to the film's realism, however, came not from reviewers but from men involved in the battle itself. Rowland Fielding wrote to his wife in September 1916 that he had seen *Battle of the Somme* at an open-air cinema at Morlancourt in France – where it formed a somewhat incongruous double bill with a Charlie Chaplin film – and thought it was 'really a wonderful and most realistic production'.[45]

A small minority of responses to the film were more critical, however. There were some complaints that the inclusion of images of dead British troops was in bad taste. One such voice was the Dean of Durham who protested that 'crowds of Londoners feel no scruple at feasting their eyes on pictures which present the passion and death of British soldiers in *Battle of the Somme*'.[46] This even prompted a leading article in *The Times*, which after assessing the evidence decreed that 'there is nothing ... to gratify the morbid, nothing to leave a sense of "bestial horror", nothing but must make the spectator a better and a braver man'.[47] The author Sir Henry Rider Haggard noted in his diary that the film 'does give a wonderful idea of the fighting'. 'The most impressive [shot] to my mind', he averred, 'is that of a regiment scrambling out of a trench to charge and of the one man who slides back shot dead'. 'There is something appalling', he concluded, 'about the instantaneous change from fierce activity to supine death'.[48]

There is an irony here in that the scenes in *Battle of the Somme* that provoked these responses – the sequence of troops going 'over the top' at the beginning of part three of the film – are now widely believed to have been faked. There are several clues. The trench is rather too shallow for the front line and there is no barbed wire on the parapet; the troops who scramble out of the trench are not wearing field backpacks and are carrying only their rifles with no other equipment such as trenching tools or spades; and the camera position as they advance into No Man's Land would have been dangerously exposed if it were the real thing. Perhaps the clinching detail is that one of the soldiers who falls forward onto barbed wire, apparently dead, crosses his legs and looks back at the camera! There are other inconsistencies in *Battle of the Somme*, including in uniforms and equipment, which suggest that some scenes may have been staged for the camera. The evidence for such reconstructed scenes notwithstanding, however, film archivist Roger Smither concludes that *Battle of the Somme* should be regarded as an authentic record as 'the proportion of such film to the whole work is actually quite small'.[49]

For Smither, *Battle of the Somme* 'may be acclaimed with hindsight as the first feature length British battle documentary and thus the direct ancestor of such notable Second World War films as *Desert Victory* and *The True Glory*'.[50] Its historical significance is attested to by the fact that it was the first film selected for UNESCO's Memory of the World Register, where it is described as 'the first feature-length documentary film record of combat produced anywhere in the world'.[51] *Battle of the Somme* features prominently in historical discourses of 'film and history' focusing on the role of film as a record of the past. Curiously, however, it is usually overlooked in histories of documentary film such as those by Erik Barnouw and Paul Rotha. There are various possible reasons for this. One is that *Battle of the Somme* does not fit the traditional Griersonian idea of documentary as 'the creative treatment of actuality': much of the film, in fact, is visually quite dull. The authentic scenes of combat, for example, are shot from such a distance that the action is barely distinguishable. Another reason is that *Battle of the Somme* was quite explicitly a propaganda film: it was released with the intention of mobilizing the public behind the war effort and as a counter to the casualty lists that were appearing in the press. Hence the film presents the opening day of the Somme offensive as a military success and makes no reference to the scale of the casualties.

These caveats aside, however, there is just as strong a case for *Battle of the Somme* as marking the origin of documentary film-making – as it came to be understood – rather than the more usual suspects such as *Nanook of the North* or *Drifters*. The film's reception discourse focused on its qualities of realism and authenticity rather than its occasional resort to reconstruction: in fact there is no evidence that contemporary audiences recognized the staged material. And, in a sense, *Battle of the Somme* is more authentic than a film such as *Nanook of the North*, where Flaherty directed the action to fit a narrative pattern and where most sequences were staged for the camera. In contrast, the structure of *Battle of the Somme* is much more fragmentary, reflecting its status as an edited compilation of (mostly) actuality footage. While it may lack the self-conscious aestheticization of films such as *Nanook of the North* and *Drifters*, there is nonetheless a rawness and immediacy about *Battle of the Somme* that makes it seem closer to the events it depicts. For example, the shots of troops waiting to go into battle – gazing into the camera and thereby establishing a sense of intimacy with the spectator that is also seen in the Mitchell and Kenyon films – acquire an added poignancy in the knowledge that some of those men would not survive the day. And some impression of the experience of combat is etched into the dazed and confused expressions of the wounded of both sides in the scenes at the field hospital. For all these reasons, *Battle of the Somme* may legitimately be claimed as an early example of documentary film.

The enormous success of *Battle of the Somme* inevitably prompted attempts to repeat that success. The curiously titled *Battle of the Ancre and the Advance of the Tanks* (1917) is a direct sequel to *Battle of the Somme* that depicts the later stages of the offensive and adopts a near-identical structure in the compilation of material. *Battle of the Ancre* generated further interest as it included images of the new British weapon – known as the tank – in action for the first time. Interestingly the film's publicity included an assertion of its authenticity: 'General Headquarters is responsible for the censorship of these films and allows nothing in the nature of a "fake" to be shown. The pictures are authentic and taken on the battlefield.'[52] This might suggest some concern in official quarters over the inclusion of reconstructed scenes in *Battle of the Somme*. *Battle of the Ancre* would appear to have been nearly as successful as *Battle of the Somme*, if not quite matching its impact on audiences. According to the official records, the two films had grossed some £65,000 between them during the first three months of their exhibition.[53] *The*

German Retreat and the Battle of Arras (1917) completed a trilogy of official feature-length actuality compilation films, though by the time it
was released in the summer of 1917 there is evidence to suggest that
cinema audiences were tiring of the genre. This, at least, was the opinion of press baron Lord Beaverbrook, chairman of the newly instituted
War Office Cinematograph Committee, who suggested that 'the present
style of films is played out. The public is jaded and we have to tickle its
palate with something a little more dramatic in the future if we are to
maintain our sales'.[54]

It was at Beaverbrook's suggestion that in 1917 British official film
propaganda policy switched from the issue of occasional feature-length
'specials' to inclusion of regular short items in an official newsreel.
The War Office took over the production and distribution of a British
newsreel known as *Topical Budget* and relaunched it under the title *War
Office Official Topical Budget*. The creation of an official newsreel was
part of a rationalization of all propaganda activities that also resulted,
in March 1918, in the establishment of a Ministry of Information under
Beaverbrook. *War Office Official Topical Budget* was issued twice weekly
until the end of the war, though in February 1918 its name changed
to *Pictorial News (Official)*. By this time there were seven official cameramen in different theatres of war: four on the Western Front, one
in Egypt, one in Mesopotamia and one with the Royal Navy at sea.
Beaverbrook claimed, perhaps with some exaggeration, that '[the] Topical Budget shown in every picture palace was the decisive factor in
maintaining the morale of the people during the black days of the early
summer of 1918'.[55] Among the items included in the newsreel were General Allenby's entry into Jerusalem in February 1918 and the signing of
the Treaty of Versailles on 28 June 1919. After the war, as the official
propaganda machinery was wound up, the War Office sold its interest
in the company and the newsreel reverted to its original name of *Topical
Budget* in which form it continued until 1931.

British Instructional Films and the documentary
reconstruction

The tradition of documentary production established in the official
films of the First World War would continue into the 1920s with a
cycle of documentary reconstructions of the war produced by British
Instructional Films (BIF). Paul Rotha described these films – including
The Battle of Jutland (1921), *Armageddon* (1923), *Zeebrugge* (1924), *Ypres*
(1925), *Mons* (1926) and *The Battles of the Coronel and Falkland Islands*

(1927) – as 'excellent examples of the documentary film'.[56] Yet, like *Battle of the Somme*, the BIF films have been left out of the standard histories of documentary film-making. This is surprising because the films can be seen to anticipate the techniques of narrative storytelling and documentary reconstruction adopted by the Crown Film Unit during the Second World War. Again, they demonstrate the existence of a pre-Griersonian tradition of documentary film in Britain.

British Instructional Films was founded in 1919 by Harry Bruce Woolfe, a non-fiction specialist, and his business partner H. M. Howard. The post-war film industry was becoming increasingly institutionalized as larger producers such as Gainsborough Pictures and the Stoll Film Company adopted more streamlined production methods and led a trend towards higher production values in an attempt to compete against Hollywood in the home and international markets. BIF was a rather different sort of undertaking in that from the outset its production strategy was geared towards factual subjects rather than fictional drama and star vehicles. It produced relatively few films but focused on quality. In particular, BIF pioneered the natural history documentary with its series entitled *Secrets of Nature* for which nearly 100 one-reel films were made between 1922 and 1929.[57] While lacking the social dimension that Grierson saw as an essential part of the documentary project, he nevertheless admired *Secrets of Nature* for its 'very frequent beauty and very great skill of exposition'.[58] However, Woolfe had loftier ambitions than supplying what the trade referred to as 'interest' subjects. In 1921 he and cameraman Herbert Lomas produced a three-reel reconstruction entitled *The Battle of Jutland*, using maps and models to tell the story of the major naval engagement of the war. It was to be the first of a cycle of films that became longer, more sophisticated and more expensive over the next six years: *Armageddon* cost £3,000 in 1923, *Zeebrugge* £8,000 in 1924, *Ypres* £12,000 in 1925 and *The Battles of the Coronel and Falkland Islands* £18,000 in 1927.[59] To put these figures in context, they were towards the higher end of the cost range for British features but were still less than the average Hollywood picture.

The BIF reconstructions were notable for their considerable degrees of innovation in documentary technique. *The Battle of Jutland* was mostly a compilation of models and maps, but the later films included a combination of reconstructed incidents and actuality footage of the war provided by the Imperial War Museum. An emphasis on authenticity differentiated the films from the fictional war dramas of the 1920s such as *The Guns of Loos* (1927) and *Blighty* (1927). Hence the BIF films were often enacted by veterans who had participated in the events rather than by well-known actors. Walter Summers, who directed *Zeebrugge*, *Ypres*, *Mons* and *The Battles of the Coronel and Falkland Islands*, was himself a veteran of the Western Front.[60] The films are early examples of the hybrid between the documentary and the story film that would later be known as drama documentary. On the one hand they adopt the conventions of 'classical' narration: participants behave as if they were real people, for example by not looking into the camera as in *Battle of the Somme*. On the other hand their narratives follow the actions of combatants en masse rather than focusing on personal stories. There are dramatizations of individual acts of heroism but overall the films are histories of campaigns rather than individuals. To this extent they shared something in common with the celebrated Soviet films of the 1920s such as *Battleship Potemkin* (1925) and *The End of St Petersburg* (1927). Woolfe and Summers would almost certainly have been aware of these films though it is unclear whether they had seen them as most were not screened in Britain until after 1927.

The BIF war reconstructions might be described as semi-official films in the sense that from *Armageddon* (which documents the campaign in Palestine) they all received – and in their credits acknowledged – the support of the Army Council or Admiralty. This official co-operation reached its fullest extent in *The Battles of the Coronel and Falkland Islands* for which BIF was allowed to film on board the Mediterranean Fleet and at naval bases in Malta and Portsmouth. The use of real ships – including HMS *Barham* as the battlecruiser *Inflexible* and the cruisers *Ceres* and *Coventry* as the German cruisers *Gneisenau* and *Scharnhorst* – is crucial to the realism of *The Battles of the Coronel and Falkland Islands*, in contrast to the models used in many naval war films.[61] So close was the association between BIF and the services that questions were even asked in the House of Commons whether the government had subsidized what were, after all, commercial film productions (it had not: though it is very likely that the 'services' provided for the film-makers were charged at a minimal rate as the departments concerned saw their participation as a means of generating favourable publicity and ensuring their interpretation of the wartime record was presented on screen).[62] The role of the service departments in assisting these films also ensured that the narrative of the war that emerged from them accorded with official views of how and why it had been fought.

Michael Paris has argued that the ideological project of the BIF reconstructions was to present 'the War as a national achievement – an adventure in which brave young Britons won immortality. They did not seek to disguise the human cost, but suggested that those who fell did so in a noble cause'.[63] This is, of course, a very different narrative of the First World War from that which came to predominate in literature from the late 1920s – exemplified by memoirs such as Robert Graves's *Goodbye To All That* (1929), Siegfried Sassoon's *Memoirs of an Infantry Officer* (1930) and Vera Brittain's *Testament of Youth* (1933); novels such as Ernest Hemingway's *A Farewell to Arms* (1929) and Erich Maria Remarque's *All Quiet on the Western Front* (1929); and plays such as R. C. Sherriff's *Journey's End* (1928) – and which also found expression in an international cycle of anti-war films in the early sound period, including *Journey's End* (1930), *Westfront 1918* (1930) and *All Quiet on the Western Front* (1930), where the dominant narrative of the war is a tragic waste of human lives rather than one of nobility and sacrifice. This probably helps to explain why the BIF films have been overlooked in most film histories. However, it would be misleading to regard the BIF films as crude propaganda. Instead they demonstrate a mixed understanding of war as both a tragedy but also characterized by bravery in what many at the time still regarded as a just cause. The films may be related to the cultural discourses of war commemoration that were emerging during the 1920s and have been analysed in Jay Winter's book *Sites of Memory, Sites of Mourning*.[64] Woolfe evidently intended the films as a lasting testimonial to the men who had fallen during the war: hence the subtitles of *Mons* ('The Story of the Immortal Retreat') and *Ypres* ('The Story of the Immortal Salient') and the films' recasting of bitterly fought campaigns as British victories.

The BIF films became increasingly prestigious affairs that were afforded high-profile promotional campaigns with extensive press coverage and culminating in a royal premiere at Balmoral for *The Battles of the Coronel and Falkland Islands*.[65] Their critical reception was mixed. On the one hand reviewers in the trade and popular press acclaimed them as patriotic epics and admired their cinematographic qualities. *The Bioscope* welcomed *Mons* in the sort of terms that its producers intended – as 'tragic and glorious' and demonstrating the qualities of a 'Homeric struggle'.[66] And the *Illustrated London News* was positively rhapsodic about *The Battles of the Coronel and Falkland Islands*, which it felt 'has been seen and moulded with such rare vision that at times it rises to the height of tragic beauty'.[67] On the other hand the quality press and the emerging intellectual film culture represented by the avant-garde film journal *Close Up* was critical of what they regarded as the too patriotic tone of the films. The reviewer 'Bryher' (a pseudonym for the pacifist journalist Winifred Ellerman) thought that *Mons* revealed 'the kind of sentimentality that makes one shudder...a mixture of a Victorian tract for children and a cheap serial in the sort of magazine one finds discarded on the beach'.[68] And *The Observer*'s review of *The Battles of the Coronel and Falkland Islands* was critical of 'the humbug now evident in the way war films are now described'.[69]

The Battles of the Coronel and Falkland Islands was the most successful of BIF's documentary reconstructions: Woolfe claimed that it grossed £70,000 in the home market.[70] Yet it was also the last. It is not immediately apparent why the cycle came to an end at this point, though the imminent arrival of talking pictures and the costs associated with converting to sound was probably a factor. Another company, New Era, released two films in a similar style to the BIF films, *The Somme* (1927) and *'Q' Ships* (1928). Geoffrey Barkas, who had started his career at BIF and had been involved in the production of both the New Era films, would also direct action sequences for the early talking picture *Tell England* (1931), which BIF had originally planned as an epic of Gallipoli in the same semi-documentary mode as their battle reconstructions but which ended up an uneasy mixture of melodramatic fiction and realistically staged combat scenes. The intellectual ascendancy of the Griersonian idea of documentary in the 1930s would cause the BIF films to be forgotten when the first histories of documentary were written. Nevertheless, as Low suggests, Woolfe and BIF made an important contribution to British cinema and can be seen as 'a link in the chain of factual film from the Charles Urban Trading Company and others of the early days to the documentary movement of the thirties'.[71]

Epics of exploration

Another tradition of documentary film-making that predates the Grierson school can be seen in the various accounts of polar and other exploration in the 1920s. These films – including Frank Hurley's *South* (1919), Herbert Ponting's *The Great White Silence* (1924) and J. B. L. Noel's *The Epic of Everest* (1924) – yet again demonstrate a different mode of documentary. On one level they can be seen as linking back to early travelogues and scenics shot in foreign countries and often notable for their highly pictorialist qualities: such films were promoted as 'attractions' that showcased the landscapes and customs of other lands. However, the films of the 1920s can also be seen as part of a discourse of national achievements in exploration and adventure that emerged after the First World War. Hence the subjects of these films were the polar explorers Sir Ernest Shackleton (*South*) and Captain Robert Falcon Scott (*The Great White Silence*) and the mountaineers Mallory and Irvine (*The Epic of Everest*). The sense that these films – like the BIF reconstructions – were understood as memorials to their subjects is evident in the review of *The Great White Silence* from *The Times*:

> One of the greatest achievements of the Kinematograph to-date has been to make Captain Scott's Expedition imperishable... [It] is wonderful to think also that 100 or 500 years hence future generations will be able to see the pictorial record and gaze upon Scott and his comrades trudging over the ice to glorious death.[72]

The films of the Scott expedition, in particular, make an interesting case study of how the same actuality material could be presented and represented in different forms. Ponting, who accompanied Scott's expedition to the Antarctic in 1910–1913, shot 25,000 feet of film as well as taking hundreds of still photographs. The expedition had two reasons for including an official cinematographer: previous polar expeditions had demonstrated the need for proof of their achievements but there was also a genuine scientific interest in researching the flaura and fauna of the Antarctic.[73] The first film from the expedition, *With Captain Scott to the South Pole* (1911), was released by the Gaumont Company before Scott's attempt at the Pole. Following the news of the death of Scott and his colleagues Gaumont reissued the material as *The Undying Story of Captain Scott* (1914). Ponting bought the rights to his film back from Gaumont and used it in illustrated lectures during and after the First World War. In 1924 – no doubt influenced to some extent by the critical acclaim heaped upon Flaherty's *Nanook of the North* – he released the feature film *The Great White Silence*. This is essentially a travelogue, showing the outward journey of Scott's expedition on the *Terra Nova* and including much footage of seals and penguins in their natural habitats as well as some breathtaking shots of the Antarctic landscape. *The Great White Silence* might be seen as an attempt to counter the criticisms of Scott's preparation by emphasizing the scientific purpose of the expedition and presenting the attempt to reach the South Pole as a coda illustrated through maps and extracts from Scott's journals. In 1933 Ponting issued a re-edited sound version entitled *90° South*, replacing the intertitles with commentary and adding an on-camera introduction by Scott's colleague (now Vice Admiral) E. R. G. R. ('Teddy') Evans.

Sight and Sound admired the film for its pictorial qualities, noting its 'fine natural photographic flair' and praising Ponting's 'distinct personal artistic craftsmanship'.[74]

The polar exploration films hold a special place in the history of British silent cinema, partly on account of their subject matter and partly by dint of their continued visibility due to restoration by the National Film Archive, but they represent only the tip of an iceberg of films of exploration and travelogues in the 1920s. These ranged from series illustrating the natural landscape of the British Isles such as *The Beauty of Britain* (Humfriese Films, 1920) and *Wonderful Britain* (Harry B. Parkinson, 1926) to expedition films such as Angus Buchanan's *Crossing the Great Sahara* (1924) and Frank Hurley's *Cape to Cairo* (1926) – the latter being a record of an epic car journey by Major and Mrs C. Court Treatt. The expedition film seems to have been particularly prolific during the mid-1920s but like other genres of silent cinema was a victim of the arrival of talking pictures as it was not technically possible to record synchronous sound on location. The rapid institutionalization of sound in the film industry at the end of the 1920s, and the public's wholehearted acceptance of 'talkies', would curtail both the extent and the range of non-fiction film as the market for silent 'interest' and topical subjects all but disappeared. Henceforth, the place for non-fiction in cinema programmes was increasingly taken by the major national newsreels.

It will be clear even from this much-truncated survey that there existed a wide and diverse field of non-fiction film in Britain before the emergence of the documentary movement in the 1930s. The extent to which early non-fiction film can be seen as part of the same historical lineage as the Griersonian tradition of documentary is open to debate. On the one hand the 'primitive' style of much early cinema and the absence of social commentary in the films is at some remove from Grierson's mantra of 'the creative treatment of actuality'. These films are perhaps better understood not as prototypical examples of documentary film but rather as part of a longer and broader history of non-fiction film-making in Britain that encompasses but is not solely defined by the documentary idea. On the other hand it is clear that Grierson was certainly not the first to recognize the social value of film: pioneers such as Charles Urban were early advocates of the adoption of film in education and as a medium of propaganda. And actuality compilation films such as *Battle of the Somme* and the battle reconstructions of British Instructional Films clearly aspire to being more than simply films of record: they employ aspects of film form and technique to represent a particular ideological perspective. In this sense they have more in common with subsequent developments in documentary film than the standard histories have generally allowed. At any rate, the still largely prevalent view that it was only the production of Grierson's *Drifters* in 1929 that marked the origin of any meaningful tradition of non-fiction film-making in Britain can no longer be sustained.

2
Documentary in the 1930s

> It may therefore be worth recalling that our British documen-
> tary group began not so much in affection for film as in
> affection for national education. If I am to be counted as the
> founder and leader of the movement, its origins certainly lie in
> sociological rather than aesthetic aims.
>
> John Grierson[1]

While there were important antecedents, such as the documentary
reconstructions of British Instructional Films and the polar exploration
epics, the emergence of British documentary as a distinct mode of film
practice in its own right is generally held to have been in the 1930s
when a combination of factors – including a growing awareness of the
potential of film as a medium of mass communication, a progressive
outlook by both the public and private sectors towards commissioning
films for publicity purposes, a realist tendency in the arts in general,
and the rise of an intellectual film culture that saw films as an art form
rather than purely as a business – created the circumstances in which the
documentary 'movement' took shape. All accounts of the origins and
early history of the British documentary film movement privilege the
role of John Grierson (1898–1972) who is widely referred to – including
by himself – as its 'founder' or 'leader'. In the standard historiography
Grierson is seen as laying down both the sociological and the aesthetic
principles of documentary film. This is despite the fact that he directed
only one major film (*Drifters*, 1929) and that his career as a hands-on
documentary producer was in fact quite short. Yet Grierson's influence
on documentary was so pervasive that the label 'Griersonian' is regularly attached to an entire tradition of film-making and even extends to
include many productions in which he had no involvement at all.

It is not the intention here to attempt to debunk the Grierson 'myth': there is abundant evidence that Grierson was indeed a prime mover in the initiative to establish Britain's first publicly funded documentary film production unit and was without doubt the documentary movement's most influential theorist and able publicist. That said, however, Grierson alone did not create the British documentary film any more than D. W. Griffith invented the art of narrative film or Charlie Chaplin was the sole pioneer of screen comedy. The origins of the documentary movement should, rather, be seen as the outcome of a set of ideological and cultural processes that came together in interwar Britain. The fact that this coincided with a period of social and economic depression is largely responsible for the association of documentary film in the 1930s with social problems – though in reality most of the films produced under the broad umbrella of the documentary movement really had little to say about 'the burning issues of the day'. The documentary movement has variously been understood as a progressive vehicle for exploring social democratic ideals, as an instrument of state publicity and propaganda, and as a medium of national cultural projection. It was to an extent all of those things: documentary film-makers cut their cloth according to their circumstances and were to prove remarkably adept in squaring the ideological and economic demands of their sponsors with their own social and aesthetic concerns. In order to assess the achievements of the documentary movement, therefore, it is necessary in the first instance to consider the various contexts – ideological, institutional and cultural – in which it took shape.

The contexts of documentary

The documentary movement was both formed within and in turn responded to the ideological contexts of interwar Britain. It is impossible to understand the nature of documentary film in the 1930s without also understanding something of the politics and society of the time. This is a period that provokes very different responses from historians and cultural commentators. On the one hand the 1930s have often been characterized as a period blighted by economic depression, mass unemployment and social distress: this was the decade of the Jarrow march and Walter Greenwood's classic novel of the Salford slums *Love on the Dole* (1933). On the other hand it was also a period that saw the growth of consumerism with increasing levels of home ownership, the rise of the motor car and the advent of seaside holiday camps. As is so often the case, the historical evidence is complex and even contradictory:

while the national picture was one of economic growth and rising living standards overall, this disguised long-term structural decline in staple industries such as textiles and shipbuilding and the consequent social problems in the regions dependent on those industries. In politics the ascendancy of the coalition National Government (1931–1940) and the failure of political extremism (neither the Communist Party of Great Britain nor the British Union of Fascists were able to mobilize much popular support) suggests that this was a period of consensus.

The role of the cinema in British social life during this period was profound. The historian A. J. P. Taylor aptly described cinema as 'the essential social habit of the age' in interwar Britain.[2] In 1934 (the first year for which reliable statistics exist) there were some 903 million cinema tickets sold and over 4,000 cinemas operating in Britain.[3] The cinema was foremost an entertainment medium and what it offered its patrons was escapism: not for no reason were the Odeons and other luxury cinemas of the 1930s known as 'dream palaces'. With a few exceptions – notably the historical epics of Alexander Korda and the polished thrillers of Alfred Hitchcock – British feature films were generally not well regarded by either critics or audiences, who viewed them as shallow and inferior imitations of the populist fare offered by Hollywood. In his influential book *The Film Till Now* (1930), for example, Paul Rotha averred that 'the modern British cinema is extravagantly artificial' and bemoaned 'the conservative and narrow-minded outlook of the producing executives'.[4] To be fair to British producers the possibility of making the type of films that the more progressive critics wanted was severely restricted by the institutional and ideological contexts in which they operated. The British Board of Film Censors actively discouraged the production of films dealing with what its president, Lord Tyrrel, called 'the burning issues of the day': for example, it blocked attempts to make a film of *Love on the Dole* during the 1930s.[5] At the same time, however, the commercial imperative of the film industry meant that most British producers were themselves disinclined to provoke controversy: the film trade's view was that audiences wanted escapism rather than social realism. Hence British cinema of the 1930s was a vehicle for the promotion of consensus: its ideological outlook was to support the status quo.[6]

A common charge levelled against British films was that their content was trivial: West End farces, Art Deco musicals and society melodramas proliferated at the expense of more serious and socially edifying fare. In particular the working classes – the very people who comprised the bulk of the cinema audience – were an almost invisible presence in British films, and when they were present were usually treated as comic relief. It should be pointed out that this did not seem to bother the millions of working-class patrons who attended the cinema each week; but it was a bone of contention for those progressive critics who advocated a more realistic and socially responsible cinema. John Grierson, for example, damned Alfred Hitchcock with faint praise as 'the world's best director of unimportant pictures'. Grierson felt that Hitchcock 'is the only English director who can put the English poor on the screen with any verisimilitude', but wondered whether he would ever 'give us a film of the Potteries or of Manchester or of Middlesborough – with the personals in their proper place and the life of a community instead of a benighted lady at stake?'[7]

In this sense documentary was an alternative to the commercial mainstream of British cinema in that it was posited on the idea of a socially purposeful and aesthetically innovative film practice. Its primary objective was the representation of the lives and experiences of ordinary people. Most of the best-known documentary films of the 1930s are those depicting groups such as factory workers (*Industrial Britain*), miners (*Coal Face*), shipbuilders (*Shipyard*), fishermen (*North Sea*) and postal workers (*Night Mail*), or exploring social issues such as slum housing (*Housing Problems*), unemployment (*They Who Live*) and education (*Children at School*). There is much truth in Harry Watt's claim that documentary films

> were revolutionary because they were putting on the screen for the first time in British films – and very nearly in world films – a workingman's face and workingman's hands and the way the worker lived and worked ... [Any] working-class people in British films were the comics. There was the funny taxi driver or the butler who dropped the tureen or the comic waiter or the postman who got bitten by the dog. But we, with *Coal Face* and little things like *Housing Problems* ... and *Night Mail*, started to give the workingman, the real man who contributed to the country, a dignity.[8]

Later ideological critiques of documentary would argue that its representation of the working classes was as artificial in its own way as the comic caricatures of feature films and that the documentarists themselves – most of whom were middle-class and university-educated – could hardly claim to speak for their working-class subjects.[9] However, there is no reason to doubt that the documentarists' intentions were anything but genuine.

It was not only in its content that documentary marked an alternative to mainstream British cinema. The movement has also been associated with the intellectual film culture that emerged in interwar Britain. This was exemplified by organizations such as the Film Society in London, which showed foreign, especially Russian and German, and avant-garde films, and by publications such as the journal *Close Up* (1927–1933) and Rotha's *The Film Till Now*, which championed film as an expressive art form. This film culture was characterized by its rejection of American cinema, tainted by its vulgar commercialism, and by the cultural and aesthetic value attached to the 'art' cinemas of Europe.[10] The failure of British cinema to produce its own stylistic movement comparable to German Expressionism or Soviet montage cinema has led some critics to claim documentary as Britain's art cinema. Lovell and Hillier, for example, suggest that documentary 'captured the interest in film as an art that was developing in Britain in the late 1920s' and that consequently 'the documentary film became the British art film'.[11] This is not merely a retrospective assessement. The association between documentary and the intellectual film culture of the interwar period was established early in the movement's history when *Drifters* was shown at the Film Society on the same programme as *Battleship Potemkin*.[12] Furthermore, early documentary was influenced by the montage techniques of Soviet cinema, which can be seen in the structural form and rhythmic editing of films such as *Drifters*, *Industrial Britain* and *Night Mail*.

Documentary therefore came to enjoy a privileged place in the British film culture of the 1930s. Its cause was championed by the film critics of the quality press such as Robert Herring (*Manchester Guardian*), C. A. Lejeune (*Observer*) and Graham Greene (*Spectator*) and by the progressive film journals *Cinema Quarterly* (1933–1936) and *World Film News* (1936–1939), which were closely associated with the movement and its objectives.[13] British documentaries were regularly shown at the Film Society where they found a place alongside films such as *The Cabinet of Dr Caligari* and the Soviet classics. Grierson's *Drifters* was immediately canonized as the foundational film of the documentary movement. Paul Rotha, for example, averred that *Drifters* marked 'the beginning of a wholly new movement in film-making in Britain'.[14] The status of documentary films with ordinary cinemagoers, however, is more difficult to assess. *Drifters* appears to have been a popular success but otherwise documentary encountered stiff resistance from commercial distributors and exhibitors, who maintained that the films were difficult to book because cinemagoers wanted escapism rather than educational fare.

As well as its place in film culture of the interwar period, the documentary movement also needs to be understood in relation to other social processes. One of these was the growth of social investigation, especially in the 1930s, exemplified through the work of sociologists such as Seebohm Rowntree and organizations like the Carnegie Trust and Mass-Observation. The link between documentary and social investigation is best exemplified by Humphrey Jennings, co-founder of Mass-Observation – the independent social survey organization set up in 1937 to provide 'an anthropology of our own people' – who would became one of the movement's most individualistic talents.[15] Jennings's *Spare Time* (1939) for the GPO Film Unit is often referred to as his 'Mass-Observation film'.[16] Documentary's interest in representing the lives and conditions of ordinary people can itself be aligned with other forms of cultural practice in the 1930s, such as the photography of Bill Brandt and Humphrey Spender, and the tradition of social journalism exemplified by J. B. Priestley's *English Journey* (1933) and George Orwell's *The Road to Wigan Pier* (1937).

Finally, the documentary movement may also be seen in relation to other progressive groups in the arts such as the Left Book Club (founded by publisher Victor Gollancz in 1936) and the works of poets and writers such as W. H. Auden (who wrote the lyrical commentary for *Night Mail*), Stephen Spender and Christopher Isherwood. The conventional view of the documentary movement is that it was a broadly left-wing grouping with a progressive social and political agenda. Harry Watt, one of the group who clustered around Grierson at the Empire Marketing Board in the early 1930s, averred that 'we were left-wing to a man. Not many of us were communists, but we were all socialists, and I'm sure we all had [police] dossiers because we demonstrated and worked for the Spanish War'.[17] However, it would not do to overemphasize the political views of the documentarists themselves, which – with occasional exceptions such as Rotha's *People of Britain* (1936) – only rarely found direct expression in their films. Instead the documentary movement is perhaps best understood as a broad umbrella whose individual members ranged from committed socialists (such as Rotha and Ralph Bond) to left-leaning liberals (Edgar Anstey and Arthur Elton). Grierson, for his part, was careful never to declare support for any political party. Where the documentarists' politics did find expression was in their interest in social problems and their commitment to film as a vehicle for the promotion of democratic ideals and progressive aesthetics.

Documentary and mass communications

Another important intellectual context for the documentary movement was the development of mass communications theory during the interwar period. This grew largely out of the United States and was a

response both to the growth of the mass media in the early twentieth century and to the spread of liberal democracy in most Western
societies after the First World War. Broadly speaking there were two
academic mass communications discourses. On the one hand there
was a liberal view, which maintained that political propaganda was
essentially undemocratic and should have no place in the machinery of the state. In 1935, for example, US academic Leonard Doob
wrote that 'the word propaganda has a bad odor. It is associated with
war and other evil practices.'[18] On the other hand political scientists
such as Walter Lippmann and Harold Lasswell believed that effective
political communication was essential for participation in the democratic process.[19] They argued that the liberal democracies could learn
from the propaganda techniques employed by totalitarian states such
as Soviet Russia and Nazi Germany. In particular there was a view that
cinema was the most potent of all the mass media for influencing public opinion: film was a universal medium that appealed to the masses
and affected its audiences on an emotional rather than an intellectual
level.

The contexts for the emergence of mass communications theory were
technological developments in the mass media (especially cinema and
radio) that enabled the rapid growth of those media, and therefore an
increased exposure to them for the public at large, and at the same
time the rise of totalitarianism in Europe (Soviet Russia, Fascist Italy,
Nazi Germany) and its enthusiastic embracing of mass media as an
instrument of propaganda and social control. Mass communications
theorists advocated the adoption of modern techniques of 'persuasion'
and 'publicity' – they largely avoided the term 'propaganda' due to its
pejorative connotations – in order that democratic states could reach out
to their electorates. R. S. Lambert, for example, suggested that a consequence of the expansion of the electorate – universal suffrage had been
introduced to Britain in 1918 – was that the modern state faced 'problems of publicity which are wholly novel to it ... the old policy of saying
as little as possible to the public has proved inapplicable in the case of
the newer, wider government and public utility enterprises, which have
to make direct contact with the voter'.[20] Some of the more progressive
theorists argued that the role of official publicity in a democracy should
be to promote social improvement. In a study of political propaganda
published by Victor Gollancz, for example, Amber Blanco White wrote:
'We want the electorate to feel, and feel passionately, that they desire
a better order than the present social system and are prepared to make
sacrifices in order to get it.'[21] The notion that propaganda could be tied

to a discourse of social improvement and progress was also to inform documentary film.

These were not just theoretical ideas: even before the emergence of the documentary movement there was evidence in Britain of a growing acceptance of the role of the mass media in political communications. In fact the most enthusiastic early convert to the cause of film publicity was the Conservative Party, which in the 1920s began to use mobile projector vans to show specially made short films in its election campaigns. As *The Times* somewhat presciently remarked: 'The Conservative Party are now making use of the cinematograph regularly in propaganda work. Political propaganda seems to be the thin end of the wedge, the other end of which may be national propaganda.'[22] It has been claimed that the Conservative and Unionist Film Association (CUFA) was 'one of the most effective disseminators of political views then available' and played an important role in the party's success in the general election of 1935.[23] The CUFA was closely associated with the National Publicity Bureau – the Conservative Party's strategist-in-chief Sir Joseph Ball held senior positions in both – set up in 1935 ostensibly for the purpose of presenting the policies of the National Government to the public. The National Publicity Bureau established close links with those whom Ball called the 'leaders' of the film industry – including commercial producers such as Alexander Korda and the major newsreel companies – evidenced by the way in which the newsreels supported the National Government's rearmament programme from 1935.[24]

This was the context in which John Grierson's advocacy of documentary film must be understood. Grierson, the son of a Scottish schoolmaster, had studied at Glasgow University after the First World War and then, for two years in the mid-1920s, in the United States at the University of Chicago on a Rockefeller scholarship. It was in America that Grierson met and was influenced by Walter Lippmann, to the extent that he changed his field of research from immigration to the study of public opinion.[25] Unlike Lippmann, however, who was sceptical in the extreme about liberal democracy as an effective model of political organization, Grierson believed that public education could bolster democratic processes and institutions. In his view, the most effective means of achieving this was through the medium of film. Upon his return to Britain in 1927 Grierson began to develop a theory of documentary practice, which he articulated through lectures and essays in a range of newspapers and periodicals. It was this work that established Grierson's reputation as the intellectual driving force behind the documentary movement in Britain.[26]

Grierson's theory of documentary was never static but rather was constantly evolving, reflecting his view that documentary practice itself should adapt to changing circumstances. The fullest early expression of his ideas was an article for *Cinema Quarterly* in 1932 entitled 'First Principles of Documentary' in which he described documentary as 'a new and vital art form' that offered the possibility of 'opening up the screen on the real world' – and rather than filming in the studio in the style of feature films 'would photograph the living scene and the living story'.[27] Here he defined the three underlying principles of documentary as location shooting, photographic naturalism and the use of 'the original (or native) actor' rather than professional performers. He admired the films of Robert Flaherty, especially *Nanook of the North* (1922), for their pioneering approach to location-based ethnographic film-making, and Walter Ruttmann's *Berlin: Symphony of a City* (1927), though in the latter case he felt that the 'poetic' effects were achieved at the expense of a deeper social purpose.[28] And like most members of the Film Society he admired Soviet cinema of the 1920s, though his preference was for later films such as Victor Turin's *Turksib* (1929) about the building of the Trans-Siberian Railway rather than revolutionary classics such as *Battleship Potemkin* (1925).

From the mid-1930s the social and educational role of documentary became more central to Grierson's thinking and his writing emphasized this aspect of the medium rather than its formal properties. He argued that cinema was a vital medium for the promotion of good citizenship and that the real purpose of documentary lay in explaining social processes to the public. He believed that film 'was much more suited to the specific purposes of education than any of the other arts'.[29] He advocated the use of film 'to create appreciation of public services and public purposes' and 'to create a more imaginative and considered citzenship'.[30] By the Second World War he was claiming 'that the documentary idea was basically not a film idea at all' but simply 'happened to be the most convenient and most exciting [medium] available to us'.[31] He now argued, in retrospect, that documentary 'was developed as a movement, and deliberately in order to "bring alive" to the citizen the world in which his citizenship lay, to "bridge the gap" between the citizen and his community'.[32] Grierson's later writings, especially during the Second World War, often focused more on the nature of democratic social processes and sometimes made only tangential reference to film. Nevertheless, he evidently believed that documentary had succeeded as an agent for social reform in the 1930s: 'Without *Housing Problems* and the whole movement of social understanding such films helped to articulate, I think history would have found another and bloodier solution when the bombs first rained on the cities of Britain.'[33]

It is important to understand that Grierson was not a revolutionary in a political sense: his views were broadly to the left of the political consensus of the time but did not embrace the Marxist dogma of the radical left. Grierson and the documentarists are best understood as social democrats in so far as what they stood for was progressive reform rather than radical change through revolutionary processes. To this extent the documentary movement may be aligned with the new pressure groups that arose in the 1930s such as Political and Economic Planning and the Next Five Years Group, which advocated a greater role for the state in social and, especially, economic planning. Grierson held an essentially corporist view of the state as an instrument for planning but did not advocate state ownership of the means of production:

> My view, if any, would be that we are entering upon a new and interim society which is neither capitalist nor socialist, but in which we can achieve central planning without loss of individual initiative...I think we are entering upon a society in which public unity and discipline can be achieved without forgetting the humanitarian virtues.[34]

For Grierson, the closest to this ideal had come with the New Deal in the United States during the 1930s and in the adoption of centralized planning by the government of Ottawa in the early 1940s.

The most controversial aspect of Grierson's theory of documentary practice was his preference for state funding over the commercial sector. To some critics this compromised the independence of the documentary movement: its reliance on public subsidy meant that it became an agent of government propaganda. However, Grierson realized that the commercial sector of the film industry was not inclined to support the kind of socially purposeful cinema that documentary represented. In contrast, state sponsorship would free documentary from the dictates of the box office: it allowed the production of films that were not necessarily driven by commercial considerations. Moreover, what Grierson advocated were semi-autonomous production units where film-makers were able to follow their own convictions. In hindsight, he believed this had been achieved at the EMB Film Unit in the early 1930s:

> What was important was that this was the only group of its kind outside Russia: that is to say, the only group devoted deliberately,

continuously, and with hope, to the highest forms of documentary. And its policy was in this respect unique, that so long as the film's general aim was served, no consideration of a mere popular appeal was allowed to enter. The director, in other words, was free in his manner and method as no director outside the public service can hope to be. His only limits were the limits of finance, the limits of his aesthetic conscience in dealing so exclusively with an art of persuasion, and the limits of his own ability.[35]

It seems likely that what Grierson would have preferred for documentary was something similar to the BBC: an organization that was publicly funded but remained politically independent and free from direct state control. This would have been consistent with his corporist view of the role of the state as a sort of benign managerial bureaucracy rather than – as in the Soviet model – exercising direct control over film production.

Documentary and the projection of Britain

The origins of documentary also coincided with a growing awareness of the potential value of film as a medium of national projection. In the 1920s, especially, a public debate emerged over the nature of cinema as a vehicle for the 'projection of Britain'. The dominant view of the cinema among social and political elites ever since its emergence as a mass popular entertainment was that its social effects, especially for juvenile audiences, were harmful and pernicious: this view lay behind the formation of the British Board of Film Censors in 1912, whose role was to regulate film content in order to protect public morals from corruption by the cinema.[36] While this view persisted throughout the interwar period, there was a growing acceptance, however, that the opposite could also be the case: that the wide popular appeal of the cinema made it an ideal vehicle for promoting positive images of society and nationhood. This was the view, for example, of Sir Stephen Tallents – the forward-thinking civil servant who played a crucial role in the origins of the documentary movement, first as secretary of the Empire Marketing Board and later as public relations officer at the General Post Office – who argued in his pamphlet *The Projection of England* (1932) that 'we must master the art of national projection and must set ourselves to throw a fitting presentation of England upon the world's screen'.[37] This view was shared elsewhere within the political classes. In 1927, for example, in the course of a parliamentary debate over the Cinematograph Films Bill, which proposed introducing a degree of protection for the British film industry, Sir Philip Cunliffe-Lister, the President of the Board of Trade, declared that 'the cinema is today the most universal means through which national ideas and national atmosphere can be spread... Today films are shown to millions of people throughout the Empire and must unconsciously influence the ideas and outlook of British people of all races.'[38]

The background to this debate was an economic crisis in the British film industry in the mid-1920s. British domestic production had declined sharply due to a combination of the underlying structural weakness of the film industry, which had not yet developed a model of vertical integration as the US industry had done, and the perceived technical inferiorities of British films, which were regarded as slow and dull in relation to their American competitors. In 1926 British domestic production hit a low of only 37 feature films, and it was calculated that American movies accounted for 92 per cent of those shown in British cinemas.[39] This was the context for the Cinematograph Films Act of 1927. This legislation – popularly known as the Quota Act – was enacted in order to protect the domestic film production industry by introducing a minimum quota of British films for both distributors (initially set at 7.5 per cent and rising to 20 per cent by 1936) and exhibitors (5 per cent rising to 20 per cent).[40] The reason for the introduction of the quota was primarily economic in that it was intended to boost British production – an ambition in which it was successful even if some of the films were of low quality (the notorious 'quota quickies' produced as cheaply as possible to exploit the new legislation) – but there was also a cultural dimension in concerns that the dominance of Hollywood movies was bringing about the 'Americanization' of British audiences. This point was made by several Members of Parliament in the course of the debate over the Films Bill, including Colonel R. V. K. Applin (Conservative) who quoted an article from the *Daily Express* to the effect that 'the bulk of our picturegoers are Americanized to an extent that makes them regard a British film as a foreign film... We have several million people, mostly women, who, to all intent and purpose, are temporary American citizens.'[41]

The challenge for British cinema, then, was to offer an alternative to Hollywood that combined the best of British culture and values with the popular appeal of American movies. The strategy of British film-makers during the 1920s had been to produce a style of 'heritage' cinema characterized by its pictorialism and adaptations of English literature: this had by and large proved unsuccessful as the films were regarded as slow-paced and stylistically retarded in comparison to American films.[42] Some commentators suggested that the best course for British cinema would be a straightforward imitation of Hollywood. John Buchan, the novelist and Conservative MP, for example, maintained that 'the American producers have shown a real understanding in spite of their many crudities. It seems to me that it is the American tradition which in the main must be followed, if we are to use films for Imperial purposes.'[43] This was also the view of the film committee of the recently formed Empire Marketing Board when it agreed at its first meeting in February 1927 upon 'the desirability of the Board's undertaking propaganda by means of a film in which intrinsic entertainment value would be paramount, and which would be suitable for distribution on its merits in the ordinary commercial way to the trade'.[44] The eventual outcome was *One Family* (1930), a stodgy imperial pageant based on an idea by Rudyard Kipling about collecting the ingredients for an 'Empire Christmas Pudding' in which various society ladies symbolized the dominions ('Lady Keele as Canada, Baroness Ravensdale as New Zealand...'). Its utter critical and commercial failure dissuaded the EMB from embarking upon any similar enterprises.

Even before the filming of *One Family* an alternative approach to the use of film for national projection had already been suggested. In 1927 John Grierson was invited to prepare a paper on film publicity by EMB secretary Stephen Tallents. The paper, entitled 'Notes for English Producers', was a wide-ranging survey of film culture that included Grierson's observations on the nature of the appeal of American cinema as well as his suggestions for how British films could compete with it. He argued that what was most admirable about American cinema was its visual naturalism, exemplified by the western (he mentioned in particular *The Covered Wagon* from 1923), and that it was to this tradition, rather than to its melodramatic plots, that 'English' film-makers should look for inspiration:

It is obvious that the naturalistic manner of cinema must touch the English mind very nearly, engaging as it does the English love of the open, the English feeling for the more empirical forms of poetry, and the English respect for authenticity. It is clear too that it is the cinema tradition which lends itself best to the visually dramatic material in which the Empire is so rich: to the adventures of discovery and colonisation, to the sweep of commerce, to the dynamics of industry: to the ships, the docks, the factories, the furnaces, the streets, the canals, the plains, the plantations, the caravans, the parades, the dams, the bridges, all over the earth ball that carry the flag of English energy and sum up whatever significance may attach to the national spirit.[45]

Grierson felt that 'the real England has not been touched' and that '[a] naturalist approach to cinema would serve to rectify this'. Evidence that this view was not his alone but was shared widely within British film culture is provided by other critics such as C. A. Lejeune of *The Observer*: 'What we want from the British cinema is *real* films ... We want our own country put on the map, our cities, our pasturage, our machinery, our railways, our fisheries, our workers, our traditions, gnarled and rooted in the soil as grand old forest trees.'[46] These were precisely the images of Britain that the documentary movement sought to project.

Grierson also saw – perhaps more clearly than other commentators – that such subjects were not likely to be forthcoming from the feature film industry but rather through a different type of film. He suggested two types of 'naturalistic production': longer feature films that 'ought to be dramatic in the usual sense with a powerful story and clear characters carried along on the tide of a great event, a stirring adventure, or a large scale enterprise', and shorter films that 'would be in the nature of a glorified news reel and would extend properly to two, three, or four reels'. He laid particular emphasis on the shorter form because such films 'could afford to dispense with the powerful story and the main appeal would be quite frankly to the spectator's curiosity rather than to his emotions'. At the same time he recognized that such films would have to adopt an original approach in terms of their technique: 'The secret of success is to realise that, even when there is no story, the visual aspects of a seemingly prosaic subject can be orchestrated into a cinematic sequence of enormous virtuosity.' As an example of such 'virtuosity' he cited the sequence in *Battleship Potemkin* of the ship setting out to sea, which – in preference to the more famous Odessa steps sequence – he considered 'the most exciting piece of cinema ever shot'.[47]

Grierson's paper was widely circulated and seems to have been well received in official quarters: it no doubt gained currency from the fact that it coincided with the passing of the Cinematograph Films Act. One immediate consequence was that Grierson was invited to join the Empire Marketing Board's film committee in an advisory capacity: later he was formally employed as its films officer following the departure of Walter Creighton, who had directed the poorly received *One Family*. In the longer term it provided intellectual ballast for those within government who saw the potential of film for national publicity. It was not only the Empire Marketing Board that embraced film in this way: the Travel Association was another convert and also employed Grierson as an advisor. In 1936 a Joint Film Committee was established, including representatives from the Department of Overseas Trade, the Travel Association, the British Council and the British Film Institute. Although the committee would be riven with interdepartmental rivalries – rivalries that were exacerbated by some members' personal antipathy for Grierson himself – the simple fact of its existence points to the growing recognition within government of the value of film publicity.[48]

The acceptance of film as a medium of national projection did much to enhance the critical standing of documentary. The feature film – at least until the Second World War – was outside the remit of official propagandists, partly on account of the expense of production and partly because of the prevailing view that the commercial industry was best left to its own devices when it came to the projection of Britain. But documentary was another matter: most documentaries were shorts (typically one or two reels) and could be produced quickly and at much less expense than features. Furthermore, the documentarists' concern with the realistic representation of different aspects of British society was more suited to the needs of official publicity. Grierson claimed that *Industrial Britain* 'was hailed as a patriotic picture and is still one of the films most widely circulated for British prestige abroad' and that documentary films 'are widely recognised for the aesthetic as well as for the national character they have brought to the British cinema'.[49] While it is only to be expected that the documentarists themselves would make such claims for their own work, evidence that documentary was indeed regarded as a potent medium of national projection is also provided by this sober assessment from *The Times*: 'It is the short films of the documentary kind, and not the popular feature film, that presents the most authentic picture of our national life.'[50]

Drifters (1929) and the Empire Marketing Board

It was under the auspices of the Empire Marketing Board (EMB) that documentary first developed as a medium of national publicity. The EMB was created in 1926 for the purpose of promoting trade within the British Empire. It grew out of the Imperial Conferences of 1923 and 1926, which had urged the introduction of trade tariffs and had supported the doctrine of Imperial Preference. When these measures were rejected by the Conservative government of Stanley Baldwin, the emphasis switched instead to advertising imperial goods and produce. The EMB undertook a wide range of publicity activities and – due in large

measure to the influence of its visionary secretary Stephen Tallents –
made extensive use of the mass media, including posters, pamphlets
and films.[51] Paul Swann suggests that in the field of publicity the EMB
'was in many ways without precedent. Never before had such an elabo-
rate domestic publicity machine been operated by a British government
department in peacetime.'[52] And Grierson described the EMB as 'the
only organisation outside Russia that understood and had imagination
enough to practise the principles of long-range propaganda'.[53]

The adoption of documentary film by the EMB needs to be seen in
the context of a broad-based approach to its publicity activies.[54] The
EMB consulted experts from the world of commercial advertising such
as Sir William Crawford, who acted as an advisor to various government
departments, and Frank Pick, Director of the London Passenger Transport Board, who had pioneered corporate sponsorship of the arts, for
instance in employing avant-garde sculptor Jacob Epstein in the design
of the London Underground. From the outset, film was one of the media
that the EMB sought to employ. One of its first projects was to fund a
cinema at the Imperial Institute in South Kensington, which opened
in 1927 and ran four shows per day of films on imperial subjects. This
was followed in 1931 by the establishment of the Empire Film Library,
whose aim was to build a 'library of films illustrating the economic
geography of the Empire'. By 1932 the Empire Film Library held 550
prints – mostly acquired from external sources – and had arranged 1,873
bookings, mostly to schools, which it estimated had reached an audience of 517,000.[55] Not for the last time there is evidence to suggest that
the largest audience for documentary films was among schoolchildren.

The EMB also commissioned its own publicity films, for which it had
a budget of between £20,000 and £25,000 per year. Until the establishment of its own in-house film unit in 1930, the commissioning of films
by the EMB seemed to be on a somewhat ad hoc basis. In 1928 it commissioned 'two short films on the subject of the Herring Industry and
Empire Plum Pudding'.[56] These eventually became *Drifters* and *One Family*. In 1929 it approached the Gaumont Company to produce 'a film
to illustrate the every day life of children at work and at play throughout the Empire'.[57] Occasionally the EMB was approached by commercial
producers with a view to supporting their films: for example it turned
down an approach by the Glory Film Company regarding its fiction film
Land of Hope and Glory (1927).[58] Among several projects that did not see
fruition was 'a talking film for education of natives' planned to accom-
pany a visit to the Sudan by the EMB's Mr Vischer but not completed

due to an explosion at Gaumont's premises in Holborn, which destroyed much of its equipment.[59]

It was the success of *Drifters* that established the EMB's reputation in the field of documentary film-making. Yet in certain respects *Drifters* was atypical of the EMB's film activities. It was not a direct marketing film but instead was conceived, in Tallents's words, as 'a background film, designed to create an atmosphere by presenting English [*sic*] life and character'.[60] It has become part of the folklore of the documentary movement that the choice of the herring fishing industry as a subject was due to the fact that this was the pet subject of A. M. Samuel, who, as Financial Secretary to the Treasury, had to approve the expenditure.[61] *Drifters* was commissioned from a production company that specialized in factual subjects (New Era Films) and was intended from the outset for cinema release. The EMB Film Committee minutes reported 'that the contract ensured that it was to the interest of the producing company to keep down costs of production and also that the producing company had a direct interest in the commercial success of the film'.[62] The final cost was a modest £2,948, and the EMB received £1,194 from its theatrical distribution.[63]

As the only major film directed by Grierson himself, the making of *Drifters* deserves special attention. The first important point was that Grierson, inexperienced in film-making, worked alongside an experienced cameraman (Basil Emmott) whose contribution to the film has often been forgotten. Yet reviewers at the time all praised the cinematography: the trade paper *Kinematograph Weekly*, for example, thought the film was 'outstandingly good' and remarked that 'Basil Emmott's camerawork helped the clever direction of John Grierson'.[64] Another significant point is that even during the shooting of the film it soon became evident that what Grierson had in mind was not necessarily a strictly authentic picture of the herring fisheries but rather an idealized representation of them. The unit travelled to Lerwick in the Shetland Islands where it hired a trawler 'chiefly on the strength of her crew's supposed photogenic quality'.[65] As it proved impossible to shoot inside the trawler's cabin while at sea, a set was built on the quayside for the interiors. The 'underwater' shots of fish were taken in a tank at a marine research institute in Plymouth. Grierson moved on to Great Yarmouth where he shot scenes in the fish market. While in Norfolk he decided that he wanted the film to include 'a real storm, an intimate storm, and if possible a rather noble storm. I waited in Lowestoft for weeks till the gale signal went up, and I got it'.[66]

The filming of *Drifters* was completed by late 1928 but it would be a full year before it was ready for release. Grierson and Margaret Taylor (whom he later married) spent over six months editing 10,000 feet of raw footage into a film of four reels that ran for one hour. It was during the editing of *Drifters* that Grierson had the first practical opportunity to explore his theory of 'the creative treatment of actuality'. His adoption of highly formalist Russian-style editing prompted some concern that the film would not be accessible to general cinema audiences. New Era's Sir Gordon Craig reported that the 'quality is first rate, and compares very favourably with the better class commercial films now being produced here', but added that 'I find it somewhat slow in action, and the titling "over the head" of the ordinary man in the street'.[67] Nevertheless, following its premiere alongside *Battleship Potemkin* at a private screening for the Film Society on 10 November 1929, *Drifters* was shown publicly at the Avenue Cinema and subsequently received quite a wide release in Britain. In January 1930 the EMB Film Committee 'noted with satisfaction the number of bookings which had been made to date of the Herring film – "Drifters" '.[68] It was one of the last silent films to reach a wide audience in Britain: most cinemas were converting to sound in 1929–1930.

There is good reason to believe that *Drifters* was more influential in relation to the development of film form and technique than it was in promoting sales of North Sea herring. The contemporary reception of *Drifters* focused on its contribution to the art of cinema: it was admired for its formal qualities rather than for the intrinsic interest of the subject matter. *The Manchester Guardian*'s review, for example, called it 'that rare thing . . . a film growing out of a knowledge of what films are for, out of a theory which is used to achieve expression, and expressing therefore a portion of life which contains wider implications than its actual action'.[69] The mass-market magazine *Film Weekly* noted its 'tremendous dramatic power' and felt that 'although it has no story in the accepted sense, [it] is one of the most thrilling, entertaining, and completely satisfactory pictures I have seen'.[70] It accorded with the views of film art held by the Film Society and other proponents of the intellectual film culture. For Paul Rotha, '*Drifters* is the only film produced in this country that reveals any real evidence of construction, montage of material, or sense of cinema as understood in these pages.'[71]

The trend in more recent critical discussion of *Drifters* has been to see it as an example of avant-garde film practice rather than as the foundational film of the documentary movement.[72] It exemplifies Grierson's idea of 'the creative treatment of actuality' in so far as the film's impact arises more from the formal components of editing and *mise-en-scène* than from the raw filmic material. In particular, Grierson adopted techniques associated with Soviet cinema such as montage and typage. The editing style of *Drifters* is closer to the 'structural montage' of Pudovkin than to Eisenstein's 'montage of attractions' in that individual shots are used as building blocks and there are no violent 'shocks' between images: indeed *Drifters* sometimes uses fast dissolves to smooth the transition from one shot to the next. It is slower-paced than the Russian films and more pictorialist. Grierson occasionally uses images for symbolic effect: the cutaway shots of waves crashing against rocks, for example, are unrelated to the narrative and might be understood as a visual metaphor for the hardships of the fishermen's lifestyle. The device of typage – the use of people not as individual characters in their own right but rather as representative social types – is seen in the use of 'nobility' close-ups of the skipper and members of the crew as they go about their work. This reflected Grierson's own rather idealized idea of the working classes: '*Drifters* is about the sea and about fishermen and there is not a Picadilly actor in the piece. The men do their own acting, and the sea does it ... Men at their labour are the salt of the earth.'[73] In this context *Drifters* was the first instance of a trend that would be very prominent in the early history of British documentary: the representation of the working classes as romanticized 'heroic' archetypes.

Yet the formalism of *Drifters* should not detract from its status as documentary. As an account of the herring fisheries the film is built around the relationship between tradition and modernity. This theme is introduced in the opening caption: 'The herring fishing industry has changed. Its story was once an idyll of brown sails and village harbours – its story is now an epic of steam and steel.' Elsewhere the film contrasts the historic roots of the fishing industry ('Fishermen still have their homes in the old-time village') with its place in the modern world of international trade ('And the sound of the sea and the people of the sea are lost in the chatter and chaffer of a market for the world'). *Drifters* also contrasts the natural environment (sea, birds, fish) with machine technology (the recurring montages of the trawler's engine with its pumping pistons and the funnel billowing steam). In this sense *Drifters* exhibits something of a tension between the historical process of modernization on the one hand and the persistence of traditional values and ways of life on the other. Grierson also uses montage to imply social comment: the scenes of the catch being boxed and sold in the market at the end of the film are intercut with shots of the men at sea hauling fish in a gale, which suggests that what is really being sold is the labour of the fishermen themselves.

It might have been thought that the success of *Drifters* would prompt the EMB to the whole-hearted adoption of the documentary method in its film publicity. In fact it was just one of several styles that were tried, with varying degrees of success. Grierson's next project was 'a film to illustrate the development of communications within the Empire'.[74] This film – eventually known as *Conquest* (1930) – was rather different to *Drifters*: it was compiled from existing footage, much of it from American westerns, and became a documentary about the history of Canada. However, the EMB Film Committee expressed reservations about its length and 'felt that the question of the historical accuracy of the incidents to be portrayed should be investigated'.[75] There is no record of the film having been shown publicly: it was regarded as a failure and persuaded Grierson that future films should be compiled only from original material. The ill-starred *One Family* was finally completed in 1930 at a cost of £15,740: the expense was due mostly to the addition of a soundtrack after shooting had been completed. There had been concerns about the quality of the film for some time: these fears were realized when it was reported 'that the film had not been well received and the Company responsible for its distribution did not regard its prospects favourably'.[76] This was something of an understatement: the film took only £334 at the box office and did not even recoup the cost of its premiere. Its failure persuaded the EMB that 'second-feature films (i.e. films of the "Drifters" type)' were better suited to its purposes as they were cheaper to produce and had better prospects of securing commercial distribution.[77]

Another lesson drawn from these various projects was that the EMB's interests would be better served if it was able to produce its own films rather than commissioning them from outside contractors whose efforts (as in the case of *One Family*) did not always match their expectations. This was the impetus behind the establishment of an in-house film unit in 1930. This was initially set up on a trial basis for six months with a budget of £2,350 to include the rental of office space in Wardour Street.[78] A programme of six films was planned and it was suggested 'for the work to be done by several young beginners, employed at very small fees'.[79] This explains the recruitment of 'promising young men' fresh out of university and with no experience of the film industry such as Basil Wright, Edgar Anstey and Arthur Elton. Other early recruits included Grierson's sister Marion and brother-in-law John Taylor, while Stuart Legg, Paul Rotha (briefly) and Harry Watt joined later. The group assembled by

Grierson at the EMB Film Unit would become the core of the early British documentary movement.

The EMB Film Unit initially turned out short 'poster films' and compilations from existing footage, but an increase in its budget in 1931 allowed it to embark upon a programme of more ambitious films – known as the 'Imperial Six' – intended for theatrical exhibition.[80] However, the EMB films struggled to find an audience in commercial cinemas as they were shot as silents – the film unit's budget did not extend to sound-recording facilities – for which there was no longer a market. Instead, the EMB films were shown through the non-theatrical circuit where there was still demand for silent films in 'substandard' (usually 16 millimetre) prints. Other than *Drifters* the only EMB film of any real note was *Industrial Britain* (1931). Grierson, perhaps mindful of the inexperience of his own colleagues, hired Robert Flaherty, then down on his luck and out of favour in Hollywood, to make a film exploring Britain's industrial heritage. Flaherty shot location footage, mostly in the north of England, which was edited into coherent shape by Edgar Anstey with the addition of music and commentary (by actor Donald Calthrop). This was at the insistence of the distributor, Gaumont-British.[81]

Industrial Britain can be seen as a transitional film in the development of British documentary between the avant-garde formalism of *Drifters* and the more didactic style of films such as *Coal Face*. It develops the technique of *Drifters* with its montages of machinery and its 'nobility' close-ups of workers in the coal, glass and steel industries. Again it emphasizes the links between tradition and modernity: the commentary asserts that today's workers 'stand for the continuity of English craftsmanship and skill, for an emphasis on quality, which only the individual can give'. In particular, the film focuses on the making of 'beautiful things' such as aerodrome lenses that require skill and precision. For this reason *Industrial Britain* has sometimes been seen as working against the social purpose of documentary: its emphasis on traditional craftsmanship has the effect of detaching the labour force from the economic contexts of modern industry. In hindsight, the absence of any reference to the problems affecting manufacturing industry following the economic crisis of 1931 is striking: the film focuses exclusively on work without mentioning that millions had no work. Like *Drifters*, *Industrial Britain* romanticizes the working classes: it is, above all, a paean to 'the personal skills of so many first-rate English workers'.

The *succès d'estíme* of *Drifters* – and to a lesser extent *Industrial Britain* – would save the film unit when the Empire Marketing Board was wound up in 1933. Despite its innovative approach to publicity the EMB had failed to make any tangible impact on the worsening trade depression: hence it became a victim of economies when the new National Government sought to cut public expenditure. In any event, the existence of the EMB had never sat easily with advocates of a free market. Nevertheless there was a view that the film unit was worth preserving. Tallents and Grierson lobbied behind the scenes to save the unit from the wreckage of the EMB. Their campaign was successful: it was decided that the film unit and its film library should be transferred to the General Post Office (GPO). The Post Office was looking to develop its own publicity activities and had already commissioned two films from the EMB Film Unit (*Telephone Workers* and *The Coming of the Dial*) towards this end. The acquisition of the film unit provided a ready-made agency to further this aim.

Robert Flaherty and *Man of Aran* (1934)

Man of Aran is something of an odd-film-out in the history of British documentary during the 1930s. Although acclaimed at the time as an important and prestigious film, its reputation seems to have diminished in hindsight, to the extent that it barely receives a passing mention in the histories of British documentary by Aitken and Swann. This is likely because *Man of Aran* was made by a director (the American Robert Flaherty) outside the British documentary movement and was produced for a commercial studio (Gaumont-British Picture Corporation) rather than for the EMB or GPO Film Unit. The film is also difficult to position in formal and aesthetic terms: its style of reconstructed naturalism is more a throwback to the ethnographic interest of Flaherty's *Nanook of the North* (1922) and *Moana* (1926) than a counterpart to the modernist aesthetic of *Drifters*. Yet the film's uniqueness demands attention.

Man of Aran was a prestige undertaking for Gaumont-British, the leading British film studio of the 1930s, and for its head of production Michael Balcon. Gaumont-British's output consisted mostly of popular genre films: thrillers, romance, musicals, comedies. *Man of Aran* would be its one venture into documentary and resulted from Balcon's own admiration for Flaherty, who had become interested in what he had heard about the people of the remote Aran Islands off the Galway coast of Ireland. According to Balcon's autobiography:

> This, as described by Flaherty, was enough. I did not ask him for any written story. It would have made no difference in any case as Bob did not work in a conventional way, and I had decided almost

immediately to go ahead and make a film simply about the struggle for life of the Aran Islanders.

In purely commercial terms, Bob was looked upon as a risk by those contolling the distribution and exhibition of films... I suppose I was taking a great chance with my own prospects in agreeing to an outlay of £10,000. Bob did not worry too much about money, either his own or what was spent on the film. He looked upon the costs as my problem and, needless to say, the money was exhausted long before the film was completed, and the project became known as 'Balcon's Folly'.[82]

The escalating cost was due to Flaherty's notoriously slow way of working – the unit was on location for over six months – and his habit of shooting without a script. Harry Watt, who was loaned to the unit as an assistant director in order to gain experience, estimated that Flaherty shot 250,000 feet of film. Watt averred that editor John Taylor, also loaned from the EMB, 'deserved just about equal credit with Flaherty'.[83] Balcon viewed the rushes as they were shipped back to London and recalled that Gaumont-British chairman Isidore Ostrer and his wife were 'absolutely enthralled by the uncut scenes of seascape and the wonderful performances of the cast Bob had assembled from among the islanders'.[84]

   Man of Aran demonstrates a rather different concept of documentary practice than the other British documentaries of the time. Flaherty was interested in traditional practices and customs and was not averse to reconstructing them for the camera. For example, the islanders themselves had not for many years hunted basking sharks with harpoons from small boats but Flaherty brought in an expert to teach them how to do it. This has inevitably raised questions about the authenticity of the film as an anthropological documentary depicting the lives and customs of the islanders. And in contrast to the films of the Griersonian school, *Man of Aran* makes no comment, either explicit or implicit, about the social and economic structure of the community it depicts. Hence *Man of Aran* had a mixed reception from documentary purists. Grierson felt that it 'was not altogether the film some of us expected. It made sensation of the sea, it restored shark-hunting to the Arans to give the film a high-spot, but Flaherty's genius for the observation of simple people in their simple manners was not, we felt, exercised to the full'. Nevertheless he still described *Man of Aran* as 'the British commercial cinema's only work of art' and was critical of distributors who 'cut down the film and billed it below the line as a subsidiary feature'.[85] Rotha was much less impressed by a film that he saw as a 'reactionary return to the worship of the heroic' and felt that at a time of economic depression documentary 'should not ignore the vital social issues of this year of grace'.[86]

The somewhat equivocal response to *Man of Aran* within the documentary movement highlights the extent to which British documentarists by the mid-1930s positioned themselves as distinct not only from the commercial cinema but also from their predecessors within the documentary mode. Flaherty's essentially romantic outlook towards his subjects now seemed dated: the more progressive outlook of the British documentary school would cause it to turn more towards social subjects as the decade progressed. In later years the reputation of *Man of Aran* rested largely on its beautifully naturalistic cinematography rather than on any ethnographic import. André Bazin admired 'the photrographic splendour of the films of Flaherty' and cited 'the shots of the basking sharks of *Man of Aran* floating drowsily on the Irish waters', but was critical of the methods employed to achieve this and expressed a preference for documentary that 'does not falsify the conditions of the experience it recounts'.[87] At the time, *Man of Aran* was a commercial failure though it achieved some critical recognition when it was awarded the Mussolini Gold Cup at the Venice Film Festival ('It made quite a useful and impressive ashtray', the staunch anti-fascist Balcon remarked). Gaumont-British would not attempt any further forays into documentary. Flaherty was involved in one more British film, shooting the location footage in India for what became Alexander Korda's *Elephant Boy* (1937), before he returned to the United States where his last completed film was *Louisiana Story* (1948).

The GPO Film Unit: The 'Voice of the Nation'

The GPO Film Unit has become more or less synonymous with the documentary movement during the 1930s even though it was responsible for only slightly more than one-quarter of the approximately 300 documentary films produced in Britain during the decade.[88] This is due partly to the fact that most of the core members of the documentary movement worked at the GPO Film Unit at some point – Paul Rotha was the one major exception – and that it produced most of the 'classic' documentaries of the time: *The Song of Ceylon*, *Coal Face*, *Night Mail*, *North Sea*, *Spare Time*. Under Grierson's direction the GPO Film Unit embraced a collaborative method of working that might be seen as his way of ensuring that no authorial signature other than his own was imprinted on its films: this would later lead to some dispute over the 'authorship' of films such as *Night Mail*.[89] Most of the key personnel of the GPO Film Unit were inherited from the Empire Marketing Board, though there were two important new recruits: Alberto Cavalcanti, a Brazilian film-maker associated with the avant-garde movement in France during the 1920s, and Humphrey Jennings, the Cambridge-educated intellectual aesthete who had convened the International Surrealist Exhibition in London in 1936 and co-founded Mass-Observation. Cavalcanti and Jennings would both depart from the Griersonian idea of documentary: hence the GPO Film Unit would become the focus of an ideological and aesthetic split within the documentary movement in the later 1930s.[90]

Its move to the GPO was much to the benefit of the film unit. The Post Office spent more on publicity than other government depart-ments and allocated more funds to the film unit than the EMB had done.[91] The film unit acquired larger office premises in Soho Square and an old art studio in Blackheath, south London, that was equipped for sound recording. The adoption of sound – even in the form of the Visatone-Marconi system that was technically inferior to the sound facil-ities of the commercial studios – meant that the unit would finally be able to make full 'talkies' for theatrical release.[92] Furthermore, the GPO Film Unit also produced films for external bodies – these included the Ceylon Tea Propaganda Bureau (*The Song of Ceylon*) and the BBC (*BBC: The Voice of Britain*) – and for other government departments, notably the Ministry of Health (*Health of the Nation*, *Welfare of the Workers*), as well as for the Post Office. It was often the films for external bod-ies that were released theatrically and were consequently most widely reviewed: hence the GPO Film Unit's reputation was built largely on a small number of 'prestige' films that were not representative of its work overall.

The GPO Film Unit's enhanced status was not achieved without some controversy. It faced opponents both inside and outside government. There were some voices within the film industry who objected to the existence of a state-funded film unit that would be making films in competition with the commercial sector. One particularly vocal oppo-nent was M. Neville Kearney, secretary of the Film Producers Group of the Federation of British Industries, who complained that the GPO Film Unit was 'highly prejudicial to the interests of the tax-payer and to the development of an important and growing industry in which many millions of British capital have been invested'.[93] The film trade did not object to the production of films by government departments but believed that they should be contracted out to commercial producers on a competitive basis. This may help to account for the resistance to GPO films from trade interests who were reluctant to book them for commercial exhibition. It may also explain why some GPO films, including *Coal Face* and *The King's Stamp*, were released under the label 'EMPO' without a GPO credit. If this was an attempt to disguise their origins it failed: none of the EMPO films were picked up by a commercial distributor.

The film unit also ran foul of its paymasters at the Treasury, who cast a critical eye over its expenditure and its operating practices. In 1934 the unit came under scrutiny from the Select Committee on Estimates, which was concerned by its loose terms of reference and what it called the unit's 'semicommercial' activities. The Select Committee recommended that the unit should not undertake any further production for external bodies without first seeking the Treasury's approval and insisted that its management should be reorganized in order to conform to civil service protocols. Grierson and Tallents had established the film unit on somewhat unorthodox lines in that most of its personnel were contracted to New Era Films rather than being on the civil service payroll. This enabled them to take on consultancy work for other organizations: Edgar Anstey and Arthur Elton, for example, also advised the British Commercial Gas Association on documentary film. In the short term, Grierson and Tallents were able to delay implementing the Select Committee's recommendations, though in the longer term their obstructive tactics and suggestions that they had misled the Select Committee sowed the seeds of distrust of the film unit within the Treasury.[94]

It would seem that what the Treasury objected to most was the management structure of the film unit rather than its costs. In fact the GPO Film Unit was an economical operation, not least because its members accepted an ethos of 'long hours and low wages'.[95] Basil Wright recalled that, before making *The Song of Ceylon*: 'I invested quite an amount of my money in buying my own film camera, a Newman Sinclair which was of a very advanced nature at the time.'[96] (The Newman Sinclair, introduced in 1927, was a 35 millimetre camera that was particularly favoured by documentarists due to its relatively light weight and robust construction.) The unit was also able to make films at very low cost. According to Harry Watt, the two-reeler *Night Mail* cost only £2,000 – 'it may have been less'.[97] This represented a cost of around £1 per foot that was the benchmark for the cheapest commercial films. It may have been that the low budgets of the GPO films were a deterrent to their securing a wide commercial release: certainly they often suffered from poor-quality soundtracks in comparison with other films. Nevertheless, it would seem that the film unit's survival in the face of the Treasury's hostility was largely down to the fact that the same sort of films could not be made cheaper elsewhere.

The strategy of the GPO Film Unit initially was to produce half a dozen shorts for commercial release each year (from 1934 these were handled by Associated British Film Distributors) as well as occasional longer films – though production for external bodies was abandoned after *The Song of Ceylon* and *BBC: The Voice of Britain* in response to the Select Committee's report. In fact it was only in 1934 that it managed to release six films (known collectively as the 'Weather Forecast' group) and then only because the Board of Trade made a special dispensation to allow them to be registered for quota under the Cinematograph Films Act (short films were excluded from quota unless deemed to be of 'special exhibition value').[98] From the mid-1930s the strategy changed with selected two-reel (*Night Mail*) or three-reel (*North Sea*) films for commercial release on an individual basis. Otherwise the GPO focused on the non-theatrical market: it held film shows in public halls and sent mobile projectors to schools and film societies. In 1936 the Post Office was operating four cinema vans, which reached an estimated audience of 500,000 schoolchildren and 25,000 adults.[99]

The work of the GPO Film Unit both built upon the achievements of its predecessor at the EMB and at the same time developed the documentary film in new directions. Any full assessment of its achievements must take into account both the public service role of the film unit (institutional context) and its contribution to documentary practice (form and aesthetics). Many GPO films, especially in the unit's early years, were fairly routine informational films on aspects of Post Office work such as the repair of underwater telephone lines (*Cable Ship*) or collecting weather reports for the Meteorological Office (*Weather Forecast*), while others explained the operation of telecommunications technologies such as the direct-dial telephone (*The Coming of the Dial*) and telegraph (*CTO: The Story of the Central Telegraph Office*). A style of humorous whimsy emerged in films promoting the domestic telephone service (*Pett and Pott*) and explaining telephone etiquette (*The Fairy of the Phone*). Paul Rotha disliked these two films, which he felt were 'errors of judgement ... whimsical attempts at comedy reminiscent of amateur charades'.[100] One of the roles of the GPO Film Unit was to act as an advertising agency for its parent body. This was most apparent in a cycle of films promoting the Post Office Savings Bank (*John Atkins Saves Up*, *The Saving of Bill Blewitt*) and services such as the Speaking clock (*At the Third Stroke*). Indeed one of the reasons advanced by the trade for its reluctance to book GPO films was that they were unwilling to pay for advertising films. Cavalcanti's *Pett and Pott* (1934) even addressed this point when the judge presiding over the trial of two burglars – who have been apprehended due to the telephone – declares: 'It is possible that at this stage of the proceedings the court and public have drawn the inference that this case and the incident apertaining thereto savour strongly of what I believe is commonly known as "advertisement" on behalf of the Post Office telephone service.'

However, to see the GPO Film Unit as nothing more than a semi-public advertising agency would be to take a very narrow view of its work. Grierson encouraged experimental film-making and gave opportunities to some film-makers whose work belongs more to the realm of avant-garde practice than classic documentary. The films of New Zealander Len Lye (*A Colour Box, Rainbow Dance, Trade Tattoo*) pioneered the technique of what later came to be known as 'Direct Cinema' (achieved by painting on and scratching a strip of celluloid) and anticipated later artist film-makers in their use of 'found footage'. Lye's films have more in common with abstract painting than documentary: indeed he had exhibited work at the International Surrealist Exhibition in 1936.[101] The GPO Film Unit also provided an outlet for animators Lotte Reiniger (*The Tocher, The HPO*) and Norman McLaren (*Love on the Wing, Money a Pickle*): Grierson met Reiniger, a German émigré, at the Film Society, and came across McLaren's work through judging the Scottish Amateur Film Festival in 1936. These films may have been regarded as minor and tangential but they helped to establish the GPO Film Unit's reputation as a centre of formal and aesthetic experimentation.

The main business of the GPO Film Unit, however, was to inform the public about the work of its parent body. In particular it faced the task of explaining how the Post Office was adapting to the new world of modern communications – a task that fitted the agenda of modernization associated with Postmaster General Sir Kingsley Wood. As Tallents declared in a pamphlet *Post Office Publicity* (1934): 'We need to build up, piece by piece, a picture for our own people, and also for others, of what this country has done, is doing and seeks to do in its endeavour to equip itself . . . to meet a wholly new range of modern conditions.'[102] The underlying theme that links most of the GPO films is the idea of the Post Office as an essential institution at the heart of British life. Hence the Post Office enables people of all classes to communicate with family and friends, whether by letter (*Letters to Liners*), postcard (*Penny Journey*), telegram (*Sixpenny Telegram*) or telephone (*Community Calls*). A recurring theme of the GPO films is the role of the Royal Mail in

connecting communities, especially providing a lifeline for isolated set-
tlements in the Outer Hebrides (*The Islanders*) or a village cut off by
flooding (*The Horsey Mail*). Another group of films focus on transport –
including roads (*Roadways*), railways (*Night Mail*), air (*Air Post*) and sea
(*SS Ionian*) – and its importance to modern communications. Collectively the GPO films promote the idea of a nation united not just by
culture and tradition but by its institutions and public services: to this
extent the GPO Film Unit fulfilled Grierson's idea of the role of documentary as a means of explaining social services and institutions to the
public.

The projection of Britain – or at least a certain idea of Britishness – was
central to the ideological project of the GPO Film Unit. Two themes in
particular are emphasized. The first is social cohesion and unity. While
social inequalities are acknowledged in GPO films, including 'letters for
the rich, letters for the poor' (*Night Mail*), the overriding impression is
one of cohesion and consensus. GPO films portray British society united
by its affection for radio (*BBC: The Voice of Britain*) and its love of sport
(*What's on Today*), while the GPO's network of postal and telephone
services unite people of all classes (*Calendar of the Year*). The fullest
expression of this theme is Stuart Legg's *BBC: The Voice of Britain* (1935),
the most ambitious and, at a cost of £7,500, also the most expensive
of the GPO Unit's films of the 1930s.[103] The film chronicles a day in
the life of the British Broadcasting Corporation and has been seen as an
early prototype of the 'fly-on-the-wall' documentary – though it is clear
that the scenes showing senior BBC personnel in conference have been
staged for the camera. It stresses the role of radio as a force for national
unity – through shots of people of all classes, ages and backgrounds listening to the wireless – and gives equal prominence to popular culture
(Henry Hall and the BBC Dance Orchestra, comedians Clapham and
Dwyer) and high culture (including classical music and a production
of *Macbeth* featuring Humphrey Jennings as one of the witches). It is
also notable for the appearances of various public luminaries, including G. K. Chesterton, J. B. Priestley, George Bernard Shaw and H. G.
Wells. There is an irresistible parallel between the role of the BBC under
Director-General Sir John Reith 'to inform, educate and entertain' and
Grierson's understanding of the role of documentary as a vehicle for the
promotion of good citizenship.[104] In this sense the GPO Film Unit, as
much as the BBC, could be said to represent 'the voice of Britain' in the
1930s.

The second recurring theme of GPO films is modernity: Britain is
represented as a nation connected by modern telecommunications
(telephone, telegraph, radio) and leading research into science and

technology. 'Research – the creative power behind the modern world', declares the commentary in *The Coming of the Dial* (1933). There is an emphasis throughout on the idea of the new, whether the 'new world of modern roads' (*Roadways*) or 'a modern system of communications' (*Weather Forecast*). To this extent the GPO films mark a shift of emphasis from those of the EMB, which had emphasized continuity with the past in films such as *Drifters* and *Industrial Britain*. The GPO Film Unit's projection of Britain as a technologically progressive nation is supported by its adoption of modernist aesthetics. The modernist impulse was exemplified by the recruitment of graphic designers such as Patrick Keely, who produced striking posters for GPO films and exhibitions, while the Hungarian avant-garde artist László Moholy-Nagy designed a montage sequence for *The Coming of the Dial*. The painter William Coldstream worked on several GPO films and received a directing credit for *The King's Stamp* (1935): he said he was drawn to the unit by 'the opportunity to work in a medium which seemed technically and socially appropriate to the times'.[105]

Within the standard historiography of British documentary and the GPO Film Unit a critical orthodoxy has emerged that distinguishes between the 'lyrical' or 'poetic' style of directors such as Basil Wright (*The Song of Ceylon*) and Humphrey Jennings (*Spare Time*) on the one hand and the preference for more structured storytelling in the films of Harry Watt (*North Sea*) and Pat Jackson (*The Horsey Mail*) on the other. While differences in style are certainly evident, however, it would not do to overemphasize this distinction, which is more apparent in hindsight – and then only in relation to certain films – than perhaps it was at the time. The fact that Watt and Wright collaborated in making *Night Mail* – and that Cavalcanti also made a significant contribution to the same film beyond his official credit for 'sound direction' – suggests that the differences between their approaches should not be exaggerated. Indeed, one reason why *Night Mail* has come to be seen as the exemplar of the GPO Film Unit might be that it fits equally into both the 'poetic' and 'story' modes.

The GPO films are perhaps better understood as exploring the various possibilities of the 'creative treatment of actuality' than as conforming to any particular style or approach. This is evident in the differences of style that characterize its best-known films. The unit's first major film, Basil Wright's *The Song of Ceylon* (1934), was inherited from the Empire Marketing Board and can be seen as a transitional film between the EMB and GPO. It was sponsored by the Ceylon Tea Propaganda Bureau who had envisaged four short films, but Wright – who spent five months shooting on location in Ceylon – saw greater potential in the material, which he edited into a four-reel film rather like *Drifters* though with the addition of a soundtrack and commentary. *The Song of Ceylon* can be placed in the same formal tradition as *Drifters* in so far as there was no scenario prepared in advance and the structure of the film emerged at the editing stage. It combines the naturalism of location shooting with the formalism of montage and is particularly notable for its experimental use of sound. Walter Leigh's score combines genuine Sinhalese music with orchestrations and both natural and synthetic sounds. The juxtaposition of images of workers harvesting tea by hand with voices reciting the prices on the commodity markets, for example, develops Eisenstein's idea of 'polyphonic montage' in that meaning arises from the relationship between image and sound. Here the device links the labour of the workers to the commercial trade in tea – it implies that the profits of the tea trade arise from the exploitation of an underdeveloped economy – though this element of social criticism is undercut by the film's insistence on the spirituality of the Ceylonese people and their traditional way of life. *The Song of Ceylon* won critical plaudits, including the Best Film Prize at the Brussels International Film Festival in 1935. It was much admired for its formal qualities: Graham Greene called it 'an example to all directors of perfect construction and the perfect application of montage'.[106]

The Song of Ceylon stands out among other 1930s documentaries for its aesthetically satisfying formal structure. Wright later suggested that this emerged as if by osmosis:

> If we take all the titles off *Song of C*. & joined it front to end it would have a continuous and permanent whole – the forward & backwards relationships being evened out into the 'magical' form of the mandala. This may be the reason why JG and I, *at the last minute*, put in the titles *in order to codify it in Western views* [*sic*] rather than leaving it in its oveural [*sic*] continuum. *And* of course to 'hide' the magic (circle). The 'instinctive' and 'instinctual' construction of *S of C*. is fully explained by the mandala idea. One does not *consciously* make a mandala.[107]

Wright's comparison of the film to a mandala – a term from Buddhism that refers to a spiritual space characterized by its formal symmetry that creates a sense of wellbeing – was influenced by his reading of Carl Jung's commentary on Richard Wilhelm's translation of the Taoist text *The Secret of Golden Flower* (1932). It is a retrospective reading that Wright laid onto *The Song of Ceylon* after reading Jung and, in that sense, may represent a post-hoc rationalization of the creative decicions taken along the way.

The experimental use of sound that characterized *The Song of Ceylon* was developed further in Grierson's *Granton Trawler* (1934) and Cavalcanti's *Coal Face* (1935). These films were again compiled from actuality footage with sound added at the editing stage: they are especially notable for their combination of montage and non-naturalistic sound. *Granton Trawler* dispenses entirely with voice-over commentary and employs abstract sounds to represent the thumping noise of the engines and the howling wind. Its disjointed montage and fragmented *mise en scène* represent perhaps the fullest incorporation of Soviet methods into the British documentary film. *Coal Face* was described as 'a new experiment in sound' when it was shown at the Film Society: its soundtrack combines discordant music (by Benjamin Britten), choral singing and colloquial dialogue. It maintains voice-over commentary but employs it sparingly. Like *Granton Trawler* it mixes 'nobility' close-ups of workers with montage, while its iconography of pit heads and slag heaps provides a powerful visual record of 1930s Britain that is rather less idealized than the landscapes of *Industrial Britain*. *Night Mail* (1936) famously combines rhythmic narration and montage as W. H. Auden's poetic commentary is matched to shots of the train steaming up an incline ('This is the night mail crossing the border/ Bringing the cheque and the postal order ... '). At the same time, however, *Night Mail* has a more structured narrative than *Granton Trawler* or *Coal Face* – following the journey of the 'postal special' from London to Glasgow – and its protagonists are more individualized. With its scenes of staged dialogue shot on a studio set, *Night Mail* anticipated the emergence of the story documentary in the later 1930s.

Night Mail was a more representative example of the films of the GPO Film Unit than either *The Song of Ceylon* or *Coal Face* because it focused on an aspect of the Post Office's work. It was one of several GPO films focusing on activities of mail sorting (*6.30 Collection*) and distribution (*Air Post*). *Night Mail* was promoted as something of a prestige film and met with generally positive reviews, though a dissenting note was sounded by Arthur Vesselo in *Sight and Sound* who felt that its use of real people struck a false tone: 'The difficulties of introducing ordinary railway employees at work, and of recording their movements and voices without making both seem oddly colourless (especially the latter, which at times seem positively disembodied) are the most obvious part of a comprehensive general difficulty in the handling of natural material.'[108]

Others criticized the film for its lack of social comment. Rotha averred that *Night Mail* 'has no social purpose whatsoever...It's beautifully made, superbly made, but what does it do in the end? It merely tells you how the postal special gets from Kings Cross to Edinburgh [*sic*]. It cannot possibly tell you about the conditions of postal workers or anything of that sort'.[109] Rotha felt that the public funding of the GPO Film Unit prevented it from adopting a more critical perspective towards its subjects: hence its preference for self-conscious aestheticism rather than sociological investigation.

The charge that the GPO Film Unit lacked social purpose is more than a little unfair, however, as some of its films did address social issues. The commentary of *Coal Face*, for example, highlights the dangers of the job ('Every working day four miners are killed and over 450 maimed or injured – every year in Great Britain one in every five miners is injured') and emphasizes the dependence of whole communities on the mines ('The miner's life is bound up with the pit. The miner's house is often owned by the pit. The life of the village depends on the pit'). And Ralph Elton's *The City* (1939) contrasts the lives of the wealthy residents of the West End of London ('Only the boss can afford to live here') with the slums of the East End ('Our bit of England is a rented room in one of the dilapidated houses...We live here huddled amid London's dirt, buried in the smoke and grime'). The GPO films are best understood not as belonging to either an aesthetic or a sociological trend within documentary but rather as texts that attempt to work through the tension between aesthetics and social comment that runs throughout all documentary films.

By the late 1930s there is evidence that the GPO Film Unit was starting to divide into different groups along ideological and aesthetic lines. This reflected a wider split within the documentary movement as a whole. On the one hand Grierson and his closest associates (Anstey, Elton, Legg) were favouring a more didactic style that eschewed narrative altogether and saw the future of documentary as being outside commercial cinemas. On the other hand Cavalcanti and Harry Watt felt that the best way for documentary to reach its audience was through incorporating some of the techniques of the fiction film in order to secure a cinema release. Grierson's resignation from the GPO Film Unit in 1937 – he had grown resentful of the civil service bureaucracy that had slowly eroded the relative autonomy he had enjoyed at the beginning – and Cavalcanti's promotion to the role of supervising producer in 1938 meant that the second view would prevail. The story-documentary mode emerged in films such as Watt's *The Saving of Bill Blewitt* (1936)

and *North Sea* (1938), Evelyn Spice's *A Job in a Million* (1937) and Pat
Jackson's *The Horsey Mail* (1938). These films were characterized by their
more structured narratives and largely abandoned Soviet-style montage
in preference for the continuity editing style of the fiction film. They
also made use of scripted dialogue and a greater amount of studio work.
They focused more on individuals (*The Saving of Bill Blewitt*, *A Job in
a Million*) or on groups where individual characters are delineated (the
trawler crew in *North Sea*), though true to their documentary roots they
used non-professional actors. Watt explained how the approach to story
documentary differed: 'I found that filming a story was quite different
from our usual general sort of atmospheric shooting. Your audience is
interested in your principal artist only and, through them, follows the
story.'[110]
     The critical and popular success of *North Sea* indicated that the story-
documentary mode could indeed reach out to the general audience that
had so often proved elusive for the documentarists. This was yet another
account of the fishing industry, though its treatment was very different from *Drifters* or *Granton Trawler*. Watt scripted the film in advance,
drawing on reports of distress signals and storm warnings from vessels
that occurred every winter, but dramatized these events through the
specific episode of one trawler caught in a gale. Most of the film was
shot on location in Aberdeen and off the Scottish coast using real fishermen, with some scenes then reconstructed in the studio. *North Sea*
does not entirely reject montage – the sequence of the crew pumping
water and dumping coal overboard demonstrates the persistence of the
Soviet influence – but formally the film is structured around narrative
and continuity editing. It also represented a shift away from the heroic
but somewhat abstract representation of working-class protagonists in
films like *Coal Face* and *Industrial Britain* to a more character-based style
that invites closer identification with the subjects as individuals. The
success of *North Sea* was timely for the GPO, which in the late 1930s was
again coming under scrutiny from the Treasury. Its publicity department
could claim that

the GPO Film Unit has now a high and well established reputation
as a producer of documentary films. None of its products has been
a palpable failure, and many of these have been strikingly successful. *North Sea* in particular has earned over £4,000 in rentals (a sum
believed to be a record for a documentary film) and has been generally acclaimed by the press as setting a new standard in this field,
despite the fact that its release coincided with the release in this

country of the far more costly film *The River*, produced under the auspices of the American Government and heralded with a remarkable amount of publicity.[111]

One admirer was Robert Flaherty, who felt that it marked a new direction for documentary: 'If there could only be here and now a series of films running through the cinemas like *North Sea* all at the same time, I am sure a vast new audience would plump for them at once.'[112]

Yet the success of *North Sea* was something of an exception: the majority of GPO films were still destined for the non-theatrical circuit. Nor did the story-documentary mode become dominant: it co-existed with the more discursive style of films such as Cavalcanti's *We Live in Two Worlds* (1937) – 'a film talk by J. B. Priestley' that promoted his particular brand of internationalism – and the impressionistic style of Humphrey Jennings's *Spare Time* (1939). The latter film, produced for the New York World's Fair, was the first in which Jennings's distinctive authorial voice can be heard. *Spare Time* draws upon Jennings's experience with Mass-Observation in its exploration of working-class leisure and popular culture ('Between work and sleep comes the time we call our own – what do we do with it?'). For some critics, such as Basil Wright, it exhibited 'a patronizing, sometimes almost sneering attitude towards the efforts of the lower-income groups to entertain themselves'.[113] This now seems an absurd judgement of a film that is notable above all for its complete lack of condescension towards its subjects. It may be that documentary purists disliked the film because it departs from the Griersonian ethos of exploring the social and economic contexts of its subject matter: *Spare Time* has no interest in the working lives or material conditions of the working classes. But it also rejects straightforward narrative in its apparently unstructured sequence of social activities, including a brass band, darts, football, dance hall, fairground, male-voice choir, puppet show and even a kazoo band. In this sense *Spare Time* can be seen both as a link back to the early history of documentary in the films of Mitchell and Kenyon, and as anticipating Jennings's wartime masterpiece *Listen to Britain*.

Independent documentary units: Shell, Strand, Realist and others

Some three-quarters of the documentary films produced in Britain in the 1930s were made outside the public sector. Most histories of British documentary identify an 'independent' strand of the documentary movement existing separately from though running in parallel with the GPO Film Unit. And it was this independent documentary sector that was responsible for a more direct engagement with social problems in films such as Arthur Elton and Edgar Anstey's *Housing Problems* (1935) and Paul Rotha's *Today We Live* (1937). In fact there was no clear distinction between public-sector and independent documentary. The major independent documentary units of the 1930s were all to some extent offsprings of the GPO Film Unit. Grierson acted as a consultant for the petroleum company Shell when it set up its own film unit in 1934, and Basil Wright founded the Realist Film Unit in 1937 after leaving the GPO. The Strand Film Company – originally set up as a feature film producer in the late 1920s but reinventing itself as a documentary unit in 1935 – also employed several former GPO film-makers, including John Taylor, Alexander Shaw and Ruby Grierson. Furthermore, many documentarists crossed over freely between the GPO and other producers, including Edgar Anstey, Arthur Elton, Stuart Legg and Ralph Bond. And, finally, some films initially intended for production at the GPO, such as Elton's *Workers and Jobs* (1935), were instead assigned to outside producers. Hence there was significant crossover in personnel and consequently in form and style between the GPO and other production units.

The context for the emergence of the independent documentary sector is to be found in the expansion of public relations during the 1930s. This period saw major industries (gas, oil, aviation) and semi-public agencies (such as the National Council for Social Service) take an interest in documentary film. This was due in large measure to the influence of a group of enlightened public relations executives – such as Jack Beddington of Shell-Mex and British Petroleum, Snowden Gamble of Imperial Airways and A. P. Ryan of the Gas, Light and Coke Company – who held to the view that industry should also have a social conscience. Basil Wright attributed the adoption of documentary by the private sector to the example of the EMB and GPO Film Units: 'The success of the EMB and GPO led to other big organisations (monopoly capital organisations and so on) realising that it was good public relations to set up their own use of film (I'm thinking particularly of the Shell film unit, which eventually grew into one of the most important documentary units ever).'[114] However, there already existed a tradition of sponsorship of advertising films by commercial concerns such as the LMS Railway Company and Cadbury's Chocolate. The difference between these films and the sponsored documentaries of the 1930s was that the documentaries related their content to wider social issues. For example, Sir David Milne-Watson, the director of the Gas, Light and Coke Company, believed that films such as *Housing Problems* helped to foster 'improved understanding and increased confidence between our industry and its public'.[115]

There were various models of documentary sponsorship. Shell Oil, after sponsoring a film in association with Imperial Airways (*Contact*), set up its own in-house production unit in 1934. The Shell Film Unit was headed by Alexander Wolcough and employed both Anstey and Elton as producers. Its stated aims were: 'To improve the efficiency of the Shell organisation by creating a greater knowledge of its products, and by teaching modern methods of marketing; to help improve the demand for Shell products; [and] to create general goodwill with perhaps no immediate or directly traceable return.'[116] To this end the Shell Film Unit exemplified the tension between commercial advertising and social utility that characterized the field of sponsored documentary production. From the outset a characteristic of the Shell Film Unit was the low profile in its films of the name of their sponsor. It specialized in technical and scientific films, exemplified by *Transfer of Power* (1939) and *Transfer of Skill* (1940), which were characterized by their high production values, though it also produced the well-received *Airport* (1935) for general exhibition.[117]

Other sponsors commissioned films from independent contractors. It was in this way that several particular associations between sponsors and film-makers emerged in the 1930s. Imperial Airways, one of the major commercial sponsors, provided a regular income for the Strand Film Company with a cycle of films including *Air Outpost* (1937), *The Future's in the Air* (1937) and *African Skyways* (1939).[118] The aim of these films was to promote air travel, a new and luxury commodity. They can be seen within the tradition of the travelogue in that their appeal arose in large measure from their pictures of distant overseas locations such as Sharjah and Cape Town, which would have seemed exotic to the vast majority of British cinema audiences. The British Commercial Gas Association sponsored several films from Grierson's close associates, including Arthur Elton (*Housing Problems*, *Enough to Eat*) and Basil Wright (*Children at School*, *The Smoke Menace*). The growth of industrial sponsorship prompted Grierson to set up an organization known as Film Centre in 1938. This was described as a 'film consultancy' whose role was to act as a co-ordinating body for sponsors and producers of documentary films. It was not a production organization, though it did have a credit on some films, for example the Realist Film Unit's *Children at School* (1937). Film Centre was also the mover behind one of Grierson's pet projects: the Films of Scotland Committee. This commissioned several films in 1938–1939 from various producers including Realist (*The Face of Scotland*), Strand (*The Children's Story*) and GB Instructional (*They Made the Land*).[119]

GB Instructional was something of an anomaly in the documentary field in the 1930s in that it was a subsidiary of one of the major commercial companies. The Gaumont-British Picture Corporation was the largest producer-distributor-exhibitor in Britain at the time. Its establishment of a factual subsidiary, alongside a specialist distributor (GB Screen Services), was initially geared towards the provision of 16 millimetre films and projectors for schools, but it soon branched out into documentary films for general release. In 1933 it took over British Instructional Films from which it inherited the *Secrets of Nature* series – rebranded as *Secrets of Life* – and production supervisor Harry Bruce Woolfe. GB Instructional has usually been seen as outside the mainstream of the documentary movement, presumably on account of its connections with the commercial film industry, but it was a major producer with over 100 short factual films during the 1930s. Its films were well regarded: *The Mine* (1936), for example, won a medal of merit at the Venice International Film Congress. GB Instructional also provided Paul Rotha with his first opportunity as a director. In 1932 Rotha was hired to direct *Contact* for Shell and Imperial Airways. Rotha explained how the film came to be made for British Instructional:

> Shell could not contract with me to produce the film. A contract must be made with a company. I could have proposed New Era but because of its EMB relations decided against it. Looking around the industry, I could find only one company which had some kind of an honest reputation and which would give me services without any control over the making of the film ... A contract was drawn up between the Shell Company and British Instructional Films, by which they provided technical services for the production in return for 10 per cent of the contract price. My own fee was agreed at £200 for what eventually came to be a year's work of direction and editing.[120]

Rotha's association with British Instructional Films would continue with GB Instructional for whom he made *Shipyard* (1935) and *The Face of Britain* (1935) before leaving the unit to become director of production for the Strand Film Company. These were again produced for commercial sponsors – *Shipyard* was a joint venture for shipbuilders Vickers Armstrong and the Orient Shipping Line – but were notable for the degree of social comment that Rotha was able to introduce into the films. *Shipyard*, for example, contrasts the luxury liner being built with the lives of the workers ('This bloomin' ship will 'ave seen more of the bloomin' world than I'm ever likely to!') and ends on a sombre note with the realization that the launching of the ship means that many of those who built it are now without work. The shipbuilding industry was one of the most depressed industries in 1930s Britain and *Shipyard* highlights the cyclical nature of employment in the town of Barrow-in Furness.

Rotha was never one of Grierson's inner circle: his background was in art school and he first established his reputation as a critic with *The Film Till Now* before a very brief spell at the EMB Film Unit in 1931. Rotha's achievements have often been overshadowed by the towering presence of Grierson but he deserves recognition as a major figure in the early history of the independent documentary movement. He was the founder of Associated Realist Film Producers in 1935 and was the group's spokesman before the Moyne Committee in 1936. Rotha sought to distance himself from what he regarded as the aestheticism of the GPO Film Unit and instead set out to make films with a clear social purpose: 'When I started up the Strand Film Company, I had as a result of my journeys into the Midlands and into Scotland, seen so much of the unemployment and the ghastly state that people were in, that I was determined to make films about these things.'[121] His most important film of the 1930s was *Today We Live* (Strand, 1937), which Rotha produced with Ralph Bond and Ruby Grierson directing. *Today We Live* was sponsored by the National Council for Social Service, a semi-public organization set up to encourage self-help among the unemployed. The film is a formal hybrid between the story documentary (using unemployed miners from the Rhondda and the people of a small village in Gloucestershire) and the more didactic sociological style of documentary associated with the independent sector. It is notable for placing present-day economic problems in a historical context, taking a distinctly jaundiced view of the Industrial Revolution and exploring the consequences of the Great War. It particularly highlights the regional impact of unemployment, noting that South Wales and other depressed areas have been left 'without a share in the revival of work', and the plight of the long-term unemployed whose 'hands have lost their skill'. While the message of the film is the positive role that social services can play in fostering a spirit of self-help in building community facilities such as a social centre and village hall, it nevertheless concludes that 'social services cannot do everything. There are fundamental problems that strike at the very root of our existence. Only by working together, with unsparing energy, can we hope to solve them.' *Today We Live* was one of the few independent documentaries to secure a commercial release and was well received by critics. *The Times* felt that its message was more uplifting than novels such as *Love on the Dole*:

> This impression of life in the distressed areas is not propaganda; it is a film with a purpose... [This] encouragement to the men to work out even part of their salvation is immeasurably more important than, say, the agonizing pictures painted by those serious novelists who have looked on unemployment and despaired.[122]

The independent documentary movement of the 1930s was characterized by a degree of formal innovation in the examination of social problems. Arthur Elton's *Workers and Jobs* (London Film Productions, 1935) combined location shooting and direct sound recording. It includes scenes shot at the Poplar Employment Exchange in which the unemployed 'speak' for themselves. The staged dialogue seems naturalistic and unscripted: it is also notable for the paternalistic outlook of the officials towards the unemployed ('Off you go, son, and wish you the best of luck') and the deferential attitude of the unemployed themselves ('Much obliged, thank you') that may seem patronizing to modern eyes but may also be representative of the social attitudes of the time. *Workers and Jobs* was sponsored by the Ministry of Labour and ultimately gives the impression that the role of the employment exchange was as much to help firms in filling vacancies as it was to assist the unemployed in finding work: 'The employment exchanges of Great Britain have on their books workers trained for every type of labour... They can fill almost any vacancy.' Elton and Edgar Anstey developed the technique of direct address in *Housing Problems* (British Commercial Gas Association, 1935). This is notable for the inclusion of interviews with slum dwellers in which they speak directly to the camera in what amounts to an early example of *vox populi*: the interviewees were given guidelines on what to say but their comments were unscripted and in that sense can be said to represent the authentic 'voice' of the poor. The interviewees include Mr Norwood ('The two rooms which I am in now, I have to pay ten shillings a week and I 'aven't room to swing a cat... I'm not only overrun with bugs, I've also got mice and rats') and Mrs Hill ('It gets on your nerves, everything's filthy – dirt, filthy walls, and the vermin in the walls – it's wicked'). As in *Workers and Jobs*, however, *Housing Problems* is mindful of its sponsor, which it positions as a progressive and socially responsible industry. Hence there are shots of new model housing developments, while a voice-over tells us: 'The gas industry has designed suitable appliances for cheap cooking and for room and water heating explicitly to meet the needs of slum clearance schemes.'

The standard histories of British documentary in the 1930s tend to position films such as *Housing Problems* and Anstey's *Enough to Eat?* as outstanding examples of the documentary with a social purpose. Richard Griffith averred that films 'like *Housing Problems* and *Enough to Eat?* have already influenced national policy, and all of them have contributed to the reputation of the documentary film as an agency for bringing the ordinary citizen in touch with the forces which govern his life'.[123] *Housing Problems*, for example, was shown to MPs at the House of Commons and seems to have been favourably received.[124] However, it would probably be more accurate to suggest that such films informed public debate rather than influencing government policy directly. *Housing Problems* was actually produced after the National Government had earmarked significant funds towards a major slum clearance campaign between 1933 and 1938. In this sense, the social purpose of the film and other less well-known films on the same subject – such as *The Great Crusade* (British Pathé, 1936) – was not so much to advocate the need for slum clearance and a programme of new house-building but rather to show how these activities were already being carried out.[125]

It has been suggested that the sponsorship of documentary by commercial industries limited its potential for genuine social criticism. Brian Winston, for instance, has argued that 'Grierson brilliantly squared the circle for the entire tradition – right-wing money, left-wing kudos and films of dubious social worth in the middle.'[126] It is undeniable that documentary films, both public and private sector, often revealed a tension between the social and political concerns of the documentarists on the one hand and the ideological or economic imperatives of their sponsors on the other. However, the criticism of the films for being of 'dubious social worth' is entirely unfair. It is important to evaluate the documentaries of the 1930s in their historical context: these were the only films at the time that attempted to address 'the burning issues of the day'. The overriding impression of *Housing Problems*, for example, remains the testimony of conditions in the slums rather than its platitudes about the social utility of the gas industry. The films may have promoted consensual social politics – given the ideological contexts in which they were produced it would be unrealistic to expect anything else – but they should be recognized for their ambition rather than criticized for their limitations.

Documentary and the trade: distribution and exhibition

A criticism often levelled against the documentary movement – including by the Treasury and also by some historians arguing for the reclamation of the British feature films of the 1930s – is that, despite the claims of its adherents, documentary was essentially a marginal mode of film practice that made little impact on the wider film culture. In other words, these were films that critics loved but no one wanted to see. The fact that only a handful of documentaries received a wide theatrical release – including *The Song of Ceylon, Night Mail* and *North Sea* – has served to reinforce this impression. The failure of documentary to secure its place in the commercial cinema raises the issue of the relationship between the documentary movement and the film trade. Some documentarists regarded the trade as hostile and blamed the commercial distributors for failing to secure release for their films. Paul Rotha, for example, believed that the distributor of *Contact* (Wardour Films) 'dislike the film and all it stands for because it is a new kind of film-making which they are incompetent to market'.[127] However, Grierson, in his evidence to the Moyne Committee in 1936 – set up to review the operation of the Cinematograph Films Act – sounded a more mollifying tone: 'Without special protection of the type suggested, the documentary film has had a satisfactory growth. Its reception by the trade was bound to be slow, but it has been more sympathic than some of us expected.'[128]

Paul Swann claims that the 'evidence is overwhelming that exhibitors and distributors had little time – or space in their film programs – for the documentary film'.[129] There is much anecdotal evidence, certainly, that exhibitors were reluctant to book documentaries. The exhibitors' trade paper *Kinematograph Weekly* consistently argued that their audiences came to the cinema to be entertained rather than for education. It should be borne in mind that a majority of the cinemagoing audience was working class: it was widely believed that such audiences did not wish to see films reminding them of their own social conditions or hardships. As the producer Dallas Bower observed: 'You rarely see a genuine documentary film in a popular cinema-hall. The miner does not want to see his own backyard and precious few viscountesses are interested in or care two hoots in hell about slum clearance.'[130]

However, this view must be qualified to some extent. The documentarists argued that as their films were so rarely accorded a cinema release, the point about public indifference could not be proven one way or the other. Rotha told the Moyne Committee that there were 'many cases...where exhibitors have taken some of their short documentary films and have not even advertised these films to a public which wishes to see them'.[131] He cited the case of *Shipyard*, which had been shown only briefly and without publicity in a Newcastle cinema. Rotha's testimony was supported by the Tyneside Film Society, whose secretary reported that it 'is anxious to see the widest possible distribution of good films, negating the anomaly of the Quota Act whereby many British-made films of documentary class are considered ineligible for "quota" '.[132] It would seem, therefore, that there were some audiences who were interesed in documentary. Even some sections of the trade recognized this. *The Cinema* remarked in 1936: 'When the documentary film deals with real life in a way which is vital and entertaining, as in *Shipyard*, it can no more fail to secure a circulation among the general public than does the well-edited and keenly-written newspaper.'[133]

Given that some documentaries, notably *Night Mail* and *North Sea*, did indeed secure successful theatrical bookings, it becomes necessary to look for other reasons for exhibitors' resistance to documentary. These can be found in the nature of exhibition practices in Britain in the 1930s and in the operation of the quota system. The introduction of the double bill – offering two feature films for the price of one – meant that shorter supporting films were squeezed out of many cinema programmes. Hence the market for all short films, not only documentaries, was contracting during the 1930s. The Board of Trade's own Cinematograph Films Advisory Committee recognized in 1935 that 'the substantial production of short films in Great Britain under existing conditions does not appear to be commercially practicable'.[134] Another factor was that films under 3,000 feet in length were excluded from quota under the terms of the Cinematograph Films Act. It is no coincidence that most of the documentaries that did secure a theatrical release were longer than 3,000 feet and therefore counted towards quota: these included *The Song of Ceylon, BBC: The Voice of Britain* and *The Future's in the Air*. The documentarists held that they were at a commercial disadvantage because the Cinematograph Films Act 'was framed before the Documentary Film became an important feature in British production as a medium of entertainment and public value'.[135]

It was the exclusion of documentaries and other short films from the quota legislation that brought about a campaign to revise the Cinematograph Films Act when it was due for renewal in 1938. Here the documentary movement found allies both in the commercial sector and in the trade union movement. A range of arguments were mobilized in support of the extension of full quota status to shorts and documentaries. Associated Realist Film Producers suggested that documentary should be afforded special status on account of its value as a medium of cultural projection, its civic value and as 'a source of prestige to British Cinema in the international field'.[136] The Strand Film Company argued that granting full quota status to documentaries and shorts 'would stimulate production in this country which is ever at the moment leading the world in documentary film production, and would create a new growing point for the film industry'.[137] And the Trades Union Congress averred that 'the need to encourage the production and exhibition of short British films of exceptional merit and of high social, educational and cultural value, is as great if not greater than the need to maintain and develop an intelligently conducted film production industry'.[138] The opposition was led by the Cinematograph Exhibitors' Association (CEA), which maintained that 'British shorts are not forthcoming in sufficient numbers because there is no money in them' and suggested that they should be excluded from the quota rather than 'trying to prop up something which is not economic'.[139] So little value did the CEA attach to documentary that its memorandum of evidence did not even mention it.

On this occasion the documentarists and their allies won the argument over the CEA. The Moyne Committee recommended that short films should be eligible for quota, subject to the same 'quality test' that it advised for feature films, as an attempt to rid the industry of the notorious 'quota quickies'. This would be assessed by a special panel including film-makers, exhibitors and others with no commercial connection with the film industry: the criteria for shorts were understood as 'meaning either box office value, special cultural or economic value, or special value from a national or Imperial point of view'.[140] These measures were duly reflected in the revised Cinematograph Films Act of 1938, which set a short films quota of 15 per cent for distributors and 10 per cent for exhibitors. The immediate effect was a marked increase in the number of documentaries registered for distributors' quota from 5 in 1936 and 7 in 1937 to 12 in 1938 (8 after the new act came into force on 1 April) and 13 in 1939.[141] This was due in some measure to more of the big American distributors, including MGM and United Artists, picking up British-made documentary films in order to fulfil their quota obligations.

However, there were still various obstacles for documentary to overcome in securing theatrical distribution. Oddly enough some of these were created by documentary producers and sponsors themselves. *North Sea* provides a case in point. This was the GPO Film Unit's most successful film but its overseas sale was very nearly wrecked by the

incompetence of the GPO, who mistakenly offered it to MGM as a feature film and then made a ham-fisted approach to Paramount who had
distributed the acclaimed American documentary *The River* (1938).[142]
In the event, the US rights were sold to a minor British distributor
(World Wide Pictures) for just £100. Evidence that little importance was
attached to overseas sales is that negotiations were left in the hands of
the GPO Film Unit's office manager, Stanley Fletcher, who evidently had
little experience in this regard and who complained that the bureaucratic procedures of the civil service meant that opportunities were lost
as 'the majority of overseas sales are agreed by telephone for as often
as not an immediate decision is required as dealers are in London only
for a few days and probably only effectively available for a few hours'.[143]
Nevertheless, the film also secured a commercial release in France, where
the distributor reported: 'Your film *North Sea* is having an unheard of
distribution throughout the whole of France and in every circuit. I am
personally very pleased with the result and, in my opinion, it constitutes
a happy augury to our future collaboration.'[144] However, the Second
World War brought an end to further plans for distribution of GPO films
in Europe.

Documentary and the public: audiences and reception

If the attitude of the trade towards documentary veered between indifference and hostility, how did the public respond to the films? The
anecdotal evidence of the popular reception of documentary is both
sketchy and contradictory. Thus, on the one hand, a cinema manager
from the West Country clearly felt that there was a receptive audience:

> In my encounters with all types of cinema patrons in the provinces I
> have been surprised at the enthusiasm which often permeates a cin-
> ema from the front row of the 'sixpennies' to the back row of the
> 'two shillings' when a good 'interest' or one of the many admirable
> British documentary shorts is flashed upon the screen. Cinema man-
> agers and cinema patrons have both combined to convince me (the
> former by their advertising of them and the latter by their applause)
> that the interest and documentary short is a valuable asset to the
> entertainment offered and purchased.[145]

This contradicts Rotha's testimony that cinemas were tardy in advertising documentaries and might indicate that the situation overall was
more varied. On the other hand, however, other sources suggest that

popular documentaries were very much an exception. According to Leslie Halliwell, then a young film buff growing up in Bolton in the 1930s:

> The majority of British shorts were excruciating, the *Secrets of Nature* series with its stop-frame nature photography being an honourable exception. Very occasionally the GPO Film Unit would come along with an eye-popping item like *Night Mail*... In Mum's words it was almost as good as a real film, even if it didn't have a story. Of course we did not then understand the word 'documentary'; non-fiction films were usually labelled 'interest', which is something they rarely did.[146]

The significant point here, perhaps, is that documentary was not necessarily understood as a separate category by audiences who instead saw them as just one type of short subject.

The surveys of cinemagoing habits and preferences conducted by Mass-Observation, while revealing in other respects, yield little evidence about documentary. The 'Worktown' survey of three cinemas in Bolton in 1937 did not include documentary as a category: while the overwhelming preference of cinemagoers was for 'musical romance' first with 'drama and tragedy' a distant second, 7 per cent of respondents nevertheless nominated 'nature and reality' films as their favourites.[147] This presumably meant, again, the likes of *Secrets of Nature*. Documentaries featured more prominently in Mass-Observation's nationwide survey of favourite films in 1943 when *Desert Victory* and *Target for Tonight* were often mentioned. While these films were, arguably, a departure from the pre-war documentary movement, the qualitative comments suggest that by the Second World War audiences had become used to documentaries in the cinemas: 'Documentary films have a great appeal to me'; 'The film was of course purely documentary'; 'First class "documentary" shooting and editing'.[148]

The limited theatrical exhibition of documentary during the 1930s might cause us to assume that the films were not widely seen. However, it was not only in commercial cinemas that documentary films were shown: indeed there is evidence that more documentaries were seen outside the cinemas than inside. The growth of non-theatrical distribution is sometimes overlooked in histories of British documentary that prioritize film-making over exhibition. This is due in part to the difficulties of estimating the size of the non-theatrical audience and assessing just how widely films were shown. Yet the documentarists always believed there was enormous potential in the non-theatrical market. Grierson, for example, came around to the view by the mid-1930s that non-theatrical was the way forward:

> As I see it, the future of the cinema may not be in the cinema at all. It may even come humbly in the guise of propaganda and shamelessly in the guise of uplift and education. It may creep in quietly by the way of the YMCAs, the church halls and other citadels of suburban improvement. This is the future for the art of cinema, for in the commercial cinema there is no future worth serving. It represents the only economic basis on which the artist may expect to perform.[149]

Grierson's emphasis on the non-theatrical market reflects to some extent his disappointment that documentary had not been able to secure a stronger foothold in the commercial cinema. But it also shows, again, how his concept of documentary as a social practice was constantly evolving: documentary needed to be able to adapt to the circumstances, and if the theatrical market was closed off this meant trying other avenues.

The most extensive non-theatrical distribution scheme was the film library that had been inherited from the EMB by the GPO. In 1935 this amounted to 850 films that were loaned to schools, technical colleges, workers' educational institutes, rotary clubs, YMCAs, YWCAs, local councils, chambers of commerce and industrial firms.[150] The library and loan system was administered by the Imperial Institute, which reported growing demand as more schools and societies acquired 16-millimetre sound film projectors: the total number of loans rose from 14,550 in 1934 to 22,785 in 1936.[151] In addition, the Post Office – following the example of the Conservative Party – deployed mobile projector units to take its films 'on the road'. J. B. Holmes wrote that this 'continues the policy of bringing the Post Office before the public by going out to the audiences as well as bringing the audiences to the cinema'.[152] There were special screenings of GPO films at events such as the Olympia Radio Exhibition in 1936 and the Glasgow British Empire Exhibition in 1938. However, evidence of how well such exhibitions were attended is again contradictory. On the one hand it was reported that 15,000 tickets were alloted in advance for a three-month display of GPO films in Manchester in 1935.[153] On the other hand a Treasury official attending the same event reported: 'On the day on which I went to Manchester there was in the hall on the two occasions when I passed through only a mere handful of spectators.'[154]

Even if one accepts the (probably inflated) figure of 3.5 million that the Post Office claimed as the total audience for its non-theatrical film shows in 1938 this is dwarfed by the 987 million cinema admissions in the same year.[155] However, there is reason to believe that non-theatrical audiences, while much smaller, may have been more receptive to documentary films. The documentarists believed that non-theatrical distribution reached a more specialist audience that was better aligned with their social interests than the general cinema audience. According to the post-war survey *The Factual Film*: 'This was a logical step in documentary development because the non-theatrical audiences were found in schools and at the meetings of societies and trade unions where they could be appealed to along the line of their special interests, unlike the average cinema audience.'[156]

However, the evidence would suggest that the largest constituency for non-theatrical film shows were school-age children. In 1934, for example, over 50 per cent of GPO Film Library loans were to schools.[157] Schools from all over the country borrowed films, including both state and public schools: to this extent the non-theatrical audience was genuinely national and extended across classes. Among the many testimonials from schoolteachers, this letter from the headmaster of Tupsley Church of England School is typical:

> May I once again express my appreciation of the GPO Films which are proving to be a very valuable aid in teaching in my school. They have been used with other classes than those originally intended and approximately two hundred children each week have seen those films already loaned.[158]

While schools accounted for the majority of loans, other organizations that made use of the GPO Film Library included the Royal Empire Society, the Oxford Radio Recreation Club, Deptford Men's Institute, Lincoln Co-operative Society, the Institute of Electrical Engineers and a firm of sausage makers called Dickie, Paterson & Riddick – and these were just during the first quarter of 1940. All the thank-you letters testify that the films were liked and appreciated, and some yield anecdotal evidence of the qualitative reception of documentary films. Naomi Mitchim, for example, ran a film club in rural Argyll:

> Many of the people here have never been to a big town at all, and films such as these are wonderfully widening to the outlook. Personally, I always enjoy your films so much because of the real people

in them; if one wanted to show a foreigner what British men and women were really like, the GPO Films would be what I should choose. I have seen *Night Mail* several times, and have always found it equally thrilling.[159]

Here, there is evidence that the films were appreciated in the sort of terms that their makers intended: for their educative value, their realism and their representation of British life. The fact that Ms Mitchim singles out *Night Mail* for special praise, furthermore, as Mrs Halliwell had also done, demonstrates that the status of this particular film in the documentary canon was recognized at the time and is not merely a retrospective evaluation.

Any attempt at an overall assessment of the achievements of the documentary movement of the 1930s must necessarily deal in generalizations. On the one hand the failure to secure a foothold in the commercial cinema meant that documentary would always be something of a marginal presence in the British film industry. On the other hand, however, the progressive ethos of documentary, both socially and aesthetically, ensured that it enjoyed an influence in British film culture that extended beyond the circulation of its films. This can be seen in the gradual infusion of documentary techniques into the commercial film industry. The fact that Robert Flaherty was hired by two commercial producers in Gaumont-British (*Man of Aran*) and London Films (*Elephant Boy*) is evidence that the film industry was attracted by the prestige attached to documentary even if the films themselves had problematic histories. Flaherty's influence can also be seen in Michael Powell's documentary-style feature film *The Edge of the World* (1937). The influence of documentary was perhaps most evident in the extent to which by the late 1930s there were signs that a more realistic and socially relevant popular cinema on the lines that Grierson and others advocated was starting to emerge in British feature films such as *The Citadel* (1938) and *The Stars Look Down* (1939). And in 1940, following the outbreak of war, and when mass unemployment was no longer a social problem, the British Board of Film Censors lifted its ban on the filming of *Love on the Dole*. At long last British cinema would see the production of socially purposeful films that were realistic in style and addressed 'the burning issues of the day'. It is impossible to say whether this would have happened without the presence of documentary, but it seems reasonable to suggest that the process was hastened by the films of the documentary movement.

3
Documentary at War

> The documentary movement represents a special expertness in the use of films for propaganda and informational purposes. For eleven years its members have been working to a thesis of public enlightenment which now fits closely to official needs; so much so that many things which documentarists have urged long and vainly now look like being created as a result of the war urgency.
>
> *Documentary News Letter*[1]

In most histories of British cinema the Second World War is regarded as a 'golden age' when the social practice of cinema-going was at its height (annual cinema admissions reached their peak at 1,632 million in 1945) and when British films, long dismissed as pale imitations of Hollywood, enjoyed a hitherto unprecedented level of both critical and popular acclaim.[2] The war also marked a high watermark for the British documentary movement, whose skills and experience were now much in demand for the provision of 'propaganda for democracy'. It was during the Second World War that documentary films reached their widest audiences and that documentary entered into the mainstream of British film culture. Documentary films such as *Britain Can Take It!*, *Target for Tonight* and *Fires Were Started* became synonymous with the ideological project of British wartime cinema to represent the 'people's war', while critics at the time and since have identified a 'wartime wedding' between documentary and the fiction film in which the style and ethos of the former infused the latter.[3]

The ideological and cultural circumstances of war affected documentary film-making in several ways. The most immediate impact was that the state became the main sponsor of documentary film. Some 1,887 films were officially 'presented' to the public in Britain and overseas

during the Second World War.[4] The majority of these were short informational and instructional films commissioned by the Ministry of
Information (MOI) or other government agencies. These official films
ranged from short 'trailers' appended to newsreels containing messages
of immediate public importance (for example, the 'food flashes' produced for the Ministry of Food) to feature-length war documentaries
for commercial distribution such as *Target for Tonight* and *Desert Victory*. Such was the need for official films that several new independent
documentary units were set up during the war, including Greenpark,
Merton Park, Paul Rotha Productions, Seven League Productions, Spectator Films and Verity Films. Most of the commissions for these companies
came from the public sector, though a degree of industrial and private
sponsorship remained throughout the war. In terms of ideology and aesthetics, the war served to widen the split that had started to emerge in
the documentary movement in the late 1930s. On the one hand the trajectory towards the story documentary, signalled by the GPO Film Unit's
North Sea, reached its fullest extent in wartime films such as *Men of the
Lightship*, *Target for Tonight*, *Coastal Command* and *Western Approaches*.
These films were complemented by the re-emergence of actuality compilations such as *Desert Victory* and *The True Glory*. These were the 'big'
feature-length documentary films that figure prominently in the standard historiography. On the other hand the far-reaching social changes
experienced during the war allowed scope for documentarists to pursue
their own progressive social and political agendas. A significant trend
of wartime documentary was the emergence of films exploring wartime
collectivism and projecting this forward to lay down a manifesto for
social reform and reconstruction. This trend, particularly evident in
films for non-theatrical distribution, was supported by *Documentary
News Letter*, a new journal published from 1940 by Film Centre, which
succeeded *Cinema Quarterly* and *World Film News* as the voice of the
progressive element within British film culture. The intellectual project
of *Documentary News Letter* during the war was twofold. It revisited the
ideological and aesthetic debates of the 1930s in order to present a revisionist view of the documentary movement as a more unified voice than
it was in reality. And it set itself up as an unofficial watchdog and critic
of the MOI and its policy for film propaganda.[5]

The Ministry of Information and documentary film

The wartime role of documentary film-making is inseperable from the
history of the Ministry of Information (MOI), the new department with

overall responsibility for the control and direction of official propaganda policy (or 'information' as the British preferred to call it in order
to differentiate themselves from the activities of the German Ministry
of Popular Enlightenment and Propaganda) whose offices were based
in the Senate House building of the University of London.[6] The MOI's
Films Division was charged with commissioning films on behalf of the
government and advising feature film producers on the sort of subjects it
felt would help the war effort. The history of both the MOI and its Films
Division were troubled, to say the least. The MOI never fully shook off
the reputation it acquired in the early months of the war as the 'Ministry of Dis-Information' or 'Ministry of Muddle'. Foreign Secretary Lord
Halifax described it as 'a body without a head and not very effective
limbs either'.[7] Its first minister, the wholly ineffectual Lord Macmillan,
became the object of public ridicule after admitting that 'I have considerable difficulty in ascertaining what are its functions'.[8] The Films
Division similarly acquired a reputation for bureaucratic inefficiency:
Paul Rotha later complained that 'a film tended too often to become a
file rather than a film'.[9]

   As ever with British documentary it is important to take into account
that the history of the movement was originally written by the
documentarists themselves. The negative view of the MOI that informs
all the standard accounts of wartime documentary was coloured by
the documentarists' sense of exclusion from the official film-making
machinery at the start of the war. They believed – not without good
cause, it has to be said – that this exclusion was politically motivated.
'The documentary people, all of us, were left in the wilderness', Edgar
Anstey averred. 'We weren't used because the Chamberlain government
was very much opposed to everything we stood for, and they had their
own film people, who moved into the Ministry of Information and were
powerful in other quarters.'[10] There was indeed a sense that the Films
Division was an outpost of Conservative Central Office. Its first director, Sir Joseph Ball, had previously been Director of the Conservative
Party Research Department and Deputy Director of the National Publicity Bureau, while other Films Division officers included D. K. Clarke,
General Secretary of the Conservative Research Department, and Oliver
Bell, on 'loan' from the British Film Institute, who had once been a press
officer for the party. Ball expressed a preference for working with the
'leaders' of the film industry – by which he meant commercial feature
film producers and the newsreel companies.[11]

   The government's initial reluctance to employ documentarists for
official propaganda was to a large extent a legacy of its problematic

relationship with John Grierson during the 1930s. Ball evidently shared his civil servants' antipathy towards Grierson. In October 1939, for example, he poured cold water on a proposal from Grierson regarding the non-theatrical distribution of British films in North America:

> Experience of Mr Grierson during his connection with the Unit inspired in the officers of the Post Office closely concerned with the matter very little confidence either in his reliability as an adviser in the matters in question, or in his discretion as an executant of the extremely delicate mission which he has proposed for himself.[12]

Grierson's absence from Britain for the duration of the war – he took up appointment as Canadian Film Commissioner in the autumn of 1939, in which role he was instrumental in setting up the National Film Board of Canada – was a mixed blessing for the documentary cause. On the one hand the documentary movement's most able publicist was not present to promote its cause inside Whitehall – even though, as Jo Fox has demonstrated, Grierson sought to influence the policies of the MOI Films Division from a distance.[13] On the other hand, however, the fact that Grierson was no longer present to antagonize the civil service probably helped to facilitate documentary's acceptance by the MOI.

Not that there was much sign of this acceptance in the early months of the war. The inertia that seemed to grip the MOI Films Division in 1939 was felt most acutely at the GPO Film Unit. Although it had been expected that the GPO Film Unit would be at the centre of the official film-making effort during wartime, the unit initially found itself underemployed. According to Harry Watt – admittedly never the most reliable witness – its members passed the time 'watching the tarts in the street below ... [and] running a book on their activities'.[14] It was largely the unit's own initiative that resulted in the making of the first documentary of the war. *The First Days* was a two-reeler shot on location in the streets of London in the early autumn of 1939. It was an impressionistic film that provides the first example of the theme of the people's war – people from all social classes and backgrounds coming together in the common good – that would be the dominant narrative of wartime propaganda. However, as no formal agreement had yet been arranged for the screening of MOI films, Cavalcanti and Watt 'hawked the first British official movie up and down Wardour Street, like a couple of hard-up producers!'[15]

However, the MOI was not quite as blind to the potential of documentary as it might have first appeared. At an early meeting with the

British Council – which was responsible for the selection of films for showing in the British Pavilion at the World's Fair in New York – it was reported that 'the Ministry of Information was anxious that documentary film companies should, if possible, be kept going' and that 'it was important that small companies such as British Films, Realist Film Unit and the Strand Film Company, etc should be given a chance to produce films'.[16] The recruitment of Joseph Reeves – former Secretary of the Workers' Film Association, the film education body of the Trades Union Congress – went some way towards redressing the Conservative dominance within the Films Division. Reeves's role was to be 'the selection and distribution of instructional and educational films by non-theatrical means, largely to self-educating societies of the working classes'.[17] Sir Joseph Ball himself did not survive the year's end, being replaced by art historian Sir Kenneth Clark, Director of the National Gallery, who, according to his own account, was appointed on the grounds that 'in those days films were spoken of as "pictures", and I was believed to be an authority on pictures'.[18] Even so, Clark's appointment was welcomed by the *literati* and, more to the point, by *Documentary News Letter*, which believed there 'is every hope that he will take immediate steps to end the inertia which has till now more or less immobilised the personnel of (among other branches of cinema) documentary'.[19] Clark drafted a 'Programme for Film Propaganda', which identified specific roles for each of the three main modes of film practice – newsreel, documentary and feature film – in projecting the war effort.[20]

There is no doubt that Clark sought to promote the cause of documentary. That said, his efforts were to some extent thwarted by the interests of cinema exhibitors who continued, as they had during the 1930s, to resist documentary films. This was highlighted by the case of the GPO Film Unit's *Squadron 992* (about the role of the balloon barrage in the defence of the Forth Bridge) and *Men of the Lightship* (a dramatic reconstruction of the bombing of the East Dudgeon lightship). These were both completed in the spring of 1940 but their theatrical release was delayed by several months while the MOI negotiated terms with distributors. *Documentary News Letter* said of *Squadron 992*: 'At the time of its completion, it would have been an important contribution to the maintenance of public confidence in the defence of Britain. Today, though the fine qualities of Watt's direction retain their vitality … it has lost the gripping topicality which it derived from being based on the Forth Bridge raid.'[21] In the event, Sir Kenneth Clark did not last much longer in post than his predecessor. He was replaced in turn by Jack Beddington, former Director of Publicity for the Shell

Group and, crucially, a known supporter of documentary. *Documen-tary News Letter* averred that Beddington 'has done more for the British artist than any other figure in industry' and that he 'will bring to his new post both taste and a sense of public need – two qualities only too rarely associated with commercial ability'.[22] Beddington recognized the need to work with both the commercial sector of the film indus-try and the documentarists: his regime sought to bring both into the official fold. A broad parallel might be drawn between the reorganiza-tion of the government under Winston Churchill, who brought Labour ministers such as Clement Attlee, Arthur Greenwood and later Ernest Bevin into the War Cabinet, and the changes Beddington introduced to the Films Division. In particular, he turned to Film Centre, hitherto ignored, and recruited Arthur Elton as Supervisor of Production early in 1941. Elton was an astute choice because, as Nicholas Pronay puts it, he 'appeared to be the least associated with the more extreme and dogmatic political activities of the documentary group'.[23] Another recruit was Thomas Baird, hired to supervise the MOI's non-theatrical distribution programme.

By the winter of 1940–1941, then, documentarists no longer had rea-son to feel isolated from the MOI. Indeed, so complete had been the transformation that there were some commentators who believed the documentarists had all but taken over the Films Division. M. Neville Kearney, who as we have seen had been a staunch opponent of docu-mentary during the 1930s, had recently been appointed Director of the British Council's Film Department. Kearney saw a 'Film Centre conspir-acy' taking over the production of MOI films. He complained to the Foreign Office (parent body of the British Council) that 'the Film Centre attitude and atmosphere pervades the whole outfit'.[24] Kearney held a deep antipathy towards the 'Documentary Boys', as he rather contemp-tuously referred to them. He clearly did not share the documentarists' commitment to progressive social reform, fearing that official film policy was being hijacked to pursue their own ideological agenda: 'One cannot avoid the suspicion that the ultimate object is eventually to centralise in the hands of one body – i.e. Film Centre "Documentary Boys" – the whole influence of films in the reordering of things social both during the war and when it comes to an end.'[25] Against this, however, can be set the opinion of Harry Watt, who later complained that Beddington 'wanted to be in with the newsreels' and always put their interests before those of documentary.[26]

In fact there is no evidence whatsoever of favouritism towards the newsreels in the commissioning of MOI films. Between 1940 and 1945 the leading suppliers of films for the MOI were the GPO/Crown Film Unit (65 films), Strand (59 films), Realist (50 films), British Movietone (41 films), Verity (37 films), Spectator (33 films), Films of GB (32 films), Paul Rotha Productions (31 films), GB Instructional (26 films) and the Shell Film Unit (24 films).[27] The MOI tended to turn to newsreel companies such as British Movietone for films about the war fronts, and to documentary for films about the home front. According to Paul Rotha:

> When in 1941 I set up my own unit with several others, including Donald Alexander, we declared a policy that we would make films at the commission of the British Ministry of Information, but we would not make films about the combat fronts. We would make films about what was happening in Britain under the influence of a world war. This was accepted, and all the films we made in the subsequent years were about such things as day nurseries and public health and schools and education and so on. Never once did we make a film about any of the [armed] services.[28]

The documentarists were in their element in exploring the effects of war on British society: to this extent it was in the films of the home front rather than the more celebrated service and combat films that the energies of the independent documentary movement were focused.

A few examples must serve to illustrate the range of subjects explored in wartime documentary. One recurring theme was to show how civilians adapted to wartime conditions. *Transfer of Skill* (Shell Film Unit, 1940), for example, demonstrates how watchmakers switched to producing fuses and how jewellery craftsmen turned their skills to making precision instruments. This film represented continuity with pre-war documentaries such as *Industrial Britain* with its emphasis on the role of skilled craftsmanship in industry. Another theme – again consistent with pre-war documentary – was the role of social services in wartime. *Citizens' Advice Bureau* (GB Screen Services, 1941) resulted from an approach by the organization itself, which suggested that a film explaining its activities would 'provide an opportunity for nationwide publicity in order to make the Bureaux known just at this time when the need for them is likely to be greater than ever'.[29] *Words and Actions* (Realist Film Unit, 1943) used a series of dramatized incidents to demonstrate both the importance of community action (for example, people setting up their own fire-watching group) and how social services could help those in need (such as a housewife threatened with repossession of her furniture by a bullying hire-purchase company). This film exemplified the persistence of commercial sponsorship of documentary film: it was produced for the Gas Association, which believed 'that a public service should concern itself with the problems of the community'.

Documentary was also concerned to demonstrate the contribution to the war effort of groups who would not otherwise receive their due recognition. In particular there was a clear effort to recognize the wartime role of women – whom it would probably be fair to say had quite often been a marginal presence in pre-war documentary – both in the home and in the workplace. *They Also Serve* (Realist Film Unit, 1940) was a tribute to the housewives of Britain: *Documentary News Letter* approved because 'it takes the simple story of an ordinary house-wife and makes it dramatic by focusing our attention on the ordinary human kindliness which may be found daily in the millions of semi-detached houses in our cities'.[30] This was the last film directed by Ruby Grierson who died later that year in the sinking of the liner *City of Benares* while escorting evacuee children to Canada. *Night Shift* (Paul Rotha Productions, 1942) focused on the role of women working in the munitions industry. The film employs a female commentary and is notable for adopting an assertively feminist position in relation to women's labour ('Blondie's been on that for six months, and she's as good as any man at her job'). It was seeing *Night Shift* that prompted Frank Launder and Sidney Gilliat to produce the documentary-style feature film *Millions Like Us* (1943) about a group of women working in an aircraft factory – an example of the 'wartime wedding' between the feature film and documentary.[31]

Most of these films were produced for non-theatrical exhibition, though a number of documentaries did make it into the cinemas. In July 1940 Beddington brokered a deal with the Cinematograph Exhibitors' Association whereby an official film of approximately five minutes would be included weekly in all cinema programmes.[32] The 'five-minute films' in 1940–1941 included, on the one hand, morale-raising films by the GPO Film Unit (*Britain at Bay*, *Britain Can Take It!*, *Christmas Under Fire*, *The Heart of Britain*) and, on the other, short fiction films from commercial studios (*Channel Incident*, *Miss Grant Goes to the Door*) that were derided by critics for their unrealistic storylines. Sydney Box's Verity Films was able to find a middle ground between the documentary and story modes in a series of short dramatizations of real incidents such as *Dai Jones Lends a Hand* and *Shunter Black's Night Off* (both 1941). In late 1942 the five-minute films were replaced by a monthly fifteen-minute film. This was in response to research into the reception of MOI films by Mass-Observation, which indicated that

> there is much to be said for having quite considerably longer MOI films, if that were possible, especially films of an informational type, dealing with subjects like war economics, news service, the integration of war strategy, war production, and the many other things which are of general interest and which people need to know about.[33]

This brought about a shift from the exhortational style of some early wartime films to the more factual treatment of films such as *War in the Pacific* (Shell Film Unit, 1944) and *Stricken Peninsula* (Seven League Productions, 1944).

However, it was in the field of non-theatrical distribution that the documentarists' influence upon MOI policy was perhaps most keenly felt. In 1940 they won a significant political victory. The MOI's ambitious plans for non-theatrical distribution – which envisaged over 100 mobile projector units and a free loans system – had been singled out for criticism by the powerful Select Committee on National Expenditure, which felt that the estimated £172,000 cost of running it was 'difficult to justify ... in time of war' and recommended that 'no further commitments be entered into unless very clear evidence is obtained from experience that the scheme is making a contribution to the war effort commensurate with the expenditure'.[34] Nevertheless, the MOI pressed ahead with its non-theatrical programme in spite of the opposition. At its height in 1943 the MOI operated 150 mobile projectors showing films in locations such as factory canteens, schools and village halls. It is difficult to gauge the size of the audiences for these shows. The total non-theatrical audience of 18.5 million claimed by the authors of *The Factual Film* for 1943–1944 is certainly a significant exaggeration: the Arts Enquiry Survey was written by documentarists who had a vested interest in presenting the programme as an outstanding success.[35] William Farr, Head of the Central Film Library, offered a rather more conservative estimate of 2.5 million regular attendees.[36] However, the real value of the non-theatrical programme was not the size of its audience but its composition. Helen Forman, recruited to the MOI from the Imperial Institute, explained that the aim of the programme was to reach audiences who could not easily attend cinemas, such as shift workers in factories and those living in rural areas. And the nature of the films produced specifically for non-theatrical exhibition – as opposed to films like *Britain Can Take It!* that were made for theatrical release but also often included in non-theatrical programmes – was different in that 'it was possible to show films with far more detailed information than would have been possible to a cinema audience'.[37] A series entitled *Worker and Warfront* (Paul Rotha Productions, 1942–1945), for example, was produced specifically for showing in factories in order 'to link the home front with the combat front'.[38] The fact that film shows would often be accompanied by lectures and discussions prompted *Documentary News Letter* to remark that 'the public forum is returning to the village and the town alike with a new orator – film, to lead a lively and well-informed discussion of the country's wartime problems'.[39]

The Crown Film Unit

The Crown Film Unit – as the GPO Film Unit formally became on 1 January 1941 – was the MOI's principal production agency. It produced 65 films for the MOI, mostly shorts but also including five feature-length story documentaries (*Target for Tonight, Coastal Command, Close Quarters, Fires Were Started, Western Approaches*) and several 'featurettes' (*Ferry Pilot, The Silent Village, A Diary for Timothy*). The MOI tended to assign its more important films to the Crown Film Unit, especially those intended for theatrical release, on the grounds that the unit 'has in its wartime form evolved a technique and skill regarded as more suitable for producing the special type of high quality film required than that possessed by outside studios'.[40] Yet for the first year of the war the future of the unit was far from certain: it was regarded as an expensive luxury by the Treasury and was the target of an aborted takeover attempt by a commercial producer.[41] Against this uncertain background the unit's survival was due to its ability to deliver films that not only fulfilled the propaganda objectives of the MOI but also met with a high level of critical and popular acclaim. In particular, its series of story documentaries about the armed services marked the emergence of a new documentary form and aesthetic perfectly suited to the ideological contexts of war.

At the outbreak of war the GPO Film Unit was placed at the disposal of the MOI while remaining under the formal control of the Post Office. It soon became apparent that the 'extraordinary complexities' of this arrangement were too unwieldy to work effectively.[42] Accordingly it was agreed that, with effect from 1 April 1940, control of the GPO Film Unit would be formally transferred to the MOI 'on the understanding that the Unit would be kept together and without prejudice to the question of control of the Unit after the war'.[43] Shortly after the MOI took control of the unit it was announced that Alberto Cavalcanti was to leave to join Ealing Studios.[44] It has often been assumed that the reason for Cavalcanti's departure was his status as a foreign national: indeed Cavalcanti himself lent credence to this view.[45] However, the MOI itself 'was anxious...that Mr Cavalcanti should be retained'.[46] He was regarded as 'the best Producer in the country and it is vital that the Film Unit should continue to have use of his services'.[47] Cavalcanti's move to Ealing seems to have been linked to an attempt to take over the GPO Film Unit by Michael Balcon, Ealing's Head of Production, who proposed that the unit should be based at Ealing under Cavalcanti's supervision.[48] Jack Beddington poured cold water on the idea on the grounds that Balcon's plan seemed to involve Ealing assuming control of the unit.[49] Balcon replied angrily that 'it was your idea that I should take over the GPO Unit and not mine' and told Beddington somewhat presumptuously 'that the primary function of the Films Division is to get films made and not to make them'.[50] Balcon was concerned that the MOI was entering into direct competition with the commercial film industry: he felt that it should commission films from commercial producers rather than produce films directly itself. His attempt to take over the GPO Film Unit was driven in part by an ambition to secure facilities for the studio. Balcon's rebuttal by Beddington would cause a rift between Ealing and the MOI: Balcon announced in December 1940 that henceforth Ealing would go its own way in the production of documentaries.[51]

Cavalcanti's replacement was Ian Dalrymple, who had worked as a writer, editor and associate producer for Alexander Korda during the 1930s. Dalrymple had been involved in the production of Korda's *The Lion Has Wings* (1939), the first propaganda feature film of the war. *The Lion Has Wings* was something of a hodge podge – it combined actuality footage and extracts from newsreels with fictional scenes shot at Denham Studios with Merle Oberon and Ralph Richardson – but it represented an early attempt at the story-documentary form that would become the hallmark of the Crown Film Unit. Dalrymple later admitted that he had 'little experience of non-fictional production' and that he thought some members of the unit 'must have some qualms about accepting a supervisor from the commercial industry'.[52] Harry Watt, for one, said that he found Dalrymple 'cold, distant and discouraging – to me at any rate'.[53] Watt would follow Cavalcanti to Ealing Studios in 1941. However, the view of others at the unit was 'that Dalrymple would do as well as anyone'.[54]

The early wartime films of the GPO Film Unit can be seen as transitional in both their content and their form. Some, such as Humphrey

Jennings's *SS Ionian* (1939), an account of the British merchant navy, were pre-war films not released until after the outbreak of war. *The First Days* (1939) remains an evocative time-capsule of the period known as the 'phoney war' in which the British public prepared for hostilities that did not immediately break out. It is a Janus-faced film in many respects. On the one hand its observational mode and detached commentary is indicative of the GPO films of the 1930s, while on the other hand it anticipates later wartime films in its striking visuals – barrage balloons silhouetted against the sky and a shot of children playing on Great War field guns at the Imperial War Museum – and in its emphasis on social cohesion: the act of filling sandbags becomes a metaphor for class solidarity ('The thousand classes of London, some from their damp basements and some from their luxury flats, came together to work for the public good'). The three-reeler *Men of the Lightship* (1940) was the first instance of the story-documentary technique of dramatized reconstruction being adapted to wartime circumstances. It was produced towards the end of Cavalcanti's time in charge of the unit and he was keen to emphasize the need for realism. After seeing some early rushes featuring professional actors, Cavalcanti cabled the director David Macdonald (an outside recruit from the commercial film industry): 'Your sailors totally unconvincing, suggest you sack entire cast and use real people.'[55] Cavalcanti also resisted pressure from the Air Ministry to introduce a scene of the raiders being shot down by the RAF, as

> to introduce a dog-fight into the picture really meant, from the propaganda angle, a recasting of the whole story and therefore a departure from the original intention of authentically reconstructing what happened and substituting a picture which an audience would be inclined to regard as introducing the usual element of 'movie fiction'.[56]

These early films were all very much products of the 'phoney war': the moral outrage of a film such as *Men of the Lightship* would come to seem mild indeed in the wake of the Blitz and later war atrocities. It was during the Battle of Britain and the Blitz, however, that the GPO Film Unit really hit its stride. *Britain at Bay* (1940) is essentially a compilation stitched together from library footage: its effect resides in the evocative commentary of J. B. Priestley, which turns it into a visual equivalent of his 'Postscript' broadcasts on the BBC. *The Story of an Air Communiqué* (1940) now seems quite risible with its posh-accented young RAF pilots and its insistence on the rigorous cross-checking of combat reports: the official claim that 185 enemy aircraft were destroyed on 15 September 1940 is now known to have been a gross exaggeration. More representative of the unit's five-minute films is *The Front Line* (1940). Harry Watt and cameraman Jonah Jones went to Dover with instructions 'to cover everything we found interesting or exciting, and try to make a film out of it'.[57] The film mixes actuality footage of aerial combat with some rather artificial *Housing Problems*-type scenes in which people speak directly to the camera, expressing their contempt for 'the Jerries'.

The GPO Film Unit's most successful wartime film from a propaganda perspective was *Britain Can Take It!* (1940). This film, originally entitled *London Front* and then *London Can Take It!*, was originally commissioned from Gaumont-British News but was 'removed' and placed with the GPO Unit.[58] This was because the Blitz footage shot by the newsreel cameramen was held to show too much bomb damage to be considered good for morale.[59] *London Can Take It!* was a combination of actuality footage with an understated commentary by American journalist Quentin Reynolds that was earmarked for exhibition in the United States. A slightly shorter version entitled *Britain Can Take It!* was released in the five-minute programme at home. *Britain Can Take It!* was universally well received: its tone of stoic defiance perfectly caught the mood of the British public in the autumn of 1940. Basil Wright admired its 'pellucid and brilliant camerawork, its leisurely and emphatic cutting and its economy of emphasis... It states facts, but with the addition of true drama and true poetry'.[60] Mass-Observation found that it was 'the most frequently commented on film, and received nothing but praise'.[61] The unit followed it with *Christmas Under Fire* (1941), which used the same techniques – striking visuals accompanied by a dry, restrained commentary by Reynolds – to show how Britons celebrated Christmas during the Blitz. Harry Watt averred that the film was intended 'especially for the super-sentimentalists of the United States. With them Christmas becomes positively orgiastic in its slush, and a film timed right after Christmas, showing Britain carrying on the tradition in its dugouts and outposts is an obvious tear-jerker'.[62] The film's ending – a tracking shot through a crowded Underground station used as an air-raid shelter to the refrain of 'O Come All Ye Faithful' – has become one of the defining images of the British wartime experience.

The 'morale' films were successful but short-lived: by early 1941 the MOI felt that the 'Britain can take it' theme had run its course and that official films should look to present Britain taking the offensive. The Crown Film Unit co-operated with the Army Film Unit in editing front-line actuality footage into films such as the five-minute *Lofoten* (1941) about a Commando raid in Norway and the feature-length *Wavell's 30,000* (1942) about the defeat of the Italian army in Libya. But it was the home front that provided the unit with most of its subjects, especially once the service film units had overcome their initial teething troubles. A film such as J. B. Holmes and Jack Lee's *Ordinary People* (1941) – largely overlooked in histories of wartime documentary in preference for the 'morale' films – demonstrates how Crown's technique and style evolved. It eschews the 'poetic' commentary style of *Britain Can Take It!* or *Christmas Under Fire* in favour of recorded dialogue between its subjects ('That's all right, lady – it's my lucky day' a taxi driver assures his nervous passenger) and focuses on individuals rather than on 'the people' en masse. The film's dedication ('To the future historian – this film was played by the ordinary people of London') draws attention to how it has been constructed as a propaganda piece, but it is no less effective than the more famous 'morale' films in showing how Londoners carried on during the Blitz. Pat Jackson's *Builders* (1942) is different again. Jackson employed the direct-to-camera technique of *Housing Problems* but developed it so that the subjects engage in a dialogue with the narrator (''Allo guv'nor, fancy meeting you down here!'). *Builders* was produced ostensibly to show the essential work of construction workers on the home front but it also intimated that a bigger task of reconstruction lay ahead after the war. As one of the subjects remarks: 'But we don't have to have a nation at war to get us all united, or to have a common aim to work for, surely?' This theme would become increasingly prominent in documentary as the war went on.

Humphrey Jennings and the people's war

The wartime films of Humphrey Jennings have come to represent the crowning achievement of British documentary during the war. Jennings directed a series of films for the Crown Film Unit that reveal a complex intellectual and aesthetic response to the conditions of war. After collaborating with others on *The First Days* and *London Can Take It!*, Jennings developed his 'poetic' style in an unmatched sequence of films whose thematic and stylistic unity mark them out as the work of a true *auteur*. *The Heart of Britain* (1941) for the five-minute film programme was a vivid account of the Blitz in the Midlands and north of England, making imaginative use of music and commentary. *Words for Battle* (1941), another five-minute film, matched images of the nation at war to inspirational extracts from English literature (Milton, Blake,

Browning, Kipling) and history (Churchill, Lincoln) recited by Laurence Olivier. *Listen to Britain* (1942) dispensed with commentary altogether and instead fused music and natural sound to capture the spirit of Britain and its people at war. This two-reel film is regarded by many as Jennings's masterpiece. *Fires Were Started* (1943), about the Auxiliary Fire Service during the London Blitz of 1940–1941, was Jennings's only full feature film and marked his fullest adoption of the story-documentary technique. *The Silent Village* (1943) was an imaginative reconstruction of the Lidice massacre in Czechoslovakia relocated to a Welsh mining village. *The True Story of Lili Marlene* (1944) dramatized the story of the famous song that became a favourite with British as well as German troops. *The Eighty Days* (1945) was an account of the V-1 blitz on southern England in 1944, narrated by American journalist Ed Murrow. And *A Diary for Timothy* (1946) was a moving account of the last months of the war presented in the form of a diary written for a newborn baby. Most of Jennings's films were made in collaboration with editor Stewart McAllister, who, like Jennings, had a highly pictorial imagination and was willing to experiment with unconventional editing techniques.[63]

Basil Wright would later write that Jennings 'found in the circumstances of war an inspiration which exactly matched his own personal feelings about his country'.[64] Jennings was a highly intelligent and complex artist whose feelings towards his country ran very deep. On the one hand he was a left-wing intellectual who despised the class system and admired the down-to-earth qualities he saw in the working classes. This admiration is evident in the sincere yet unpatronizing portrayals of ordinary people in his films such as the firemen of *Fires Were Started* and the Welsh miners of *The Silent Village*. His films focus exclusively on the home front. Even his notes for an unmade film of the Royal Marines suggest that his interest was in the people rather than the fighting: 'My idea is to avoid at all costs making another ruddy documentary service picture; but at the same time not to fall back on a fictional story with action as the only alternative – because it isn't.'[65] On the other hand, Jennings had a great love for English history and culture: his films mobilize both traditional signifiers of Englishness (such as the cultural texts of *Words for Battle*) and popular culture (such as Flanagan and Allen performing 'Underneath the Arches' in *Listen to Britain* and the communal singing of 'One Man Went to Mow' in *Fires Were Started*). For Jennings – as for his contemporary George Orwell – there was no intellectual contradiction between socialism and patriotism. While living in South Wales filming *The Silent Village*, for example, he wrote to his wife:

I never really thought to live to see the honest Christian and Communist principles daily acted on as a matter of course by a large number
of British – I won't say English – people ... From these people one can
really understand Cromwell's New Model Army and the defenders of
many places at the beginning of the Industrial Revolution.[66]

The organizing principle of Jennings's films is creative montage: the
juxtaposition of both familiar and unfamiliar images whose combination creates new meanings. Perhaps the most famous example is the cut
from Flanagan and Allen to a piano recital by Dame Myra Hess in *Listen
to Britain*: the fusion of popular and high culture links their audiences
and so suggests social unity and national cohesion. Pat Jackson recalled:
'Humphrey would interpret a situation in disconnected visuals, and he
wouldn't quite know why he was shooting them, probably, until he got
them together. Then he would create a pattern out of them.'[67] In many
respects Jennings stood outside the mainstream of the documentary
movement: his 'poetic' style fitted neither the story-documentary mode
favoured by other Crown directors nor the more didactic style of independent documentarists. Indeed the formalism of Jennings's films did
not meet with the approval of some of his documentary colleagues.
Edgar Anstey famously dismissed *Listen to Britain* as 'the rarest piece
of fiddling since the days of Nero'.[68] *Documentary News Letter* thought
Words for Battle nothing more than 'an illustrated lantern-slide lecture'.[69]
The same journal also disliked 'the strangely oblique approach' of *The
Silent Village*.[70] Even its review of *Fires Were Started* – which it conceded
featured 'the best handling of people on and off the job that we've seen
in any British film' – added a caveat that 'Jennings must be held entirely
to blame for the three or four occasions when ... (in his worst *Words for
Battle* manner) he goes all arty for a moment'.[71]
      However, there was a significant divergence between the view of
documentary purists and the reception of the films by contemporary
audiences. Donald Alexander reported that *The Silent Village* was well
received in the north of England: 'I saw the film in Sheffield (a city
surrounded by coal-mines incidentally) and I felt that it was a success; it was accepted, and it was not dismissed as phoney.'[72] Nor was
this an isolated view. All the evidence points towards the films of this
most intellectual of directors striking an emotional chord with audiences across the country. Roger Manvell, a regional films officer for the
MOI during the war, found that Jennings's films were consistently popular in non-theatrical shows: 'I can testify personally that they were
the ones we constantly showed that immediately stirred emotions,

not only in the West Country but in the far tougher Northeast of Britain (Tyneside) which I also came to know well at the time.'[73] And Helen Forman recalled that *Listen to Britain* was 'liked and applauded' because it resonated with people of different backgrounds: 'All sorts of audiences felt it to be a distillation and also a magnification of their own experiences of the home front. This was especially true of factory audiences ... Films got very short shrift if they touched upon any area of people's experiences and did not ring true.'[74]

As Jennings's only feature-length film, *Fires Were Started* – sometimes also known as *I Was A Fireman* in its non-theatrical version – particularly stands out among his work. Roy Armes describes it as 'a perfect fusion of documentary and narrative'.[75] Jennings researched the film exhaustively by reading official and anecdotal accounts of the Blitz. In shooting the film he remained true to the Crown tradition of using real people – in this case actual firemen – while the fire sequences themselves were reconstructed on location at St Katharine's Dock in London.[76] Unlike some of his other films, where a pattern emerged at the editing stage, *Fires Were Started* was constructed at the script level. It demonstrates a classic three-part structure: the first part of the film is a leisurely intro- duction to the firemen, focusing on the induction of a new recruit; the second part – in which both the narrative pace and editing tempo accel- erate to create a sense of greater urgency – shows the firemen in action and ends in the death of one of their comrades; and the shorter final act deals with the aftermath of the fire and Jacko's funeral. Yet within this highly structured narrative there are many characteristic Jennings moments: these include an almost surreal shot of a frightened horse in the smoke (an image that his script notes reveal Jennings wanted in the film from an early stage) and the heroic shots of the firemen sil- houetted against the skyline. The film's ending is a bravura example of associative montage as Jennings cuts between Jacko's funeral and the munitions ship that the firemen saved sailing down the Thames: the implication here clearly is that Jacko's death has not been in vain. Like other Jennings films, *Fires Were Started* evidently struck a chord with audiences who regarded it as a realistic account of their experiences. One respondent in a Mass-Observation survey said: 'Having lived through the London blitz we naturally enjoyed this film. We were impressed with the way things were done and with the lack of heroics.'[77] And another paid it perhaps the highest compliment: 'The best wartime documentary yet: never have ordinary people been more convincingly done (Humphrey Jennings's M-O training?) and the film is nevertheless "poetic" in its treatment.'[78]

Target for Tonight (1941) and the story documentary

The style that became most associated with the Crown Film Unit was the story documentary, exemplified by its five feature-length films that were all accorded a theatrical release: *Target for Tonight, Coastal Command, Close Quarters, Fires Were Started* and *Western Approaches*. The ascendancy of the story-documentary mode, involving studio reconstruction and scripted dialogue, has usually been seen as continuing a lineage that began in pre-war films such as *North Sea*. In fact only one true story documentary was produced at the GPO/Crown Film Unit between *North Sea* in 1938 and *Target for Tonight* in 1941, and that film, *Men of the Lightship*, was made by a director from the commercial film industry (David Macdonald). The Crown story documentaries were as much a product of the ideological circumstances of war as they were the continuation of a pre-war trend. They were particularly associated with Ian Dalrymple's period as head of production at Crown: all the features were initiated under Dalrymple even if the last of them (*Western Approaches*) was released after his departure. However, the production history of the first of these, *Target for Tonight*, shows that it was not originally conceived as either a story documentary or a feature film.[79]

The initiative for the film that became *Target for Tonight* came from the Air Ministry and was for a two-reel instructional film documenting the history of Bomber Command since the mid-1930s and justifying Lord Trenchard's foresight in advocating a strong bomber arm. The first treatment included an account of Bomber Command operations since the outbreak of war and concluded with a reconstruction of a daylight raid over France to 'show our major striking weapon actually on the job'.[80] Harry Watt was chosen to direct, and the film was commissioned as a two-reeler entitled *Bomber Command* at a cost of £3,000. However, Watt evidently had different ideas about what sort of film should be made. He envisaged 'a prestige film of Bomber Command, not a factual resumé of the long term policy'.[81] This was consistent with the MOI's Programme for Film Propaganda, which had foreseen a series of 'full and carefully worked out films of each of the fighting services'.[82] Thus the film became a dramatic reconstruction of a 'routine' bombing raid over Germany focusing on the crew of a single Wellington bomber ('F for Freddie'). Watt followed documentary practice of using real people, with the crew played by serving RAF personnel, and even persuaded Sir Richard Pierse, the Commander-in-Chief of Bomber Command, to appear in the film as himself. *Target for Tonight* was shot partly on location at Mildenhall airfield, while a reconstruction of the Bomber

Command Operations Centre at Denham Studios was 'the biggest set ever built by documentary'.[83] The film's length grew in line with its ambition: it ended up as five reels and its direct cost of £6,406 was twice the original estimate.[84] Nevertheless, it went on to be a major hit on its commercial release, returning £73,636 to the Treasury.[85] It was a critical success in Britain and in the United States, where it was voted best documentary of 1941 by the National Board of Review of Motion Pictures. And it found a champion in Lord Beaverbrook, the Minister of Aircraft Production, who thought it 'a picture which must move and interest audiences wherever it is shown'.[86]

Eric Rhode writes that *Target for Tonight* 'now seems as evocative of its period as an ugly, narrow-armed utility chair. The bleakness of its aerodrome setting and the awkwardness of its editing and camera placements capture the austerity of the period with a zeal so puritannical that it begins to assume the conviction of a style'.[87] In comparison to feature films of the time it now seems technically crude: the awkward editing includes several jump cuts in shots of the Wellington in flight. However, this has been seen as a deliberate device to 'insist upon the individuality of each shot, and hence to the aircraft as a material prerequisite for that shot rather than to the purely notional aircraft entailed in its construction as fiction'.[88] In other words, the jump cuts are a technique to differentiate it from the 'invisible' editing of the classical feature film. *Target for Tonight* is a model of narrative economy: it is spare and concise, with no superfluous scenes, and detached in its characterization of men simply going about their jobs with a minimum of fuss. Its austere realism and the absence of sensational heroics is the antithesis of early wartime features such as Ealing's *Convoy* (1940) and *Ships With Wings* (1941), which were popular with audiences but criticized in some quarters (including *Documentary News Letter*) for resorting to melodrama rather than realism.[89]

The success of *Target for Tonight* – by some measure the most profitable of Crown's theatrical releases – was due in large measure to its historical timing: it was the first film to show Britain hitting back rather than merely 'taking it'. No matter that it exaggerates the accuracy of the RAF's strategic bombing: in 1941 the bombing offensive was the only means by which Britain was able to take the war to Germany. In the United States – where it was distributed by Warner Bros and reportedly shown in some 12,500 cinemas – it 'rode out on the wave of admiration for British pluck and endurance that was sweeping the country'.[90] It was reported that Alfred Hitchcock re-edited the film for American consumption.[91] At the same time as showing Britain 'hitting back', however, *Target for*

Tonight also indicated the potential of the longer story-documentary form for reaching a wider general audience in the cinemas. It was significant in this regard that the film was critically well received not only by the quality press, who had often championed the cause of documentary in the past, but also by the popular press, which had not. For example, the editor of the *Daily Express*, following an ecstatic review by his film critic Jonah Barrington, wrote to Sidney Bernstein at the MOI: 'It is a truly magnificent film, and the "Daily Express" if anything underplayed it. Just the same I think, after seeing the paper this morning, it would be only right and proper if we were to change the title from "Daily Express" to "Crown Film Unit Gazette".'[92]

Harry Watt left for Ealing Studios after completing *Target for Tonight* – his first film for the studio would be the documentary-style feature *Nine Men* (1943) – but the template for the wartime story documentary had been set. Pat Jackson's *Ferry Pilot* (1941) had a similar production history to *Target for Tonight*: it was conceived originally as a five-minute film and grew to a four-reel 'featurette'.[93] In contrast, J. B. Holmes's *Coastal Command* (1942) was planned as a feature film from the outset. It had a bigger budget than *Target for Tonight* (the final direct cost was £16,646), due to a unit being sent to Iceland to shoot aerial footage. Like *Target for Tonight*, *Coastal Command* focuses on the crew of one Sunderland aircraft ('T for Tommy') and the actors were actual RAF personnel, including Sir Philip Joubert, the Commander-in-Chief of Coastal Command. The film dramatizes the sinking of a U-boat and an attack on a German warship alongside the more routine convoy protection patrols. *Coastal Command* is a more polished film than *Target for Tonight*: it is particularly notable for its sharp cinematography and for its epic score by Ralph Vaughan Williams. It was another critical and popular success, with receipts of £47,797.[94]

However, the success of the Crown documentary features – Jack Lee's *Close Quarters* (1943) completed a triptych about branches of the services – prompted some jealousy on the part of other producers. Paul Rotha later described Crown as 'the luxury unit' because they had preferential treatment in the allocation of resources.[95] In 1942 the unit moved to the requisitioned Pinewood Studios, which was closed to commercial production during the war. And some commercial producers were of the view that the Crown features represented unfair competitition. Michael Balcon, no doubt smarting from his earlier rebuttal by the MOI, complained about 'competition from official film units, such as the Crown Film Unit, making short features of the *Target for Tonight* length (six reels) with the assistance of Treasury backing and other facilities not open to commercial producers'.[96] *Close Quarters*, for example, was seen as competing directly with Gainsborough Pictures' submarine drama *We Dive at Dawn* (Gainsborough Pictures), while *Fires Were Started* preceded Ealing's fire service drama *The Bells Go Down* into cinemas. The MOI replied that 'a film like *Target for Tonight* when commercially distributed only displaces commercially made productions on its own merits'.[97] The case of *Fires Were Started* marked the first instance of trade resistance to the Crown features. General Film Distributors thought it was too slow-paced and wanted to cut it: in the event, a longer version was shown non-theatrically as *I Was A Fireman*.[98]

Pat Jackson's *Western Approaches* (1944) was the last of the big story documentaries produced by the Crown Film Unit. It was the most ambitious project undertaken by the unit: shot in Technicolor and featuring extensive location shooting in the North Atlantic. Like the other Crown features it is realistic, spare and austere: even Jack Cardiff's cinematography is subdued, its colour tones appropriately cold and desaturated. *Western Approaches* had started production in 1942 but was beset by problems – including weather conditions and delays in processing the camera negative, which had to be done by Technicolor's own laboratories – that meant it did not reach the screen for two years.[99] There was a growing feeling during the course of its production that it would mark the end of Crown's feature film experiment: 'The Treasury emphasised that we were risking a good deal by putting all our eggs in one basket and that if this film did not come up to expectation, the whole programme of the Unit would have to be reconsidered.'[100] The delays to the film and its alarmingly escalating costs – it finally cost over £86,000 – meant that *Western Approaches* was the last film of its kind. Nevertheless, it was another popular and critical success. Lord Beaverbrook thought it was 'one of the best films of the war, if not the very best'.[101] And John Shearman felt that it was 'perhaps the perfect example of the feature-like documentary'.[102]

There was a sense towards the end of the war that the Crown Film Unit had somewhat lost its way. Ian Dalrymple left in 1943: J. B. Holmes assumed the role of senior producer but proved a less effective manager than he was a director. This was evident in the unusually high number of aborted projects in 1944.[103] The MOI's Director-General reported 'that 1944 was a poor year for the work of the Crown Film Unit ... We knew at the time that they were inadequately employed and a lack of leadership was getting business into some confusion and holding up production.'[104] However, its decline in the later years of

the war should not overshadow the very real achievements of the official film unit between 1940 and 1943. The popular success of films
such as *Target for Tonight* raised the public profile of documentary after
a decade as a marginal mode of film practice. And the Crown feature films also marked documentary's entry into the mainstream as
their fusion of documentary techniques and character-driven narratives
would become the preferred aesthetic of British films during the war (*In
Which We Serve, Millions Like Us, Nine Men, San Demetrio, London, The
Way Ahead*) and after (*The Overlanders, The Blue Lamp, White Corridors,
The Cruel Sea*).[105]

Desert Victory (1943), the Army Film Unit and actuality documentary

An alternative to the reconstructed story documentaries of the Crown
Film Unit was to be found in the work of the film units of the armed
services, particularly the Army Film Unit, which from 1941 became the
Army Film and Photographic Unit (AFPU) and specialized in the production of documentaries compiled from actuality footage shot at the
front by service cameramen. The AFPU expanded from four cameramen
in 1940 to over 80 by 1943.[106] To some extent it stood apart from the rest
of the documentary movement: in fact the directors responsible for the
compilation of the AFPU's footage (including David Macdonald and Roy
Boulting) tended to be recruited from the feature film industry rather
than documentary. Yet in a sense they belong to an older documentary
tradition than the work of the Crown Film Unit. Indeed the films of the
AFPU can be seen in a direct line of descent from the actuality films
produced during the Great War such as *Battle of the Somme*.

   Like the British Army itself, the Army Film Unit (AFU) had an inauspi-
cious start to the war. Its early efforts were not effective. It was a cause of
some embarrassment, for instance, that the only film of the Dunkirk
evacuation was taken by a newsreel cameraman (Charles Martin of
British Pathé) rather than by army cameramen. Early AFU films were
deemed inferior to the newsreels, which were able to process their film
and get it into cinemas more quickly. It was reported that some cinema exhibitors were reluctant to take the AFU film *Lofoten* (1941) – an
entry in the MOI's five-minute film series about a Commando raid in
Norway – 'on the grounds that their audiences had seen the material in
the Newsreels'.[107] When the first Soviet war documentaries were shown
in Britain, press baron Lord Kemsley complained that their actuality

footage made British films look 'feeble and ill-nourished efforts' in comparison.[108] One of the problems was that in the early years of the war there was little in the way of British military success for official cameramen to record. And even when there was a rare success – such as the offensive against the Italian armies in Libya in 1941 – there was trade resistance to the official film, *Wavell's 30,000* (1942), on the grounds that it did not count for British quota because it was shot overseas! An MOI memorandum expressed polite incredulity: 'It seems rather absurd that a film put out by this Ministry because of its propaganda value should be penalised in this way by the operation of an Act which was drafted when the circumstances of the present time could not possibly have been foreseen.'[109]

In the event, the debacle of *Wavell's 30,000* did little damage as subsequent reverses in the Western Desert meant that the film 'dated quickly and had to be withdrawn'.[110] It was the success a year later of *Desert Victory* (1943) that put the AFPU on the map. This film was compiled from footage of the Eighth Army's breakthrough at the Battle of El Alamein shot at the front by No 1 Army Film and Photographic Section under the command of Major David Macdonald. It was planned to edit the footage into a two-reeler entitled *The Battle of Egypt*, but, rather like *Target for Tonight*, the film grew during production to a one-hour feature that was released in March 1943. Churchill took a personal interest in the film and even recorded his El Alamein speech for inclusion in the version for US distribution.[111] The Prime Minister had prints sent to Roosevelt, Stalin and the prime ministers of the Dominions. *Desert Victory* was widely distributed in Britain – though not without the MOI having to prevail upon the Board of Trade to exempt it from quota regulations – and again like *Target for Tonight* was a significant commercial success with box-office receipts of £77,250.[112] It was also successful in the United States where it won an Academy Award for 'Most Distinctive Documentary of 1943'. To a large extent the success of *Desert Victory* was down to the simple fact that it was an account of the first major British land victory of the war. But critics and audiences also responded to its status as actuality rather than reconstruction. *The Times* was impressed by its dramatic front-line footage: 'The desert is not a stretch of country which lends itself easily to photography . . . but *Desert Victory*, which is a kind of elongated newsreel, is made with such intelligence and sincerity that it is not only a valuable document but actually succeeds in being good "cinema".'[113] There were in fact a few reconstructed scenes shot at Pinewood, but unlike *Battle of the Somme* the film acknowledges this in the credits.

The impact of *Desert Victory* on wartime documentary film was profound. Its success paved the way for a series of 'Victory' films in the later years of the war – *Tunisian Victory* (1944), *Burma Victory* (1945) and *The True Glory* (1945) all followed – though none of these caught the moment in quite the same way as *Desert Victory. Tunisian Victory* was produced in association with the US Office of War Information and was compromised to an extent by political rivalries between the allies as well as by the insertion of some moments of misplaced sentimentality by Colonel Frank Capra of the US Army Signal Corps.[114] *The True Glory* was compiled by Britain's Carol Reed and America's Garson Kanin from over 5 million feet of film shot by British and US army cameramen during the D-Day Landings and the campaign to liberate Western Europe. Its positive critical reception once again disguised a degree of inter-service and inter-allied rivalry in the making of the film.[115] *Burma Victory*, a wholly British affair, was again well received by critics but was not released until after the end of the war, by which time the public appetite for war documentaries had waned.[116]

There are two general points to be made about the AFPU's actuality documentaries. One is that they more or less displaced the dramatized story documentaries of the Crown Film Unit in official propaganda policy: no new Crown feature-length documentaries started production after the release of *Desert Victory*. Harry Watt felt that the success of *Desert Victory* signalled the end of films like *Target for Tonight*: 'The moment they appeared, the real thing, the front line shot by real army men who were being killed while doing it, the reconstructed documentary, as such, was dead, to my mind.'[117] The second point is that, alongside the Crown films, the AFPU films demonstrated that, contrary to the views of distributors and exhibitors, there was a market for documentary – or at least a particular type of documentary – in the commercial cinemas. As Paul Rotha observed: '*Target for Tonight, Desert Victory, Western Approaches* and other famous feature-length documentaries received a wide commercial distribution in the cinemas earning considerable revenue ... The public wanted to see these films because they were dramatized actuality, with all the physical excitement and dramatic action of raid and battle and shipwreck.' Yet, as he also noted, these films stood apart from the mainstream of the documentary movement in that 'they were not in the traditional line of peace time documentary and, with some exceptions, they were not made by technicians from the pre-war British documentary group'.[118] There is a certain irony in that the films that did most to raise the profile of documentary during the war were in fact atypical and not representative of the work of the documentary movement as a whole.

The progressive voice of wartime documentary

For Rotha, as for other documentarists, the real work of documentary during the war was on the home front. Documentarists saw their role as being to observe the social changes taking place as a consequence of wartime conditions and – consistent with the progressive ethos of the movement – to support the case for social reform. The first issue of *Documentary News Letter* published a manifesto entitled 'War Aims for Documentary':

> War, whatever its immediate aims, tends to produce dislocation – economic, social and moral. To wage war successfully it is neces- sary to overcome these dislocations...It is necessary, therefore, to study the impact of war on the social scheme, and to do it cease- lessly throughout the period of conflict. Here the documentary idea in film has a great contribution to make...Nothing could be better propaganda – both internal and external – than a wide analysis of the war on our democratic state, and of the constructive actions which a nation can – if it will – initiate in the midst of a world which seems bent on self destruction.[119]

This manifesto, which clearly linked to Grierson's idea of the social pur- pose of documentary, was a typical statement of the documentarists' view about their own role during wartime. It would be reiterated time and again in the pages of *Documentary News Letter* and would also inform the content and tone of the wartime films of the documentary movement.

It soon became evident that the documentarists would not be con- tent just to produce propaganda films: they were concerned to raise awareness of wartime social developments and to lay down a progres- sive agenda for the future. A recurring theme of many home-front documentaries was to look to the future and to speculate how the spirit of wartime unity and collectivism could be carried forward into the task of post-war reconstruction. One of the strategies they employed was to contrast the social achievements of the war with the future task of peacetime reconstruction. The first clear expression of this idea was in *The Dawn Guard* (Charter Films, 1941), produced for the five-minute programme by two film-makers from the commercial industry (John and Roy Boulting) but who shared the progressive outlook of the documentarists. The film takes the form of a dialogue between two Home Guard sentries who start to discuss what the war is being fought for. The older of the two men (actor Percy Walsh) sees it in traditional terms as the defence of a way of life ('It's the liberty we had and never thought about we got to fight for, to get our lives back to where they was'), but his younger companion (Bernard Miles) suggests 'that isn't enough' and argues the need to carry on beyond the defeat of the Nazis: 'We made a fine big war effort, well when it's all over we got to see it we make a fine big peace effort... Ay, there'll be work enough, too, when this lot's over, building up something new and better than what's been destroyed.' *Documentary News Letter* approved of *The Dawn Guard* 'because it comes very near to expressing the feeling of ordinary people as regards what sort of future is to come out of the war'.[120]

The dialectical structure of *The Dawn Guard* – contrasting two profoundly different ways of understanding the war – echoed the views of other progressive commentators in the early period of the war. In particular, it recalls one of J. B. Priestley's radio broadcasts in the summer of 1940 in which he discussed the 'two ways of looking at this war'. The 'official' view, Priestley explained, 'is to see this war as a terrible interruption' and to fight in order that 'we can have done with Hitler and his Nazis and go back to where we started from'. He contrasted this with what he believed was a 'more truthful way of looking at this war', which was 'to regard this war as one chapter in a tremendous history, the history of a changing world, the breakdown of one vast system and the building up of a new and better one'.[121] The war saw the emergence of a popular discourse of reform and reconstruction – sometimes, it has to be said, quite vaguely expressed – that in turn generated an expectation of a more just and egalitarian society after the war. In particular, the policies of the pre-war National Government – both in relation to the appeasement of Germany and in domestic and economic affairs – were discredited. There was a reaction against the 'Guilty Men' – a term popularized in a polemical tract by 'Cato' (a pseudonym for three Beaverbrook journalists: Michael Foot, Peter Howard and Frank Owen) published by Victor Gollancz – and a determination not to return to the bad old days of dole queues and hunger marches. It was this popular mood that would ultimately bring about the election of the Labour government in 1945. As the historian Paul Addison has remarked:

The year 1940 has gone down in our annals as the time when all sections of the nation put aside their peacetime differences, and closed ranks under the leadership of Churchill – 'their finest hour'. It should also go down as the year when the foundations of political power shifted decisively leftward for a decade.[122]

The Dawn Guard was an early example of what would becomer a steady trickle of documentary films addressing people's hopes for the future. A few examples must once again suffice to illustrate the trend. Ralph Bond's *Post 23* (Strand, 1941) focuses on the men and women brought together as air-raid wardens. They are a broad social mix (bus conductor, clerk, stockbroker, architect, telephonist) representing a cross section of middle and working classes. They discuss how the war has made them feel more connected to their community, and the film ends with the chief warden (actor John Longden) declaring to camera: 'The qualities we've learned from comradeship and common suffering are not going to be wasted after this war. It's out of experience like ours that the new world will be built.' Paul Rotha's *They Speak for Themselves* (Seven League Productions, 1942) similarly features a group of young people discussing what they expect for the future and their role in shaping it. Donald Alexander's *Five and Under* (Paul Rotha Productions, 1941) concludes its account of wartime nursery provision with a polemical aside against social deprivation and a declaration that the 'new Britain' after the war 'must have health and education for all'.

These were all examples where documentarists seem to have inserted their own social concerns into films about other subjects: here the references to post-war social reform have been tacked on to films about different aspects of the home front. However, the progressive voice of documentary was not limited to films about the civilian experience. The AFPU's *ABCA* (1943) illustrates the work of the Army Bureau of Current Affairs, an organization set up to further the education of servicemen by introducing topical discussion and debates into their training. ABCA was credited with raising the political awareness of servicemen and may have influenced the outcome of the 1945 general election in which many servicemen voted Labour.[123] The film shows a session in which a group of soldiers discuss the Soviet war effort and what they can learn from it. The commentary asserts the inevitability of post-war reform: 'We recognise that the new world is in the building now. ABCA is helping to win the war by giving the soldier the weapon of truth and understanding. It is also laying the foundations of an enlightened society which will one day enjoy the peace.'

The extent to which these films were an expression of official MOI policy is unclear. On the one hand the wartime government was reluctant to make specific promises about jobs and housing that it might not be able to meet: Churchill, in particular, was wary of the 'homes fit for heroes' promised after the First World War.[124] For this reason, the Prime Minister had even wanted to prevent copies of the Beveridge Report from being distributed to servicemen. Sir William Beveridge's Report on Social Insurance and Allied Services (1942) – which suggested a comprehensive system of social security 'from the cradle to the grave' – focused the hitherto rather vague aspirations for the future into a concrete plan for a post-war Welfare State. On the other hand, however, the MOI was dependent upon progressive artists such as the documentarists for its publicity work. As George Orwell observed:

> The ideal, from the official point of view, would have been to put all publicity in the hands of 'safe' people . . . but since not enough of these were available, the existing intelligentsia had to be utilised, and the tone and even to some extent the content of official propaganda have been modified accordingly. No one acquainted with the Government pamphlets, ABCA lectures, documentary films and broadcasts to occupied countries which have been issued during the past two years imagines that our rulers would sponsor this kind of thing if they could help it. Only, the bigger the machine of government becomes, the more loose ends and forgotten corners there are in it.[125]

The sense that documentary, especially non-theatrical documentary, was one such forgotten corner was endorsed by Helen Forman, who said that 'we enjoyed a great deal of freedom. We were not told what to do or plagued by theories of morale.'[126]

As the war went on, documentary films became more assertive in their promotion of a reformist agenda of social and economic reconstruction. Basil Wright and Max Anderson's *The Harvest Shall Come* (Realist Film Unit, 1943) was a four-reel story documentary about the agricultural industry, focusing on the experiences of farm labourer Tom Grimwood (John Slater). The film pays particular attention to the poor living conditions and low pay of many rural workers. It is critical of the neglect of agriculture between the wars and contrasts this with the wartime emergency that has 'forced us to take stock of our agriculture and the men who live by it'. The film concludes with a direct call for social improvement:

> The farm labourer, like any other worker, has a right to a secure job, good wages, regular hours, and a yearly holiday with pay. He has a

right to a well-built home with good water supplies, drains, light-
ing and heating...These things are the responsibility of the British
people and we must see that they are done.

The Harvest Shall Come was sponsored not by the MOI but by the
chemicals industry (ICI) who had apparently thought they were commissioning a film about fertilizer. The sponsor allegedly regarded the
film as 'communist propaganda': it was released only through the
personal support of Robert Hudson, the Minister of Agriculture.[127] *Documentary News Letter* thought it 'the first genuine story film made with the
documentary purpose and by the documentary method' and, despite
some technical shortcomings, felt that 'its closeness to the hopes and
fears of ordinary people, its reflection of the nobility of the working
man, will reach out to the hearts of any audiences'.[128]

John Ellis has argued that one of the issues facing wartime documentary was that 'a new regime of representation of voice was required to
produce an acceptable and intelligible "we" that could speak out for
the British nation, from the British nation'.[129] There were two strategies
through which this was achieved. One was a move away from the patri-
cian tones of the newsreels and even of some documentaries towards
the adoption of regional accents. The 'rustic' Somerset tones of Bernard
Miles in *The Dawn Guard* may seem mannered to modern ears but a
more authentic regional voice was to be found in John Eldridge's *Wales –
Green Mountain, Black Mountain* (Strand, 1943), which featured a poetic
commentary written and narrated by Dylan Thomas. The film explores
the legacy of unemployment in the mining and farming industries of
Wales: Thomas's eloquent yet bitter commentary ('Remember the procession of the old young men/ From dole queue to corner and back
again...Nothing in their pockets, nothing home to eat/ Lagging from
the slag heap to the pinched, packed street') serves both as an indict-
ment of pre-war economic policies and as an assertion of the need for
change ('Remember the procession of the old young men – It shall never
happen again').

Another strategy of wartime documentary was to explore the use of
both diegetic and non-diegetic voices. Sometimes these voices are set
up in opposition to one another as the 'authentic' voices of ordinary
people challenge the 'official' voice of commentators. Perhaps the best
example of this technique was Gilbert Gunn's *Tyneside Story* (Spectator,
1943). The film describes the neglect of the Tyneside shipbuilding industry before the war and shows how workers from the Eldon yard were laid
off until it was reopened to meet the demand for new ships during the

war. However, a triumphalist commentary about the regeneration of the industry ('As long as Britain calls for ships the call will be answered by the ring of steel on steel in the shipyards of the Tyne') is undercut by one of the workers who is rather more sceptical as he speaks direct to camera:

> Ay, but wait a minute. Tyneside's busy enough today, old 'uns and young 'uns hard at work making good ships. But just remember what the yards looked like five years ago – idle, empty, some of them derelict, and the skilled men that worked in them scattered and forgotten. Will it be the same again five years from now?

Hence the film expresses doubt about the prospects for industrial regeneration and full employment after the war – and so challenges the 'official' point of view of the commentator. The worker 'Fred', with his authentic Geordie accent, is played by a member of the Newcastle-upon-Tyne People's Theatre Company, one of several left-leaning groups associated with the documentary movement during the war: others included the Unity Theatre, a socialist collective that had close links with the Co-operative movement.[130]

One possible explanation for the insertion of what amounted to left-wing politics into official film production during the war was that as most of these films were made for non-theatrical distribution they passed under the radar. As for the 1930s, however, the evidence is mixed regarding the popular reception of these films. On the one hand there is anecdotal evidence that some audiences were sceptical about even the vague promises of reform held out in films like *The Dawn Guard*. One of the MOI's own travelling projectionists reported that the film was not well received by an audience of Scottish miners, who thought it was 'insincere': 'A film like *Dawn Guard* leaves them with the idea that someone is trying to put something over on them.'[131] On the other hand the documentarists themselves felt, naturally, that their efforts made a positive contribution to a public discourse about the effects of war on British society. *Documentary News Letter* felt that the non-theatrical film programme 'has brought into being machinery for public enlightenment on a scale hitherto unprecedented in any country' and that the MOI 'has become a major sponsor in the field of democratic education by film as regards civic responsibilities, social reform and social progress'.[132]

It has sometimes been suggested that documentary film contributed to the victory of the Labour Party in the general election of 1945: Paul Rotha, for example, later averred that Labour politician Stafford Cripps had said as much.[133] There was certainly an association between the outlook of progressive documentary films and the social and economic policies of the Labour Party. Nicholas Pronay contends that 'by the close of World War II, significant sections of the British people had been treated to visions of a grandiose post-war Utopia' and that 'it had been given a very clear and specific party-political identification: if you want this wonderful future, you can only have it if you vote Labour'.[134] It is impossible to ascertain the extent to which documentary films may have influenced voters' behaviour: did they help to shape people's expectations about the post-war world or did they just reflect a popular view that was already quite widespread? Toby Haggith concludes his study of wartime home-front documentaries on a sceptical note: 'All the evidence shows that the effect of MOI film on the outcome of the election was negligible.'[135] The truth probably lies somewhere in between. Documentary may not have won the election for the Labour Party, but it surely helped to frame the ideological context in which the election was fought, as voters chose the progressive agenda of the Labour Party (exemplified in its manifesto, entitled *Let Us Face the Future*, which focused on jobs, health and housing) over a tired and backward-looking Conservative Party (whose manifesto, *Mr Churchill's Address to the Electors*, focused on foreign policy and made little mention of social reform). To this extent documentary should be seen as one of many progressive voices in wartime Britain – others included J. B. Priestley, George Orwell, 'Cassandra' of the *Daily Mirror* and the BBC's 'Brains Trust' – which in their different ways focused attention on how the war was changing British society.

And some documentary films were quite explicit in their politics. *World of Plenty* (Paul Rotha Productions, 1943) may be the only example of socialist economic propaganda sponsored by the British government and afforded a widespread theatrical release. This was a 'food propaganda' documentary that offered a stinging critique of pre-war conditions of food poverty in the midst of plenty and called for a planned economy in agriculture and food distribution. Rotha suggested the film to the MOI after producing a short documentary covering a conference held by the British Association for the Advancement of Science in 1941, where one of the speakers, Sir John Boyd Orr, had spoken about the dietary deficiencies among poorer sections of the population and had called for a state-controlled food production and distribution policy during and after the war.[136] Rotha collaborated with Orr in preparing the script, though the film encountered numerous political obstacles in its path to the screen. The Ministry of Agriculture disliked the film on the grounds that 'undue prominence is given to unofficial speakers on the subject of the future of the food situation in Europe'.[137] And the MOI's special advisor on films, Sidney Bernstein, was worried that references in the script to the dumping of food in America – a policy the US government officially denied – 'would be extremely embarrassing'.[138] However, Rotha was supported by Jack Beddington and by Lord Woolton, the Minister of Food. *World of Plenty* was completed early in 1943 and premiered at the World Food Conference in Hot Springs, Virginia, USA.

It was in *World of Plenty* that Rotha developed the dialectical style of documentary for which he is best known. It combines actuality footage with animated diagrams and uses no fewer than six narrators who present different points of view as they debate the world's food problem. This results in a constantly shifting mode of address whereby no single voice is ever in control or regarded as totally authoritative.[139] Hence the film begins with the 'official' Voice One (E. V. H. Emmett of Gaumont-British News) establishing the subject matter in the conventional manner only to be interrupted by the sceptical Voice Two (Yorkshire journalist Eric Knight) who asks 'Let me see that again' and questions the official statistics ('You can prove anything with diagrams – give me half an hour with Walt Disney and I could pay my income tax and never feel it!'). *World of Plenty* therefore takes the form of a 'film argument' in which different points of view are heard rather than a straightforward statement of the case. Other 'voices' heard in the film include Lord Woolton and Orr himself, who argues that the distribution of food has been made more equal and efficient under wartime conditions and asserts that the state should continue to exercise control over food distribution after the war. This was a more radical policy than even the post-war Labour government undertook: its nationalization programme never extended to the food industry. William Whitebait, the film critic of the *New Statesman*, thought it an excellent example of how to present an argument to the public: 'No meatier piece of exposition and propaganda has ever forced its way into our cinemas... *World of Plenty* is a front-page story and a leading article thrown at the heads of cinema-goers, and, whatever its success or failure as entertainment, it will plant a seed.'[140]

What conclusions can be drawn about the achievements of wartime documentary? There is no doubt that wartime conditions provided important opportunities for documentary that had not existed before the war. The scale of documentary production increased, documentarists had an opportunity to work with bigger budgets and better facilities, and documentary found an audience in commercial cinemas that it had not reached before. *Documentary News Letter* believed that the success of the major war documentaries had overcome the antipathy of the film trade: 'In the public cinemas there can be no doubt that the [Films] Division's notable series of feature documentaries including *Target for Tonight, Western Approaches* and *World of Plenty* ... have created a taste for documentary which even the most stick-in-the-mud exhibitor can ignore no longer.'[141] Against this must be set the facts that the film trade was still resistant to documentary (witnessed in distributors' reluctance to pick up official films unless they were eligible for quota) and that the effectiveness of the non-theatrical exhibition programme is impossible to ascertain. Nicholas Pronay asserts that documentary films, in the end, had little effect on public morale: 'As far as the war effort was concerned, the country could have dispensed with the whole lot without an iota of difference. The real propaganda *war* was carried out in the commercial cinemas and by the newsreels, not in any significant way by the documentary film.'[142] However, this seems an unduly negative assessment. There is clear evidence that some documentaries made a significant impact on audiences (*Britain Can Take It!, Target for Tonight, Desert Victory*) even though that impact was often specific to the moment. The effect of the social documentaries on public attitudes is more difficult to assess and may in any event have been more cumulative in nature. Whatever the effects of its films, however, the documentary movement had prospered under wartime conditions. It had served the ideological needs of the state in the production of propaganda films and at the same time had also furthered its own progressive social agenda in contributing to public discourse around the nature of the post-war world. Perhaps the most significant outcome of the war was that documentary had finally been embraced by the government as an important instrument of official publicity. After its uncertain start the MOI's support of documentary had developed into one of the most extensive programmes of official film-making by any liberal democracy in the twentieth century. Indeed it may have been the fullest adoption of documentary film by the state seen outside the Soviet Union and Castro's Cuba. This in turn fuelled an expectation that the post-war Labour government would look to develop the wartime project of documentary into the task of post-war reconstruction.

4
Post-War Documentary

> And in Documentary it means more interesting films, films
> with a sense of humour, films which do not try to preach, but
> just do what is the necessary function of every good film – to
> wit, to entertain. The people stood for a lot of propaganda dur-
> ing the war. But now it has a chance to prove that it has grown
> up – that it can make films the public will enjoy seeing.
>
> *Documentary Film News*[1]

The orthodox view of British documentary after the Second World War
is that it was a period of stagnation and decline – a narrative summed
up in the title of Elizabeth Sussex's book *The Rise and Fall of British
Documentary*.[2] Basil Wright, for example, believed that 'exhaustion set
in' after the war and 'we were over the peak'.[3] This was not merely a
retrospective view. A contemporary report on documentary for the Central Office of Information was dismissive in the extreme of 'the old Soho
Square gang': 'They are stale. They have no new ideas. They are content
to plough the same somewhat arid furrows that they have ploughed
for these many years.'[4] It would probably be fair to say that few if
any post-war documentary films deserve a place in the canon alongside classics such as *The Song of Ceylon*, *Night Mail*, *Fires Were Started* or
Desert Victory. In the standard historiography two events – the death of
Humphrey Jennings in 1950 and the closure of the Crown Film Unit in
1952 – have come to represent, symbolically at least, the end point of
the documentary movement of the 1930s.[5]

However, the narrative of decline does not withstand close scrutiny.
In terms of actual production the post-war period saw the expansion of
the documentary sector in the British film industry with the emergence
of new production units including (but not limited to) Anvil Films, Basic

Films, DATA (Documentary and Technicians Alliance), Merlin, Rayant and World Wide Pictures. Much of the work for these units came from government sponsorship: from 1946 the new Central Office of Information embarked upon an extensive programme of public information films that surpassed even the height of wartime production in its quantity. And there was also a significant increase in industrial sponsorship of documentary, including by major corporations such as Imperial Chemical Industries, Unilever and the Ford Motor Company, and by the newly nationalized coal and railway industries. Nor does the narrative of stagnation and decline take account of the emergence of new talent into the documentary field: notable new directors included Lindsay Anderson, Terry Bishop, Paul Dickson, John Eldridge, Geoffrey Jones, Derrick Knight, John Krish and Karel Reisz. And, while some of the 'old Soho Square Gang' may indeed have been 'over the peak', as Wright put it, others – notably Edgar Anstey at British Transport Films and Arthur Elton at the Shell Film Unit – adjusted successfully to the new landscape of post-war documentary. If the post-war period remains the 'unknown' chapter of British documentary cinema this is due largely to the perception that documentary had lost its progressive social purpose and had instead become an adjunct of the commercial advertising industry that – as *Documentary Film News* had predicted in 1948 – attached more significance to entertainment value than it did to public education. However, a more appropriate way of understanding the trajectories of post-war documentary is to see it not as a period of decline but as one of transition.[6] This is evident in the divergent tendencies that can be identified within documentary. On the one hand the post-war period saw a decisive break with the Griersonian tradition of documentary as a social practice and the embracing of other modes and styles more suited to the ideological needs of the time. These included the task of economic reconstruction after the war, and the promotion of British culture and heritage for audiences at home and abroad. On the other hand the legacy of Humphrey Jennings and other more 'poetic' documentarists can be seen in the highly individualistic and personal films of the Free Cinema movement in the 1950s.[7]

Documentary and the post-war British film industry

The post-war history of documentary needs to be understood in relation to the fortunes of the British film industry as a whole. British cinema, including documentary, had emerged from the Second World War with its critical reputation significantly enhanced. British films had not only provided much-needed escapism during the dark days of the war but had also served the national need in promoting the British war effort in films such as *Target for Tonight, In Which We Serve, Millions Like Us, Desert Victory* and *The Way Ahead*. Michael Balcon, who as Head of Production at Ealing Studios had been a major player in the renaissance of British cinema, summed up the critical consensus of the time when he wrote in 1946: 'Undoubtedly it is the influence of realism on the British film in wartime which has given it a new and individual character and which has weaned it away from being an amateur and clumsy pastiche of its Hollywood counterpart.'[8] British cinema was at the height of its popularity in the decade after the war: cinema attendances peaked at 1,632 million in 1945 and remained above their pre-war level until the late 1950s. The new cultural prestige attached to British cinema was reflected in the institution of the Royal Film Performance (1946) and the British Film Academy (1948), while the emergence of a tradition of 'quality' film-making with films such as *Henry V, Brief Encounter, Odd Man Out* and *Great Expectations* was seen to herald a bright future for the British film industry.[9]

Yet the apparently buoyant condition of the British film industry disguised a number of deep-rooted economic and structural problems. The domestic production sector contracted during the war and was slow to revive afterwards: the increase in cinemagoing was fuelled largely by American films. Like all sectors of the industry, documentary was affected by the increasing costs of labour, film stock and studio rental. The average cost of a theatrical one-reel documentary film in 1947 was around £3,000 – twice as much as before the war.[10] Furthermore, the rise of the Rank Organization as the leading producer-distributor-exhibitor in Britain had significant consequences for the whole industry.[11] Paul Rotha expressed the growing concern over Rank's near-monopoly when he wrote in 1945 'that so much power vested in one group is an unhealthy and precarious state for an industry which can so widely reflect the characteristics and opinions of a country's people'.[12] In particular, Rank's entry into the field of non-fiction film-making represented a direct challenge to documentary. *This Modern Age* (1946–1949) was a topical monthly news cinemagazine in the style of *The March of Time*. It was produced on a larger budget than the documentarists could hope for (£15,000 per two-reel issue according to one estimate) and would have competed with documentary films for space in cinema programmes.[13] It has been suggested that *This Modern Age* was J. Arthur Rank's sop to the post-war Labour government: that it included favourable coverage of its policies in return for leaving his empire intact.[14] For example, 'Homes for All' (No. 1, September 1946) supported the government's plans for rebuilding inner cities; 'Coal Crisis' (No. 8, April 1947) defended nationalization of the coal industry; and 'Development Areas' (No. 9, May 1947) endorsed state subsidies to support industrial regeneration in depressed regions. *This Modern Age* was discontinued in 1949 when Rank implemented a strategy of retrenchment following losses sustained in its feature film production programme – and when it had become apparent that there was no political will to dismantle its empire.

The foremost concern for documentary in the immediate post-war period was that, having gained a foothold in the commercial cinema during the war, it would now once again find itself relegated to the margins of the industry. In this context the resistance of exhibitors to documentary films remained a major problem. It soon became apparent that exhibitors wanted to ease themselves out of the wartime 'gentlemen's agreement' to put aside space for a monthly official film in all cinema programmes. In 1946 this space was taken by the official newsreel *Britain Can Make It*. The argument, as it had been during the 1930s, was that audiences frequented the cinema for entertainment rather than education. As one civil servant put it: 'One of our problems is that the subjects about which we make films are sometimes unpalatable in themselves and not well suited to be the middle of a sandwich consisting of Rita Hayworth and a gangster Second Picture.'[15] At the same time there was opposition from the documentarists to the free distribution of official films, which it was felt displaced other shorts. The newly formed Federation of Documentary Film Units – an organization set up at the end of the war, representing eight of the leading independent documentary producers – argued that free distribution hindered documentary as a whole because it squeezed them out of cinemas: 'The principle of free distribution to the cinemas has had the effect of depressing the general market for documentary films, and of fixing the upper limit to the number of films which the Government can get into the cinemas.'[16]

A combination of several factors therefore – including an ailing production sector, the continued dominance of American films and a depressed market for British films – created a sense of almost permanent 'crisis' in the film industry in the late 1940s: this certainly was the impression given by headlines and leaders in the trade press.[17] It was against this background that in 1947 Hugh Dalton, the Chancellor of the Exchequer, announced the imposition of an *ad valorem* duty of 75 per cent on the earnings of overseas films in Britain. The

'Dalton duty' was an attempt to address the chronic post-war balance of payments deficit and was aimed principally at American distributors who remitted most of their revenues from the British market back to the United States. In 1947 it was estimated that remitted revenues amounted to some $70 million.[18] The US film industry, through its trade association, the Motion Picture Association of America, retaliated with a boycott of the British market. The British government had hoped that the domestic film industry, including documentary, would be able to step up production. Harold Wilson, the President of the Board of Trade, suggested 'that the Central Office of Information should attempt to arrange for a greater production of documentary films even if it involved the other sponsoring Departments in spending more money in commissioning films'.[19] Wilson evidently had faith in the popular appeal of documentary: 'The average cinemagoer would rather see a good English documentary film than much of the big feature stuff which he is now asked to look at.'[20] Of course, this may have been an expedient view given his expressed desire to increase documentary production. However, his suggestion was rebutted by the Director of the COI's Films Division:

I am surprised that the President of the BOT should be so ill-informed, and should write so glibly so far off the target! Mr Wilson...is in fact suggesting that the Government should spend more money on films in order to help absorb unemployment in the Documentary industry...I cannot believe that the Treasury would take very kindly to such a suggestion – nor indeed would it be proper to use the tax-payer's money for such a purpose.[21]

In fact the entire film industry had been caught off guard by the Dalton duty: it had not been consulted and lacked the capacity to meet the public demand for films once the US boycott took effect. A compromise was reached with the Anglo-American Film Agreement of 1948, whereby the duty was removed in return for a limitation on the remittance of revenues.

Hence the place of documentary in the post-war film industry remained as parlous as it had been during the 1930s. The imperative, for both official and independent documentary, was to hold its own in the cinema programme against commercial competition. In 1947 the Director-General of the Central Office of Information claimed that 'we have been selling official films to the trade during the last year in quantities greater than have ever before been achieved in the history of British documentary'.[22] Yet to a large extent this was due to the need for renters to fulfil their quota obligations at a time of reduced output from the British studios. The abolition of renters' quota under the Cinematograph Films Act of 1948 would change the game. This marked a decisive shift in the film industry that enhanced the position of distributors (no longer required to handle British films) at the expense of producers (often dependent upon a distribution guarantee to secure funding for their films). Robert Angell, an independent documentary producer who specialized in films sponsored by industry, painted a gloomy picture of the economics of the documentary industry:

> It used to be possible to get films with a running time under thirty minutes released as supporting programmes in cinemas, provided they were made as entertainingly as possible and the sponsors' message was not too intrusive. The returns to the producer for any short were minimal after the distributor had paid for the prints of the film and other charges and subtracted their percentage from the small part of the box office take negotiated with the exhibitor. If the short had latched itself onto a very successful feature (a matter of luck and nothing to do with the quality of the short) some money might be made over a year or two but nothing approaching that spent on production.[23]

There is much anecdotal evidence that distributors, once freed from the obligation to handle British films, were resistant to documentary. Lindsay Anderson recalled that his documentary *Thursday's Children* (World Wide Pictures, 1954), which he co-directed with Guy Brenton, about the Royal School for the Deaf in Margate, was rejected by all the major distributors: 'We hawked it about in the traditional way, and everyone was very moved, and all the distributors cried, but said of course it wasn't entertainment, and they were very sorry....'[24] It was only when *Thursday's Children* won an Academy Award for Best Short Subject of 1954 that it was retrospectively afforded a theatrical release. Even the introduction of the British Film Production Fund in 1950 – also known as the Eady Levy (after Treasury official Sir Wilfred Eady who devised it) – that offered a subsidy to British producers and distributors arising from an additional tax on ticket sales did little to remedy the problem as, according to Angell at least, distributors would sometimes try to buy out producers for a lump sum 'which was technically illegal, but often proved a temptation for the producer'.[25]

The Central Office of Information and documentary film

The election of the Labour government in July 1945 is widely regarded as marking a decisive shift in the political landscape of Britain. Labour was elected on the promise of an ambitious pro-gramme of reform whose key policies were the introduction of a comprehensive system of National Insurance, nationalization of major industries (coal, steel, electricity, gas, railways) and the establish-ment of a National Health Service providing free health care for all. So far-reaching were these reforms and so widespread was the popular support for them that when the Conservative Party was re-elected in 1951 it pledged not to reverse them. Hence 1945 has been seen as marking the emergence of a new consensus in British politics that lasted until the 1970s. It is perhaps no coincidence that this period also coincided with the peak years of documen-tary film production: the new public utilities and social services were major sponsors of documentary between the late 1940s and early 1970s.

It was only to be expected that the documentary movement would have welcomed the election of the post-war Labour government. Its social and economic policies – including the expansion of the Wel-fare State and the adoption of Keynesian economic controls – reflected the reformist agenda that progressive documentarists had been advocat-ing during the war in films such as *World of Plenty*. The expectation was that the Labour government would look to place documentary at the centre of a new national publicity strategy. Paul Rotha later said that 'we optimistically thought that the new government would have a really imaginative, progressive attitude towards information services... We were very bitterly disappointed.'[26] The first indication of this disappointment was the government's decision in 1946 to close down the Ministry of Information (*Documentary News Letter*, once the MOI's fiercest critic had called for its continuation in peacetime) and to replace it with a new Central Office of Information (COI). The COI was a compromise between those who argued for maintaining a gov-ernment publicity organization and those who felt that propaganda was a necessary evil in war but had no role in peacetime.[27] Unlike the MOI, however, the COI was not a ministerial department responsible for policy but rather a service department whose role was to facilitate the publicity needs of other departments. Its role has often been compared to a public-sector advertising agency. The documentarists felt that the absence of a policy-making remit for the COI meant their influence was diminished. This was certainly the view of John Grierson, who returned to Britain in 1945:

> I keep on feeling that the documentary group as a whole is not at the centre where political and social planning is being thought out and legislated, or not close enough to the centre. It is not good enough to be on the outside looking in, waiting on someone else's pleasure for an opportunity to serve social progress.[28]

The establishment of the COI necessitated a rethinking of the relationship between documentary and the state. Grierson – employed first as an advisor and then as Controller of Films for the COI between 1948 and 1950 – argued that state sponsorship of documentary was more crucial than ever 'for the strengthening of the national spirit, its projection abroad and the development of the national economy at home and in the colonies'.[29] He advocated an increase in official sponsorship and the adoption of a policy-making role for the COI. His views were no doubt informed by his experience at the National Film Board of Canada, which was now held up as a model of progressive state sponsorship of documentary film. However, Grierson's proposals were opposed by Bernard Sendall, the COI's existing Films Officer, who felt that the postwar expansion of the documentary sector meant that it needed to look for other sources of funding:

> It does not seem to me to be in the least bit realistic to expect that the Documentary film industry at the dimensions it has now reached can be preserved by a reshaping of Government sponsorship... To my mind, the trouble today is that an industry which was quite rightly given over to State purposes during the war has failed to find a peacetime basis – unrelated to the activities of the State – upon which to thrive.[30]

The nature of the relationship between documentary and the state was itself a matter of some controversy. Some Conservative MPs charged the COI with wasting public money. Anthony Marlowe, for example, averred 'that the Central Office of Information are not making films with anything like the success of the wartime Ministry of Information' and that 'films made by this organisation are very seldom seen by the people, although they cost a vast amount of money'.[31] He was especially critical of the reported £30,000 cost of the 'Charley' films, a series produced by the animation studio Halas & Batchelor about a comic everyman character sceptical about the welfare reforms (*Charley's March of Time*, 1947) and National Health Service (*Your Very Good Health*, 1948). The subtext of such criticisms was that the COI was in effect producing publicity for the Labour Party – a reversal of Labour's complaint that the MOI Films Division in 1939 had been too closely aligned with the Conservative Party. Peter Thorneycroft complained about 'a film on the Transport Act which was straight, clear-cut political propaganda'.[32] The film in question was not named in the course of the debate but was very probably *Transport* (Pathé Documentary Unit, 1950). This film, produced by Peter Bayliss and directed by Peter Bradford for a series entitled *The Wealth of the World*, set out to explain the nationalization policy enacted by the Transport Act of 1947. It was critical of the unrestricted free enterprise that sustained the railway boom of the nineteenth century ('a race that moved too fast') and endorsed the idea of an integrated national transport policy as advocated by the government ('Road transport, railways, canals and docks – to view them all together and make them work as one – that is the task'). Thorneycroft alleged that the film 'was pretty much the Minister's speech, only on celluloid; it looked better on celluloid and lasted only 20 minutes'.

However, the COI was rather more concerned about the flak it received from the documentary movement than with accusations of partisanship from the Opposition benches. By 1947 it was clear that an ideological rift was emerging between the COI and the documentarists. The documentarists' complaints included the lack of direction from the COI, the lengthy and bureaucratic commissioning process, and what they regarded as inadequate payment for preliminary work on projects that were often then abandoned. Paul Rotha further blamed the COI for the perceived decline in quality of post-war documentary:

The fact that the COI's production programme is not conceived on a national level or geared towards the realities of Britain's position in the world has brought about a sense of frustration among the technicians which, together with the delays and financial arguments associated with so many COI films, has done much to undermine the goodwill of the documentary movement...As the major sponsor of documentary films, the COI must be held responsible for the lack of drama and vitality that regrettably characterises its current product.[33]

The Federation of Documentary Film Units complained so loudly that the Cabinet Office even launched an investigation into relations between the COI and the documentarists. Sendall blamed the agitation on what he called 'the Rotha faction' and felt that the COI needed to be robust in its response: 'It is necessary to rebut emphatically the idea that the documentary film in Britain is degenerating as a result of incompetence and lack of imagination on the part of the Central Office.'[34] Grierson tried to calm the situation, writing to the COI's Director-General, Sir Robert Fraser:

> I am worried about this mix-up with the documentary people and don't like it degenerating into hard feelings which can't help anyone... Also I have a strong feeling that the documentary film itself needs a revival, and a deliberate one, if it is to do the big job it certainly can at the present juncture.[35]

For its part, however, the COI maintained that the needs of government had changed since the war and that new approaches to publicity were necessary to reflect this. The techniques that had served documentary so well in the past were not suited to the ideological contexts of the post-war world. Ronald Tritton, who had been a publicity officer for the War Office during the war and now headed the COI's Films Division, put it thus:

> It is impossible to exaggerate the difference between the war years and to-day in reaching inspirational level with the documentary technique. Warfare is rich documentary material ('The dramatic interpretation of reality'). White papers are not. There are few real visuals that properly support economic exposition, there are even fewer that have any inspirational quality. We are in a period of blue-print publicity, a period of ideas and plans for the future. Since these plans are at root social, they can often be interpreted into terms of human drama; since they are often not visible to the eye a documentary interpretation is often impossible (New Towns, National Health Insurance, Incentives, Consultative Machinery, etc, etc.)[36]

Tritton was sceptical that the pre-war documentarists would be able to adapt to the new conditions: he felt that 'we can expect no response to such a challenge from Soho Square'. He averred that government public relations officers

> have, in most cases, a greater awareness of what the public will like than the Documentary boys whose knowledge of this is woefully sparse... It is because [Denis] Forman, [Philip] Mackie, Graham,

etc, have been full of ideas and out of sympathy with old-style documentaries that we are getting more films made with greater entertainment value, however much the boys may dislike it![37]

This view was shared by Jack Beddington, a long-time friend of documentary as the Director of Publicity at Shell in the 1930s and then as Director of the MOI Films Division: 'The trouble with the documentary film world today is that the old gang is still in charge.'[38]

In the event, the COI's view would prevail over the documentarists: by the late 1940s the influence of the 'old gang' was waning. Grierson's attachment to the COI lasted only until 1950 when he left to take charge of Group 3 – a feature film production unit set up by the newly established National Film Finance Corporation to support new talent in the industry.[39] Basil Wright, who had been appointed as supervising producer in charge of the Crown Film Unit towards the end of the war, stood down after a year and set up a new documentary unit (International Realist) but made only one more significant film, *World Without End* (1953), which he co-directed with Paul Rotha for UNESCO. Most of the key pre-war and wartime GPO/Crown directors moved into the feature film industry, including Pat Jackson, Jack Lee and Harry Watt. Rotha, for his part, produced a brace of important films about economic reconstruction in 1946–1947 (*Land of Promise*, *The World is Rich*) before his company, Films of Fact, went into liquidation. In 1953 he joined the BBC to set up its own documentary unit. The only members of the 'old gang' to adapt to the new conditions were Edgar Anstey, who became Films Officer for the British Transport Commission in 1949, in which role he would continue until his retirement in 1974, and Sir Arthur Elton, whose association with the Shell Film Unit lasted until his death in 1973.

The Crown Film Unit after the war

The post-war history of the Crown Film Unit played out the ideological and political tensions that affected documentary as a whole after 1945. At the end of the war, any notion that the official film unit might be returned to the control of the Post Office was quietly forgotten. It was envisaged that Crown would play a central role in post-war film policy under the COI. Ronald Tritton, for example, felt that 'Crown is the best instrument for the production of the main effort films'.[40] However, Crown would struggle to rediscover either the ideological or the aesthetic pre-eminence that it had enjoyed during the war. There was a sense that the unit had lost its sense of purpose and that morale had suffered as a consequence. Alexander Shaw, who succeeded Wright as an interim supervisor in 1946, diagnosed the problem thus:

> I compared its problems with other Units which I have known (notably Realist and the IFI of India), all of which employed the same type of people as are at Crown, and searched for a solution. Finally, I went back to the basic principles which apply to any group of people working together to do creative work, and found that the two Units I had in mind, one of which it must be remembered was under Government control, had something which Crown had not. They had a feeling of freedom and a sense of responsibility... The members of the Units knew that it was up to them to make the system work and that there were no alibis to make, no THEY to be blamed.[41]

Shaw – who did not wish to take on the role in a long-term capacity – suggested that either Humphrey Jennings, Harry Watt or Donald Taylor should be approached to take on the senior producer's job. In the event, however, it was Grierson's brother-in-law, John Taylor, who succeeded Shaw as producer in charge of the Crown Film Unit in 1948.

There is a sense in which the post-war history of the Crown Film Unit is less a history of film-making than one of continuous institutional reorganization. Shaw drew up a 'charter' that envisaged a significant degree of autonomy for the unit: it detached Crown from the control of the COI Films Division by placing it under the direct authority of the COI's Controller and Director-General.[42] Bernard Sendall approved of detaching Crown from the Films Division as he thought it would negate 'the anti-Establishment notions which prevailed under the Beddington regime'.[43] In contrast to the speed and efficacy with which changes had been effected during the war, however, discussions over the wording and implementation of the Crown charter dragged on for 18 months. There were also concerns that the unit was underemployed. Shaw argued that the cost of running the film unit (around £150,000 per year) 'can only be justified if sufficient work is produced': hence he suggested that all projects coming to the COI should be offered in the first instance to Crown 'so that the Producer can balance his programme according to the needs of the Unit'.[44] However, Shaw's successor, John Taylor, resisted a suggestion to split Crown into a number of separate units in order to maximize its production capacity on the grounds that it 'would involve too drastic a change in the basis of the documentary film industry'. 'If it was put into operation', the minutes record, 'most of the commercial units which had specialised in Central Office of Information work might find themselves unable to carry on and the final result might be that the Central Office itself would not be able to obtain films of the same quality as it had previously.'[45]

It is evident that in the late 1940s Crown suffered from an almost permanent state of instability. John Taylor held that 'the Unit had been depleted of directors and script-writers, and there had been a shortage of work for those who remained; producer had followed producer in quick succession; [and] there had been uncertainty about the future of the Unit'.[46] Grierson's appointment to the COI caused a rift with his brother-in-law. Grierson felt 'that there was dead wood at Crown... Geniuses had come out of it in the past, but he had a feeling that they were not there now'.[47] It is tempting to speculate that what Grierson really meant was that the unit was no longer staffed mostly by his own acolytes. There were further problems associated with Crown's move to new studio premises at Beaconsfield. The studio was too large for Crown alone, though the overheads were included in Crown's operating costs. Grierson suggested bringing other documentary units to Beaconsfield to form a loose federation and that contracts should be awarded to any units that 'could produce better work cheaper'.[48] Grierson effectively undermined the position of Taylor, who left to join the somewhat less prestigious Colonial Film Unit. One brother-in-law was replaced by another: Donald Taylor (married to Grierson's sister Marion) took over in 1950.

Against this background of constant institutional upheaval it is hardly any wonder that Crown's post-war films should prove to be something of a mixed bag. Humphrey Jennings's *A Diary for Timothy* (1946) is a transitional film that was begun during the last months of the war: it is a bittersweet film whose overriding impression is not the ultimate victory but rather how hard-won that victory was. Jennings followed it with *A Defeated People* (1946) about the post-war occupation of Germany. It was not an easy subject for Jennings, who surprisingly felt little sympathy for the privations of the German people.[49] There are echoes of this in the film's commentary ('You'll never get Nazi ideas out of the heads of some of the adults') and its association between ideology and disease ('We must prevent not only starvation and epidemic but also diseases of the mind – new brands of fascism – from springing up'). Jennings's last film for Crown was *The Cumberland Story* (1947) on the history of coal mining, from the Workington pit disaster of 1837 to the nationalization of the industry in 1947. The film struggled to find a distributor on the grounds that 'it was too political and too dull a subject'.[50] Richard

Winnington's review of *The Cumberland Story* for the *News Chronicle* saw it as a symptom of a wider post-war malaise that failed 'to rediscover the dynamic missing since the war from British Documentary films'.[51]

Crown's post-war films reflected the diverse range of subjects that characterized the output of the COI. They ranged from serious treatments of juvenile delinquency (*Children on Trial*, 1946) and mental health (*Out of True*, 1951) to somewhat melodramatic accounts of women's sexual health (*The People at No. 19*, 1949) and the nursing profession (*Life in Her Hands*, 1951). There are echoes of Crown's wartime films in Ronald Stark's *Men of the World* (1950), which illustrates the role of National Servicemen in the British Army's post-war deployments in the Mediterranean and the Far East. A more outward-looking perspective was evident in films such as Jill Craigie's *Children of the Ruins* (1948), illustrating the work of UNESCO in reconstruction activities in Europe, and Terry Bishop's *Daybreak in Udi* (1949), which demonstrated the opening of a maternity hospital in Nigeria. The latter film won an Academy Award for Best Documentary Film of 1949 – an effective rebuttal to criticisms that post-war British documentary had lost its way. That said, however, the distinctiveness that characterized Crown's wartime films was no longer in evidence. A late Crown film such as *From the Ground Up* (1950), for example, commissioned by the Economic Information Unit to demonstrate the regeneration of post-war British industry, is indistinguishable in technique from many similar films made by independent units such as DATA or Greenpark.

The sense that Crown was no longer producing films of outstanding or special quality inevitably focused attention on its operating costs. Crown was always a more expensive outfit than the independent units, because it carried overheads of a permanent staff and studio facilities. In 1947 Crown employed 121 permanent staff and its overheads (not including the costs of films) amounted to £98,500 per year.[52] And its films were at the upper end of the cost bracket for documentary: a theatrical one-reeler such as *Men of the World* cost £3,023, while *From the Ground Up*, also one reel, was budgeted at £4,500. This was nearly three times the amount for which DATA was contracted to produce the one-reel *Mining Review* for the National Coal Board. For some critics the last straw was the feature-length *Four Men in Prison* (1950), which cost £16,000 but fell foul of magistrates who considered it 'useless and inaccurate and a waste of public money'.[53] It was little wonder that in the post-war climate of austerity the future of the official film unit should come under intense scrutiny.

It was the election of a Conservative government in October 1951 that spelled the end for the Crown Film Unit. This has sometimes been presented as a political decision in that the Conservative Party was hostile to the documentary movement and Crown was made the scapegoat.[54] However, the archival evidence suggests that the motive was simply economic. The incoming administration accepted most of Labour's social reforms but set its sights on efficiency savings in the running of government: publicity and film-making were easy targets. The new government took the view that 'film production is an expensive medium of information and will have to be cut down to the bare minimum for essential Departmental requirements'.[55] The Treasury – which had always regarded the film unit as an expensive luxury – produced figures indicating that in the financial year 1950–1951 the production costs of Crown films amounted to £218,000, while salary costs amounted to a further £78,500.[56] The same evidence indicated that total commercial earnings of Crown films had dropped from £25,000 in 1946–1947 to £4,000 in 1950–1951. This was attributed to the fact that wartime films such as *Target for Tonight* and *Western Approaches* were still in circulation after the war and 'were mainly responsible for the high figures in 1946–47 and 1947–48'.[57]

As might be expected, the decision to close the Crown Film Unit drew criticism from the documentarists themselves and from the unions, while the cessation at the same time of the COI's mobile film service disappointed many of the film societies who made use of the free loan system.[58] A letter to *The Times* protesting against the closure as 'an ill-considered economy' was signed by (among others) Michael Balcon, Thorold Dickinson, David Lean, Roger Manvell, Carol Reed, Paul Rotha and Basil Wright.[59] Unusually, civil servants also became involved in the debate. Ralph Nunn May, who had been Deputy Director of the MOI Films Division towards the end of the war and whose association with the Crown Film Unit had continued post-war as its general manager, made what he described as a 'desperately unorthodox approach' to R. A. Butler, the new Chancellor of the Exchequer:

> There are, alas, few things remaining of which it can truly be said that Britain has the best in the world. The Crown Film Unit has an unchalleneable [*sic*] position as the best short film unit in the world. In war it has proved itself a vital weapon; and in peace a skilful and adaptable instrument, making films of many different kinds for almost every Department; making them all well; and not only doing a thoroughly

practical and useful job, but winning awards the world over for the
quality of its films – in itself no bad thing for British prestige.[60]

Nunn May's passionate intervention on behalf of the official film unit
casts him as the heir of enlightened civil servants such as Sir Stephen
Tallents. Butler was advised not to reply on the grounds that Nunn
May 'is a civil servant, who has no business whatever to make direct
representations to a Minister about a matter affecting his work'.[61]
   However, the protests against the abolition of the Crown Film Unit
fell on deaf ears. The official position was that 'the decision to ter-
minate its existence has been taken with regret; but...it is a decision
which has been forced on the Government by the hard facts of the
economic situation'.[62] The fact that another publicly funded documentary unit (British Transport Films) had recently been set up and that yet
another would shortly be established under the aegis of the National
Coal Board was an irony that seems to have been lost on the Treasury.
Alternative suggestions to re-establish the Crown Film Unit as 'Group 4'
under the National Film Finance Corporation, or that the British Film
Institute should take over some of its work (in return for an additional
grant), came to nothing.[63] Thus the history of the official documentary
unit that extended back in an unbroken lineage to the establishment
of the EMB Film Unit in 1930 came to a somewhat abrupt and rather
anticlimactic end.

Land of Promise (1946) and documentaries of reconstruction

The major ideological project of documentary film in the immediate
post-war period was to explain the task of economic recovery and reconstruction. The extent to which this was an official mandate is unclear.
The MOI, in its twilight months, had argued that the new social and economic conditions of peacetime 'point to an increasing service of public
information through film. The complexities of the post-war world will
underline the need for a public informed of the problems which the
nation faces and the plans being made to solve them'.[64] However, there
was never an equivalent of the MOI's Programme for Film Propaganda
for post-war film-making. In expositionary terms, furthermore, reconstruction was a more difficult theme to put across than the wartime
narratives of national unity and the people's war. Hence documentarists
adopted different formal strategies to explore post-war problems. One
group of films, focusing particularly on industrial activity, adopted a
didactic factual style that recalled wartime documentary (*Britain Can*

Make It, Mining Review, From the Ground Up). Another strategy, mostly exemplified by the longer films of Paul Rotha, was the dialectical 'problem' style of documentary (*Land of Promise, The World is Rich*). And a third strategy was the more contemplative, poetic documentary, best exemplified by the late films of Humphrey Jennings (*The Dim Little Island, Family Portrait*).

The absence of an official mandate and the adoption of different techniques both help to explain the mixed messages of post-war reconstruction documentaries. On the one hand the official newsreel *Britain Can Make It* (Films of Fact, 1946) – its title evoking memories of the wartime spirit in *Britain Can Take It!* – was commissioned to 'carry the story of the British people gearing themselves to the task of converting a nation mobilised for war into a country constructing for peace'.[65] *Britain Can Make It* was released in 12 monthly issues throughout 1946 and mostly covered subjects related to the regeneration of industry. The tone of the music (by William Alwyn) and commentary is relentlessly upbeat: the emphasis is always on productivity and the adoption of new efficiency methods (such as time-and-motion study). On the other hand, however, this may be contrasted with a film such as *The Balance* (Films of Fact, 1947), which was commissioned by the Board of Trade to explain why most British manufactured goods were destined for export rather than for the home market. Sir Stafford Cripps, the Chancellor of the Exchequer, delivers a stern homily to austerity: 'We're living on tick – on loans from America and Canada, and that must not go on. We must pay our way as a nation, just as you do as a family – and nothing but our own hard work can do it.' Similarly, *From the Ground Up* (Crown, 1950), while upbeat about the prospects for economic recovery, also endorses the culture of austerity: 'It's worth denying ourselves now to assure for ourselves and our children a future peaceful and plentiful.'

The dominant political and economic doctrine of the post-war period was 'planning': this was what Tritton meant by 'a period of blue-print publicity'. The mantra of planning was a recurring theme of post-war documentary, especially those focusing on the rebuilding of Britain's cities.[66] Again, different strategies were employed in representing the task of urban reconstruction, though the ideological effect of these films – conditioned as it was by the immediate post-war context – was generally much the same regardless of their producers or sponsors. *A City Reborn* (Gryphon Films, 1946), about the building of prefabricated houses in blitzed Coventry, is a story documentary seen through the eyes of a soldier on leave (Bill Rowbotham). It concludes with a clear call for a progressive approach to planning: 'After the war there can be no thinking of returning to the good old days of cramped houses in crippling streets, of slums still living on...And this will happen again if we don't plan.' *The Way We Live* (Rank, 1946) is more in the style of social documentaries such as *Housing Problems*: director Jill Craigie incorporated *vox populi* opinions of local residents into a film about the development of the rebuilding plan for Plymouth. *A City Speaks* (Films of Fact, 1947) was an example of a film commissioned by a local authority (the City of Manchester Corporation) rather than through the COI. It exemplifies the dialectical strategy of Paul Rotha's films in its comparison between the city's Victorian past, associated with social problems and poor planning, and the view that a coherent programme of urban planning would deliver better living conditions – represented by the model suburb of Wythenshawe.[67] *A Plan to Work On* (Basic Films, 1948) is different from other town-planning documentaries as it focuses on the mistakes of the past rather than the efforts of the Luftwaffe. It is a part-story documentary using actors to dramatize the development of the town plan for Dunfermline in Scotland: 'We're going to plan a new town – the way it should be to live in.' Like *The Way We Live*, the film insists upon the importance of involving communities in the planning process: 'Our plan must be for the benefit of everyone who lives and works here.'

Rotha's *Land of Promise* (Films of Fact, 1946) was the most radical of the post-war reconstruction documentaries. Rotha had conceived the film during the late stages of the war as a sequel of sorts to *World of Plenty*. His intention was to use the same techniques to examine the housing shortage that he had previously applied to food distribution. Rotha again consulted experts including Sir John Boyd Orr and Otto Neurath, an Austrian émigré who had developed the Isotype ('International System of Typographic Picture Education'), which established a set of conventions for the visual representation of statistical data.[68] On this occasion, however, Rotha had to find private sponsorship and an independent distributor:

About two-thirds of the finance had been put up by the gas industry, who thought they were getting a film on housing, which they were. But I ran out of money and had to put money from my company into it to finish the film. I was determined it should be finished. Then George Hoellering who ran the Academy Cinema in Oxford Street saw it and liked it very much. He had a renting company called Film Traders and they took the film, and he distributed it both theatrically and non-theatrically after that.[69]

While the combination of its theme and sponsorship by the (pre-nationalization) gas industry might suggest continuity with pre-war films such as *Housing Problems, Land of Promise* is better understood as a development of the more dialectical technique that Rotha had started to develop in his wartime films and which reached perhaps its fullest extent here.

Land of Promise was billed as 'an argument about our homes and houses': to this end it employs the technique of multiple narrators who argue over the evidence presented in the film. There are three entirely abstract voices – 'History', 'Hansard' ('The voice of the Mother of Parliaments – I am record') and 'Isotype' ('I use symbols to make diagrams') – and four other 'real' voices who represent different ideological standpoints. While some other films had acknowledged that planning was not universally popular – some, especially on the political right, resented what they regarded as state interference in the lives of individuals – *Land of Promise* tackles this issue directly. 'Voice One' (John Mills) represents an everyman character who offers a broadly progressive point of view and who is willing to listen to the arguments of experts. He is contrasted with 'Know-All' (character actor Miles Malleson, who collaborated on the script), who represents the voice of conservative Middle England: he is complacent, resistant to change and rejects the arguments advanced in favour of planning, which he regards as unwarranted intrusion by the state ('You simply cannot muck about with other people's lives like that!'). The remaining two voices are a quietly spoken Women's Institute-type ('Could men not learn without a war?') and a working-class housewife who feels disenfranchised from the political system ('They're all alike those politicians'). These voices are overlaid onto a history of housing development and policy in Britain, illustrated by a combination of library footage and animated diagrams provided by the Isotype Institute.

Land of Promise is structured in three parts. 'Homes As They Were' documents the familiar history of the promises of 'homes for heroes' after the First World War and lays the blame on the timidity of politicians and on the self-interest of the construction industry, which claimed it could not build new houses due to the lack of demand – despite unemployment in the industry itself. There are echoes of *Housing Problems* in the account of 'forgotten people' living in slums and in the campaign for tenants' rights led by Father John of Stepney. 'Homes As They Are' documents the effects of the Blitz and asserts that wartime evacuation and conscription have revealed the poor health of Britain's slum-dwellers. At the same time, wartime collectivism had demonstrated what could be achieved through centralized planning. This section ends by raising the question of expectations for the post-war world familiar from wartime documentaries, as the middle-class female voice asks: 'They're coming back – the men and women, the boys and girls, the people who've been fighting this war for you – they're coming back. What have you got to show them?' The final part of the film, 'Homes As They Might Be', is an unequivocal call for a planned economy in housing, including compulsory land purchase to facilitate construction. To this end *Land of Promise* advocated a genuinely radical solution to the housing problem: even the post-war Labour government never contemplated nationalization of house construction, or compulsory purchase.

Land of Promise was widely – and for the most part favourably – reviewed. For Roger Manvell:

> *Land of Promise* is an example of the true documentary film built up in Britain during the ten years before the war and matured in the service of the community during the last seven years. It takes its problems and its facts and its audience seriously, but it never forgets, in the best sense of film-journalism, that the facts and the statistics represent human lives lived in certain ways in certain conditions.[70]

Dilys Powell described it as 'the pictorial equivalent of a White Paper' and though she detected 'a touch of condescension towards its audience' she nevertheless felt that in all it produced 'an overwhelming argument in favour of planned rebuilding of our cities'.[71] It was variously described as a 'clever documentary' (*Daily Mirror*), a 'vigorous argument' (*Sunday Express*) and 'an important and stimulating film' (*News Chronicle*). The left-leaning press (*Tribune, Daily Worker, Daily Herald*) were the most favourably inclined towards the film, whereas the *Daily Telegraph* took against its 'generally pretentious treatment' and deemed it 'unworthy of Paul Rotha's talent'.[72]

Land of Promise is a film very much of its time: it captures the mood of optimism for a more egalitarian society that accompanied the election of the Attlee government before the harsh realities of post-war economic problems had begun to bite. Rotha followed it with *The World is Rich* (Films of Fact, 1947), in which he returned to the problem of world hunger explored in *World of Plenty*. This was commissioned by the COI and reunited most of the key people involved with *World of Plenty*, including Sir John Boyd Orr (who appears in his capacity as Director of the United Nations Food and Agriculture Organization) and writer Arthur Calder-Marshall. An indication of the importance attached to

The World is Rich is that it was budgeted at £25,000.[73] However, as Rotha complained at the time, its production 'has been a history of hold-ups and frustrations which more than once brought its producer to the point of resignation'.[74] In particular, Rotha blamed the protracted commissioning process and delays to payments for the bankruptcy of his company Films of Fact.

The World is Rich follows the same formal strategy as *World of Plenty* and *Land of Promise* with a three-part structure ('The World in Famine', 'The World in Subsistence', 'The World in Full Health') and seven narrational 'voices' who express different views about the global food shortage. However, the film met with neither trade nor official approval. Ronald Tritton reported that '*The World is Rich*... a grim and harrowing piece full of social conscience, having been rejected by all the major renters, has just now found a potential dealer who strongly recommends heavy cuts and the removal of "some of all that misery".'[75] Following an intervention from the Labour MP Woodrow Wyatt, a shortened version of *The World is Rich* received a limited distribution in London in 1948.[76] Its failure seems to have persuaded the COI to focus on short films rather than features for public exhibition: there would be no further theatrical features after *The World is Rich*.

By the late 1940s, the COI evidently felt that documentary was in danger of placing too strong an emphasis on Britain's economic problems. It realized that the public was beginning to resent the continued austerity of the post-war years and had no appetite for films suggesting that conditions might get worse before they improved. Hence the COI sought to encourage what it called films of 'uplift'. In this sense documentary was to return to the morale-raising role it had played during the war. *Chasing the Blues* (DATA, 1947), for example, employs upbeat jazz music in its promotion of ideas for improving the welfare of workers in order to increase production. It was sponsored by the Cotton Board and combined documentary with part-animated sequences directed by Jack Ellitt, who had collaborated with Len Lye at the GPO Film Unit in the 1930s. *What a Life!* (Public Relationship Films, 1948) was conceived as 'an attempt to cheer people up by poking fun at the prophets of doom'.[77] This short comedy features two men (played by Richard Massingham and Russell Waters) who have become so miserable with their dull daily routine ('Everybody's gloomy these days – why should I be out of fashion?') that they decide to end their lives. But their suicide attempt ends in a moment of high comedy: their attempt to sink their rowing boat (carrying a Union flag) fails because the water is too shallow, whereupon the two men collapse into uncontrolled laughter.

Humphrey Jennings's *The Dim Little Island* (Wessex Films, 1949) also set out to raise the spirits of the public – though did so in a characteristically complex manner. This film was part of a COI-mandated initiative 'to divert the mind of the audience from the austerities of the economic situation towards the fund of opportunity for enjoyment that lies open to anyone in Britain today'.[78] Originally entitled *The Eye of the Beholder*, *The Dim Little Island* is described in its titles as 'a short Film compiled on some thoughts of our Past, Present and Future by Four Men': these are composer Ralph Vaughan Williams, naturalist James Fisher, industrialist John Ormston and cartoonist Osbert Lancaster. They respond to 'the illusion that Great Britain is quite a dim little island...that the country is going to the dogs' by eulogizing the natural environment (Fisher), highlighting the great improvements in health and living conditions since the nineteenth century (Ormston) and celebrating the heritage of folk songs 'which had a special appeal to me as an Englishman' (Vaughan Williams). It has been argued that the film undermines its own message with its concluding shot of Ford Madox Brown's painting *The Last of England*, which shows nineteenth-century Britons forced into economic exile.[79] Yet the elegiac tone and open ending ('What will befall Britain?' asks Lancaster) is entirely consistent with Jennings's later films, especially *A Diary for Timothy*.

Documentary and the Festival of Britain

If the late 1940s was a period characterized by continued austerity and an underlying mood of gloom and despondency about Britain's future, the early 1950s in contrast was a period of renewed optimism and hope. Two events – the Festival of Britain in 1951 and the coronation of Queen Elizabeth II in 1953 – came to symbolize the mood of confidence and renewal. It was the first of those events that had the greatest impact on the documentary movement. The Festival of Britain had been conceived by the Labour government as 'a showpiece for the inventiveness and genius of British scientists and technologists'.[80] As designed by architect Hugh Casson it presented a future of modernist art and architecture exemplified by the Dome of Discovery and the futuristic Skylon. It was also intended to act as a tonic to a tired nation: to help raise spirits by providing people with an opportunity for patriotic celebration. It is no wonder that the somewhat contradictory discourses of the Festival of Britain – to look to the future while also celebrating the past – caught the imagination of Humphrey Jennings.

Family Portrait (Wessex Films, 1950) – 'a film on the theme of the Festival of Britain' – is not generally one of Jennings's most admired films but it is perhaps his most personal. In particular it has been seen as a filmic expression of his (uncompleted and unpublished) work *Pandaemonium*, an immense history of the Industrial Revolution compiled from a myriad of official reports, diaries, letters, novels and poems exploring the impact of technology and industrialization on British life and society.[81] It exemplifies Jennings's characteristically highly formalist style in that it mobilizes symbols of Britain's cultural heritage (Shakespeare, Elgar) and scientific legacy (Newton, Darwin, Watt) alongside modern technological developments in line with the themes of the Festival of Britain. Hence Jennings's familiar association between past and present is seen again in the parallel between Drake's 'magic mirror' in the defeat of the Spanish Armada and the deployment of radar during the Battle of Britain. The underlying theme of the film is the construction of the nation as a family: hence the Festival of Britain is 'a kind of family reunion' that unites people from diverse backgrounds. There are echoes of previous Jennings films in the images of working-class leisure activities (*Spare Time*) and the celebration of popular culture (*Listen to Britain*), but unlike the wartime films *Family Portrait* acknowledges social and economic inequalities ('rifts in the family we're having to repair') and accepts the fact of Britain's declining power in the world by advocating its integration into 'the family of Europe'.

It was only due to Jennings's tragically early death that *Family Portrait* was his last completed film, but in many respects it can be seen as a summation of his life's work in film. The reviews – and *Family Portrait* had probably the most favourable critical reception of any of Jennings's films since *Fires Were Started* – certainly constructed it in that way. His former colleague Stuart Legg wrote: '*Family Portrait* is, I think, the most advanced point he reached in putting prose and poetry together in a new way. He could not at this time have left a richer gift to the England he loved so dearly.'[82] The *Monthly Film Bulletin*'s verdict was that it was 'continuously fascinating, sharp and evocative; the last film of a director without doubt among the most talented that Britain has ever produced'.[83] It is rather a bitter irony that only with his death did Jennings receive the critical recognition he had so long deserved. While the Griersonian purists had often regarded him as a dilettante, a new generation of post-war critics admired him as a truly individual talent. Gavin Lambert, editor of *Sight and Sound*, felt that Jennings's death 'deprives the British cinema of one of its most adventurous spirits, [and] British documentary of its most gifted artist'.[84]

It is a curious fact, however, that while the critical reputation of Jennings's wartime films has grown in retrospect, the reputation of his post-war films has diminished. Lindsay Anderson, for example, felt that both *The Dim Little Island* and *Family Portrait* 'can be dismissed. In fact they must be. They demonstrate only too sadly how the traditionalist spirit was unable to adjust itself to the changed circumstances of Britain after the war'.[85] It is a harsh and unfair verdict. Jennings's final films demonstrate the maturity of a style that had been developing continuously since *Spare Time* and exemplify an artist at the height of his creative powers. The ambiguity that some critics detect in these films is not an indication of creative decline but rather a consequence of the fact that Jennings no longer had to meet the ideological demands of wartime propaganda with its unambiguous assertion of national unity. In fact the more questioning tone of *The Dim Little Island* and *Family Portrait* can in hindsight be seen to have begun with *A Diary for Timothy*. Keith Beattie counters Anderson's view by arguing that *Family Portrait* is as closely attuned to ideologies of Britishness as the wartime films and 'analyses what the film proposes as essential, continuous components of national identity in relation to suggestions concerning Britain's future'.[86]

Family Portrait was not the only official film of the Festival of Britain. John Boulting directed the feature film *The Magic Box* (1951), a biopic of the British film pioneer William Freese-Greene, produced as a non-profit-making enterprise by a collective of major industry figures, while the Telekinema on the South Bank screened a range of short films especially commissioned for the festival. These included several films by the animators John Halas and Joy Batchelor as well as films by the Shell Film Unit (*Air Parade*), Petroleum Films Bureau (*Forward A Century*) and the Port of London Authority (*Waters of Time*).[87] The most notable of the documentaries commissioned for the festival, other than *Family Portrait*, was Paul Dickson's *David* (World Wide Pictures, 1951). *David* was commissioned through the COI to 'show Wales to the world' and in that context it provides an alternative view of (national) identity in that it focuses on a nation-within-the-nation rather than projecting an overarching view of nationhood as in *Family Portrait*.[88] The film chronicles the life story of Dafydd Rhys, a thinly disguised characterization of Welsh poet D. R. Griffiths, brother of Jim Griffiths, the long-standing Labour MP for Llanelli, played by himself. Dickson's style is less austere and more romanticized than the story documentaries of the Crown Film Unit: *David* is very much the story of a personalized individual rather than an archetype representing a particular social class.

Dickson also employs a more subjective style of narration, including flashback scenes, telling David's story both from his own perspective and through the eyes of a young boy Ifor Morgan (John Davies) at the school where David works as caretaker. *David* was released in cinemas as a supporting item to Michael Powell and Emeric Pressburger's *The Tales of Hoffman*: admired for its effective integration of a political narrative with a personal story, it is a highly evocative and emotionally moving film that demonstrates the persistence of social documentary after the Second World War, but in a style removed from the Griersonian otthodoxy.

A Queen is Crowned (1953) and the heritage documentary

A Queen is Crowned (Rank Organization, 1953) hardly merits a mention in most histories of British cinema even though it was one of the most unique films ever released in the country. Produced and directed by Castleton Knight for the Rank Organization, *A Queen is Crowned* was a Technicolor record of Elizabeth II's coronation. It is the only non-fiction film ever to top the British box office (there are no reliable statistics for *Battle of the Somme*) and it was a surprise success in the United States where it was voted Best Foreign Film of 1953 by the National Board of Review of Motion Pictures.[89] *A Queen is Crowned* was in fact just one of several film records of the Coronation – others included another feature, *Elizabeth is Queen* (Associated British Pathé, 1953), and the short *Coronation Day* (British Movietone, 1953) – but it was by some measure the most popular. Leslie Halliwell, who at the time was manager of the independent Rex cinema in Cambridge, suggested that 'it quickly became clear to press and public alike that *A Queen is Crowned* was the one to see, mainly because it was longer'.[90] It was received by some critics in tones of the highest reverence, while even those who were less awestruck by the spectacle of its royal pageantry recognized its importance as a historical record and admired its technical achievements.[91]

On one level, of course, it might be claimed that *A Queen is Crowned* is not really a documentary at all in a strict sense but rather a feature-length newsreel. It can be placed in a tradition of film records of royal ceremonial extending back to Cecil Hepworth's film of the funeral procession of Queen Victoria (1901) and Charles Urban's Kinemacolor film of the Delhi Durbar of 1911. However, *A Queen is Crowned* was culturally more ambitious than a newsreel and owed something to the 'creative treatment' of the documentary school. It contextualizes the Coronation by locating the event itself within historical and cultural motifs of nationhood. Hence the Technicolor footage of the Coronation is book-ended with shots of the British countryside and heritage sites such as the royal castles of Windsor and Balmoral, while narrator Sir Laurence Olivier recites John O'Gaunt's valedictory speech from *Richard II* ('This royal throne of kings, this sceptred isle/ This earth of majesty, this seat of Mars... This blessed plot, this earth, this realm, this England'). Olivier's commentary provides a direct link with wartime documentary (*Words for Battle*), while the Shakespearean quotation also evokes British feature films of the Second World War.[92] *A Queen is Crowned* is nothing if not conservative in both cultural and aesthetic terms: but its popular success is testimony to the prevalence of a traditional view of nationhood as well as to the prestige of the British monarchy in the 1950s. Its significance is to be found not in its formal properties but rather in its ideological import as a commemoration, preserved in a kind of Technicolor aspic, of an event that the historian David Cannadine has described as 'a retrospectively unconvincing reaffirmation of Britain's continued great-power status'.[93]

A Queen is Crowned may also be seen as part of a lineage of British film-making that for want of a better term might be called the heritage documentary. This tradition – which represents an alternative to the Griersonian modernist aesthetic of films like *Coal Face* and *Industrial Britain* – can be traced back to the cultural propaganda films produced by the British Council during the Second World War. The British Council held a remit for the projection of British life and culture overseas and to this end it sponsored films for overseas distribution in allied and neutral countries. However, its films had attracted scorn for their conservative outlook and for not engaging with the impact of the war on British society. The MOI had castigated the British Council for making films such as *London River* (British Films, 1941), *Western Isles* (Merton Park, 1942) and *Song of the Clyde* (Merton Park, 1942) on the grounds that it was

> a fatal weakness to suggest that peacetime culture persists unchanged in a war, because this suggests that the people are not spiritually at war at all... A film on the Clyde which does not show a single warship, a single sailor or even a convoy, will come as a shock to every neutral.[94]

For its part the British Council – which in any event was severely hamstrung by an arrangement whereby it was responsible for 'cultural' propaganda while the MOI reserved unto itself 'war' propaganda – argued that 'the presentation in the Empire and foreign countries of a picture of the British way of life...is bound to form an essential part of any intelligently conceived policy of short-term wartime propaganda and it is the very essence of long-term peacetime propaganda'.[95]

The MOI's view had prevailed during the war when there was an urgent need to project the national war effort for consumption at home and abroad. But after the war it was the British Council's image of Britain that regained the ascendancy in official film-making. The incoming Conservative government instituted a review of the work of the COI with a view to reducing the cost of official publicity. The Drogheda Report of 1954 recommended that the main effort of official film-making activity should be directed into promoting Britain overseas.[96] This signalled a decisive shift away from official films examining economic and social problems for domestic consumption to films intended primarily for overseas audiences and focusing instead on the projection of Britain as a prosperous and welcoming nation. The role of films such as *An English Village* (Anvil Films, 1956) and *Oxford* (Greenpark, 1958) was firmly within the documentary tradition of 'the projection of Britain': but the Britain they project is an idealized land of buccolic pursuits and traditional institutions that presents an image of a stable society at ease with itself. The latter film, sponsored by the Foreign Office, was part of a campaign to encourage foreign students to study in Britain. The Foreign Office also saw film as a means of promoting immigration in order to address labour shortages in key British industries. The British Nationality Act of 1948 had extended British citizenship to Commonwealth subjects who chose to settle and work in Britain. Hence a film like *Moslems in Britain – Cardiff* (United Motion Pictures, 1961) is at pains to present a positive image of well-paid work and social integration: the commentary asserts that the Arabic-speaking population of Cardiff lead 'not the life of an immigrant but of a local citizen', while Yemeni immigrants aver that 'work is good and everything is good'. This might seem a rather naive view in light of the backlash against immigration that would follow later in the 1960s.

Like the wartime films of the British Council, post-war heritage documentaries have been the object of scorn for their safe and cosy representation of Britain. Karel Reisz held that documentarists had lost their old sense of social purpose:

> Where in the thirties they made valuable films about life as it was lived in this country...today they make at best the (admittedly valuable) scientific films or, at worst, spend their time 'projecting Britain'. This means films about the Lake District, Stirling Moss, old trams and the beauties of spring.[97]

(The film about 'old trams' that Reisz mentions is probably John Krish's *The Elephant Will Never Forget*: there was apparently some animosity between the two as Krish had publicly voiced his distate for Free Cinema – a movement in which Reisz was a major participant.)

An even more trenchant criticism of this style of film has been made by Brian Winston, who focuses on the Foreign Office-sponsored *Today in Britain* (World Wide Pictures, 1964) as an example of the ideological shortcomings of official documentary films in this period:

> *Today in Britain*, conservatively clinging to the traditional norms of 'professional' film-making, quite seriously belies the state of the nation in 1964. Exports were stalled, the balance of payments was dire, prices were rising... *Today in Britain* says none of this because it is, in fact, a government recruitment piece designed to attract Commonwealth students to the then expanding tertiary education sector... It certainly fits into the emerging official narrative of gracious imperial withdrawal and denies the all too often bloody end of Empire which actually took place. Just as illusory are the film's images of welcome for people of colour in the UK, giving the impression, utterly false in my view, of a multi-racial society at ease with itself.[98]

For Winston, the film's distance from social reality (or at least his own memory of it) fatally compromises its status as a documentary: hence he finds it wanting on both ideological and aesthetic grounds. Yet to condemn these films – or worse still to deny them their place in the history of documentary cinema – is to ignore the historical and ideological contexts in which they were produced. If the COI responded tardily to the end of empire, and downplayed the racial tensions that attended Commonwealth immigration, this was not just a shortcoming of its films but of British society as a whole as it sought to come to terms with its new post-imperial identity. In this sense the 'projection of Britain' in the films of the COI was no more partial and selective than its predecessors at the EMB or GPO.

The NCB Film Unit and British Transport Films

The closure of the Crown Film Unit in 1952 did not mark an end to the state sponsorship of documentary film. Quite the contrary in fact: two of the newly nationalized industries were to embark upon extensive programmes of documentary production. The National Coal Board (NCB), established in 1947, sponsored around 900 films between then and 1983, including some 400 issues of its monthly cinemagazine *Mining Review*, while British Transport Films, founded in 1949, sponsored around 700 films between then and 1986. For each industry this represents a numerically far greater output than the combined total of the EMB/GPO/Crown Film Unit, yet these films have been entirely overlooked in most accounts of British documentary film. The British Transport films, especially, have been ignored by documentary critics on account of their lack of social purpose. Nevertheless, the films of the nationalized industries can be seen as marking a continuation of the tradition of public service documentary that had begun with the GPO Film Unit in the 1930s. This is evident not only in some of the personnel involved – Edgar Anstey at British Transport Films was a veteran of the documentary movement of the 1930s – but also in the style of the films, which continued the tradition of documentary as a vehicle of both social education and national projection.

The National Coal Board's initial interest in documentary was for recruitment to the industry but this soon developed into a much broader ambition to explain the role of the coal industry in national life and its importance to the British economy. The main vehicle for this was *Mining Review*. The origins of this monthly cinemagazine, which would run until 1983, were complicated. A Board of Trade memorandum of December 1947 refers to 'an industrial news magazine of achievements in production, technology, and other fields [that is] now in preparation and efforts are being made to persuade the exhibitors to give it a general showing once a month in addition to the free ten-minute film'.[99] At the end of the year the CEA was asked to accept 'a new monthly industrial news review … The project, which is being handled by the Crown Film Unit, has the strong personal blessing of the Chancellor of the Exchequer'.[100] This would seem to refer to *Mining Review*, which other sources confirm was backed by Sir Stafford Cripps, who had recently succeeded Hugh Dalton as Chancellor of the Exchequer.[101] *Mining Review* would replace the recently discontinued *Britain Can Make It*: exhibitors accepted it because it was free and counted towards their quota. Each ten-minute issue would usually feature three stories – carefully chosen to represent all the coal-producing regions – though occasionally a whole issue was given over to one item.

The production of *Mining Review* was initially entrusted to the Crown Film Unit but after six issues the contract was given to DATA, which continued to produce the series until 1961. The reason for the switch from Crown to DATA is unclear but it may well have been economic: DATA was contracted to produce *Mining Review* for £1,600 per issue (rising to £1,850 in the 1950s), which was only slightly over half the cost of a one-reel film by Crown in the late 1940s.[102] DATA (Documentary and Technicians Alliance) was a film-makers' co-operative set up in 1945 by a group of former Paul Rotha employees headed by Donald Alexander. Its early films included commissions for the Board of Trade (*Cotton Come Back*, 1946) and the Economic Information Unit (*All Eyes on Britain*, 1947) about the regeneration of post-war industries. It was on the strength of these films that DATA won the contract for *Mining Review* in 1948. The connection between DATA and the NCB was strengthened in 1951 when Alexander left the co-operative to take up post as the NCB's Films Officer. By the 1950s *Mining Review* was DATA's primary source of income and the annual renewal of its contract had become a point of some anxiety for general manager Terrick FitzHugh: 'The magazine is no longer just a contract to us. After four years of monthly issues, it has become, for our directors and cameramen, quite a way of life.'[103]

The NCB's objective in sponsoring *Mining Review* was explained by its Director of Public Relations Noel Gee:

> We produce *Mining Review*, as we do *Coal* magazine, to show the industry to the miners and their families, to give them a sense of belonging to a progressive undertaking, to make them realise that they are no longer a forgotten part of the British community and to suggest that, in return for being treated as normal citizens they owe the community a responsibility to act as good citizens. And to do this we try to picture modernisation schemes, mechanisation, research, improved welfare and health amenities, increased safety and so on. To lighten the propaganda, as I have said, we introduce sport, musical and similar light items.[104]

The subjects covered by *Mining Review* ranged from improvements in safety ('Safety First', Year 2, No. 11) and the opening of a new health centre in South Wales ('Miners' Health Centre', Year 2, No. 3) to recreational holidays ('Holiday Camp', Year 2, No. 12) and the visit of singer and actor Paul Robeson for a special performance for miners and their families at the Usher Hall in Edinburgh in 1949 ('A Star Drops In', Year 2, No.11) – the last item now chiefly notable for the (albeit no doubt unintended) racism of its commentary: 'When you see a film star and a miner together, the dusky one's the miner – well, usually!'

Mining Review was nothing if not propaganda for the nationalized mining industry. It sought to promote the benefits of nationalization for the industry – focusing especially on the welfare of miners and the increased levels of productivity – and to place coal at the centre of post-war industrial regeneration. 'Replanning a Coalfield' (Year 2, No.10), for example, contrasts the pre-war slump and pit closures with the creation of 11,000 new jobs arising from the rationalization of the coalfields of Fife. Lord Balfour, the chairman of the NCB's Scottish Division, asserts the value of miners to the national economy: 'Coal may be scarce – but from a national point of view, miners are scarcer.' While the NCB always maintained that *Mining Review* was produced primarily for the miners themselves, it seems apparent that the series was also a means through which the NCB sought to present itself to the public. As Noel Gee remarked in 1958: 'Especially at periods like the present when the National and Provincial press is tending to run down the Board and the mining industry for political reasons, I consider that this is of real importance.'[105] Even in the 1960s – when the industry was faced with economies as the demand for coal declined – *Mining Review* was still seeking to justify the policy of nationalization. Thus 'A Story from South Wales' (Year 16, No. 6) sought to present the closure of Aberaman colliery in a positive light by focusing on the relocation of labour to neighbouring pits. The voice of an 'old' miner attests: 'It's only since the days of nationalization that I've known of measures of this sort being taken.'

There is much evidence to indicate that *Mining Review* was a considerable success. In 1951 it was estimated to be seen by one million cinemagoers per month: Alexander noted 'the greatly increased showing of *Mining Review* at leading cinemas in the West End of London'.[106] While its distribution was no doubt helped by the fact of it being given away free to cinemas, *Mining Review* was nevertheless in competition with other cinemagazines and newsreels for screen time. By 1957 the NCB was claiming a circulation of around 350 cinemas per issue ('mostly in the mining and industrial areas') and noted that these included some large cinemas such as the New Palace in Carlisle (with a capacity of 1,000 seats) and the Haymarket in Newcastle (over 2,000 seats).[107] Like other industrial sponsors the NCB also ran its own non-theatrical distribution scheme. In 1951 it was estimated that there were 400 non-theatrical shows of *Mining Review* a year, reaching an audience of around 20,000 but that the bulk of these 'would appear to be external shows, i.e. to schools and so on, rather than to miners'.[108]

While *Mining Review* was at the heart of the NCB's film programme, it was far from the only aspect. From the outset the NCB had also sponsored stand-alone films, beginning with *King Coal* (1948) by the animator Jules Pinschewer. As NCB-sponsored film production increased in the early 1950s there was discussion about setting up an in-house film unit. Donald Alexander weighed up the pros and cons:

> I am personally always disturbed at the general plushness (if I may use the word) which always seems to supervene, abetted by the ease with which expenditure is concealed in overheads and establishments, directly a sponsoring body sets up its own unit. Shell is a notable exception, and Crown the most disastrous example. Nevertheless, properly handled, production by direct labour *should* be at best far more economical, and in many ways easier for all concerned, than production through contractors.[109]

The initial outcome was a halfway house whereby the NCB continued to use external contractors for films intended for public exhibition but set up its own unit for internal films. In 1953 the NCB Technical Film Unit was established for the production of films 'for use in training not only new entrants to the Industry, but miners and technicians of all grades'.[110] In 1961 all production, including *Mining Review*, was brought in-house under the auspices of an expanded and renamed NCB Film Unit.[111] DATA was wound up shortly afterwards but many of its staff found new employment – with the NCB Film Unit.[112]

The films of the NCB demonstrate a range of formal strategies. An early film such as Paul Fletcher's *Nines Was Standing* (Greenpark, 1950) adopts the familiar technique of story documentary in order to dramatize the role of newly created consultative committees of management and workers in finding a solution to a closed coalface. ('Nines' is a coalface – reflecting the custom in the mining industry of referring to particular seams by a number in the plural – while 'standing' means that it was not being mined.) In contrast, Stuart Legg's *Plan for Coal* (DATA, 1952) employs graphs and diagrams to demonstrate rising demand for coal and increasing production. *Plan for Coal* is highly didactic in its insistence on the importance of the industry to the British economy: coal is nothing less than 'the bedrock of British wealth and welfare'. The *Mining Review* item 'Hungarians in Britain' (Year 10, No. 8) adopts the style of television news reporting as presenter John Slater interviews with a hand-held microphone a group of miners who have fled the Hungarian Uprising and have found work in Britain. And Alun

Falconer's *New Power in Their Hands* (NCB Film Unit, 1957) employs direct address to camera in imagining the spectator as a visitor to a mine. For all its insistence on the value of mechanization the film concludes with a eulogy to the camaraderie of the miners themselves:

These men look the same as they have always looked, they talk as they have always talked, they have the same imperishable loyalty to each other – and against you if necessary – but before your eyes they are changing, taking the new power in their hands, and becoming the miners of the twentieth century.

It is in the films produced for the NCB that the legacy of the social documentary of the 1930s is most evident. The images of heroic working-class archetypes in films like *Coal Face* are echoed in the persistence of 'nobility' close-ups in NCB films such as *New Power in Their Hands* and Richard Mason's *Portrait of a Miner* (NCB Film Unit, 1966). The latter film is also reminiscent of the style of Free Cinema and the British new wave in its 'poetic' representation of a supposedly ordinary miner. The film focuses on a day in the working life of Pat Leigh, who is standing for election as a union representative at Thoresby colliery. It combines scenes of Pat at work with testimonies from family, friends and colleagues: these include the contrasting views of his wife ('Pat's a good husband and father – I love him') and a fellow trade unionist ('Pat Leigh's an opportunist – I dislike him as much as any man I've ever met'). A recurring theme of *Mining Review* is the presentation of miners at play, as in 'The Art of Mining' (Year 13, No. 4) – celebrating the Ashington painters – and 'Whitehaven Whippets' (Year 15, No. 7). *A Time to Heel* (Derrick Knight & Partners, 1963) demonstrates the work of the NCB's rehabilitation service in caring for injured miners and getting them back to work. It again emphasizes the benefits of nationalization ('When I started work there was no such thing as an ambulance car – if you had an injury they'd take you home on a horse', recalls an older miner) and suggests that improvements in miners' health and welfare should be attributed to the National Health Service. The overriding impression of the NCB films is the presentation of miners as a special breed of men set apart from others by virtue of the dangerous nature of their work and their importance to the national economy.

Yet the NCB films also document the history of an industry that was undergoing very profound change. By the late 1950s the days of a national coal shortage were finished: indeed supply now outstripped demand as the ascendancy of coal was challenged by other fuels such as oil and gas. NCB films therefore had to switch from promoting the importance of the industry to the national economy to urging the need for economies of production. This also implied a shift from a general audience to one consisting primarily of miners themselves. Peter Pickering's *Nobody's Face* (NCB Film Unit, 1966) was a case in point. This film was introduced by NCB chairman Lord Robens who advocated the need for greater efficiency – no longer presented as a means of increasing coal production but rather to reduce costs in order that the price of coal could be kept competitive. The film documents a 'typical' shift in which time is lost through myriad delays caused by inefficient planning, faulty equipment and human error. It is particularly notable for the liberal smattering of expletives ('Get tha bloody stuff moving and don't bloody argue!') and for its somewhat less than deferential tone towards management ('No wonder Lord Robens is closing the bloody pits!'). It concludes that routine delays and hiccups can lose some two-and-a-half hours from a six-hour shift and suggests that 'planner, management and miner have all contributed' to the problem.

The visual style of the NCB films is spare to the point of austerity: they picture an often stark landscape of pit heads and winding machinery while their protagonists are usually coated in coal dust and dirt. To a very great extent this style is technologically determined: the difficulties of shooting underground in cramped conditions and poor light mandates the austere 'look' of the films. The NCB Film Unit continued using the silent Newman Sinclair camera with its clockwork mechanism long after it had become obsolete, as safety regulations prohibited electric cameras and sound equipment to be taken underground. Several directors, including Peter Pickering and Alun Falconer, enjoyed long careers with the NCB. Hence they developed an understanding of miners and their communities that was invaluable for their work. As Donald Alexander recognized: 'Film-makers with experience of coal-mining, while not as rare as abominable snowmen, are less common than blackberries.'[113]

The other major state industry sponsor of documentary film, British Transport Films (BTF), was set up as an in-house production unit by the British Transport Commission in 1949. The official records pertaining to BTF are much less extensive than for either the GPO or NCB film units, but according to Donald Alexander: 'The British Transport Commission has capitalised its own unit at what must be considerable cost (the premises which belonged to "This Modern Age", and which included a recording studio, have been taken over and considerably enlarged), and must now be spending annually as much as Shell or Anglo-Iranian.'[114]

Edgar Anstey, who was appointed as British Transport Films Officer, said that he took the Shell Film Unit as his example:

There's absolutely no doubt that the view of the Shell oil group which is held in the world is conditioned in some measure by the distinction and objectivity, and humanity, too, of the films that the Shell Film Unit had made over these years. And we hope that the view of British Rail here and the other nationalized transport industries, is being conditioned internally and externally to some extent by the work that's being done by film.[115]

In fact BTF combined aspects of the tradition of industrial film-making (it absorbed the small film unit set up before the war by Southern Railways, for example) with talent recruited from the old documentary movement (including former GPO directors J. B. Holmes, Ralph Keane, John Taylor and Alexander Shaw). Its roster of permanent staff was quite small so BTF balanced in-house production with commissions from freelance directors. Among those who established their reputations with films for BTF were directors John Krish, Joe Mendoza and John Schlesinger, and cinematographer David Watkin.[116]

BTF's remit included all publicly-owned transport, including buses, canals and road haulage, though the vast majority of its output would focus on the railways. The unit became renowned for the production of rail travelogues characterized by what has been described as 'a recognisable BTF house style of documentary classicism'.[117] For documentary purists the BTF films are regarded as a departure from documentary's true purpose of socially engaged film-making and are dismissed as little more than glorified commercials for British Railways. Yet these were some of documentary's most prestigious films and were regularly nominated for – and won – international awards and festival prizes. These included the Golden Lion for Best Documentary at the Venice Film Festival for John Schlesinger's *Terminus* (1961) and an Academy Award for Best Short Subject for Peter Scott's *Wild Wings* (1965), in addition to several British Film Academy awards. BTF was also successful in getting its films in front of audiences: in the early 1960s it claimed a total cinema audience of six million and estimated that each title had an average non-theatrical audience of three million.[118] BTF films were also shown on television, which had strict regulations regarding paid advertising but could justify these documentaries on account of their public-information content.

In the content, form and ideology of its films BTF may be seen as the inheritor of the legacy of the GPO Film Unit of the 1930s. Its films explaining the running of the rail network (*Train Time*, 1952), the daily operation of a major network station hub (*This is York*, 1953), the maintenance of the railways (*Making Tracks*, 1956) and the task of cleaning locomotives (*Wash and Brush Up*, 1953) recall how GPO films had demonstrated the varied work of the Post Office. The critically acclaimed *Elizabethan Express* (1954) – a three-reeler chronicling the non-stop journey of the special summer express from London to Edinburgh – was a *Night Mail* for the 1950s replete with rhyming commentary and elegantly composed shots of the train in motion. Moreover, the ideological strategy of the films – to promote the nationalized railways as a public service at the heart of national life – has clear echoes of the GPO films. The glorious colour travelogues of the 1950s – including *West Country Journey* (1953), *The Heart of England* (1954), *Any Man's Kingdom* (1956), *The England of Elizabeth* (1957) and *A Letter for Wales* (1960) – demonstrate how the railways link all parts of mainland Britain. They can be seen as part of the same heritage documentary project as the films of the COI, in that the nation they present is mostly buccolic and rural: a land of meadows, hills, valleys and country lanes. It is also apparently a nation of perpetual sunshine: the BTF films were usually shot during the summer months when the landscape and natural scenery could be filmed to best effect. The advertising slogan for BTF was 'See Britain by Train': the travelogues focus exclusively on leisure travel at a time before the motor car had become commonplace and when the railways offered access to a wonderful world of holidays and sunshine.

To watch the BTF films today is to evoke a sense of nostalgia for a bygone era of rail travel: they picture an age of luxurious Pullman carriages, full-service dining cars with elegantly attired stewards and top-hatted station masters. Yet at the time BTF was setting out to present a picture of a national rail network embracing modernization. The films span the period that saw the phasing out of steam locomotives and the introduction of diesel-electric trains. In fact there is little nostalgia in a film such as *Service for Southend* (1957), which follows the last steam train from Liverpool Street to Southend and presents the electrification of the line as 'part of a vast scheme for modernizing British Railways'. The acclaimed *Blue Pullman* (1960) illustrates the introduction of a new diesel-electric luxury train for business travellers, featuring such mod-cons as air conditioning and noise insulation: this is expressed impressionistically as natural sound is phased out by music and sound effects. Even a minor film such as *Diesel Trainride* (1959), which captures the sheer joy of two children taken on a train journey by their parents, notably features a new diesel multiple-unit train that allows a view from the front of the train in a manner that recalls the old 'phantom rides'.

Not all BTF films necessarily conformed to the unit's house style, though, that said, it is significant that more 'personal' directors such as John Krish and John Schlesinger made fewer films for BTF than journeymen such as Michael Clarke and James Ritchie. Krish's *The Elephant Will Never Forget* (1953) – an elegiac and evocative account of the last days of the tram service in New Cross, south London (the title refers to the Elephant & Castle Inn) – is much celebrated but entirely atypical of BTF's output. Krish had been sent simply to record the ceremony of the chairman of London Transport shaking hands with the driver of the last tram but instead he 'borrowed' stock, and shot eight reels of film over five days, including a sequence of an elderly couple enjoying their last tram ride. The film's nostalgia for the trams ('It was one day not long ago London had to say goodbye to her last tram. Sometime, some day, it had to come') evidently did not accord with the progressive foward-looking ethos of BTF: the story goes that Anstey fired Krish immediately after seeing the film.[119] Schlesinger's *Terminus* (1961) – an account of a day in the life of Waterloo Station – is closer in style to Free Cinema than it is to the work of BTF. The film eschews commentary altogether and instead uses a blues/jazz score (composed by Ron Grainer with songs by Julian Cooper) as it narrates the incidents and events of the day. Schlesinger took advantage of technological developments to employ a hand-held camera and portable sound-recording equipment to capture snatches of dialogue and overheard conversations. The style of *Terminus* is reminsiscent of Jennings's *Listen to Britain* in that it creates drama from the everyday: a passenger who has missed her train; a bag lady rummaging among the rubbish bins; a group of West Indians performing the calypso 'Jamaica Man'; a lost boy reunited with his mother (though this scene would appear to have been staged for the camera judging by the use of close up). *Terminus* was critically acclaimed and would provide Schlesinger with a ticket into the feature film industry, where he joined Free Cinema directors Tony Richardson, Karel Reisz and Lindsay Anderson as a key figure in the British new wave.

The restructuring and rationalization of the railways in the 1960s under the aegis of Dr Richard Beeching – a former ICI executive who became chairman of the British Railways Board in 1961 and presided over the closure of uneconomical branch lines and small stations – would bring about a reorientation in the films of BTF. To watch a film such as *John Betjeman Goes by Train* (1962) today is to be reminded that the rural halts he visits such as Wolferton and Snettisham would not survive the 'Beeching axe'. In a sense the most important of BTF's films of the 1960s was also one of its dullest: *Reshaping British Railways* (1963). This was directed by Anstey himself and takes the form of an extended illustrated lecture by Beeching, arguing the economic case for discontinuing underused passenger services and focusing on freight ('British railways are the busiest in the world and yet they lose enough money to put something like ninepence on the income tax'). The structural changes to the railway network would result in BTF becoming 'more functional in its aim – films aim at creating interest and getting traffic, and are more directly aimed at appropriate sections of business than they used to be'.[120] The film unit was obliged to reduce budgets and to focus more on information and training films: the glossy prestige documentaries became fewer in the 1960s. Its last film shot on 35 millimetre for cinema release was the impressionistic *Overture: One-Two-Five* (1978), produced to mark the introduction of the new InterCity 125 service between London and Bristol. The decline of the theatrical market for shorts in the 1970s affected BTF as much as other documentary producers, though it was able to diversify into the production of television commercials. Anstey's retirement in 1974 did not spell the end of the line for BTF – the unit continued in existence until 1986 – but its golden age, like the railways themselves, had long since passed.

Documentary and industrial sponsorship

The expansion of the documentary sector after the Second World War was due in very large measure to the growth of industrial sponsorship. It was not only the nationalized industries that saw the potential of documentary film for public relations and training: there was also a significant increase in sponsorship of documentary by the private sector. Existing corporate sponsors such as Shell (that had set up its own film unit in 1934) and ICI (which had started commissioning films during the war) were joined by newcomers to the field including the Ford Motor Company (that sponsored several of the Free Cinema films of the 1950s) and Unilever (a dual-listed company that backed films in Britain and the Netherlands). To some extent the growth of industrial sponsorship can be seen as an extension of the pre-war interest in visual publicity by bodies such as the London Passenger Transport Board, while the post-war generation of film officers – including Gordon Begg at ICI, Laurence Mitchell at Unilever and Norman Vigars at Ford – were the successors to enlightened public relations men such as Jack Beddington and Frank Pick. There was considerable crossover and fluidity between the public and private sectors: Ronald Tritton, for example, left the COI in the late 1940s to become films officer first for Anglo-Iranian Oil and, later, for British Petroleum.

There were several reasons for the growth of industrial sponsorship of documentary. A report for the British Productivity Council – a semi-public body set up by the Conservative government in 1952, which commissioned over 100 films before its closure in 1975 – declared that:

> film is by far the most versatile of all visual methods. It can provide, among other things, a record of an operation, an inspection of a pro-cess, a demonstration of a product, an explanation of a balance sheet or of a technique, an encouragement to progress or an epic of an enterprise.[121]

As this suggests, the range of sponsored documentary was broad, extend-ing from training and instructional films produced solely for internal consumption to others intended for public exhibition. At the top end of the scale were prestige films for cinema release such as the Shell Film Unit's *The Rival World* (1955) and *Shellarama* (1965), though the major-ity of films were booked through non-theatrical distributors. Evidence of the continued demand for 16 millimetre prints for educational use is seen in the establishment of film libraries by organizations such as the Gas Council and the Petroleum Films Bureau. It was estimated that films booked through these and other libraries reached an audience of 17 million per year.[122] Most corporate sponsors observed Arthur Elton's 'First Law of Industrial Sponsorship' that 'the impact of a sponsored film upon its audience will be in inverse ratio to the number of times the sponsor insists on having his name mentioned'.[123] The aim was to raise the profile of an industry rather than to make money from exhibition. According to one commentator: 'No sponsor would ever, twice, expect his films to pay.'[124]

There were two models of industrial documentary sponsorship. While Shell and ICI, for example, set up their own film units, other companies commissioned films from outside contractors. Hard evidence regard-ing the costs of industrial film operations is scarce. In 1952 Donald Alexander estimated that the production costs of the Shell Film Unit (excluding overheads) were around £50,000 per year and that the Anglo-Iranian Oil Company, which contracted out its films, 'must by now be spending nearly as much money'.[125] Many of the small documentary producers established after the war specialized in industrial film-making. These companies were used to working on tiny budgets and could be jealous of the resources allocated to the larger units. The managing director of the Big Six Film Unit, for example, claimed in 1951 that his company had produced 68 industrial documentary films since the end of the war at an average cost of 17s. 7d. per foot in contrast to the £2 18s. 7d. per foot of COI-commissioned films and the £3 3s. 4d. per foot of the Crown Film Unit. Edward Cook felt that there 'has been a considerable waste of money' in official film-making: but the fact that his own unit's films were made so cheaply may perhaps explain why none of them are remembered today.[126] Films intended for theatrical release were afforded higher production values: by the early 1960s a cost of at least £30,000 per reel had become the benchmark for 'an ambitious piece of industrial communication'.[127]

The growth of sponsored documentary needs to be understood in relation to the state of the post-war industrial landscape in Britain. On the one hand the nationalization of certain industries brought massive investment and increased productivity: the coal-mining industry in the 1950s was perhaps the best example. On the other hand some industries were caught in a political tussle that created instability. The steel industry was a case in point: nationalized by Labour in 1951, denationalized two years later by the Conservatives and nationalized for a second time by Labour in 1967. This background informs films such as Jack Howells's *The Sea Shall Test Her* (British Films, 1954) sponsored by the British Iron and Steel Federation and Paul Dickson's *Stone Into Steel* (Wallace Productions, 1960) for the United Steel Companies. These films present an image of successful and productive industries flourishing under private ownership: their ideological import seems to be to assert that there is no need for nationalization. At the same time, the Tory government of the 1950s was haunted by the spectre of industrial unrest. It promoted a consensual approach to industrial relations through mechanisms such as works councils and consultative committees. The British Productivity Council sponsored films such as Peter Bradford's *People, Productivity & Change* (World Wide Pictures, 1963), which used *vox populi* to air grievances and suggest solutions that 'value the opinions of both management and unions'. The Ministry of Labour sponsored Paul Dickson's *The Film That Never Was* (World Wide Pictures, 1957), which uses the format of a film-within-a-film as a director called Gregson (played by actor Gordon Jackson) is hired to make a film on the subject of 'consultation in industry', only for his ideas to be rejected as 'too melodramatic' by the film's sponsors. Hence the film-within-the-film remains unmade ('We can't make a film – how can we get agreement?').

The ideological objectives of sponsored documentary are often quite transparent from the films themselves. A recurring theme is to present industry as a progressive undertaking and to emphasize its role in creating jobs and wealth. Peter Pickering's *The Island* (Data Film Productions, 1952) for the Anglo-Iranian Oil Company, for example, focuses on the benefits of building a new oil refinery in Kent ('It's great to see a new life for the whole island', one character remarks) as a means of responding to the opposition of some local residents ('We don't really like change'). The oil industry was particularly concerned with its public image, especially following the rise of the environmental movement in the 1960s. Derek Williams's *The Shadow of Progress* (Greenpark 1970) for British Petroleum was made 'as a contribution to European Conservation Year'. It exemplifies perfectly the tension in much sponsored film between the sponsor's ideological objectives on the one hand and wider social issues on the other. The film presents pollution as an inevitable consequence of urbanization and the public's demand for consumables rather than something for which industry alone is to blame. The commentary implies a collective responsibility for the proliferation of junk and waste, which it describes as 'a comment on the generation which put man on the Moon without cleaning up its own back yard'. And the film presents the oil industry as leading attempts to develop solutions to pollution while reminding audiences of the cost ('We can have a cleaner world if we are willing to pay for it'). In this sense, the film can be seen as an heir to films of the 1930s such as *The Smoke Menace*, which had also identified an urgent matter of public concern before explaining how the sponsor was leading the way in addressing it.

The relationship between industry and documentary producers involved negotiating a delicate balance. On the one hand many documentarists were dependent on sponsorship from industry and were therefore obliged to make the films that their paymasters wanted. On the other hand sponsors needed the expertise of the documentarists to put their case across. This could sometimes create uncomfortable compromises. Robert Angell cited the case of Imperial Tobacco, who 'wanted a film to show to "opinion formers" to put across two things: first their side of the smoking and health story and secondly, the fact that they were a well-run happy company and not in need of nationalization'. Angell took a pragmatic approach to the ethical questions raised by working for the tobacco industry:

I have normally viewed the role of the sponsored film producer as being similar to an advocate – not necessarily agreeing with the client's point of view but as a paid professional, doing the best job possible. Politics seems to me to be fair game for parties of most persuasions but health and smoking with people's lives at stake was another matter... [Imperial Tobacco] recognised the problem, did as much possible to research the reasons for what they described as 'connections between smoking and ill-health' and were prepared to change the 'product', i.e. cigarettes, drastically if necessary. Their main argument was that if they accepted without question that cigarette smoking of any sort and in any circumstances is lethal and closed down all their operations, the loss of jobs, revenue from taxes and even, they maintained, some consumer benefits would be enormous. All in all, quite a tricky film which we tried to present in a balanced, investigative way as a television style documentary directed by an ex-BBC man, Richard Collins, and presented by Raymond Baxter.[128]

Angell conceded, however, that in light of later evidence that emerged about the connection between smoking and lung cancer 'I don't think I would accept the job.'

The sponsored documentary has been almost invisible in standard histories of British documentary. This is no reflection of the quality of the best films – Shell, especially, always had a high critical reputation – but rather because, rather like the output of BTF, they have been deemed to lack the social purpose of true documentary. Brian Winston, for instance, is critical of the 'debilitating effects of sponsorship', which he sees as robbing the sponsored documentary of any real social import.[129] He cites *Stone Into Steel* as 'as good an example of the flight from social meaning as any film made in the tradition'.[130] For Winston, the film's emphasis on industrial processes and products (including the liner *Oriana* and the Jodrell Bank radio telescope) takes depersonalization to its extreme: it is an account of industry from which actual workers are more or less invisible. Against this can be set the alternate view of journalist John Chittock, editor of *Screen Digest* who also wrote a column on 'industrial film' for the *Financial Times* and who cited Shell as a company who 'were very clever in their marketing strategy, but I admire them all the more for that. I think that it demonstrates that there are ways of marrying commercial purposes to genuine social good'.[131]

For all their ideological limitations, the sponsored documentaries of the 1950s and 1960s should not be dismissed just because they do not conform to one particular idea of what documentary is or should be. It seems rather peculiar that admirers of the documentary movement of the 1930s often cite its adoption of commercial sponsorship as a progressive alternative to state support but then use commercial sponsorship as a stick with which to beat post-war documentary. This might be down to the perception that the documentarists of the 1930s had been able to set the ideological agenda, whereas after the war control over form and content shifted away from the film-maker in favour of the sponsor. However, without commercial sponsorship, documentary production would not have been nearly so voluminous as it was in the quarter of a century after 1945 and many documentary film-makers would not have enjoyed such long and successful careers.

Post-war social documentary

Perhaps the main reason why the critical reputation of post-war documentary has suffered in comparison to the documentaries made in the1930s and during the Second World War is the decline (real or perceived) of the progressive and socially purposeful documentary film. As early as 1946 *Documentary News Letter* had observed 'that social documentary films like *Housing Problems, Enough to Eat?* and *The Harvest Shall Come* are diminishing in number instead of increasing with the increasing size of documentary'.[132] There are various explanations for the apparent decline of social documentary after the war. One was that the shifting ideological needs of the public sector (the public information films of the COI) and the growth of commercial sponsorship of documentary mandated a different style of film. Another was simply the difficulties that post-war social documentaries like *The World is Rich* experienced in securing distribution. A broader reason might be, however, that the social problems that had informed progressive documentary during the 1930s – unemployment, slums, malnutrition – were much less acute after the war. The Welfare State did not abolish poverty any more than the National Health Service cured all illnesses: but the fact that they were available for all meant that the need for films such as *Housing Problems* or *Enough to Eat?* had been significantly diminished.

In fact the social documentary did not disappear after the war. Instead it shifted focus to examine not general social problems but rather specific issues affecting particular social groups. Even in the brave new world of Attlee's Britain there were still people who were in various ways disadvantaged or marginalized by society. And there was no shortage of subject matter for the socially committed documentary film-maker in the post-war period. These included the physically disabled (*The Undefeated*), the mentally handicapped (*There Was a Door*), disadvantaged children (*They Took Us to the Sea*), refugees (*Return to Life*) and the elderly (*I Think They Call Him John*). The persistence of social documentary was to a large extent made possible through sponsorship by charitable organizations. Among the charities that sponsored documentary films were the National Society for the Prevention of Cruelty to Children (*Henry*, *They Took Us to the Sea*), the Polio Research Fund (*Four People*), the British Epilepsy Association (*People Apart*) and the Craignish Trust (*I Think They Call Him John*). It was in the realm of social documentary that several of the distinctive new talents in the documentary field made their names – including Lindsay Anderson, Guy Brenton, Paul Dickson and John Krish – while their films were often notable for their formal innovation as well as their investment in social issues. This section will consider five social documentaries that exemplify different narrative and formal strategies: *To Be a Woman*, *The Undefeated*, *Thursday's Children*, *There Was a Door* and *I Think They Call Him John*.

Jill Craigie's *To Be a Woman* (Outlook Films, 1951) is not about a marginal group as such but rather examines the sexism experienced by women in everyday life. To this extent it provides an alternate post-war perspective to wartime films such as *Night Shift*. In *Night Shift* the emphasis had been on inclusion: women's labour was presented as essential to the war effort. In contrast, *To Be a Woman* focuses on the exclusion of women from senior positions in politics, industry and national life. The film is assertively feminist in its repeated claim that women are seen as 'cheap labour' and its declaration that 'women still have to contend with a nineteenth-century outlook...a kind of Edwardian hangover'. It adopts the dialectical style of Rotha's films in its alternating of a male and female voice-over and its contrasting *vox populi* that state different points of view ('I don't believe in all this equality nonsense', declares a stay-at-home housewife). *To Be a Woman* declares its progressive credentials in its support for equal pay for women – a quarter of a century before this was enshrined in law – and demonstrates the persistence of the agitational documentary (*Tyneside Story*-style) of the war years: 'Isn't it about time that we in Britain made it a proud thing to be a woman?' It is possibly the most explicitly feminist film produced in Britain before the radical work of Sally Potter and Laura Mulvey in the 1970s: it is no surprise, therefore, that the film failed to secure a wide release. Craigie, disillusioned, directed no further films after *To Be a Woman*, thereby depriving British documentary of one of its few women directors.[133]

Paul Dickson's *The Undefeated* (World Wide Pictures, 1950) was commissioned by the Ministry of Pensions to illustrate its work in the rehabilitation of injured servicemen from the war. Dickson adopts an innovative approach to the story-documentary formula in a film that is notable for its high degree of subjectivity, including not only first-person narration but also the 'camera-eye' technique that the US actor-director Robert Montgomery had employed in his feature film *The Lady in the Lake* (1946). *The Undefeated* follows the story of a glider pilot, Joe Anderson (Gerald Pearson), who loses both legs in a crash and endures a slow and painful rehabilitation as he learns to walk on artificial legs. Joe has also lost his ability to speak – attributed to what would now be understood as post-traumatic stress disorder. Joe is a fictional character but Gerald Pearson who plays him was a Parachute Regiment veteran who lost his legs at Arnhem. The loss of his voice was invented for the film 'to make sure that the audience would be hooked on Joe's story'.[134] The aim of the film was to remove the stigma for the war disabled in accepting state support for dealing with their injuries. Joe does in the end find his voice – while a 'twist' ending reveals not only that he found work at the Ministry of Pensions but that he has been the case officer narrating the film. *The Undefeated* is an affirming and moving film that deserves to be better known: certainly it is evidence against the narrative of stagnation and decline in post-war documentary. It was critically acclaimed, including awards for Best Documentary from the British Film Academy and Berlin Film Festival, and was 'widely acknowledged as a work of considerable distinction'.[135] Its critical success ensured that it received theatrical release from Associated British-Pathé, though it was mysteriously withdrawn from circulation in 1951, allegedly due to fears that its depiction of physical injury would undermine a recruitment drive then under way for the Korean War.[136]

Guy Brenton and Lindsay Anderson's *Thursday's Children* (World Wide Pictures, 1954) demonstrates the work of the Royal School for the Deaf in Margate. There is some dispute as to the nature of the collaboration between the two film-makers. According to camerman Walter Lassally – who while shooting the film also collaborated with Anderson in making *O Dreamland*, which would become one of the first Free Cinema films – *Thursday's Children* was 95 per cent Anderson's.[137] Yet Anderson's diaries suggest differently:

> Working with Guy is not exactly a holiday: no doubt I plague him as he plagues me... The film is his creation of course, as a project completely his. After that – I suppose pretty well 50–50 his and mine. On his own he'd almost certainly have made a mess of it – buggered it up with his 'theoretical' ideas. And on my own, I'd never even have begun.[138]

The film's treatment of deaf children as marginalized due to their deafness has parallels in other films directed solely by Brenton, which suggests that it was at least as much his film as Anderson's. These include *People Apart* (Morse Films, 1957), which focuses on the stigma attached to those suffering from epilepsy ('It is often kept dark and we try to think of it not at all'), and *Four People* (Morse Films, 1962), which 'intends to show what effect disablement can have on people's lives, and how life may still be lived'. Ros Cranston has argued that Brenton developed

> a form of social documentary very different from that of the Grierson generation but equally distinctive when set against most of the output of the documentary industry around him... His interest in how society deals with those who don't easily fit into conventional patterns is at the heart of his best film work.[139]

Derek Williams's *There Was a Door* (Greenpark, 1957), sponsored by the Manchester Regional Hospital Board, was another variation on this theme. The subject is what the film refers to as 'mental deficiency': this is what would later become known as Down's Syndrome, though the condition is not named in the film. Like *The Undefeated* it is an innovative story documentary that adopts a non-chronological narrative structure, including flashbacks and multiple points of view. The film focuses on 19-year-old Johnny Harris ('a severe case of arrested mental development') and the efforts of a sympathetic GP to explore the various options for his care. The emphasis is as much on the effects on parents of caring for a mentally disabled child, especially Johnny's mother, as on Johnny himself. Indeed Johnny is the one character who does not have a 'voice' of his own. Despite the unfortunate (to modern ears) language, especially when the GP visits a hospital for 'mental defectives', *There Was a Door* is notable for its sympathy towards its subject ('mental deficiency is a sheer misfortune') and for its suggestion that institutionalization in a home would not necessarily be right for Johnny and that he should if possible be allowed to live as normal a life as he can – a progressive attitude towards mental illness at a time when there was a tendency to regard such disability as something best hidden from view. The film is also notable for its honesty in stating that even the NHS does not have finite resources and that there are others in greater need of help. The conclusion is humanistic but also highlights the limitations of mental health care: 'They [the Harris family] had given me a new respect for people – but there was nothing I could do to help them. Surely something better could be done?'

The career of John Krish is perhaps the best case study of how a socially committed documentarist was able to negotiate the competing demands of sponsors while also pursuing his own interests. Krish's oeuvre was remarkably varied: it included several feature films (the 1963 science-fiction thriller *Unearthly Stranger* has become something of a cult) and shorts for the Children's Film Foundation as well as documentaries for the Ministry of Labour (*Mr Marsh Comes to School*, 1961) and the National Union of Teachers (*I Want to Go to School*, 1959, and *Our School*, 1962). The fact that Krish was able to alternate between government and private sponsorship – and between documentary and the feature film industry – while at the same time maintaining a distinctively personal outlook would suggest that the effects of sponsorship were not necessarily so 'debilitating' as some commentators believe. His social documentaries represent his most important work. These included an account of the difficulties experienced by East European refugees in adjusting to life in Britain, notable for its refusal to idealize the refugees themselves (*Return to Life*, 1960) and a bittersweet film of an excursion to Weston-super-Mare for disadvantaged children that juxtaposes scenes of the children enjoying themselves with those left behind (*They Took Us to the Sea*, 1961).

I Think They Call Him John (Samaritan Films, 1964) is 'the most enduring item in Krish's filmography'.[140] Krish had long wanted to make a film about the plight of the elderly living alone without any family or friends: he secured funding from the Craignish Trust, a charity connected to a Scottish distilling company. *I Think They Call Him John* chronicles a day in the life of elderly widower John Ronson living alone in a high-rise flat in St John's Wood: Krish shot the film over two successive Sundays. Ostensibly *I Think They Call Him John* adopts the form of the observational or 'fly-on-the-wall' documentary that had been popularized by television, though in fact it is a highly constructed piece as Krish shot the film mute so that he could instruct his elderly subject what to do. Krish and cameraman David Muir used a 28 millimetre lens in order that three walls of the flat could be seen in every shot and thereby enhance the feelings of isolation and claustrophobia. The film that comes to mind when watching *I Think They Call Him John* is Vittorio De Sica's late neo-realist masterpiece *Umberto D* (1952). André Bazin felt that *Umberto D* marked the apotheosis of neo-realism because it succeeded in stripping away all melodrama:

One wonderful sequence – it will remain one of the high points of film – is a perfect illustration of this approach to narrative and thus to direction: the scene in which the maid gets up. The camera confines itself to watching her doing her little chores: moving around the kitchen still half asleep, drowning the ants that have invaded the sink, grinding the coffee. The cinema here is conceived as the exact opposite of that 'art of ellipsis' to which we are much too ready to believe it devoted.[141]

Bazin's description could apply to *I Think They Call Him John*: in a straightforward manner the film narrates John's daily routine of getting up, shaving, dressing, having breakfast, cleaning his flat, making lunch, watching television, ironing and going to bed. Like De Sica's film, Krish eschews montage in favour of simple long takes and moments of 'empty' action. There is no music and the only non-diegetic sound effects are the noise of machine guns as John recalls the First World War. The commentary is spare and matter-of-fact: 'John Ronson – retired. Old miner, old soldier, old gardner, old-age pensioner, widower, no children.' It concludes on a consience-pricking note: 'We can all be irritated by the old, they're too slow, too full of the past … The old are an army of strangers we have no intention of joining – but it is not that simple. If we don't care, who will learn to care?' *I Think They Call Him John* is a beautifully austere film entirely free from obtrusive stylization or directorial flourishes. Krish's simple (one might say deceptively simple) style powerfully evokes the feelings of loneliness and isolation experienced by the elderly. It is a deeply moving film and 'an acute contemplation on the state of loneliness in a modern world'.[142] The film was deemed too bleak by cinema exhibitors who declined to book it. Yet in its modest and unassuming way *I Think They Call Him John* is as effective a piece of social documentary film-making as the near-contemporaneous and much more celebrated *Cathy Come Home*.

The history of British documentary film after the Second World War is both richer and more complex than the conventional narrative of stagnation and decline would allow. This was a period of growth for the documentary sector but also a period of diversification as it adapted to changing ideological and institutional contexts. Indeed it is perhaps the greater diversity of post-war documentary that accounts for its lesser reputation as compared to the pre-war period, rather than any deficiencies (aesthetic or otherwise) of its films. While the documentary movement of the 1930s was defined by a particular ideological project – a project, moreover, that was specific to the historical circumstances of the time – post-war documentary was not tied to a particular idea of what documentary should be. On the one hand the ideological needs of the state and industry – the two major sponsors of documentary film – had changed: documentary therefore had to develop and evolve in order to respond to these changing needs. Hence the emergence of new forms, including the heritage documentary and the industrial documentary. On the other hand the persistence of the social documentary, albeit not of the same type as had emerged before and during the war, demonstrates that the progressive credentials of the documentary movement were still embraced by the second generation of documentary film-makers. As for the charge that documentary had become stale, this simply does not withstand scrutiny. Post-war documentary was characterized by a process of continuing innovation in form and technique, while films such as *Land of Promise*, *Family Portrait*, *The Undefeated*, *David*, *Terminus* and *I Think They Call Him John* – all very different examples of documentary form – are as distinctive in their own right as the classics of the 1930s.

Where there is less scope for debate is the fact that documentary production dropped sharply in the 1970s and that both theatrical and non-theatrical distribution of documentary films had more or less ceased by the end of the decade. There were various complex reasons for this but three stand out. For one thing documentary – like the film industry as a whole – was affected by the precipitous decline in cinemagoing during the 1970s and the consequent structural changes in the distribution and exhibition sectors of the film industry. In particular, the theatrical market for shorts and supporting items contracted severely before disappearing entirely in the 1980s. Another factor was that the economic downturn of the 1970s saw many sponsors withdraw from documentary film-making. ICI had sold off its film unit in 1966 (it found a new lease of life as Millbank Films, specializing in safety films), Unilever and Ford ended their film-making activities in the 1970s, and even the Shell Film Unit had to face the economic reality of budget cuts. Many of the small independent documentary units that had specialized in sponsored documentary either ceased operating or switched to making 'corporate videos'.[143] A third factor was that television had now surpassed cinema not only as the pre-eminent mass-entertainment medium but also as the major arena of documentary activity. Therefore it is to television that we should turn for the next chapter of the history of British documentary.

5
Television and Documentary

> In 29 years the word 'documentary' has spread all over the world to describe almost all films of social significance...The word has now overflowed its original intention and is often applied to radio programmes, books, articles and paintings. Indeed, it has been so tortured and transformed even within the limits of cinema that, at times, it must be a wise Grierson who knows his own child. It is, however, perfectly at home in television. Indeed, so many opportunities occur in television for 'the creative interpretation of reality' [*sic*] through the visual image that Flaherty himself has said that the eventual future of documentary lies there.
>
> Duncan Ross[1]

The emergence of television as a new mass medium that challenged and eventually surpassed the pre-eminence of cinema offered new opportunities and new challenges for documentary. Some documentarists responded enthusiastically to the promise of television. Duncan Ross, for example, who had been Paul Rotha's assistant producer for *Britain Can Make It* before joining the BBC in the late 1940s, saw television documentary in the Griersonian tradition of 'the creative treatment of actuality'. The public service ideology of British broadcasting – as mandated by royal charter for both the licence fee-funded British Broadcasting Corporation and its commercial rival Independent Television – chimed with the educative and socially purposeful ethos of the documentary project.[2] And, for the documentarists, television offered a potential audience many times larger than they could hope to reach either in the cinema or through non-theatrical distribution: 90 per cent of British households owned a television set by the 1960s. The audiences

172

for some of the landmark documentary television series such as *The World at War* dwarfed those for documentary in the cinema. For all these reasons there was much truth in the view that documentary was perfectly at home on television.

However, television documentary would take shape in a different institutional context than documentary film. It soon became apparent that television would not be able to subsist on a diet of existing documentary films: indeed the strict guidelines on television advertising disqualified most sponsored documentaries from the airwaves. Instead television would need to produce its own documentary content – which in turn gave rise to the emergence of new documentary forms and styles shaped by the specific technological and aesthetic contexts of the medium. In particular the 'liveness' of early television formalized a different relationship between the text and the spectator: and in this sense television documentary was particularly suited to the adoption of *vérité* techniques that gave rise to new documentary modes such as the current-affairs documentary and the observational or 'fly-on-the-wall' documentary. At the same time, however, the emergence of the drama-documentary mode demonstrates some continuity with existing practices in documentary film. Susan Sydney-Smith has argued 'that new forms of post-war popular television...were closely related to those documentary forms developed earlier by film and radio'.[3] This chapter maps the various different lineages of television documentary in Britain between the advent of commercial television in 1955 and the derugulation of the industry signalled by the Broadcasting Act of 1990, which brought about fundamental changes in the political and cultural economies of British television. It focuses especially on the relationship between the institutional contexts of television and documentary practice. Indeed, a feature of television documentary that has generally been overlooked is that many landmark programmes and series that have been seen as representing particular lineages or taxonomies were often in the first place the outcome of very specific institutional and ideological conditions.

Institutional contexts

Although there had been a limited BBC television service in London between 1936 and 1939, when it was suspended upon the outbreak of the Second World War, the history of television as a mass medium really begins with the resumption of regular broadcasts in 1946. Over the next decade television grew from a London-centric service for a few to a national medium. The building of a national network of transmitters between 1949 and 1954 brought television within the reach of 80 per cent of the population, while the arrival of a second channel in 1955 ended the BBC's monopoly and introduced competition into the television industry. The growth of the television audience is seen in the increase of combined 'sound and vision' licences (costing £2) from only 343,882 in 1950 to 1,449,260 in 1952, 4,503,766 in 1955 and 10,469,753 by 1960.[4] The rise of television overlapped with the decline of cinemagoing, which had peaked at the end of the war and thereafter showed a steady downward trend until a precipitous fall between 1955 (when there were 1.2 million annual cinema admissions) and 1960 (when there were only 500,000) saw over half the cinema audience disappear.[5]

The history of television broadcasting in Britain after 1955 has generally, if rather too simplistically, been categorized as a contest between, on the one hand, an ethos of 'public service broadcating', exemplified by the BBC, and, on the other, an ideology of 'populism', represented by ITV. In fact ITV also had a public service remit, while the BBC had always been alert to the desirability of providing audiences with popular entertainment alongside its more serious fare. For both broadcasters 'factual content' was seen as a means of delivering their public service mandates. In his study of historical programming on British television, Robert Dillon argues that BBC policy in the immediate post-war period was geared towards 'producing programmes based around the central themes behind the concept of a nation-state'.[6] These included one-off documentaries about London (*The Heart of an Empire*, 1946) and national institutions (*The Palace of Westminster*, 1947), and early screenings for classic war documentaries including *Desert Victory*, *Coastal Command*, *Close Quarters* and *Target for Tonight*. In 1952 the BBC also screened the American-made series *Victory at Sea*, in the process drawing criticism from Prime Minister Sir Winston Churchill on account of its bias towards the US war effort. The BBC, which at this time was unable to mount such a large-scale archive film compilation, defended itself on the grounds that

> these are American films made for the American audience, and, unless we could have felt able to refuse the free gift of them for our Television Service, we have to accept the fact and do our best to explain it to viewers and put the films in the right perspective.[7]

The place of documentary in British television during the 1950s is best understood in terms of a process of institutional negotiation. There emerged at the BBC, for example, an institutional discourse that differentiated between current affairs programming on the one hand and documentary on the other. Current affairs was the responsibility of the Talks and Features Department (an inheritance from radio broadcasting) whereas documentary initially had no recognized institutional home until the establishment of the Documentary Department in 1953. Duncan Ross categorized the difference thus: 'Whatever form of illustration is used... the first duty of "talks" is, obviously, to interpret a speaker. Documentary, on the other hand, is not concerned with speakers and is at its best when it ignores them completely and interprets the subject straight from life.'[8] Ross, perhaps on account of his film background, therefore saw documentary as distinct from the broadcasting tradition of illustrated lectures. One account of the early history of British television documentary has it that Mary Adams, the Head of Talks and Features, was an empire builder who sought to subsume documentary within her own fiefdom.[9] The 'rescue' of documentary and the establishment of its own department is attributed to Cecil McGivern, who became Director of Television Programmes in 1947. McGivern's background was in radio but he believed that television should develop its own style that amounted to more than just 'radio with pictures'. According to Norman Swallow, who produced the BBC's first major documentary series *Special Enquiry* (1952–1957): 'I think the Documentary Unit survived and flourished because of Cecil McGivern. Being a radio Features, i.e. documentary man, he therefore supported those of us who were making documentaries, and I would say historically that he was the right man in the right place at the right time.'[10] An indication of the importance that McGivern attached to documentary was that he recruited a major name to head the new department: Paul Rotha.

Like other documentarists, Rotha was initially excited about the possibilities offered by television. In 1953 he told fellow documentarist Stanley Hawes that television was 'our medium' and detected within the BBC a 'new and infectious enthusiasm... reminiscent of the '30s in documentary'.[11] However, his time at the BBC would prove brief and unhappy. The episode highlights the difficulties of adapting the working practices of documentary film (small units operating with a considerable degree of creative freedom) into the institutional structures of television (large, bureaucratic and hierarchical). Rotha evidently saw television documentary as an extension of documentary film: his major contribution at the BBC was a 12-part series called *The World is Ours*, which was produced on film and examined the work of UNESCO and other United Nations agencies. Rotha understood *The World is Ours* as a continuation of the tradition of social documentary from films such as *World of Plenty* and *The World is Rich*.[12] But younger members of the Documentary Department had different backgrounds, including theatre (Steve McCormack), journalism (Norman Swallow) and radio (Denis Mitchell), and they did not necessarily cast themselves in the same tradition of social documentary as Rotha. McCormack, who produced the magazine programmes *About Britain* and *London Town*, suggested that the impulse of early BBC documentary was journalistic rather than political: 'We were really interested in London, and how to present the variety, the endless variety, of London to the viewers. We had no political axe to grind. We didn't give a damn about anything... You could almost say we were naive.'[13]

Rotha's own account of his departure from the BBC after two difficult years suggests that he was frustrated by interference from above rather than the working envrionment within the Documentary Department itself: 'I was very proud of the programmes, mostly on social matters one way or another, that we put out... But, as time went on, over the two years I was there I found it more and more difficult from a policy point of view.' He cited the last-minute cancellation of a *Special Inquiry* report exploring 'what was wrong with the railways and what was right with the railays' that was aborted following an intervention from the BBC's Director-General. Rotha explained: 'This went on on a number of subjects. It went on over subjects we had about Cyprus and about the slums of Glasgow, and eventually it became very unpleasant for me to have to keep cancelling what I thought were extremely important programmes, and, quite frankly, I got out.'[14] However, an internal BBC report suggests that Rotha was unable to adjust to the different working environment of television:

> Mr Rotha found it difficult to adapt himself to the BBC method as opposed to the method of the film industry. Broadly speaking, the film method is to set up a unit for each film (or film series) to be made. The BBC method is to provide permanent Servicing Departments to cater for all Output Departments... These difficulties have led to a 'softening', not a strengthening, of documentary output.[15]

In particular, Rotha's preference for shooting on film, which was more expensive than studio broadcasts, did not accord with BBC practices at the time. Rather than leaving of his own accord, the BBC Written Archives reveal that Rotha's contract was not renewed.

A different set of institutional factors prevailed on the commercial network. The arrival of ITV had been welcomed in some quarters as a populist alternative to the perceived stuffiness of the BBC, but there were others who regarded commercial television as pandering to the lowest common denominators in cultural taste. The prominence of game shows such as *Take Your Pick* and *Double Your Money* on early ITV seemed to confirm this prejudice in the eyes of its critics. The Independent Television Authority (ITA), the regulator for commercial television, stipulated that ITV programmes 'ought to express the coherent policy and outlook of a group of people conscious that what they have in their hands is a social responsibility'.[16] The adoption of documentary was a means by which the regional contractors who supplied programmes for the ITV network could prove their social responsibility. Scottish Television (STV), for example, hired John Grierson to produce *This Wonderful World*, a documentary magazine programme that ran for 350 weekly episodes between 1957 and 1965. *This Wonderful World* was very much Grierson's series: he produced it, selected the subject matter, edited the film excerpts, wrote the commentary and introduced each episode himself. It was a flagship series for STV, one of the smaller ITV contractors, and one of its few programmes to be shown across the full ITV network. At the height of its popularity in the early 1960s it was among the top ten network programmes and was seen by an estimated six million viewers.[17] Jo Fox argues that *This Wonderful World* was commissioned quite consciously as a 'prestige' series to uphold the public service remit imposed on the ITV broadcasters and that its content – which included cultural, social and scientific subjects – 'reflected the contemporary need to navigate a path between "serious" content and "popular" appeal'.[18]

The institutional prestige attached to documentary within the television industry was further demonstrated in the emergence of 'event' documentaries in the 1960s. The BBC, for example, commissioned *The Great War* (1964), at 26 parts its most ambitious documentary series to date, to mark both the fiftieth anniversary of the outbreak of the war and the launch of its second channel, BBC2, while the 13-part *Civilisation* (1969), presented by art historian Sir Kenneth Clark, was produced to exploit the arrival of colour broadcasting. *Civilisation* was commissioned by BBC2 Controller David Attenborough, later to secure fame in his own right as presenter of a series of acclaimed natural history programmes, and it is a sign of the prestige attached to the project that it was afforded the large budget of £15,000 per episode.[19] The best indication of the cultural acceptance of television documentary was *Royal Family* (1969), illustrating a year in the life of Queen Elizabeth II both on and off duty. *Royal Family* was the first film or television programme focusing on the work of a reigning monarch: the producers were allowed unprecedented 'behind-the-scenes' access by Buckingham Palace. Its production was overseen by the BBC's Head of Documentary, Richard Cawston, though in a unique arrangement it was shown on both BBC1 (where it drew an audience of 23 million for its first broadcast) and on ITV (where 15 million viewers saw the repeat). *Royal Family* was seen by an estimated 63 per cent of the population – a huge audience for any television programme and the sort of figure only possible during the era of limited competition.[20]

Technological and aesthetic contexts

The institutional discourses of early television also reveal a lively debate around the nature of documentary as a form. Unlike the debates within the documentary film movement during the 1930s, however, where aesthetic concerns were generally secondary to the question of the social utility of documentary and its relationship to the state, the debates within the television industry focused primarily on form and aesthetics. This was due largely to the nature of the medium and the technologies at its disposal. The historiography of early television is marked by a strong streak of technological determinism: television form developed within the limits of what was technologically possible. Until the end of the 1950s most television – and hence most television documentary – was 'live'. It was not until 1958 that the first Ampex video-recording machines, which allowed the broadcast of pre-recorded material, were introduced into British television. The only alternative to live broadcast in the formative years was to shoot on film: this was expensive and generally took the form of short 'telecine' extracts included in a live broadcast rather than full programmes in their own right. Dai Vaughan argues that it was the simultaneous introduction of a silent-running 16 millimetre camera (the Eclair) and a lightweight portable tape recorder (the Nagra) in 1963 that created the conditions in which television documentary could flourish:

> Almost overnight it became possible to shoot synch with portable equipment...The new type of documentary, shot with small crews, which was relatively cheap and could be made in a hurry, was ideally suited to the needs of television, where the difference in definition between 16mm and 35mm was least important.[21]

The emergence of the drama-documentary mode in the 1950s was very much shaped by the technological contexts of early television. The BBC drama documentaries of the 1950s – examples include *War on Crime* (1950), *The Course of Justice* (1950–1951) and *I Made News* (1951) – feature the work of public services and institutions (police, courts, hospitals) and the usual practice was to gather case histories and then script them into stories with archetypal characters and situations that would be enacted in the studio with the occasional film insert. To this extent they were a hybrid form between the live studio drama (the 'single play' that holds particular critical currency in television history) and documentary (maintaining a sense of distance from the drama by, for example, not listing the actors' names in the *Radio Times*). Derek Paget argues that contemporary practitioners 'saw dramatisation as their means of controlling the documentary material both editorially and technically'.[22] On another level the drama documentary may be understood as an attempt to develop a formula for combining the public service ideology of television (documentary) with popular appeal (drama). A recurring feature of debates around television documentary during this period was the imperative of engaging audiences in subject matter that was not necessarily 'dramatic' in its own right. Caryl Doncaster, an early member of the BBC Documentary Department, saw 'dramatised story-documentary' as an alternative to the 'Talks' format: 'The talk informs. The dramatised story-documentary interprets. One appeals to the intellect, the other to the emotions.'[23]

The early history of television drama documentary is particularly associated with the career of Robert Barr. Barr's background was in radio journalism and as a war correspondent before joining the BBC Television Service in the late 1940s, where he headed the small Documentary Unit before it became a fully fledged department in its own right. He wrote of documentary that 'its form is the dramatisation of facts, reconstruction of events, and it uses any dramatic device to make its point. It will use (and devise) any technique that will give force and clarity to the information it seeks to convey.'[24] As a producer Barr was responsible for several early experiments in drama documentary, including *War on Crime* (1950), *I Made News* (1951) and *Pilgrim Street* (1952). It was a sign of the fluidity of the institutional contexts of early television that Barr and several of his colleagues would later move seamlessly to the BBC Drama Group, where he produced the police series *Z Cars* and *Softly, Softly*.

Even during this early period there was some disquiet about the drama-documentary mode. Some critics felt that the mixing of fact and

fiction in documentary was disingenuous. Maurice Wiggin, the television critic of the *Sunday Times*, was a sceptic: 'The whole point of
documentary is that it is literally true ... If it is not literally true, it is not
documentary but something else – a kind of play-writing ... We have
had too much fact-based fiction cooked up in the studio and played
by professional actors.'[25] However, this view was not necessarily shared
by audiences. The BBC's Audience Research Department was tasked
with monitoring popular responses to all programme types. Robert Barr
asked it to report on a repeat of the story documentary *Missing from
Home* (1955) – it was less common for documentaries to be repeated
than straight plays – as he feared the audience's view of it as being
'real' would be undermined by seeing it again. But Audience Research
reported 'that viewers are perfectly well aware that a documentary such
as this is not the same thing as an OB [Outside Broadcast], yet at the
same time this realisation does not seem in any way to impair their
capacity to be gripped by a programme'.[26] This would suggest that audiences were capable of distinguishing between what was and was not
dramatic reconstruction.

The studio-based drama documentary was a historically specific form
that would be rendered obsolete in the 1960s when technological
developments – including lightweight film cameras and portable sound
recording – allowed television documentarists to move out of the studio
and onto location. However, the influence of these early experiments
can be seen in the development of television drama in the 1960s.
Indeed the ITV Annual Report for 1959–1960 referred to the fiction
series *Emergency-Ward 10* and *Probation Officer* as 'two established documentary drama series' and even included *Coronation Street*, which started
in 1960 and would in time become Britain's longest-running soap opera,
in the category of 'documentary drama'.[27] The early *Coronation Street* can
be seen as a television example of the 'kitchen sink' tradition of British
social realism, which includes the novels of the 'northern realists' (Alan
Sillitoe, Stan Barstow, David Storey) and the British new wave films.
Michael Barry, the BBC's Head of Drama between 1951 and 1962, felt
in hindsight that the television drama-documentary experiment influenced the emergence of new wave theatre and cinema: 'If it had not
been for the audiences prepared by the television drama documentaries,
Look Back in Anger would not have found its moment.'[28]

The shift from the studio to location that became possible in the
early 1960s naturally influenced the institutional discourses of television documentary. The BBC Written Archives reveal that the corporation
was much engaged with theoretical debates around *cinéma vérité* in the

1960s. In fact, as Brian Winston has rightly pointed out, it was not the French *cinéma vérité* movement, spearheaded by documentarists such as Jean Rouch, which really informed television documentary practice, but rather the contemporaneous Direct Cinema, associated with US film-makers such as Richard Leacock and Albert and David Maysles.[29] The BBC's notion of *vérité* was closer to Direct Cinema (which aimed to observe in an 'objective' way without the camera intruding) than the French school (which involved interaction between the film-maker and the subject with the camera as a catalyst for finding some deeper 'truth'). It was during the 1960s that the idea of television as a 'window on the world' – a phrase that was institutionalized in the production discourses of current-affairs documentaries such as *Panorama* – was popularized. However, this is not to suggest that television documentary was any less mediated than its filmic counterparts. A BBC training manual from the early 1970s states that 'even the purest piece of "ciné vérité" can never be – and indeed should never be – totally free of the day-to-day business of directing'.[30] The director's role was to interpret the raw material – yet another variation of 'the creative treatment of actuality'.

However, the institutional practices of television documentary policed the extent of its 'creative treatment' quite rigorously. An example of this can be seen in the series of films that Ken Russell made for the BBC's arts documentary series *Monitor* in the early 1960s.[31] A peculiar feature of Russell's biopics of the lives of great composers, including Prokofiev, Elgar, Bartok and Debussy, was the use of actors in dramatized scenes. Russell saw this technique as a means of evoking their personalities, but the introduction of such 'fiction' challenged the accepted documentary practice of sticking rigidly to known facts and brought Russell into conflict with Huw Wheldon, the Head of Documentary. Wheldon – who admired Russell but disapproved of this particular technique – confided in a colleague that 'my main reservation...is the possible disaster that might arise from using actors in the suggested way. My own opinion is that this kind of thing would be much more effective if the people were *suggested* rather than literally seen.'[32] Nevertheless, Wheldon was willing to compromise and allowed Russell his head. The dramatized elements of Russell's biopics developed from shots of an actor's hands playing a piano in the Prokofiev film to long shots of various actors playing Elgar at different points in his life but without any dialogue. The boundary between fact and fiction was pushed further in the Bartok film, in which Russell used a shot of an actor as Bartok surrounded by a crowd of people on a moving escalator (shot at Leicester Square Underground Station) in order to represent his feeling of alienation. However, it was *The Debussy Film* (1965) that proved the most problematic and brought an end to the experiment. Russell felt that Debussy's 'complex and enigmatic' life called for a more impressionistic treatment 'that bound the hallucinatory state of his mind to the dreamlike quality of his music'.[33] The technique he adopted was that of filming a film crew making a film about Debussy – hence legitimating the use of actors – and re-creating episodes of the composer's life in dramatic form. *The Debussy Film* was the most radical of Russell's composer biopics in its departures from conventional documentary practice. However, Audience Research found that viewers were confused by the film-within-a-film format.[34]

Another factor that shaped the content and form of television documentary has often been overlooked: the practice of fixed-point scheduling that mandated programmes of a particular length. This was seen as a limitation by some documentary film producers such as Robert Angell: 'Idleness is caused by the time slots dictated by television which demands that documentaries (indeed all programmes) run to predetermined lengths of 26 or 52 minutes… A documentary particularly ought to find its own natural length and the makers should have the freedom to edit.'[35] However, the mainstays of television documentary since the 1960s have been episodic series produced for particular time slots that in some cases have enjoyed extraordinary longevity: examples include the BBC's *Horizon* (1964–) and *Tomorrow's World* (1965–2001), and Anglia Television's *Survival* (1961–2001). It was series such as these – rather than the more high-profile 'event' series – that provided the bread and butter of television documentary until the emergence of new 'reality' formats in the 1990s.

Documentary and current affairs: *Panorama, This Week, World in Action*

The institutional structures and professional discourses of the television industry meant that some programmes that might be considered documentaries were not necessarily defined as such within the industry itself. The example of current-affairs television was a case in point. This emerged in the late 1950s and 1960s with programmes such as the BBC's *Panorama* (1955–) and *Tonight* (1956–1965) and ITV's *This Week* (Associated-Rediffusion/Thames Television, 1956–1992) and *World in Action* (Granada, 1963–1998). Current affairs is a category specific to television that has no precise equivalent in film: perhaps the closest parallel would be the *March of Time* newsreel that adopted a more journalistic style and featured longer 'specials' than the regular newsreels. In the television industry, current affairs was seen as separate from documentary: at the BBC this was institutionalized in the form of the Talks Department producing topical and 'political' programmes and the Documentary Department whose remit was 'social' topics. However, the professional discourses of current-affairs television tended to describe it in terms of engaging in a mission to educate and inform the public, which had clear echoes of the Griersonian documentary project. The authors of a recent study of *World in Action* state unequivocally that 'current affairs television had its origins in the documentary cinema pioneered by John Grierson in the 1930s'.[36]

Like other forms of documentary, current-affairs television took shape within specific institutional and ideological contexts. In particular it can be seen as a means of legitimating television as a 'serious' medium. The case of *Panorama* is a good example. *Panorama* has often been cited as Britain's first current-affairs series though it was originally conceived as a topical 'magazine' programme focusing largely on arts and cultural affairs. The early history of *Panorama* is now best known for perhaps the most famous spoof in television history – Richard Dimbleby's report on the harvesting of Italian 'spaghetti trees', broadcast as an April Fool's Day joke in 1958 – but this disguises the fact that the programme was already in the process of transforming itself into a topical current-affairs series with a focus on politics. In the case of *Panorama* this was to differentiate the series from its chief rival within the BBC: *Tonight*. Presented by Cliff Michelmore, *Tonight* was characterized by its less reverent tone towards interviewees that can be seen as an early manifestation of the decline of deference that characterized British television, and the BBC especially, in the 1960s.[37] *Panorama*, in contrast, positioned itself as a more heavyweight programme: as well as its chief reporter Dimbleby (a 'heavyweight' in more ways than one) its regular contributors included political journalists such as Ludovic Kennedy, Woodrow Wyatt and Robin Day. Robert Rowland, a film producer for *Panorama* during the 1960s, credits its transformation to Michael Peacock who became its editor in 1958: '*Panorama*, under the editorship of Michael Peacock, became the heavyweight flagship, with *Tonight* its cheekier, brighter relative. *Panorama* producers were sober-suited. *Tonight* producers wore dark glasses and sports jackets.'[38]

The contexts for ITV's major current affairs series, *This Week* and *World in Action*, were different. Whereas *Panorama* changed tone and content to differentiate itself from an internal rival, ITV's embrace of current affairs was more in the way of a response to external pressures. The

Pilkington Report of 1962 had severely censured ITV for its 'triviality' and for falling 'well short of what a good public service of broadcasting should be'.[39] It was largely as a consequence of the Pilkington Report that the decision was made that the 'third channel' should be awarded to the BBC rather than ITV. Another consequence was that the regulatory body, the ITA, stipulated that ITV contractors should broaden the range of their programme content, and specifically that they should include more current affairs. It was this stipulation that lay behind the change in editorial policy of *This Week*, which, rather like *Panorama*, had started out as a more lightweight magazine programme in the 1950s. Indeed its first issue had been described by one reviewer as 'more fun than *Panorama*'.[40] The appointment of Jeremy Isaacs as producer of *This Week* in 1963 signalled a shift towards more serious and political content. Isaacs presided over changes to the format of *This Week*, shifting from multiple stories to single-issue programmes, and in production methods. In particular Isaacs embraced the shift in television documentary out of the studio and onto film. He later said: 'I had an absolute belief in the effectiveness of film to communicate life as it was lived, and that determined the choice of subject matter and the techniques.'[41]

Granada's *World in Action* – a title with a Griersonian lineage as there had been a film series of that name produced by the National Film Board of Canada during the Second World War – was even more directly a response to the requirement for the ITV network to produce more current-affairs programming. Granada was one of the original ITV franchise holders and had always been seen as more socially engaged than other contractors. Its co-founder and chairman was Sidney Bernstein, a left-leaning former cinema exhibitor, while its managing director from 1964, Denis Forman, had worked at the GPO Film Unit in the 1930s. From the outset *World in Action* set out to be even more punchy and topical than its rivals. The tone was set by its first producer Tim Hewat, whose manifesto for the programme was that it should be 'declamatory and aggressive, inquiring and insubordinate, trying to bludgeon the audience into thinking for themselves'.[42] Like *This Week* it embraced shooting on film and adopted contemporary *vérité* techniques: the Maysles brothers, pioneers of the Direct Cinema movement, were even hired to shoot the American sequences for a film on The Beatles in New York. Accounts of the making of *World in Action* in the early years suggest a somewhat seat-of-the-pants operation and it was criticized by Granada executives for going over budget due to the last-minute decision-making process.[43] But this allowed *World in Action* to steal a march on its rivals when Hewat went to Dallas only days after the assassination of President Kennedy to make a film about the city that had suddenly become the focus of world attention – 'Dallas' won the Television Guild Award for Best Factual Programme. *World in Action* was an immediate success and its audience was twice that of *Panorama*.[44]

The rivalry between the major current-affairs programmes to some extent recalls the competition between the newsreels in the 1930s. And the professional discourses of current-affairs television tended to erect institutional boundaries. Rowland testifies to the rivalry between the production teams of *Panorama* and *Tonight*: 'Both programmes engendered tribal loyalties, and mixed little in the Lime Grove bar, or the canteen. We fought our journalistic corners, believing that the distinction between us expressed that "creative tension" which was proclaimed to be the essence of what Huw Wheldon called "excellence".'[45] In practice, however, the boundaries were rather more fluid. John Morgan, a reporter for *Tonight*, moved over to *Panorama*, while Jeremy Isaacs left *World in Action* to become editor of *Panorama* in 1965. Indeed current-affairs television in the 1960s provided a fertile training ground for a whole generation of future television executives. Two *Panorama* editors, Michael Peacock and Paul Fox, would both become Controllers of BBC1, as would *Tonight* editor Donald Baverstock. Alasdair Milne, who succeeded Baverstock as editor of *Tonight*, was a future BBC Director-General, while another future Director-General, John Birt, began his career as a researcher for *World in Action*. Jeremy Isaacs would graduate to Head of Features at Thames Television in the early 1970s and later became the first Chief Executive of Channel 4 in the 1980s.

It was during the 1960s that current-affairs programmes represented the cutting edge of topical coverage on British television. At this time there was a novelty to seeing politicians on television: Anthony Eden was the first Prime Minister to be interviewed live (interviewed by Aiden Crawley on *This Week* in 1956) and *Panorama* scored something of a first when, in 1968, it persuaded Prime Minister Harold Wilson and Leader of the Opposition Edward Heath to take part in a live debate following a film item they had not seen. The topical nature of current-affairs television meant that it often courted controversy. *Panorama* withdrew an item on 'Immigration and Race' during the 1964 general election campaign, which Rowland attributed to pressure from the Labour Party that was campaigning on a platform of better race relations. That said, the major current-affairs programmes covered most of the major political stories of the time – including the Civil Rights campaign in the United States and the Troubles in Northern Ireland – while of course observing television's institutional mantra of 'objectivity'. There were also profiles of politicians and other public figures, background films on events such as the Cuban Missiles Crisis and the Profumo Scandal, and reports on controversial topics such as abortion and homosexuality. *World in Action* gained a particular reputation for consumer-themed stories. While most stories involved detailed research in the best tradition of investigative journalism, some were more hastily conceived. In March 1968 *World in Action* sent two camera crews to cover the anti-Vietnam War demonstration outside the US Embassy in Grosvenor Square: 'The Demonstration' includes footage shot in close proximity to the protest and is one of the best examples of *vérité* television in Britain.

A combination of the ideological imperative of current-affairs television to examine contemporary politics, and the nature of its format as an 'exposé', meant that it often became a site of controversy. Nowhere is this more evident than in the coverage of subjects raising questions of national security. The coverage of political violence in Northern Ireland 'posed a serious challenge to current-affairs television, which was repeatedly forced to consider which topics could legitimately be brought into the public arena for discussion and to ask who had the right to add their voice to that discussion and who might define its terms'.[46] The issues revolved around how to reflect fairly two ideologically entrenched positions (Unionists on the one hand, Republicans on the other) and, from 1968, whether the activities of the Irish Republican Army (IRA) should be reported 'in context' (in the sense of attempting to explain its motives) or condemned outright as terrorists. Rowland felt that at *Panorama* 'we failed considerably to report the festering difficulties of Northern Ireland...*Panorama* never focused on Northern Ireland as we should have done.'[47] *This Week* initially attempted to bypass political controversy by focusing on the effects of sectarian violence on communities ('What Was Lost, What Was Won?', 1969) and individuals ('Death in Belfast', 1970), though this became impractical after the events of 'Bloody Sunday' (30 January 1972) when 13 Irish civilians were killed when British troops opened fire believing protestors to be armed. *This Week* sent a crew to the Bogside, who remarkably were able to interview some of the troops involved. The announcement of a judicial enquiry meant that the material could not be edited into a report in the usual way, as this might be considered prejudicial: instead it was shown as unedited rolls of film complete with clapper board and out-takes to demonstrate there was no editorial intervention. David Glencross of the ITA felt that the programme 'was an original step forward in an area which is pretty well uncharted in television journalism'.[48]

Northern Ireland brought into sharp relief the mantra of 'objectivity' that informs the professional discourses of television journalism. There was an expectation in some quarters, including the government and right-wing media, that television should not represent the views of the 'enemy'. Lord Aylestone, the chairman of the ITA, said bluntly: 'As far as I'm concerned Britain is at war with the IRA in Ulster and the IRA will get no more coverage than the Nazis would have in the last war.'[49] The 1974 Prevention of Terrorism Act declared the IRA a proscribed organization, which effectively forbade any interviews with its members by the media. In the aftermath of the IRA's bombing campaign in mainland Britain in 1974–1975 there was understandably pressure on broadcasters to conform. Yet charges of bias persisted in the coverage of the British Army's role in Northern Ireland. There is evidence that some television journalists went against official mandates. In 1978 the Institute for the Study of Conflict, a right-wing think tank, questioned 'the political affiliations of those connected with the programmes' – referring specifically to *This Week* and *World in Action*.[50]

The presentation of Northern Ireland and the IRA caused an undercurrent of tension between television and the state for a quarter of a century. These tensions came to a head in 1988 with the controversial 'Death on the Rock' (*This Week*), which questioned the official account of the shooting of three IRA suspects by members of the Special Air Service (SAS) in Gibraltar. The programme combined a reconstruction of events leading up to the shooting and interviews with witnesses, who claimed that contrary to the official version the terrorist suspects had been shot without warning. The suggestion that what had taken place amounted, in effect, to an execution inevitably prompted outrage from the right-wing press: *The Sun* even accused Thames of peddling 'IRA propaganda'. Prime Minister Margaret Thatcher described her feelings as 'much deeper than being furious'.[51] Thames was so shaken by the backlash against the programme that it commissioned its own external enquiry by Lord Windlesham and Queen's Counsel Richard Rampton. The enquiry commended the 'thoroughness' of the research that had informed 'Death on the Rock' and concluded that the programme had acted as a 'lightning conductor...for intense feelings'.[52] Hence the furore was attributed to the wider political context rather than to any significant flaws in the programme itself.

The controversy over 'Death on the Rock' needs to be seen in the context of two decades of unresolved tensions between the television industry and successive governments over Northern Ireland. It also highlights important questions around the role of current-affairs television and its responsibilities. On the one hand the government and some elements of the press believed that television should tow the party line when it came to matters of national security: for the political right, the episode was taken as an indication of a perceived left-wing bias in the broadcast media. On the other hand the episode legitimates the role of television as an investigative medium: it was not afraid to ask questions that were in the public interest about the legality of actions by the security services and the nature of anti-terrorist policy. In this context, television's refusal to kowtow provides a counterweight to critics on the Marxist left who see the broadcast media as part of the ideological apparatus of the state.

Cathy Come Home (1966) and the documentary drama

Cathy Come Home has become such a canonical text for television studies that it would seem resistant to further analysis: surely all that can be said about it has been said? Yet on closer scrutiny the critical historiography of *Cathy Come Home* often rehearses (or re-rehearses) the same tensions apparent within the film itself.[53] On the one hand *Cathy Come Home* has been acclaimed as a landmark of television documentary: it was a hard-hitting agitational piece that had considerable social impact and contributed to a wider public debate around the issue of homelessness. To this extent it is sometimes placed in the same social-problem tradition of documentary as *Housing Problems* some 30 years before. On the other hand *Cathy Come Home* is also a seminal piece of television drama: it was produced as part of the acclaimed 'Wednesday Play' strand on BBC1 and its techniques of first-person narration and location filming are seen as bringing a new degree of realism to the single play. In almost every respect – ideologically, formally, aesthetically – *Cathy Come Home* is a perfect hybrid of the 'documentary' and 'drama' modes. It is for this reason, as much as for its impact at the time, that *Cathy Come Home* has become the focus of so much critical debate.

The production history of *Cathy Come Home* is well known. It was one of a series of plays produced under the umbrella of 'The Wednesday Play' – a new strand launched by the BBC Drama Group in 1964, characterized by its combination of social realism and formal innovation. 'The Wednesday Play' was the baby of Sydney Newman, Head of the BBC Drama Group in the mid-1960s. Newman was an outsider, a Canadian recruited to the BBC from the world of commercial television who saw drama as a vehicle for engaging with social issues, or what he termed 'agitational contemporaneity'.[54] He had pursued this agenda as Head of Drama at ABC, where he had produced the acclaimed *Armchair*

Theatre, which included social realist plays by writers such as Alun Owen
(*No Trams to Lime Street; Lena, O My Lena*). In its early years 'The Wednes-
day Play' became a showcase for work by new dramatists including
Dennis Potter (*Stand Up, Nigel Barton*), Nell Dunn (*Up the Junction*) and
David Mercer (*In Two Minds*). *Cathy Come Home* was written by Jeremy
Sandford, an Oxford graduate who had become a campaigner for the
homeless after moving from affluent Chelsea to working-class Battersea
in the late 1950s. Sandford's first outline of what would become *Cathy
Come Home* was submitted to the BBC in February 1964 but was turned
down as not its 'cup of tea'.[55] A second draft in 1965 was also rejected
on the grounds that it was 'documentary stuff' that would turn the
'Wednesday Play' slot into a 'political platform'.[56] It was finally accepted
by producer Tony Garnett in 1966. Garnett brought in Kenneth Loach,
who had cut his teeth directing episodes of *Z Cars* before moving to
'The Wednesday Play' where he had already made half a dozen films
before *Cathy Come Home*, including *Up the Junction* (1965), which had
aroused controversy for its harrowing scene of a young woman who
experiences a traumatic abortion. Loach recalled that he was introduced
to Sandford by Nell Dunn, the writer of *Up the Junction*, who was married to Sandford: 'I met him through her and he showed me a two-page
outline of *Cathy Come Home*. I remember reading it and being absolutely
bowled over by it. Tony and I were very eager to tell the story.'[57]

In institutional terms, therefore, *Cathy Come Home* originated with
the Drama Group rather than the Documentary Department. This
may explain why Sandford and Loach were afforded more leeway in
employing fictional elements than Ken Russell or Peter Watkins, another
documentary director whose film *The War Game* was censored by the
BBC in 1965.[58] It was during the filming, however, that a documentary
aesthetic emerged for *Cathy Come Home*. It was shot mostly outside the
studio, using locations in London and Birmingham, over a period of just
three weeks. A few scenes were shot in the studio due to an agreement
with the actor's union Equity: *Cathy Come Home* employed professional
actors led by Carol White as the eponymous Cathy and Ray Brooks as
her husband Reg. But Loach shot it in a *vérité* style using a hand-held 16
millimetre camera and portable sound recording. For the final scene at
Liverpool Street Station, where Cathy's children are forcibly removed by
social workers, Loach used a hidden camera in order to record the real
responses of passers-by:

> The key thing was to find a camera position that would give us good
> coverage of what was happening and wouldn't be seen by people

passing by. We gave Carol White a position with the two kids on the station seat and then let her sit there for a bit and found a way to cue the actors playing the social workers and the police to come over and take the children.[59]

Hence the effect of naturalism was achieved through artifice: in that sense *Cathy Come Home* is as much a constructed text as the studio-based drama documentaries. However, the fact that *Cathy Come Home* was shot on film imbues it with a very different aesthetic.

Cathy Come Home balances its dramatic and documentary elements so perfectly that it is difficult to separate the two in formal terms. On the one hand its status as fiction is asserted at the outset in a caption that describes it as 'A Story by Jeremy Sandford'. The play adopts the structure of a drama in the sense that it is narrative-based and character-led. *Cathy Come Home* is the story of a young woman who leaves home, marries and has three children: following her husband's accident the family become locked in a downward spiral of poverty that sees them evicted, living in a squat and a caravan, with Cathy finally ending up seeking refuge in an emergency hostel. In a sense this conforms to the structure of a classical tragedy, not least because Cathy becomes caught up in a process over which she has little control. The viewer's sympathy is directed towards Cathy as she is characterized as a basically decent person who is let down by social services as well as by her loving but feckless husband. Other devices of fictional drama include Cathy's voice-over narration and the prominence of personal spaces (flat, bedroom, caravan) rather than the public spaces of documentary. Yet the narrative is also fragmented and episodic: it is constructed in a linear pattern but elides events and compresses time more abruptly than in the 'classical' mode. And there is no sense of narrative resolution or closure: the film ends with a bleak scene in which Cathy's children are taken from her and she is left alone and homeless. There is no indication how this will be resolved: the film ends abruptly without suggesting what Cathy's fate will be.

On the other hand *Cathy Come Home* also asserts its status as documentary through a range of devices. The *vérité*-style camerawork reflects the observational documentary mode: Loach frequently shoots around objects in the foreground or through railings or trees as if his camera is spying on its subjects. The documentary element is further highlighted through other voice-overs besides Cathy's, which provide a mixture of factual information about the shortage of council housing ('In Birmingham there are 39,000 families on the waiting list, in

Leeds thirteen and a half thousand, Liverpool 19,000, Manchester nearly 15,000') and opinions about what should be done ('What's needed is a government that realizes this is a crisis – and treats it as such'). This technique grounds the drama in factual content as well as establishing that Cathy's individual story is representative of a more general experience. The scenes in which Cathy encounters officialdom – such as the building society manager who explains the problems of buying a house, and her interviews with social services – also take on a documentary aspect. Indeed they hark back to the staged dialogue scenes in films such as *Workers and Jobs* and *Today We Live*, where the role of the official is to explain the problem for the benefit of the audience. And finally the conclusion of *Cathy Come Home* anchors it firmly in the documentary mode, with captions asserting its basis in fact ('All the events in this film took place in Britain within the last eighteen months') and providing yet more statistics ('4,000 children are separated from their parents and taken into care every year because their parents are homeless. West Germany has built twice as many houses as Britain since the war').

The politics of *Cathy Come Home* reflect a progressive standpoint in the sense that Cathy's misfortune is presented not as a consequence of her own decisions but rather as the result of an underlying problem in housing provision. It is not the individual who is to blame but the system: *Cathy Come Home* constantly emphasizes the inadequacy of social services in responding to the needs of citizens. It has been suggested that *Cathy Come Home* is a critique of the welfare state: at one point a voice-over even describes the homeless as 'casualties of the welfare state – perhaps the worst casualties of all'. However, it seems clear that what is at stake is not the idea of the welfare state itself but rather its limitations. These limitations are ideological as much as economic: again, a voice-over explains that 'many social workers feel that all homeless families are problem families'. This is reflected in Cathy's encounters with offialdom throughout the film. Most of the officials – housing officers, social workers, hostel wardens, care assistants – are at best indifferent and at worst condescending towards Cathy. There is also a sense in which officialdom is presented not only as unable to help but even as contributing to the problem. The rigid enforcement of the 'women-only' policy in the hostel has the effect of breaking up the family: Cathy and Reg are at first separated institutionally and then narratively (as Cathy says: 'I feel he's drifting away').

The reception of *Cathy Come Home* has been well documented. It evidently made an impression on viewers when it was broadcast on BBC1 on 16 November 1966. Audience Research recorded an unprecedentedly high 'reaction index' of 78 among its viewing sample (the average for 'The Wednesday Play' strand in 1966 was 54) and reported that '*Cathy Come Home* made a deep impression on the vast majority as a very striking and disturbing documentary-style play, which highlighted the problem of homelessness in Britain today in such a way as to arouse intense feelings of pity and indignation'.[60] Such was its impact that *Cathy Come Home* was repeated eight weeks later on 11 January 1967: the repeat screening was seen by some 12 million viewers. It received extensive coverage in the press and mostly favourable reviews. For critics in the left-wing press such as Stewart Lane of the *Morning Star* – official mouthpiece of the Communist Party of Great Britain – it was a call to action: 'All of us in the Labour movement should do everything we can to ensure that Mr Sandford's campaign is successful, that the Government is compelled to apportion some of the money now being wasted on arms toward solving the problem of the homeless once and for all.'[61] The social import of *Cathy Come Home* was recognized across the political spectrum even by those who did not share its politics. Peter Black of the *Daily Mail* called it 'a poster play ... borrowing a good deal from the Communist Party line on housing' but nevertheless felt that 'the old Corp [*sic*] did a service. It should rightly sting us into uproar.'[62] However, a dissenting note was sounded by Philip Pursuer of the *Sunday Telegraph*, who disliked its 'communist' overtones and averred that 'I'm sure the play did a great deal of service to social education, but I am certain it did a terrible disservice to television drama'.[63]

The impact of *Cathy Come Home* extended beyond the immediate context of its reception in that it fed into a wider public debate about the homeless problem. *Cathy Come Home* has often been linked to the formation of the homeless charity Shelter, which was set up shortly after the play's first broadcast. This is not to say that Shelter was formed as a direct consequence of *Cathy Come Home* – the impetus behind the charity predated the play – though there is no doubt that *Cathy Come Home* came at precisely the right moment to help raise awareness of the homeless problem and to inform debate. Indeed, Shelter exploited the connection by running press advertisements coinciding with repeat screenings of *Cathy Come Home*, featuring pictures of Carol White and asking: 'Did you see Cathy last night?'[64] Loach has since looked to downplay the significance of the 'Cathy effect' by suggesting that it was short-lived and had no lasting impact: 'I remember that Anthony Greenwood, who was then minister of housing, asked to see us and told us how much he appreciated *Cathy*. We said, "Fine. But what are your plans to deal with homelessness?" And he ummed and ahhed and talked around it and obviously – nothing.'[65] To this extent the social impact of *Cathy Come Home* may be compared to *Housing Problems* some 30 years before: its influence was in raising awareness of the problem rather than in actively influencing policy.

The critical response to *Cathy Come Home* also ignited a lively debate around the documentary drama as a form. While reviewers were all united about its social significance, some questioned whether the documentary-drama mode was the best way of presenting such an important topic. Sylvia Clayton in the *Daily Telegraph*, for example, wrote: 'I should have preferred to see a problem of this magnitude treated as a full-scale documentary investigation rather than a tragic individual love story, but the suffering of decent, bewildered people was powerfully conveyed.'[66] Maurice Wiggin's review for the *Sunday Times* took the form of a dialogue between 'Better Self' and 'Worse Self' in which 'Worse Self' expressed preference for 'straight documentary' ('I'm uneasy about this hybrid form. It's an editing of actuality into some-thing that is neither precisely fact nor exactly fiction') while 'Better Self' reminded him that the form had been employed in literature ('Zola did it. And stuffy purists didn't like it *then*').[67] The most severe criti-cism came from Grace Wyndham Goldie, the recently retired Head of Talks and Current Affairs, who described *Cathy Come Home* as 'an early example of a new and dangerous trend in television drama'. Wyndham Goldie's objections were posited on the idea that while social advo-cacy might be acceptable in a fictional drama, it should not be allowed in documentary on the grounds that it might compromise the BBC's statutory requirement of objectivity. She argued that the hybrid form of *Cathy Come Home* blurred this distinction and that 'if you put advo-cacy into the semi-dramatic form of a semi-documentary it may in effect be by-passing the fundamental rules under which broadcasting organisations are permitted by society to exercise their privileges'.[68]

The debate over *Cathy Come Home* therefore rehearsed a wider debate in television over the role and status of the documentary-drama mode. It is a debate that continues in more recent critical assessments of the typicality of *Cathy Come Home* as a documentary drama. On the one hand Derek Paget sees it as representative of formal developments in the genre during the 1960s and calls it 'the prime example of second-phase documentary drama from British television's own "Golden Age"'.[69] This 'second phase' was characterized by shooting on location and in a 'filmic' style as opposed to the more televisual style (live, studio-based) of the 'first phase' of drama documentary in the 1950s. On the other hand, however, Stephen Lacey argues that *Cathy Come Home* is 'untypical in the ways in which it inserts documentary directly into the dramatic frame'.[70] Lacey's case is that the form and style of *Cathy Come Home* 'has not been widely imitated', including by either Jeremy Sandford, whose other notable success was *Edna, the Inebriate Woman* (1971), which did not employ the contextualizing documentary devices of *Cathy Come Home*, or Ken Loach, whose subsequent work in television, notably *Days of Hope* (1975), and film shifted more towards social-realist fiction.

Archival documentary: *The Great War* (1964) and *The World at War* (1973)

The historical documentary compiled from archival and actuality footage predates television, though it was on television that it achieved its most popular form. The archive compilation emerged on US television in the 1950s exemplified by 'event' series such as NBC's *Victory at Sea* and CBS's *Twentieth Century*. It can be seen as both ideologically and economically motivated: ideologically in the sense that at the height of the Cold War these series recounted major world events from the perspective of the United States, and economically in the sense that archive film was relatively inexpensive and could be used for the bulk of visual material. The first major British archival compilation was the BBC's *War in the Air* (1954), which was to some extent a riposte to the American-centred narrative of *Victory at Sea*. However, the benchmark for the archival compilation was set by two major documentary series – the BBC's *The Great War* and Thames Television's *The World at War* – which have never been surpassed in terms of either scale of production or popular appeal. Although the two have often been compared – with *The World at War* seen as a 'sequel' to *The Great War* in more ways than one – their institutional contexts and production histories were entirely separate.

Robert Dillon describes *The Great War* as 'a marriage of chance and opportunity'.[71] Its production was shaped by three contexts, which all came together at more or less the same time. The first context was that it marked the fiftieth anniversary of the war in 1914: it would not only be a major part of television's commemoration of the conflict but was also seen as representing a last opportunity to gather eye-witness testimony from the generation who had lived through the war. The second context for *The Great War* was the launch of BBC2 in 1964: the 'third channel' had been awarded to the BBC rather than ITV as it was felt that the BBC had a better record in the provision of educational and factual content.

The Great War could therefore be presented as a flagship for the launch of BBC2. The third context was that the Imperial War Museum offered a repository of archival film material that could be used for the series. To this extent the museum's co-operation was essential to the success of the project. Noble Frankland, the Director of the Imperial War Museum, agreed that the museum would provide film at a reduced cost in return for control 'over the quality of the programmes'.[72] *The Great War* was unprecedented in its scope, comprising 26 episodes, and represented an innovation in form as it combined archive footage with first-person accounts of veterans interviewed on camera. Michael Redgrave provided the linking commentary but otherwise the only 'voices' were those of participants: there were no academic 'talking heads'.

The production of *The World at War* was not an entirely happy process. Frankland soon came to the conclusion that 'the BBC, as represented by [series producer] Tony Essex, had less integrity than I had expected' and found that 'the quality control by the Museum, which I had made a condition in the agreement, was impossible to exercise'.[73] In particular, Frankland complained that archival film material – which included extracts from the official film *Battle of the Somme* – was used uncritically without distinguishing between actuality and reconstructed scenes. Frankland insisted that the BBC should issue a disclaimer at the start of each episode to the effect that some of the material was reconstructed: the caption states that it 'is used only when the reconstruction is so accurate as to be indistinguishable from the real thing, and when no genuine film exists'.[74] There were also tensions within the production team. The two main writers for *The Great War* were John Terraine, a journalist who had published a sympathetic biography of Sir Douglas Haig, and Correlli Barnett, a young military historian with a decidedly 'revisionist' interpretation of the First World War. Terraine and Barnett clashed with Sir Basil Liddell Hart, the distinguished military historian who acted as historical advisor for the series. Liddell Hart objected in particular to episodes on the Somme (episode 13) and Passchendaele (episode 17) and issued a public statement in which he declared that 'duty to history' had compelled him to resign from the series.[75]

For all these problems behind the scenes, however, *The Great War* was a popular and critical success. It was positively reviewed by most national newspapers and evidently made a significant impact on viewers. Audience Research found that most viewers thought it was 'brilliantly written and spoken... The film material, it appeared, could not have been better chosen... It was found surprising that so many contemporary photographs and films were available, and the quality was frequently noted as extremely good'.[76] The reception of *The Great War* seems not to have highlighted its 'revisionist' narrative of the Western Front – controversially for the time it had dared to suggest that the Battle of Somme marked the turning point of the war because despite the huge British losses it significantly eroded the strength of the German Army – but focused instead on the moving testimony of participants.[77] There was a conscious effort to present history 'from below' rather than the traditional sort of military history that focuses on commanders and campaigns. It also attempted to examine all aspects and theatres of war, though the fact that all the film material came from the Imperial War Museum meant that in the end it did lean towards an Anglocentric perspective. Nevertheless, Jeremy Isaacs felt that *The Great War* successfully refrained from 'the insouciant gung-ho of US series like *Victory at Sea*, or Jack le Vien's *Churchill: The Valiant Years*'.[78]

It was Isaacs who would produce *The World at War* – a series that surpassed even *The Great War* in its impact. *The World at War* was a sequel to *The Great War* only in terms of its content: its institutional context was entirely different as it was produced by one of the ITV contractors (Thames Television, where Isaacs was Head of Features in the early 1970s) and none of its writers or directors had worked on the previous epic. But like *The Great War*, *The World at War* came together through a combination of circumstances. There were three factors that determined its production for the ITV network rather than for the BBC (which had harboured plans to make a series about the Second World War since making *The Great War*). One was that in the early 1970s ITV was once again under pressure to prove its public service credentials, while the ITA now had the authority to require all regions to broadcast documentary and current-affairs programmes at the same time. Another factor was that Noble Frankland was reluctant to work again with the BBC following his experience with *The Great War* but had formed a good working relationship with Thames on a series about Earl Mountbatten of Burma, produced in 1968.[79] And the third factor was that in 1971 the new Conservative government reduced the levy paid by ITV contractors on their income from advertising. This move – which left the ITV companies unexpectedly cash-rich in the early 1970s – was intended 'to provide an opportunity for Independent Television to improve the quality of its programme service'.[80] According to Isaacs's account: 'The day after [Christopher] Chataway made his announcement, I went to Brian Tesler, the director of programmes at Thames, and put the idea to him.'[81]

The structure of *The World at War* was essentially the same as for *The Great War* – 26 episodes combining archive film and eye-witness interviews with a 'star' commentator in Sir Laurence Olivier – though overall the series was less Anglocentric than its predecessor. This was due in large measure to Frankland's role as chief historical advisor, who suggested that the original outline focused too much on the European theatre and had too little on the war in the Far East. Frankland also 'wanted it to be made clear that the land operations which decisively exhausted the German army were not in Africa, Italy or France, but in Russia'.[82] Unlike *The Great War*, most of the writers for *The World at War* were television journalists rather than professional historians – though specialist consultants were employed for some episodes, including Angus Calder (for the episode 'Home Fires' on the British home front) and Louis de Jong (for 'Occupation' on the wartime experiences of the Netherlands). Unlike Tony Essex, who had exercised control over all aspects of *The Great War*, Isaacs decided to 'allow the interests and preferences of different producers to be reflected in individual episodes of the series'.[83] The publicity for *The World at War* declared that the team of film researchers watched over 3.5 million feet of film: this almost certainly represents the most exhaustive job of film research ever undertaken for a television series.[84] Isaacs – no doubt bearing in mind Frankland's view of *The Great War* – impressed upon the production team the importance of absolute integrity in the use of archive film: 'I know all the difficulties, but it is important to remember that we are not making "poetic" films with a licence to use footage where we please. We are making an historic series and should not knowingly use pictures purporting to be what they are not.'[85]

The critical and popular reception of *The World at War* was even more positive than for *The Great War*. It was widely – and favourably – reviewed in the press, sometimes several times over the course of its six-month run, and regularly drew audiences of 8–10 million in a primetime Wednesday-evening slot on the ITV network. It received many public plaudits and was regarded by many historians as having 'set new standards for prodigious research and integrity of presentation'.[86] Yet *The World at War* also provoked some controversy, though in contrast to *The Great War* this was played out not within the production team but in the many letters of complaint directed to Thames and the Imperial War Museum (to be fair there were also many letters of praise for the series). These ranged from complains of omission (one correspondent demanded 'an apology or a public reference in your next programme' for the omission of one particular warship) and factual errors to charges of bias ('No where in the program did you give credit to General Patton and US forces') and even political propaganda (one viewer called it 'a

British propaganda film, it has obviously been carefully vetted by the Russians').[87] While some of these responses may seem hysterical in the extreme, what they reveal is the extent to which, even 30 years after the event, the Second World War was still a contested memory. And, overall, there is evidence of an ideological position: the overall narrative of *The World at War* is that war is a tragedy for all those involved, regardless of whether the cause is just. Researcher Susan McConachy averred that 'it was a very anti-war series'.[88]

The World at War became the yardstick against which other historical documentary series would be judged. It had a significant impact in legitimating the use of archive film in historical education and also helped to popularize oral history on television. Yet it was destined not to be repeated – at least not on the same scale. *The World at War* belonged to the period of limited competition when there were only three television channels in Britain and a historical documentary series could be shown across the full ITV network at a primetime slot on Wednesdays at 9 p.m. Moreover, the sheer scale of an undertaking such as *The World at War*, which finally cost around £1 million, became impossible after inflationary pressure later in the 1970s eroded television production budgets.[89] When Isaacs made *Cold War* in the 1990s it was for US media mogul Ted Turner rather than for the BBC or ITV, while the BBC could only afford to undertake the 26-part *People's Century* (1995–1996) – the last of the major archival compilation series – as a co-production with WGBH-TV Boston. Nevertheless, the influence of *The World at War* can be seen in the proliferation of television documentaries that have continued to mine the rich seam of archive film material of the Second World War (often, in fact, the same material as in *The World at War*) for cable broadcasters such as the History Channel as well as in occasional smaller 'event' series such as *The Nazis: A Warning from History* (BBC2, 1996) and *The War of the Century* (BBC2, 2000).

Observational documentary

The observational documentary – or what in the popular discourses of television came to be known as the 'fly-on-the-wall' documentary – has its origins in the Direct Cinema and *cinéma vérité* movements of the 1960s. The genre is particularly suited to television in two respects. First, the intimacy of television made the 'human' element more immediate: television allows a sense of closeness to the subjects that is different from cinema. Second, the episodic format of television allowed observational documentaries to follow individuals or institutions across a longer period of time than in a film: this allows more detail and moɪ Observational documentary divides commentators: for its sɪ can provide a valuable sociological experiment and insigʃ cultural politics of institutions (evident, for example, in Roger Graeɪs *Police*) while for its detractors it is often seen as little more than a soap opera (as seen in the response to Paul Watson's *The Family*).

The Family (BBC1, 1974) is often seen as the prototype 'fly-on-the-wall' television series though in fact it was inspired by a US series entitled *American Family* from 1972. Producer Paul Watson said that he 'wanted to make a film about the kind of people who never got on television'.[90] The subjects of the series were Terry and Margaret Wilkins, a working-class couple living with their children in a flat in Reading. Watson and his crew spent three months filming the Wilkinses for up to 18 hours a day: the footage was edited into 13 half-hour episodes. *The Family* was notable for its frank and candid representation of 'ordinary' people: the Wilkinses were vilified in some sections of the national press for their swearing and uncouth behaviour. (To this extent little has changed: a similar tabloid frenzy greeted the notorious 'White Dee' in Channel 4's *Benefits Street* in 2014.) However, *The Family* also reveals the constructed nature of the observational documentary in the sense that at times its subjects seem to be 'performing' themselves for the camera. It is not clear whether moments of insight such as Margaret's comment that 'no TV family ever has dirty pots and pans' is her own observation or something that has arisen through discussion with the documentary crew. *The Family* would become the model for other series, such as Desmond Wilcox's *The Marriage* (BBC1, 1986), and has been seen as the origin of the 'reality television' that emerged in the 1990s: indeed obituaries of Margaret Wilkins referred to her as the 'first lady of reality tv'.[91]

The charge that 'fly-on-the-wall' television is to all intents and purposes a soap opera may in part arise from the fact that series such as *The Family* focus on the personal spaces of home and family life rather than the public spaces traditionally associated with documentary. The late 1970s, however, saw the emergence of a cycle of observational documentaries on subjects such as the Royal Navy (*Sailor*, 1976) and the prison service (*Strangeways*, 1980). The focus of these series on institutions and professional groups rather than individuals locates them more securely within the historical lineage of British documentary practice. The most significant of these institutional fly-on-the-wall series was *Police* (BBC1, 1982) produced by the BBC's regional documentary unit in Bristol. Producer Roger Graef and his crew spent a year following Thames Valley Police's E Division based in Reading. *Police* had been supported by the Home Office, which was keen to restore public confidence in the force following the race riots in inner-city areas of London, Liverpool and Bristol in 1981. To some extent this backfired. The most commented-on episode of *Police* featured an allegation of rape made by a woman with a history of psychiatric illness. The male officers interviewing her are dismissive of her story in the extreme (one even refers to it as 'the biggest bollocks I've ever heard') and to all intents and purposes bully the woman into withdrawing the complaint. Here again the editing of the sequence – wherein the camera assumes the position of the victim (who remains unseen) and the police officers are shot in close-up while subjecting her to hostile questioning – demonstrates how aspects of form and technique can be applied to generate a particular effect even in a supposedly observational mode. 'A Complaint of Rape' prompted a public outrage and has been credited with changing the way in which the police deal with rape victims. Peter Fiddick, reviewing the episode for *The Guardian*, called it a 'uniquely valuable film' and felt that the documentary mode laid bare the police's attitude in 'a way that would scarcely have been credible in a dramatisation'.[92]

The 'fly-on-the-wall' format is popular with television commissioning editors because it is relatively cheap to produce and often generates a good deal of public attention. At its best it demonstrates television's ability to address social topics through the documentary form. Leo Regan's *100% White* (Channel 4, 2000), for example, winner of the BAFTA for Best Documentary, focused on three former members of a neo-Nazi gang. Regan's documentary adopts the *cinéma vérité* technique in which the film-maker interacts with his subjects by challenging their views on race and encouraging them to discuss their attitudes towards their friends and families. It also exemplifies a trend within television documentary in which the film-maker becomes as much the 'star' as the ostensible subjects. In Britain this is best exemplified in the series of interview-documentaries with celebrities by presenter Louis Theroux. It also became the hallmark of Nick Broomfield, a British documentarist who also worked in the United States during the 1980s. Broomfield developed a distinctive personal style in which his documentaries became films about the making of films, beginning with *Driving Me Crazy* (1988) and employed to hilarious effect in *Tracking Down Maggie* (1994), which follows his failed attempts to secure an interview with former British Prime Minister Margaret Thatcher during a tour of the United States.

Granada and the evolution of drama documentary

In Derek Paget's historical taxonomy of 'docudrama' on British and American television the 1970s are seen as a transitional period that sees a shift away from anthology series such as 'The Wednesday Play' towards the production of stand-alone 'event' programmes.[93] This process was influenced to some extent by the rise of the made-for-television film in the United States as the major networks started making their own 'movies' to make up for the shortage of new cinema films available for television broadcast. These television movies – which effectively displaced the single play – were often characterized by their engagement with social issues and their realist style. Hence the merger in formal terms between the American 'docudrama' and the British 'dramadoc'. In Britain this process is particularly associated with Granada Television, which led the way in the production of drama documentary for some three decades.

Granada's ideology has been categorized as one of 'populist radicalism': it sought to engage the public through topical and issues-led programming.[94] It had produced its first drama documentary (a reconstruction of the Great Train Robbery) in 1963 and even included dramatic reconstructions in its *World in Action*. However, the emergence of a distinctively 'Granada style' of drama documentary is generally attributed to producer Leslie Woodhead. An editor of *World in Action* in the late 1960s, Woodhead explained that he came to the drama-documentary mode as a practical solution to a particular subject:

> As a television journalist working on *World in Action*, I came across an important story, but found there was no way to tell it. The story was about a Soviet dissident imprisoned in a mental hospital. By its very nature, it was totally inaccessible by conventional documentary methods. But the dissident, General Grigorenko, had managed to smuggle out of mental prison a detailed diary of his experiences. As a result, it was possible to produce a valid dramatic reconstruction of what happened to Grigorenko.[95]

The Man Who Wouldn't Keep Quiet (1970) was the first of several historically based drama documentaries reconstructing events behind the Iron Curtain: these included films about the Cultural Revolution in China (*A Subject of Struggle*, 1972), the Polish Communist leader Edward Gierek (*Three Days in Szczecin*, 1976), the Soviet occupation of Czechoslovakia in 1968 (*Invasion*, 1980) and the rise of the Solidarity movement in

Poland (*Strike*, 1982). The content of these 'Iron Curtain' documentaries inevitably saw them positioned as political or campaigning films. But as they accorded with the ideological discourses of the Cold War, they were well received and seem not to have attracted the sort of criticism often directed at the drama-documentary mode for its resort to reconstruction.

The 'Iron Curtain' documentaries were drama documentaries (in the sense of being reconstructions of actual events) rather than documentary dramas in the style of *Cathy Come Home*. Woodhead took his responsibilities as producer-director seriously and laid down strict guidelines that came to be known as the 'Woodhead Doctrine'. He asserted that the aim of drama documentary should be 'to recreate as accurately as possible history as it happened. No invented characters, no invented names, no dramatic devices owing more to the writer's (or director's) creative imagination than to the implacable record of what actually happened'.[96] The Granada drama documentaries assert their status as fact rather than fiction through the use of authenticating documents such as Grigorenko's diary (*The Man Who Wouldn't Keep Quiet*) and trial transcripts (*A Subject of Struggle*). The subjects were thoroughly researched and efforts were made to cast actors who resembled the people they were playing. And the films employ authenticating devices such as captions and voice-overs explaining the sources and materials on which they are based. In the discourses of the television industry this marks a commitment not so much to 'truth' as to 'accuracy'. It was a mantra not to include anything that could not be substantiated in one way or another. Observing the production of *Strike* in 1982, Elizabeth Sussex averred that 'Woodhead's films now draw on so much unpublished and unassessed material as to make them not just authentic but authoritative documents'.[97] As evidence of this she cited the example of *Collision Course* (1979), a reconstruction of the events leading to a mid-air collision near Zagreb in 1976, based on the recorded transcripts of air traffic control that was reportedly used as evidence in an official inquiry.

Yet for all his commitment to a strict discourse of authenticity, Woodhead also saw drama documentary as a constantly evolving form: 'I think no two drama-documentaries are alike. They constantly reinvent the form ... Although they try to apply certain basic guide rules, no two of them are quite formally alike.'[98] Hence the relationship between dramatized and documentary elements is worked through in different ways in every drama documentary. This can be seen in the different forms of drama documentary in the 1980s by Granada and other producers. Antony Thomas's *Death of a Princess* (ATV, 1980) – about the execution of

a member of the Saudi royal family for adultery – is notorious for spark-
ing a diplomatic row between Britain and Saudi Arabia. Foreign Secretary
Lord Carrington, who was obliged to make a personal apology to the
Saudis, weighed into the drama-documentary debate when he declared
that 'the new formula of mixing fact with fiction, dramatization mas-
querading as documentary, can be dangerous and misleading'.[99] (This
might suggest that Carrington did not watch much television given that
the drama documentary was hardly a 'new formula': the debate over
'mixing fact with fiction' extended back at least as far as *Cathy Come
Home*.) However, the diplomatic storm over *Death of a Princess* has rather
obscured its innovations in form. Thomas's film dramatized not only the
execution but also his own investigation – his search for the 'truth' –
with Thomas playing a fictionalized version of himself in the character
of a film-maker called 'Christopher Ryder'. This self-reflexive technique
has the effect of problematizing the idea of documentary 'truth'. Paget
categorizes *Death of a Princess* as 'the televisual equivalent of modernist
"metatheatre" and "metafiction" (plays and novels that embed discussion of the making of theatre or fiction within their construction)'.[100]
Again, this was not a new idea: Ken Russell had employed it for *The
Debussy Film* in 1965.

   Death of a Princess also marked a new direction in its production
context in that it was a co-production between Britain's Associated
Television (ATV) and a consortium of overseas broadcasters: WGBH-TV
Boston, Telepictures (Holland), Seven Network (Australia) and Eastern
Media (New Zealand). Such co-production arrangements would become
increasingly common during the 1980s and 1990s. The advantages of
co-production were that it enabled the broadcasters concerned to share
costs (stand-alone drama documentaries are generally among the more
expensive television programmes) and guaranteed a wider audience.
At the same time, however, co-production also necessitates compromises
in order that the ideological demands of different partners can be met.
This is demonstrated in the collaboration between Granada and Home
Box Office (HBO). HBO is a subscription-based American cable broadcaster that specializes in more serious and challenging content than
the mainstream networks. The first Granada/HBO co-production was
Coded Hostile: The True Story of Flight 007 (1987) about the shooting-
down of a Korean airliner by US fighters in 1983. Woodhead described
it rather disparagingly as 'very ritzily made, high-profile actors, driving
score'.[101] The use of 'name' actors (in this case Michael Murphy and
Chris Sarandon) was a strategy of American docudramas – also exemplified by Jason Robards (*The Day After*, 1985) and Burt Lancaster (*Voyage*

of Terror: The Achille Lauro Affair, 1990) – though hitherto had tended to be less common in Britain where the preference had usually been for 'unknown' faces who did not bring the baggage of other roles and associations.

The Granada/HBO collaboration continued through a series of drama documentaries, including *Who Bombed Birmingham?* (1989) on the Birmingham pub bombings of 1974, *Why Lockerbie?* (1990) on the explosion of Pan Am Flight 103 in 1988, and *Hostages* (1992) on the kidnapping of Western journalists in Beirut. The influence of the American co-production partner has generally been understood as the reason for the shift towards more 'drama' than purely documentary elements in these films. For example, while the British version of *Why Lockerbie?* represented the crash as an image of an airliner disappearing from a radar screen, followed by a fade to graves in the Lockerbie churchyard and the victims' memorial service, the US partners considered this 'too muted' and, for the version shown in the United States, included shots of the carnage of the crash with burning houses and emergency services. Woodhead attributed this to cultural differences between the British and Americans: 'It's not a sleazy ending, just a different one, and was a very interesting difference of reading of what their audience wanted... [We] can cope with the interiorising of our feelings but they feel like they're being short-changed.'[102] The shifting balance towards drama is best demonstrated in *Hostages*, which focuses on the friendship that developed between John McCarthy and Brian Keenan and veers towards the formula of the 'buddy movie'. *Hostages* also cast name actors – including Colin Firth as McCarthy, Natasha Richardson as his girlfriend Jill Morrell, Ciaran Hinds as Keenan, Harry Dean Stanton as American hostage Frank Reed and Kathy Bates as Peggy Say – whose participation was made possible by HBO's involvement.

Hostages further raised one of the ethical issues involved in drama documentary: the extent to which the subjects themselves should be involved in the production. This is an important consideration for programme-makers where the participants are living or where the events are still quite recent. Granada and HBO went ahead with *Hostages* even though most of the former hostages themselves were opposed to the film and refused to participate. Their public explanation of objections was based yet again on the issue of fact versus fiction. Four of the hostages depicted in the film – McCarthy, Keenan, Terry Anderson and Terry Waite – challenged the claim that *Hostages* was a 'true story' by stating that 'the film contains scenes involving us that are pure fiction. Granada is grossly misleading the public by giving them the impression that they will see what actually happened.'[103] The producers blamed the adverse advance publicity for the disappointing audience ratings for *Hostages*.

British drama documentary has often been associated with campaigning issues: this is one reason for its identification as a progressive mode. *Hostages* had been conceived in 1990 with the aim of raising pressure on the British and American governments to do more to secure their release, but by the time it was made in 1992 all the hostages had been released: this might help to explain why in the end it emphasized the personal drama rather than the wider context. Jimmy McGovern's *Hillsborough* (Granada, 1996) – a dramatization of the tragedy of the FA Cup Semi-Final in 1989 that left 96 Liverpool fans dead, and its aftermath – was produced within the context of the campaign by survivors and relatives to reopen the inquest into their deaths. *Hillsborough* is an artfully crafted campaigning drama documentary that highlights the personal tragedy by focusing the narrative on selected families. Along with the use of 'talking head' interviews, with actors in character expressing their feelings about the effects of the tragedy, *Hillsborough* again shifts the balance of 'drama' and 'documentary' elements in favour of drama (personal, subjective) over documentary (public, objective). It makes a powerful case that the original verdict of 'accidental death' was flawed and that crucial evidence had been ignored. It was made with the full backing of the Hillsborough Family Support Group and – like *Cathy Come Home* some 30 years before – is credited with contributing to a changing climate of opinion around the tragedy: and to the extent that the newly elected Labour government in 1997 announced a new inquiry, it was successful in that regard. Similarly, two drama documentaries broadcast in the same week in 2002 – McGovern's *Sunday* (Channel 4) and Paul Greengrass's *Bloody Sunday* (Granada) – were produced to mark the thirtieth anniversary of the shootings in Derry. A judicial inquiry was already under way at the time and the two films were therefore made in the context of renewed interest in the incident. Like *Hillsborough* there is a campaigning or even agitational dimension to them: both films were concerned with exposing the 'cover up' by the army and discovering the 'truth', though in this case both the sequence of events and the role of various participants is more in dispute than Hillsborough. *Sunday* and *Bloody Sunday* were prepared in much the same way by scrutinizing official records and interviewing eyewitnesses, but their formal strategies are quite different. *Sunday* is a more coherent character-focused narrative, whereas *Bloody Sunday* is fragmented and frenzied: rapid ellipses, jump cuts, and shot with a shaky and often disorienting hand-held camera. *Bloody Sunday* had the greater impact – it was afforded a limited cinema release and provided Greengrass with a ticket to Hollywood where he would direct the 9/11 drama-documentary feature film *United 93* (2006) – though the more conventional *Sunday* is perhaps the better of the two films.

It would be fair to say that drama documentaries such as *Hillsborough* and the two 'Bloody Sunday' films are exceptional rather than representative of the genre: relatively few drama documentaries, in fact, are 'message' films. Indeed, for some commentators films like *Hillsborough* have been seen as marking an end-point of sorts for a specifically tele-visual style of drama documentary. The fact that *Bloody Sunday* was also released in cinemas, and the ease with which directors like Greengrass have shifted over to mainstream feature films, demonstrates the increasingly blurred boundaries between film and television. This process is also seen in the advent of digital cameras, which reduce the definitional differences between film and television. Another way of interpreting these developments, however, is to see them not as the end of drama documentary on television but as another phase in its evolution. For Paget, the 'fourth phase' of drama documentary since the end of the 1990s is characterized by hybridization and diversification as it adapts to changing contexts.[104]

Drama documentary's ability to adapt itself to changing institutional and ideological contexts was demonstrated again in 2004–2005 by a cycle of historical drama documentaries that marked the sixtieth anniversary of the last year of the Second World War. *Dunkirk* (BBC2, 2004), *D-Day* (BBC2, 2004), *When Hitler Invaded Britain* (Granada, 2004), *D-Day to Berlin* (BBC2, 2005) and *Blitz: London's Firestorm* (Channel 4, 2005) can be said to constitute a cycle, as although they were made by different hands they were all aired within a 20-month period.[105] They exemplify different production ecologies as well as representing innovations in form and technique. *D-Day*, *D-Day to Berlin*, *When Hitler Invaded Britain* and *Blitz* were co-productions with overseas partners: the £3 million *D-Day*, for example, included partners in Britain (the BBC), France (Telefrance), Germany (ProSeiben) and the United States (the Discovery Channel), with slightly different versions produced for each country. *D-Day to Berlin* was a co-production between the BBC and the History Channel. *Dunkirk* was the only one funded and produced wholly in-house as BBC commissioning editor Jane Root 'wanted to do something very British rather than a co-production'.[106]

The formal and aesthetic strategies of these drama documentaries demonstrate several innovations. As well as the usual mode of dramatic reconstruction they also include archive film and interviews with participants who are themselves represented in the films by actors. This has the effect of creating new meanings and associations between different elements. In contrast to the 'Woodhouse Doctrine' they do not distinguish between actuality and reconstruction, while some attempts have been made to 'improve' the footage. *D-Day*, for example, includes grainy colour shots of Lord Lovat leading ashore the 1st Special Service Commando Unit at Sword Beach: as the British Army Film and Photographic Unit did not have colour cameras these shots must have been either 'colourized' or reconstructed. *Dunkirk* illustrates how different elements may be combined within the formal system of the film. In one scene of the evacuation a conventional shot/reverse shot editing technique cuts between the crew of one of the 'little boats' looking at the beach and what they see: but here the point-of-view shot is monochrome actuality while the colour reaction shots are actors. Another innovation of these films is the incorporation of computer-generated imaging (CGI) in order to enhance the impression of realism. The reconstruction of Omaha Beach in *D-Day* includes CGI shots of ships and swarms of troops coming ashore. It also adopts the technique of Steven Spielberg's fictional feature film *Saving Private Ryan* (1998) in its use of a shaky hand-held camera splashed with water and sand to approximate the 'look' of actuality film – though as Toby Haggith has pointed out this effect is in fact very different from the efforts of combat cameramen who were trained to keep the camera steady.[107]

Finally, these films also offered a different narrative of the Second World War that distanced itself (if only partially) from the 'myth' of events such as Dunkirk and D-Day. *Dunkirk* endorses the familiar narrative of the evacuation as a 'miracle of deliverance' – its third and final episode is even entitled 'Deliverance' – though it also includes 'revisionist' moments that challenge the official version, for example in showing British officers shooting their own men in the back when they disobey an order to stand fast. A common feature of these films is the 'revelation' of incidents that were not made public at the time such as the massacre of British POWs by the SS at Remont (*Dunkirk*) and the deaths of American servicemen when a training exercise off the south coast of England was intercepted by a German E-boat (*D-Day*). *Blitz* is perhaps the most revisionist of the lot in that the commentary constantly calls into question the testimony of witnesses who aver to the spirit of stoicism and defiance. In fact *Blitz* seems quite consciously to be mobilizing the historical 'memory' of the Second World War for its own ideological ends. For example, it presents the German air raids on London in 1940 as retaliation for British bombing raids on Germany ('When Munich was fire-bombed, Coventry was the answer'), which is a contentious claim to say the least. Is it entirely too fanciful to suggest that the horror it repeatedly expresses at the bombing of civilians (also including references to Dresden, Hiroshima and Nagasaki) might have been a response to the US military's campaign of 'shock and awe' during the invasion of Iraq in 2003?

Continuity and change: Television documentary since the 1990s

The 1990s saw the most far-reaching changes to the ideological and institutional structures of British television since the introduction of the ITV network in 1955. The advent of cable and satellite services (the latter in the form of BSkyB – a merger between two companies: Sky and British Satellite Broadcasting) signalled the end of the era of limited competition and the BBC/ITV duopoly. The Broadcasting Act of 1990 implemented the Thatcherite principles of deregulation and competition into the television industry. Hence the existing regulatory body, the Independent Broadcasting Authority, was abolished and replaced with a new 'light touch' regulator known as the Independent Television Commission; the regulator's authority to mandate certain types of programme was removed; Channel 4 was to sell its own advertising; and the next round of franchise allocations for ITV would be through an auction with the franchises awarded to the highest bidder.[108] It was believed in some quarters that the Broadcasting Act was a response to those ITV companies such as Thames (which would lose its franchise in 1992) that had challenged the government with programmes such as 'Death on the Rock': one of its clauses was to remove the requirement to include primetime current-affairs programming. In fact there is no evidence to substantiate this, and the Broadcasting Act was entirely consistent with the policies of the Thatcher government. Nevertheless, the consequences for British television – and for the place of documentary within it – were profound.

Since the 1990s the terrestrial broadcasters have been operating within a framework of increased competition and tighter budgets. The pursuit of ratings now became the primary consideration: the traditional public-service ethos of British television had been significantly weakened by the new regimes. One of the consequences of this was the decline of current-affairs television. *This Week*, which had seen its ratings decline in the early 1990s, did not survive the demise of Thames Television: the new franchise holder Carlton had little interest in social matters and replaced it with *The Good Sex Guide*.[109] *World in Action* lasted until 1998 when it was replaced by a more populist topical programme built around a well-known presenter (*Tonight With Trevor McDonald*). Its last major coup was an exposé of the perjury and corruption of Cabinet minister Jonathan Aitken ('Jonathan of Arabia'). The old warhorse *Panorama* is now the last man standing of the triumvirate of major current-affairs series. The squeeze on budgets effectively brought an end to the big 'event' documentary series after the BBC's *People's Century*. And documentary did not fare any better on the new satellite and cable channels. The subscription revenue for sports and movie channels enabled broadcasters such as Sky to offer more specialist channels catering for niche audiences: documentary was one of those. Hence documentary was moved over to ghettos such as the Discovery Channel and the History Channel: the former offering a diet of cheaply made 'reality' subjects, the latter apparently subsisting on repeats of *The World at War*.

In these new institutional conditions it was not long before practitioners and critics alike were speaking of a 'crisis' in British television documentary. Caroline Dover has argued that television documentarists have always seen themselves as a professional community who share common working practices and ideological assumptions. In the 1990s this community felt that a combination of economic retrenchment and a new populism not only challenged the prevailing public-service ethos of television documentary but also threatened to undermine the very principles on which it was based. Two developments in particular – several exposés of documentary 'fakes' (which began with revelations about an ITV investigative programme called *The Connection* about the Colombian drugs trade, which included fabricated scenes) and the rise of what came to be known as the 'docusoap' – focused public attention as never before on the value of documentary and its role in public service broadcasting.[110]

Yet – and in line with the mantra that new challenges also create new opportunities – the imperatives of chasing ratings and cutting costs also created the conditions in which new forms of television documentary could emerge. Writing in 1996, John Corner noted that the new conditions 'threaten to reduce the presence of documentary within broadcast schedules and to modify programming by the requirements of "lightness" and "watchability"'. But he also identified positive trends in that 'it is apparent that, in Britain certainly, documentary work is showing a vigorous re-imagining of both its visual and verbal language'.[111] Corner identified three new forms – the 'emergency services' documentary (*999, Blues and Twos*), the 'do-it-yourself' documentary (*Video Diaries*) and the 'undercover' *vérité* documentary (*Disguises, Undercover Britain*) – as evidence of innovation in documentary practice.[112] Of course it is necessary to issue the regulation caution that 'new' does not necessarily equate to important or even good: but nevertheless the emergence of these new forms and styles can be seen as further evidence of the flexibility and endurability of the documentary form.

The emergence of the 'do-it-yourself' documentary was perhaps the most significant innovation of the 1990s. *Video Diaries* (1990–1992) and its successor *Video Nation* (1993–1997) emerged from the BBC's Community Programmes Unit, which had a long tradition of producing 'access' television, but the format – based on camcorder footage shot by 'amateur' documentarists – was particularly suited to the conditions of the 1990s when a combination of technological developments (small portable video cameras) and economic restraints (it was very cheap to produce) provided the ideal context for this type of programme. The *Video Diaries* format represents a form of documentary 'from below' as the participants choose the subjects. It might also be seen as linking back to the social-anthropological tradition of Mass-Observation, which of course had a close association with the documentary movement in the 1930s through Humphrey Jennings. The 'diaries' themselves were often a mix of *vérité*-style footage and *vox populi* as participants spoke to the camera. As an experiment in 'democratic' programme-making *Video Diaries* proved so popular when shown on BBC2 – usually before the *Newsnight* current-affairs discussion programme at 10.30 p.m. – that in the end over 1,300 'diaries' were broadcast. The BBC saw the series as a means of engaging those who felt they were often misrepresented on television. According to co-producer Mandy Rose:

> A fundamental aim of the project was to make a space where people from such groups could represent themselves, on their own terms. One of *Video Nation*'s starting points is that to humanise difference is a critical function for the media in a mass society. We were surprised however and then nonplussed by just how many people said that they felt their lifestyle or community was not currently reflected. Gays, single mothers – sure, but Christians and Pagans, and housewives in Cheshire and bikers and bankers – everyone seemed to feel it.[113]

The production discourses of *Video Nation* therefore position it as a reflection of the social beliefs and attitudes of a multicultural and multifaith Britain. This is probably true enough with the caveat that a process of selection has taken place to find the participants: the BBC's own account suggests that it chose one from approximately every 50 applications. *Video Nation* ran until the late 1990s when the format was rendered redundant by the expansion of the Internet and the advent of video-sharing websites such as YouTube. Henceforth it was the Internet that became the natural home of the 'do-it-yourself' documentary.

The reduction of budgets for historical documentary and the consequent eclipse of the big archival compilation series – it would be almost impossible to mount a series on the scale of *The World at War* today – has obliged programme-makers to find new ways of bringing the past alive for the audience. One strategy was represented by *The Second World War in Colour* (Carlton, 1999), an expensive series that in a sense bucked the trend in television historical documentary – though it was still only three episodes in contrast to the 26 parts of *The World at War*. This was partly an attempt to lure the interest of younger viewers who were perceived to be deterred by black and white images. It was successful enough to prompt a short-lived cycle of 'colour' archive documentaries – albeit often involving the digital 'colourization' of monochrome material as the available colour film was quickly exhausted.[114] Another strategy – and a more economical one – was the revival of the presenter-led 'talks'-type documentary based around a charismatic expert such as Richard Holmes (*War Walks, Battlefields*). This form has also employed non-historians to front history programmes, particularly television comedians such as Tony Robinson (*Tony Robinson's Romans, Tony Robinson's Titanic Adventure*) and Rory McGrath (*History Quest, Bloody Britain*). For its critics this format is seen as an example of the 'dumbing down' of television history programming; for others it is dressed up as a genuine attempt to engage younger viewers in the past.

Another distinctive development in television documentary during the 1990s was the emergence of new hybrid forms as documentary elements were combined with other genres. The most popular of these hybrids was the 'docusoap'. This was a hybrid of documentary and soap opera that adopted a *vérité*-style observational mode to follow individuals or groups in their working or domestic lives. Its mode of address crossed from the traditional public space of documentary into the personal space of the soap opera. The docusoap was not an entirely new phenomenon – it might be argued that it can be traced back to a series like *The Family* – though it proliferated in the 1990s. One of the reasons for its emergence was technological: shooting and editing on video rather than 16 millimetre film enabled the programmes to be made faster and cheaper. The arrival of the docusoap was signalled by an Australian import (*Sylvania Waters*) shown by the BBC in the early 1990s but home-grown versions followed such as *The Living Soap* (BBC2, 1993–1994), which followed the lives of six students in a rented house in Manchester. The most successful British docusoaps, however, tended to focus on institutions and workplaces: examples included *Children's Hospital* (BBC1, 1993–2000), *Airport* (BBC1, 1996–2008) and *Airline* (ITV, 1998–2006). Docusoaps were favoured by television commissioners because they were low-cost and popular with viewers: the examples cited above were shown in primetime slots and often drew audiences of eight million. They sometimes made unlikely celebrities of 'stars' such as Maureen Patton of *Driving School* (BBC1, 1997), whose incompetence behind the wheel earned her the deserved reputation of Britain's worst driver. Docusoaps are disparaged by critics but broadcasters defend them on the grounds that they have reinvigorated interest in factual television.[115]

From the artificially constructed environment of *The Living Soap* – for which the BBC bought a house and 'cast' the students – it was only a short step to so-called 'reality TV' formats such as *The 1940s House* (Channel 4, 2001) and *The Trench* (BBC2, 2002), which attempted to re-create the conditions of the past for modern audiences. It would probably be fair to say that *The 1940s House* was more successful in this regard than *The Trench*, whose authenticity was severely compromised by the producers' inability to subject the participants to real machine-gunning or gas attacks. Again it was not an entirely new development – precursors included *Living in the Past* (BBC1, 1978) – but it proliferated in the 2000s. Perhaps the best that one can say of most 'reality TV' is that it almost legitimates the docusoap as a serious genre! The most successful of all 'reality TV' was *Big Brother*, which began in 2001 and was seen by many critics as sure evidence of the 'dumbing down' of Channel 4 in the era of competition. The popularity of *Big Brother* is inexplicable to any sane person: no doubt it represents a sociological phenomenon of some sort though it has little connection to documentary as it is generally understood.

However, the emergence of new documentary forms has not totally eclipsed existing and traditional forms. The persistence of the contemporary drama documentary is illustrated by the television plays of Peter Morgan and Peter Kapinsky. Morgan wrote *The Deal* (2003) – about the alleged secret pact in which Tony Blair supposedly agreed to stand down as Prime Minister after two terms in favour of Gordon Brown – and *Longford* (2006), about the veteran prison reform campaigner and his attempts to secure the release of child murderer Myra Hindley. Kapinsky wrote and directed *The Government Inspector* (2005) dramatizing the life of Dr David Kelly, whose suicide in 2003 first called into question the British government's claims about Iraq's possession of weapons of mass destruction. These examples demonstrate yet again the constantly evolving nature of the drama-documentary mode: it would be fair to say that the balance has shifted decisively in favour of drama. Yet the topical subject matter and political interest of these films is in the best tradition of drama documentary.

The BBC's most prestigious documentaries in the 1990s and 2000s are the unmatched series of natural history programmes presented by David Attenborough, including *Life in the Freezer* (1993), *The Private Life of Plants* (1995), *The Life of Birds* (1998), *The Blue Planet* (2001) and *Planet Earth* (2006). These can be seen as continuing the tradition established by the ground-breaking *Life on Earth* (1979) and *The Living Planet* (1984) and even represent a link back to the early history of British documentary in *Secrets of Nature*. The persistence of the natural history documentary illustrates how new technologies – including infrared cameras, digital shooting and High Definition – can enhance a genre without fundamentally affecting its basic form and style. The 'Life' series has become one of the BBC's biggest 'global brands' – alongside *Top Gear* and *Doctor Who* – and it is significant that at a time when most of the BBC's factual content has been relegated to its digital channels these programmes are still afforded a primetime slot on BBC1.

Another example of continuity with the past is represented by the *7 Up* series, which by any standards must be considered one of the most innovative experiments in the history of documentary film-making. Betsy McLane suggests that '[it] would be foolish to understate the importance of "Up" in the evolution of documentary, especially on television, since the series presents a sublime example of matching distribution with both form and content'.[116] The first '7 Up' in 1964 was an episode of *World in Action*, which featured interviews with a group of seven-year-old children recording their views on subjects such as home and school and their ambitions for the future. It was intended as an experiment in social or ethnographic documentary and the participants were chosen to be representative of different social classes. '7 Up' was posited on an explicit assumption that each child's social class would determine their future life and career. As the commentary explained: 'Why do we bring these children together? Because we want to get a glimpse of England in the year 2000. The shop steward and the executive of the year 2000 are now seven years old.' It was originally intended as a one-off but it became a long-term project as the programme-makers would return to the same children (at least those who wished to continue their association with the project: most have done so) at seven-yearly intervals to document their growth into adulthood and their various life experiences. Hence there have been further episodes in 1970, 1977, 1984, 1991, 1998, 2005 and 2012. The first '7 Up' was directed by Paul Almond, whereafter the series has been steered by Michael Apted, a researcher for the first instalment who helped to choose the participants. *7 Up* has become one of documentary television's most anticipated events: it combines the drama of personal narratives with the wider tapestry of social change in Britain over half a century. And it also illustrates the changing nature of documentary itself. It may be claimed retrospectively as a forerunner of 'reality television': indeed it might indicate greater sociological potential for this much-derided genre. One reviewer of the 2012 episode '56 Up', for example, described it as 'reality television as it ought to be'.[117] *7 Up* has won numerous international awards and the format has been adopted by broadcasters in other countries including the United States, Canada, France, Germany, Sweden, Japan, Australia and the Soviet Union (where it is called *Born in the USSR*). And – although the methodology of such things is, to say the least, dubious – *7 Up* topped the audience poll of Channel 4's programme *The 50 Greatest Documentaries* in 2011.[118]

7 Up – and other examples discussed in this chapter – demonstrate the truth of Duncan Ross's claim that documentary was 'perfectly at home in television'. The most striking point of the history of British television documentary is the sheer diversity of the form in its small-screen incarnation. It has both built upon and expanded the conventions of documentary film. While on the one hand television has readily assimilated narrative forms, including both the documentary drama (*Cathy Come Home*) and the drama documentary (*Hillsborough*), it has also branched out in new directions with the current-affairs documentary (*Panorama*, *World in Action*) and the sociological documentary (*7 Up*) that have no precise equivalents in film. If this demonstrates anything, it surely has to be the flexibility of the television medium: the case could reasonably be made that television has enabled more innovation in documentary practice than film. Indeed it might be that it was only by its move onto television that British documentary could finally break with the Griersonian orthodoxy that had so long prevailed. And, finally, it was on television rather than in the cinemas that documentary finally reached a mass audience. The audiences for series such as *The World at*

War and the sustained public interest in the *7 Up* series demonstrate that the British public are not resistant to documentary, as cinema exhibitors had for so long maintained. And while these are exceptional rather than run-of-the-mill examples, the longevity and durability of other forms of documentary would suggest that there is a general audience for documentary that had only rarely been reached in the cinemas. Perhaps it is just that television has proved more successful in delivering the kind of documentaries that its audiences wanted.

6
Alternative and Oppositional Documentary

It is just over three years since we presented our first FREE CINEMA programme at the National Film Theatre – as a 'Challenge to Orthodoxy'. It made something of a stir. We were called 'White Hopes'... 'Rebels'... 'A Serious venture of enormous promise'... Audiences were large and enthusiastic. And, largely as a result of this favourable response, the thing became a movement. Now this is the sixth of these programmes. It is also the last. We have decided that this movement, under this name, has served its purpose. So this is the last FREE CINEMA...

FREE CINEMA is dead. Long live FREE CINEMA!

Free Cinema 6 manifesto[1]

While all documentary may be considered an alternative mode of film practice, in the sense that it asserts its difference – formally, institutionally, ideologically – from the fiction film, there also exists within documentary a 'tradition of independence' that runs alongside, and sometimes in opposition to, the mainstream of the movement.[2] In Britain this alternative tradition has taken various forms, including the left-wing political film-makers of the 1930s for whom documentary was a means of promoting causes such as disarmament (*People of Britain*) and addressing topical subjects absent from the newsreels such as the Spanish Civil War (*Behind the Spanish Lines, Spanish ABC*), the Free Cinema movement of the 1950s with its polemical declaration of independence both from the British commercial cinema of the time and from the Griersonian orthodoxy of documentary, the work of the Cinema Action group in the 1970s with its agitprop 'people's films' on behalf of marginalized groups such as council tenants (*Not a*

216

Penny On the Rent), the homeless (*Squatters*), students (*Hands Off Student Unions!*) and strikers (*Arise Ye Workers*), and in the emergence of the film workshop and collective movement during the 1970s and 1980s exemplified by organizations such as Amber Films, the London Women's Film Group and the Black Audio Film Collective. The alternative tradition also includes idiosyncratic individual film-makers such as Peter Watkins, whose radical approach to documentary drama challenged the orthodoxy of institutional practice in British television. To group all these movements and film-makers together is not to suggest that they constitute a linear or coherent history of alternative film practice in Britain. Quite the contrary: they encompass a wide range of formal and ideological strategies and all have their own unique characteristics. Nevertheless, they all saw themselves as being outside the mainstream of the documentary movement and consciously positioned themselves as alternative or oppositional voices.

Political documentary in the 1930s

The first alternative documentary practice in Britain can be seen in the emergence of a strand of political film-making associated with left-wing activism in the 1930s. The context for this movement was the interest taken in film by the Labour movement – encompassing the trade unions and co-operative societies as well as the socialist political parties.[3] Two factors lay behind the Labour movement's interest in the medium. One was propagandistic: to use film for promoting social and political awareness among the working classes. But there was also a recognition that film had become an integral part of working-class popular culture and that it could play an important role in the provision of leisure and recreational activities. Yet there were two major obstacles to these objectives. One was that working-class audiences by and large preferred the escapist fare of the commercial cinema over the more educational and political films sponsored by the Labour movement. The other was that the commercial film industry was so overhwhelmingly wedded to capitalist interests that there was little scope for the promotion of a socialist perspective through the cinemas. Therefore, if the political left was to use film for its own ends, political or cultural, it would need to establish its own production and distribution networks. As Paul Rotha told the Labour Party Conference in 1936: 'In its own interests, in the interests of the working class of Great Britain, I suggest that the situation is such that it is imperative for Labour to organise its propaganda without delay and to make use of the most modern and effective instrument.'[4]

There was always an association between the documentary movement and the Labour movement – many documentarists were politically
left-wing and some (such as Ralph Bond) were involved in political
activism – but the documentary films of the 1930s, including both the
GPO Film Unit and the independent documentary movement, were
largely apolitical even when they dealt with social issues such as *Housing Problems*. Hence the political films of the 1930s tend to be seen as
outside the mainstream of the documentary movement – even those
made by documentarists such as Rotha's *People of Britain* and Bond's
Advance Democracy![5] The mainstream of the documentary movement
was politically and socially progressive but advocated reform through
the existing political system and institutions. In contrast, left-wing film
groups sought to bring about fundamental and far-reaching change in
society. Unlike the mainstream documentary movement they actively
opposed the National Government and its policies. As the first newslet-
ter of the left-wing distributor-producer Kino Films asserted in 1935:
'The election is still fresh in our minds… We cannot doubt that if the
electorate had been convinced that the National Government stands for
reaction and against progress, this Government would have suffered an
overwhelming defeat at the polls.'[6]

To this extent political documentary may be seen as an alternative
to the commercial newsreels that in the 1930s were closely tied to the
policies of the National Government. There were five major newsreel
companies in the 1930s – British Movietone, British Pathé, Gaumont-
British News, Paramount and Universal – but, despite fierce competition
between them to be first with the news, they all shared a broadly conservative outlook in matters social and political. It has since become known
that there existed close personal links between the newsreels and the
National Government. In 1938, for example, Sir Joseph Ball, Director
of the Conservative Research Department, confided in Prime Minister
Neville Chamberlain that he was on good terms with the chairmen of
the newsreel companies and 'could count upon most of them for their
full support to any reasonable degree'.[7] Hence the editorial policies of
the newsreels reflected the government's view in relation to contentious
domestic issues such as strikes and demonstrations – typically presented
as mob violence rather than as expressions of political dissent – and
unequivocally supported its foreign policy.[8]

However, early efforts to develop a distinctively left-wing film culture in Britain were piecemeal and uncoordinated. This can be seen in
the proliferation of organizations and societies – including the Federation of Workers' Film Societies (FWFS), the Workers' Film and Photo

League, Kino Films, the Progressive Film Institute and the Workers' Film Association – and in the ideological differences that emerged between the Labour Party and the more radical left. In the beginning the main effort of the workers' film movement was directed towards securing screenings of Soviet films such as *Strike, Battleship Potemkin* and *The End of St Petersburg*. The revolutionary classics were banned from public exhibition by the British Board of Film Censors but could be shown privately at film clubs under special licence from local authorities. In 1930 the FWFS ventured into film-making with *Workers' Topical News*, a silent newsreel covering events such as the 'hunger marches' that were largely left out of the commercial newsreels. The most important of the left-wing film organizations of the 1930s were Kino Films, an offshoot of the Workers' Theatre Movement set up in 1934, and the Progressive Film Institute, established in 1935 by Ivor Montagu, an aristocratic socialist who had been one of the founding members of the Film Society. The main activities of Kino and the Progressive Film Institute were in distribution, but they both ventured into production of documentary films towards the end of the decade. The practice of screening films at film clubs and societies enabled the workers' film movement to bypass censorship but at the same time meant that audiences were often quite small. The Labour Party, which was suspicious of the communist influence behind some of these groups, maintained a distance from them and set up its own organization (the Workers' Film Association) in 1938.[9]

The political documentary films of the 1930s reflect the preoccupations of the British left at the time. On the one hand there is a strong investment in domestic social and political affairs: many of the films set out to promote political awareness among the working classes and to mobilize them against the prevailing political and economic orthodoxy. On the other hand there is a broadly internationalist theme expressed through opposition to Fascism and in support for the principle of collective security through the League of Nations. The films themselves range from short silent films of marches and demonstrations (the FWFS's *Against Imperialist War – May Day 1932* is a fairly representative example of this) to professionally produced sound films intended for theatrical exhibition, such as the Spanish Civil War films sponsored by the Progressive Film Institute. Rather than attempting a survey of the whole field of political documentary this section will instead focus on five films that exemplify the range of subject matter and styles: *People of Britain, Advance Democracy!, Behind the Spanish Lines, Spanish ABC* and *Peace and Plenty*.

People of Britain (1936) – sometimes also known as *Peace of Britain* or simply just as *The Peace Film* – was a three-minute short opposing the National Government's rearmament programme. The initiative came from Rotha and fellow documentarists:

> One afternoon in March 1936, two or three of us at Strand Films were looking down from the third-floor windows at the newspaper placards outside Frascarti's Restaurant in Oxford Street. They shouted BRITAIN TO REARM. One of us said (I don't remember who), 'Why the hell are we making films if we don't do something about urging people to demand peace by collective security?' It had an electrifying result. Within a few minutes we agreed to make a very short film (so it could be slotted into any cinema schedule without due interference) to be shown free as widely as possible asking the audience to write to their MP to support the policy of collective security at the League of Nations. All work on the film would be voluntary; money would only be needed for film stock, cost of laboratory processing, sound recording and copies of the finished film.[10]

Rotha estimated the cost of making the film at £250 and raised this through private donations from individuals, including Labour MP Sir Stafford Cripps. Among those involved in making the film were Ruby Grierson and composer Benjamin Britten.

People of Britain is a strident call for peace and collective security. It highlights the cost of armaments (stating this to be £2,000 million a year or £260 per second) and makes an implicit criticism of the government for spending money on arms when 'one tenth of our people are near starvation'. It employs a technique from *Housing Problems* with four people who speak directly to camera expressing their opposition to war and support for the League of Nations. It concludes with a call to direct action: 'Demand peace by reason. Write to your MP. Demand peace.' *People of Britain* may be seen as an alternative voice to newsreels such as 'Is there to be an armaments race?' (British Movietone, 7 March 1935), 'Where stands peace?' (Paramount, 16 November 1936) and 'Britain's rearmament plan' (Gaumont-British, 18 February 1937), which sought to mobilize public opinion in support of rearmament by presenting it as a necessary response to the aggressive foreign policies of Italy and Germany, and linking it to jobs. The film may also be understood in the context of a pacifist mood that had emerged in Britain in the mid-1930s and that can be seen, variously, in the election of independent candidate John Wilmott in the East Fulham by-election of 1933, campaigning on a disarmament platform, the formation of the Peace Pledge Union in

1934, and the ten million signatories of the 'Peace Ballot' calling for a reduction of armaments in 1935.

People of Britain also threw into sharp relief the role of film censorship. As it was intended for public exhibition the film was submitted to the British Board of Film Censors (BBFC), which initially declined to issue a certificate. The BBFC maintained that the reason was legal rather than political in that the film included a brief shot of tanks, which the board thought might have been under the copyright of the War Office.[11] The film was shown to the press on 7 April 1936 and the following day several papers, including the *News Chronicle*, *Daily Herald* and *The Manchester Guardian*, ran news items and editorials criticizing the BBFC's decision. The board then announced that it had passed the film uncut with a 'U' certificate. Lord Tyrrell, the President of the BBFC, denied that the decision had been in response to external pressure, stating that 'the certificate was issued for the film the day before the attacks were made in the Press'.[12] Rotha refuted this and averred that the producers were not informed that the film had been passed until the afternoon of 8 April.[13] The controversy did the film no harm: *People of Britain* was reported to have been shown in 570 cinemas, including the showcase London Pavilion in Picadilly Circus, and was seen by an estimated 4.3 million people.[14]

Advance Democracy! (1938) was written and directed by Ralph Bond for the London Co-operative Society. The Co-operative movement had a history of sponsoring films in order to publicize its trading activities extending back to the 1920s, but it was not until the late 1930s that it embraced political film-making. This was due in large measure to the influence of Joseph Reeves, a Labour Party activist who served as secretary of both the Co-operative Film Committee and the Workers' Film Association.[15] In formal terms *Advance Democracy!* is a hybrid between the story documentary – using actors from the Unity Theatre, a socialist drama collective – and a library compilation. Benjamin Britten again provided the music, which incoporates traditional anthems of the Labour movement such as 'The Red Flag' and the 'Internationale', performed by the Norbury Co-operative Choral Society. It was registered for British quota under the Cinematograph Films Act of 1938 with the Progressive Film Institute as distributor, though it is unclear whether the film was ever shown theatrically.

Advance Democracy! belongs squarely within a classic tradition of left-wing politics highlighting the gulf between rich and poor:

There are a million people living in London. Some of them have a very comfortable time staying at the best hotels and eating at the best restaurants … [But] The great majority of London's citizens must watch every penny, shop as economically as they can, and eat as cheaply as possible.

The film follows dockworker Bert (Fred Baker) and his wife May (Kathleen Gibbons). Initially Bert is politically apathetic but his attention is piqued by a radio broadcast by Co-operative MP A. V. Alexander, who talks about the suppression of early trade unionism (the Tolpuddle Martyrs) and the founding of the Co-operative movement by the Rochdale Pioneers. The broadcast concludes with a call to action ('The Co-operative movement will play its part in defence of peace, freedom and democracy – will you?') that prompts Bert to join the forthcoming London May Day Parade. *Advance Democracy!* concludes with a reconstruction of the 1938 parade, which explicitly links the defence of workers' rights to opposition to Fascism: stock shots of Hitler, Mussolini and Franco are juxtaposed with shots of demonstrators carrying placards declaring 'Irish Republicans greet Spanish Republicans – Smash *All* Imperialisms'. *Advance Democracy!* therefore associates itself with the politics of the Popular Front – the alliance of left-wing political parties in Europe united in their opposition to Fascism – and asserts the idea of an international socialist brotherhood through pictures of Clement Attlee alongside Stalin and the French socialist Prime Minister Léon Blum. It is a radical call for action: more radical than the Labour Party, which sought to distance itself from the Popular Front.

Also in 1938 the Progressive Film Institute raised £3,000 to send a film unit – headed by Thorold Dickinson and Sidney Cole – to Spain to cover the civil war. Dickinson was a writer and editor from the commercial industry who had recently directed his first feature film (*The High Command*, 1936), Cole was a union activist in the Association of Cine-Technicians. The Progressive Film Institute had a particular interest in the Spanish Civil War – a rallying cause for the British left before the Second World War – and had already distributed several Spanish-made films. In Spain the unit split into two, one shooting in the Basque Country and the other around Barcelona, Sarria and Puigcerdà.[16] Back in London the footage was edited into two short films: *Behind the Spanish Lines* and *Spanish ABC*. Dickinson, whose politics were left-liberal rather than socialist or communist, was motivated to undertake the films to redress the absence of coverage of the Republican side from the newsreels. He preferred to see them as news films rather than documentaries: 'These were not documentary films but news reports; any eloquence depended on the immediacy of the images captured on the spur of the moment, snapshots in every sense of the word.'[17] Although Dickinson and Cole share credits for direction and editing on both films, it is generally understood that Cole was responsible for *Behind the Spanish Lines* and Dickinson for *Spanish ABC*.[18] The films seem to have been shown quite widely through left-wing film societies across the country. There are records of the films being booked by the Scottish People's Film Association in Glasgow and by the Nottingham Co-operative Society, while *Spanish ABC* was shown with *Advance Democracy!* at a meeting of the Workers' Film Association in Kent.[19] Dickinson recalled: 'I saw them in the Albert Hall with five or six thousand people there.'[20]

Behind the Spanish Lines is the more overtly propagandistic of the two films. It sides unequivocally with the Republican side as the legitimate Spanish government and emphasizes its democratic credentials by focusing on its attempts to preserve press freedom and to maintain hopsitals despite constant bombing. In contrast to the newsreels, which only alluded obliquely to the involvement of other nations in the Spanish Civil War, *Behind the Spanish Lines* stresses German and Italian support for the Fascists. *Spanish ABC* focuses specifically on the Republican government's efforts to maintain schools during the war – in contrast to the Fascists who are shown to be closing them – and asserts the crucial importance of education in the democratic process. It was favourably reviewed, including by *The Manchester Guardian*, which appreciated it as an attempt to raise awareness of the subject: 'This is a stirring film, on a subject about which not enough is known in this country.'[21]

Finally, *Peace and Plenty* (1939) was the only film ever directly commissioned by the Communist Party of Great Britain. It was intended as a campaign film for the general election due to be held in 1940. Ivor Montagu produced for the Progressive Film Institute and the film was distributed non-theatrically in the summer of 1939. In his study of left-wing film-making in the 1930s, Bert Hogenkamp contends that *Peace and Plenty* 'is an exceptional film'.[22] Rachael Low similarly considers that '*Peace and Plenty* is outstanding among the political films of the time'.[23] It abandons the realist conventions of films like *Advance Democracy!* and instead combines library footage, stills, animation and a stridently assertive commentary in a savage satirical attack on the National Government in general and Neville Chamberlain – represented by a puppet caricature wearing a top hat – in particular. It examines the record of the government in home and foreign affairs, highlights the amount of land and property owned by members of the Cabinet, accuses

Chamberlain of hypocrisy over Munich ('Peace in Our Time') and asserts that the government's defence policy is led by its ties to armaments companies. It concludes with Harry Pollitt, a leading light of the Communist Party of Great Britain, urging voters to 'end profiteering' and eject Chamberlain from office – represented by the Chamberlain puppet being kicked off screen. *Peace and Plenty* was shown privately at the House of Commons in June 1939 and was booked by Communist Party branches until the outbreak of war in September 1939 meant that the election was delayed.[24]

The tradition of political film-making that emerged during the 1930s came more or less to a halt with the Second World War. Hogenkamp avers that 'the war acted as the great divide for the left-wing film movement in Great Britain'.[25] The ideological contexts of the war did not allow any scope for oppositional film-making: the Communist Party was discredited following the Nazi-Soviet Pact of August 1939 and the progressive parties threw themselves behind the war effort. The incorporation of the Labour film movement into the official fold was exemplified by the recruitment of Joseph Reeves to run the non-theatrical film programme of the Ministry of Information. Only the Co-operative Wholesale Society remained an active presence in the field, setting up its own film unit to produce films such as *Manchester Took It, Too* (1941) – a riposte of sorts to the GPO Film Unit's *London Can Take It!* – and culminating in the £15,000 *Men of Rochdale* (1944), a story documentary about the origins and history of the Co-operative movement, produced in association with Sydney Box's Verity Films.[26] That the tradition of left-wing film-making did not re-emerge after the war can be explained by the onset of the Cold War – wherein Communism replaced Fascism as ideological enemy number one – and by the fact that economic and social conditions in the post-war period were rather different from the 'hungry thirties'.

Free Cinema and its contexts

'Free Cinema' was the collective title of a series of six programmes of short films shown at the National Film Theatre in London between 1956 and 1959 combining new British talent (pre-eminently Lindsay Anderson, Tony Richardson and Karel Reisz) and the work of other contemporary international documentary film-makers (Lionel Rogosin, Georges Franju) and European 'new wave' *auteurs* (Roman Polanski, Claude Chabrol, François Truffaut), though in retrospect it is the British films that have been understood as constituting the Free Cinema corpus.[27] The programmes were put together largely by Anderson, a critic-turned-film-maker who had been one of the leading lights of the polemical Oxford University film magazine *Sequence* (1947–1952), and Reisz, who was chief programmer for the National Film Theatre. It was Anderson who coined the term 'Free Cinema', which, as he later told Alexander Walker, was invented as an attempt to generate public interest in the films: 'Without that declamatory title, I honestly believe the Press would have paid us no attention at all...it was a successful piece of cultural packaging.'[28] In this sense at least, Free Cinema was startlingly successful: it was widely reviewed in the press and the screenings were often sold out. The films also won international recognition with prizes at the Venice Short Film Festival (*Every Day Except Christmas*) and the Tours Short Film Festival in France (*We Are the Lambeth Boys*).

The corpus of Free Cinema films is small, barely a dozen in total, but even so critical attention has focused mostly on the films of Lindsay Anderson (*O Dreamland*, *Every Day Except Christmas* and, to a lesser extent, *Wakefield Express*) and Karel Reisz (*Momma Don't Allow*, co-directed with Tony Richardson, and *We Are the Lambeth Boys*) at the expense of others such as Lorenza Mazzetti (*Together*), Claude Goretta and Alain Turner (*Nice Time*), Robert Vas (*Refuge England*) and Michael Grigsby (*Enginemen*). The films themselves were produced independently over several years and were not conceived as part of a movement: it was the circumstances of their exhibition that caused them to be seen collectively as a group. As the first Free Cinema manifesto declared: 'These films were not made together; nor with the idea of showing them together. But when they came together, we felt they had an attitude in common. Implicit in this attitude is a belief in freedom, in the importance of people and in the significance of the everyday.'[29] As the critical momentum behind Free Cinema gathered, it came to be seen as a movement whose advocates were united in their rejection of the ideological and aesthetic orthodoxy of British cinema. 'This programme is not put before you as an achievement, but as an aim', declared the 'Committee for Free Cinema':

> We ask you to view it not as critics, nor as a diversion, but in direct relation to a British cinema still obstinately class-bound; still rejecting the stimulus of contemporary life, as well as the responsibility to criticise; still reflecting a metropolitan, Southern English culture which excludes the rich diversity of tradition and personality which is the whole of Britain.[30]

In fact, Free Cinema was less of a unified movement or even a style than has generally been claimed. Its practitioners came from a range of backgrounds. Anderson, Richardson and Reisz were Oxbridge men (Reisz at Cambridge, the others at Oxford), but Lorenza Mazzetti (a now largely forgotten signatory of the first Free Cinema manifesto) was from an art school background, while Robert Vas was a Hungarian émigré who came to Britain following the Hungarian Uprising of 1956 – his film *Refuge England* powerfully evokes the experience of being a refugee and the feeling of isolation upon arriving in an unfamiliar place. The films themselves were also produced under different circumstances. Anderson's *Wakefield Express* was commissioned by the newspaper of the title to mark its centenary, while Anderson and cameraman John Fletcher shot *O Dreamland* entirely at their own initiative using leftover film stock from Anderson's *Thursday's Children*. *The Singing Street*, the earliest of the Free Cinema films to be made, was shot by a group of amateur filmmakers at Norton Park School in Edinburgh who styled themselves the 'Norton Park Film Unit'. *Momma Don't Allow, Together, Nice Time, Refuge England* and *Enginemen* were all produced with grants from the British Film Institute's Experimental Film Fund. This fund had been set up in 1952 in order to support formal innovation and it provided small grants to up-and-coming non-commercial film-makers. *Momma Don't Allow*, for example, was made for a total of just £425.[31] But Free Cinema did not turn its back on conventional sponsorship: *Every Day Except Christmas* and *We Are the Lambeth Boys* were sponsored by the Ford Motor Company as the first two entries in a series entitled 'Look at Britain'. It is perhaps no coincidence that these are also the most technically polished of the Free Cinema films.

Free Cinema needs to be seen in relation to various contexts. Its polemical rejection of middlebrow orthodoxy and the 'obstinately class-bound' nature of British cinema aligns Free Cinema with the emergence of the 'Angry Young Men' of British theatre and literature – a term applied to dramatists such as John Osborne and writers like Alan Sillitoe who railed against the 'establishment' and the persistence of the class system. The first Free Cinema programme (February 1956) predated by only three months the première of John Osborne's landmark play *Look Back in Anger* at the Royal Court Theatre (May 1956). Moreover, the play had been directed by Tony Richardson – who would also direct the film version in 1959 – while other Free Cinema directors would also make feature films based on the novels of the 'northern realists', notably Karel Reisz's film of Alan Sillitoe's *Saturday Night and Sunday Morning* in 1960 and Lindsay Anderson's film of David Storey's *This Sporting Life* in 1963.

To this extent Free Cinema was a part of the seismic shift in British popular culture occurring in the late 1950s that would see the ascendancy
of working-class realism in film, theatre and television into the next
decade. It was an early indicator of the process that historian Arthur
Marwick would identify as the 'first stirrings' of cultural revolution in
Britain.[32]

Free Cinema has sometimes been associated with the emergence of
the 'New Left' – an intellectual movement that emerged in the late
1950s centred around protest movements such as the Campaign for
Nuclear Disarmament (CND) and which found a voice through journals such as *New Left Review*. Indeed the editors of *New Left Review*
cited Free Cinema in this context: 'Without CND supporters, Anti-Ugly
protesters, African demonstrators, Free Cinema and the Society for the
Abolition of the Death Penalty, we would be nowhere.'[33] The most direct
link between Free Cinema and the New Left was *March to Aldermaston*
(1959), the film of the CND-organized protest march from London
to the nuclear weapons factory at Aldermaston over the Easter week-
end of 1958. Anderson and Reisz were prominent among the group of
documentarists who worked on the film: although it was not shown
officially under the Free Cinema banner, the influence of Free Cinema
is apparent in its interest in 'ordinary people with an opinion' and its
representation of the marchers as individuals rather than as a mass. Free
Cinema was not political in the way that the political documentaries
of the 1930s were political but it shared the New Left's commitment
to the idea that artistic creativity was in its own way a political act.
Reisz, for example, argued that the documentary film-maker does more
than simply represent society: 'There is a difference in kind between a
sociological fact and poetic truth, and the artist had better remember
it if he wants to keep his audience... The strength and relevance of his
commitment and depth of his instinctive response will determine how
significant his images will be.'[34]

Free Cinema also had an international context. It can be seen as
part of a movement in international documentary film-making that
embraced a new approach towards its subjects, characterized by an
emphasis on the individual and a shift away from scripted construction
to a more observational mode. Instead of staging scenes for the camera,
documentary directors would look to let subjects speak for themselves
while searching for moments of drama or psychological insight. In this
context Free Cinema may be aligned with other contemporary movements such as Direct Cinema in the United States and *cinéma-vérité* in
France.[35] This shift was to a large extent technologically determined as

the advent of lighter and more mobile equipment enabled film-makers to undertake more location work. A shared feature of all Free Cinema documentaries is that they were shot entirely outside the studio. Most were shot using the lightweight 16 millimetre Bolex camera and hyper-sensitive Ilford HPS film stock that allowed location shooting without artificial light – even for night shoots. It is no coincidence that around half of all the Free Cinema films (*Wakefield Express, Momma Don't Allow, Every Day Except Christmas, Refuge England, We Are the Lambeth Boys*) were shot by the same cameraman: Walter Lassally. It was not until the end of the decade that it was possible to record synchronous sound on loca-tion: *We Are the Lambeth Boys* was the first Free Cinema film to do this. Free Cinema made a virtue of its technological limitations: 'With a 16 millimetre camera, and minimal resources, and no payment for your technicians, you cannot achieve very much in commercial terms... But you can use your eyes and ears. You can give indications. You can make poetry.'[36]

Another context for Free Cinema was the intellectual shift in film cul-ture towards the idea of a personal cinema. This was spearheaded in France where a group of young critics associated with the journal *Cahiers du Cinéma* – including François Truffaut, Eric Rohmer, Claude Chabrol and Jean-Luc Godard – advocated *la politique des auteurs*, which main-tained that a director with a personal vision could be seen as the true 'author' of the finished film. The first Free Cinema manifesto in 1956 had in fact embraced what later came to be known as the '*auteur* theory' in its assertion that: 'As film-makers we believe that no film can be too personal. The image speaks. Sound amplifies and comments. Size is irrel-evant. Perfection is not an aim. An attitude means a style. A style means an attitude.'[37] In this context it is important to remember that the origi-nal Free Cinema programmes had included the work of other 'personal' documentary film-makers such as Georges Franju and Lionel Rogosin. And Lindsay Anderson anticipated Truffaut and Godard in identifying a link between criticism and practice: a title card for *O Dreamland* describes it as 'A Sequence Film'.

It was Anderson who, of all the Free Cinema directors, most fully embraced the idea of a personal cinema. This is apparent not only in his own films but also from his film criticism. Anderson was one of the editors of *Sequence* in the late 1940s and, after its demise, followed Gavin Lambert to *Sight and Sound*, which in the early 1950s transformed itself from a rather dull educational journal into a lively publication focusing on international film art. *Sequence* anticipated *Cahiers du Cinéma* in its polemical defence of Hollywood cinema – now starting to be understood

as a 'classical' art form in its own right rather than merely as a philis-
tine commercial entertainment – while Anderson's appreciation of the
'poetry' of directors such as John Ford and Humphrey Jennings can
be seen as a precursor of the *auteur* theory.[38] Anderson's admiration
for Jennings is particularly significant for understanding the aesthetic
impulse of his Free Cinema films. Anderson once famously described
Jennings as 'the only real poet that the British cinema has yet produced'.
He amplified:

> His [Jennings's] subjects were thus, at least on the surface, the com-
> mon ones; yet his manner of expression was always individual, and
> became more and more so. It was a style that bore the closest possi-
> ble relationship to his theme – to that aspect of his subjects which
> his particular vision caused him constantly to stress.[39]

Jennings's influence can readily be identified in Anderson's films – *O
Dreamland* recalls *Spare Time* in its subject of working-class leisure, for
example, while the spirit of *Listen to Britain* seems to infuse every other
frame of *Every Day Except Christmas* – though to read them solely as a
homage would be somewhat reductive as there are also other influences
at work.

The style of Free Cinema has been seen as marking a decisive break
from the mode of representation associated with the Griersonian school
of documentary. This was recognized in a contemporary review of the
final Free Cinema programme in *The Times*, which felt that the films
'have brought fresh vitality into British documentary'. 'Grierson's great
conception of documentary remains monumental, unimpeachable', it
went on; 'but it is, after all, a conception of 30 years ago. Its approach
was different from Free Cinema; and it was suited to different times.'[40]
Whereas Griersonian documentary had taken shape within a context
of consensual social democratic politics, Free Cinema was aligned with
the anti-establishment voices of the 'Angry Young Men' and the New
Left; whereas Griersonian documentary represented working-class people collectively, Free Cinema saw them as individuals; and whereas
Griersonian documentary frowned upon 'artistic' flourishes and personal style, Free Cinema promoted the idea of the film-maker as an
artist who sought to 'make poetry'. The two traditions are at opposite
ends of Grierson's definition of documentary as 'the creative treatment of actuality': for Grierson it was the 'actuality' that mattered
most, whereas for Free Cinema it was the 'creative treatment' that took
precedence.

The differences between the Griersonian tradition and Free Cinema are perhaps most evident in their representation of the working classes. The classic documentaries of the 1930s had focused on the working classes at work: *Industrial Britain*, *Coal Face*, *Night Mail*, *North Sea*. *Spare Time* was the exception to this rule, and significantly it was Humphrey Jennings whom the Free Cinema directors most admired. Free Cinema is as much interested in the working classes at play as exemplified by subjects such as a funfair (*O Dreamland*), jazz club (*Momma Don't Allow*), Piccadilly Circus by night (*Nice Time*) and the Ashford House youth club in south London (*We Are the Lambeth Boys*). *O Dreamland* has been understood as a critique of crass popular entertainment in much the same tradition as Richard Hoggart's *The Uses of Literacy* (1957): Anderson contrasts the 'attractions' (including a chamber of horrors full of grotesque tortures – 'Your children will love it') with the impassive faces of visitors, while the ritualistic chanting of bingo numbers implies that the players have become automatons. *Momma Don't Allow* and *We Are the Lambeth Boys* are both notable for their closeness to their subjects: there is none of the distance that characterizes the films of the 1930s. *Every Day Except Christmas* and *We Are the Lambeth Boys* differ from most other Free Cinema films in their recourse to a voice-over commentary – apparently at the insistence of their sponsor – but they are unpatronizing and sympathetic towards their subjects. *Every Day Except Christmas* chronicles a day in the life of Covent Garden: of all the films it comes closest to the evocation of what Anderson called 'the poetry of everyday life'.[41]

Free Cinema has been subject to almost as many fluctuations in critical reputation as the documentary movement of the 1930s whose aesthetics it had so consciously rejected. At the time the films were much admired for their boldness and praised for their social import. Gavin Lambert, in a long review of the first Free Cinema programme for *Sight and Sound*, compared the films favourably with the Italian neo-realists and suggested that '*Together*, *Momma Don't Allow* and *O Dreamland* stand out sharply on their own, as the first signs for some time of a fundamentally progressive, personal approach to exploring contemporary life in this country through the cinema'.[42] For Penelope Houston, writing in the early 1960s, the films were 'directly social' and the movement was 'in step with that whole semi-cultural, semi-political wave of protest which dates roughly from the time of Suez and Hungary'.[43] And Alan Lovell noted the 'freshness and vitality' of Free Cinema and felt that the films 'have some of the qualities of the very earliest documentaries, where the camera's ability to capture the world about it surprises and charms the spectator'.[44] He suggested that most Free Cinema films 'could be described as portraits of British society in the 1950s. Like *Look Back in Anger* in the theatre, part of their impact on audiences came from the representation of the contemporary world on the screen, where before it had been firmly ignored'.[45]

Later assessments of Free Cinema were less generous. Raymond Durgnat, that most idiosyncratic of critics, wrote in 1970 that 'Free Cinema manages nothing that hadn't been done earlier and better *within* the commercial framework' and claimed that 'its achievement is minimal by contrast with the vigour and sophistication of parallel movements in France and the USA'. Durgnat felt that the treatment of the working classes in *Every Day Except Christmas* marked no advance over *Industrial Britain* and of all the films preferred *We Are the Lambeth Boys* because 'the lyricism is subtler'. He was particularly grudging about the 'aethetic limitations' of *Momma Don't Allow*, which he described as 'badly cut, badly shot, with no feelings for jazz, for dancing, for bodies, for clothes, or for pace'.[46] For Roy Armes, the problem with Free Cinema was that its proponents were middle-class Oxbridge-educated ex-public schoolboys who could not claim to speak for their working-class subjects any more than the documentarists of the 1930s could for theirs. 'For all their links with the late 1950s generation', Armes avers, 'Anderson, Reisz and Richardson in fact follow the pattern set by Grierson in the 1930s: the university-educated bourgeois making "sympathetic" films about proletarian life, not analysing the ambiguities of their own privileged position.'[47] This is a particular failing of Lindsay Anderson, who 'makes no attempt to understand the people he is filming', while in all the films, contrary to earlier assessments, 'there is little evidence of social or political analysis and the documentaries remain on the level of reporting'. Like Durgnat he concludes that 'in the overall context of late 1950s cinema the novelty of these Free Cinema documentaries is extremely limited'.[48]

In most respects these criticisms are unfair. Anderson, Richardson and Reisz could not help the circumstances of their upbringing any more than Grierson's university-educated colleagues could: in any event Armes ignores the work of other Free Cinema directors who did not share the same background. Durgnat's charge that Free Cinema pales in comparison to contemporary movements in France and the United States ignores the rather salient point that Free Cinema in fact predated those movements by several years. The major innovation of *cinéma-vérité* was to involve subjects as participants through direct address to the camera – a technique that became possible only with the advent of portable synch-sound recording that was not available until the end of the 1950s when Free Cinema had run its course. And the 'aesthetic limitations' of the films are now what makes them seem fresh and distinctive. The graininess of the cinematography and the occasional jump cuts, even in the more technically accomplished films such as *Every Day Except Christmas*, can be understood both as an indication of the conditions of low-budget film-making and as a formal strategy to differentiate the films from the polished products of the studios. It was not the aim of Free Cinema to be technically perfect: style and attitude mattered more. In this regard Free Cinema should be seen as an important stage in the development of alternative documentary practice in Britain. In particular, it provides a bridge between the 'poetic' films of Humphrey Jennings and the emergence of a more aesthetically and politically radical documentary practice in the work of the independent collectives and workshops of the 1970s and 80s.

Peter Watkins and the alternative form in documentary drama

The short but highly dramatic career of Peter Watkins demonstrates both the potential and the limitations of alternative documentary practice in British television. Watkins (born 1935) was of the same generation as Ken Russell and Ken Loach and like them joined the BBC in the early 1960s where he was recruited to the Documentary Department by Huw Wheldon on the strength of several amateur films. These included an account of life in the trenches during the First World War (*Diary of an Unknown Soldier*, 1959) and a documentary reconstruction of the Hungarian Uprising shot in Canterbury (*The Forgotten Faces*, 1961). From the start of his film-making career Watkins combined an interest in representing violence and its effects with a radically alternative approach to the notion of documentary 'truth'. An internal BBC report indicates that the Documentary Department had reservations about Watkins from the start: it was felt that his training film, which he chose to make about the torture of prisoners during the Algerian War, 'was violent to a degree which would almost certainly have ruled it out if it had been designed for transmission', while as an assistant director on a documentary about Marshal Tito he had used actuality footage 'entirely out of context, simply to illustrate points which Watkins wanted to make'.[49] Stephen Hearst, producer of the Tito documentary, recommended that Watkins should not be kept on: it was Huw Wheldon who decided that his undoubted talent was worth the risk.

Watkins initially wanted to make a film about nuclear war – which eventually became *The War Game* – but was persuaded instead to film a reconstruction of the Battle of Culloden. This was one of several topics suggested by Watkins in a memorandum that also included the Sharpeville massacre in South Africa, the imprisonment of the Suffragettes and an adaptation of Nikos Kazantzakis's controversial book *The Last Temptation of Christ* (1953). Watkins evidently had very definite ideas about documentary practice and ambitious plans for what he wanted to achieve:

> The nuclear film is not a single idea in itself. I intend it to be part of an overall framework of a film-style that I want to work in – a style of using non-professionals, quite ordinary people, to capture the inside heart-beat of other people and events, past and present.[50]

Watkins's preference for non-professional actors and filming entirely on location using lightweight cameras and portable sound-recording equipment had much in common with the contemporaneous *cinéma-vérité* movement, but where Watkins differed was that he advocated dramatic reconstruction and scripting rather than unmediated recording:

> All the internal BBC discussions about the new 'camera liberty' seem to have been dealing with the attempts to capture the passing moment as it is actually happening... My idea is to have, by re-staging, every second under total organised and pre-planned control, and yet still to give it the appearance of actually happening at that moment.

'I am convinced', he added, 'this can open up a totally new path and direction in documentary television film.'[51]

Culloden (1964) was the first opportunity for Watkins to put his theory of alternative documentary into practice. He based the 70-minute film on an authoritative study by the historian John Prebble, who acted as historical advisor, even including specific dialogue such as Lord Elcho's cry of 'Run you cowardly Italian!' as Bonnie Prince Charlie flees the field of battle.[52] Watkins made two crucial creative decisions. The first was to insist not only on using non-professionals but also to cast according to type:

> If I want to have an awkward, raw-boned, pox-scarred woman of Nairn talking to camera about what she has experienced under the English occupation troops, then a genuine Highland woman from

> Nairn, who mentally and physically fits this description, will be far
> more realistic and have far more jagged truth than could ever anyone
> from *Spotlight*.[53]

The second decision was to use a hand-held camera (*Culloden* was shot
by cameraman Dick Bush with a 16 millimetre Arriflex) and to shoot the
film as if it were a 'live' event before the camera. Watkins told Prebble
that 'every single foot of the film, be it violent action or someone
uttering forth to camera, is going to be filmed with bumpy journalistic grain and realism, exactly as though it is happening there and
then, and is being recorded by a sort of *World in Action* team'.[54] This
technique included the use of direct-to-camera interviews with participants – a significant innovation in that while it had been seen before
in contemporary documentary (*Housing Problems*, for instance) it had
never been employed before in a historical reconstruction on British
television.

Culloden may be seen as an example of what the postmodernist film
critic Robert A. Rosenstone calls 'the New History film'. This genre –
exemplified by highly self-conscious films such as *Hiroshima, mon amour*
(1959), *Memories of Underdevelopment* (1968), *Hitler: A Film from Germany*
(1977) and *Walker* (1987) – 'finds the space to *contest* history, to interrogate either the metanarratives that structure historical knowledge,
or smaller historical truths, received notions, conventional images'.[55]
Culloden is nothing if not revisionist in its representation of the past:
it shatters the romantic myths of Tartanry in characterizing Bonnie
Prince Charlie as a drunken coward and is unflinching in its depiction not only of the brutal nature of eighteenth-century warfare but
also of the savagery of the English-Hanoverian army in its reprisals
against the Highlanders. Watkins presents most of the clansmen as
joining the rebellion for economic necessity rather than romantic
nationalism and includes telling details of the social inequalities on
both sides. But *Culloden* also highlights how film technique can construct the past. Aspects such as the commentary's insistence on the
present tense ('This is grapeshot – this is what it does'), the direct
addresses to camera and the use of freeze-frame at the moment of
death make the spectator very aware that they are watching a construction. It is a radical, wholly successful approach to the historical drama
documentary.

Culloden was broadcast on BBC1 to much critical acclaim and made
such an impact that it was repeated after six weeks.[56] Its success raised
Watkins's stock considerably and enabled him to push ahead with

his cherished 'nuclear film' project. *The War Game* (1965), however, would prove to be one of the most controversial episodes in the history of British broadcasting. Watkins undertook the film as a reaction to what he saw as '[the] silence on why we possess nuclear weapons' and in order 'to make the man in the street stop and think about himself and his future'.[57] *The War Game* has sometimes been labelled 'the CND film': although Watkins himself was not a member of CND, he had contact with the movement and was sympathetic to its cause. He planned *The War Game* as a series of 'emergency reports' covering the aftermath of a nuclear strike on London. Like *Culloden* it 'would be shot entirely as though a newsreel shot under very trying conditions. Scratches, contamination streaks, bad sound quality, would all be an inherent part of the presentation of this film'.[58] Watkins undertook extensive research, reading Civil Defence manuals and consulting a wide range of experts, including scientists, doctors, psychologists and strategists, about the likely effects of a nuclear bomb. *The War Game* was shot in April 1965 on several locations in south-east England (Dover, Gravesend, Tonbridge) with a cast recruited from local amateur dramatic societies. Watkins had a first cut ready by mid-June 1965 but the BBC, which had all along been nervous about the potential political repercussions of the film, prevaricated for several months before finally deciding not to broadcast it. This decision incensed Watkins, who blamed the BBC for 'the final and effective suppression of this film'.[59]

The reasons for the 'suppression' of *The War Game* have been much debated and the episode remains highly controversial.[60] There was speculation at the time and since that the BBC had bowed to political pressure in refusing to broadcast the film. In particular it has been suggested that there was collusion between Cabinet Secretary Sir Burke Trend and BBC Chairman (and former Cabinet Secretary) Lord Normanbrook. The National Archives reveal that Normanbrook wrote to Trend expressing his concern that 'the showing of the film on television might well have a significant effect on public attitudes towards the deterrent' and, therefore, 'I doubt whether the BBC ought alone to take the responsibility of deciding whether this film should be shown on television'.[61] A number of 'senior Whitehall officials', including Trend and representatives of the Home Office and Ministry of Defence, attended a screening of *The War Game* at the BBC's Television Centre on 24 September 1965. The carefully worded official record states that 'the Government did not wish to offer any view on whether or not the film should be shown to the public'.[62] The ball was back in the BBC's court. In November 1965

Normanbrook informed Trend that the corporation had decided not to broadcast it.[63] The BBC's official reason for not showing the film was that 'it is too horrifying for the medium of television'. In particular, concern was expressed about 'the effect it might have on elderly people living alone'.[64] However, *The War Game* was afforded a limited cinema release in 1966. It won a number of awards, including a Special Jury Prize at the Venice Documentary Festival (1966) and the Academy Award for Best Documentary (1967) – the latter collected, on Watkins's behalf, by actress Elizabeth Taylor.[65]

The focus of historians, critics and conspiracy theorists on the political context of *The War Game* has tended to overshadow discussion of its qualities as a documentary. Here the BBC paid Watkins something of a backhanded compliment in suggesting that it was 'too horrifying' to be shown on television because people might think it was real. There was, of course, a precedent for this: in 1938 Orson Welles's dramatization of *The War of the Worlds* for the CBS radio network in the United States had caused panic among some listeners who, tuning in midway through the broadcast, had mistaken its technique of news reports for the real thing.[66] If nothing else *The War Game* is certainly a masterclass in film technique: it is shot in a grainy, rough-edged style that breaks up the narrative with inserts (such as extracts from Civil Defence texts) and addresses to camera from scientists, doctors and clergymen. In depicting the attack itself Watkins avoids the usual cliché of stock footage of a mushroom cloud and instead uses overexposures and negative film images to represent the heat blast caused by a nuclear explosion. A fire storm rages, doctors struggle to cope with the flood of casualties, policemen carry out mercy killings by shooting the severely wounded. The latter part of the film illustrates the onset of a 'nuclear winter' as survivors struggle to cope in the aftermath. Disease spreads, people live in squalor, social order breaks down: in one scene, civilians raid a food depot and are executed by an army firing squad for looting. As documentary, *The War Game* may be compared to films such as Humphrey Jennings's *The Silent Village* and Kevin Brownlow and Andrew Mollo's *It Happened Here* (1963) in that it applies the techniques of dramatic reconstruction to an event that did not in fact take place.

There is much evidence that while the BBC was anxious about the political aspects of *The War Game*, the film itself was admired within the corporation. Indeed there were some voices who argued that it should have been broadcast. One such was John Boorman, then the Head of the BBC Documentary Unit at Bristol:

This is a brilliantly made, carefully documented film of unprecedented importance...The Producer's [*sic*] stated intention is to attempt to break the conspiracy of silence surrounding nuclear war. In this sense it is undoubtedly a propaganda film, and compares with the finest films of this nature – Jennings's *Listen to Britain* and Leni Riefenstahl's *Triumph of the Will*. It is harrowing but not more than the programmes we have seen on Vietnam, Belsen and Hiroshima...I believe it should be shown, providing adequate warnings are given and that it is scheduled at a suitably late hour.[67]

Even those who supported the decision not to show it recognized its qualities as a film. The publisher Robert Lusty, who sat on the BBC's Board of Governors, told Normanbrook: 'It was extraordinarily interesting to see that awful film and to ponder on its problems. I am sure you were right to sanction it and also sure you are right to feel that we should not put it out under our own responsibility.'[68]

Watkins's acrimonious resignation from the BBC effectively burned his bridges as far as the corporation was concerned: the remainder of his career would be spent on the margins of the film industry developing his own particular style of fictionalized documentary in films such as *Privilege* (1966), *Gladiators* (1968) and *Punishment Park* (1970). He would never make another film with the immediacy and impact of either *Culloden* or *The War Game*. His career is significant in that it reveals the ideological limitations that apply when a film-maker presents such a radical challenge to accepted institutional practice. The BBC's management was never able to understand why Watkins was unwilling to compromise: 'A programme or a producer with a mission or a message should include in his professionalism the perception to know what concessions he must make to opinions or circumstances if his mission or message is ever to be seen and heard.'[69] Hence the combination of Watkins's refusal to compromise and the BBC's inability to accommodate his alternative form of documentary deprived British television of one of its most unique and individualistic talents.

Cinema Action and 'people's films'

In the late 1960s and early 1970s the whole context of alternative film-making in Britain was transformed by the emergence of new groups and practices that set out quite deliberately to position themselves outside and in opposition to the mainstream. This period saw the growth of film collectives and workshops that developed organizational structures and film-making practices radically different from the established film and television industries. The first such group in Britain was the London Film-Makers' Co-operative (LFMC), set up in 1966 as on offshoot of the New York Film-Makers' Co-operative, which brought together experimental film-makers including Steve Dwoskin, Peter Gidal, David Larcher, Annabel Nicolson and William Raban. While the LFMC was involved more in avant-garde artists' films, it was followed by other groups who developed a distinctive form of alternative documentary practice. Much of the initial activity was centred in London and revolved around groups such as Cinema Action (founded 1968), the Berwick Street Collective (1970) and the London Women's Film Group (1972), though regional groups followed, including Amber Films of Newcastle (1969), the Sheffield Film Co-op (1973), the Edinburgh Film Workshop (1977) and the Birmingham Film and Video Workshop (1979). These groups were all characterized by their 'democratic' notions of collective management and a flexible division of labour in opposition to the hierarchical structures of the established film and television industries. They sought to integrate the activities of production, distribution and exhibition rather than separating them. And most of them had close links with their local communities (such as Amber Films) or worked with specific constituencies such as trade unions (Cinema Action).

The workshop movement was very much a product of the ideological and cultural contexts of the late 1960s. This period saw the acceleration of the 'cultural revolution' in British society as a range of social forces combined to create the circumstances in which an oppositional film culture could flourish. Such forces included a gradual erosion of the culture of deference that had long characterized British society (best exemplified by the reaction to the Profumo Scandal of 1963), the rise of a more assertive and self-confident youth culture (focused largely around fashion and pop music), increasing recreational drug use among the young and the affluent (mostly marijuana but also LSD), a culture of experimentation in the arts (exemplified by the founding of the Arts Lab in Drury Lane in 1967), the proliferation of protest movements (for example in relation to nuclear weapons, abortion, the Vietnam War and Women's Liberation), and the increasingly confrontational nature of political protest (seen especially in student 'occupations' and the re-emergence of sectarianism in Northern Ireland).[70] The new film workshops were often closely associated with protest movements. Cinema Action, for example, came into being as a direct consequence of the student protests of May 1968 in Paris, while the London Women's

Film Group and Sheffield Film Co-op both identified closely with the women's movement.

It was also a period of radicalization in intellectual film culture. The late 1960s and early 1970s saw the rejection of conventional aesthetic debates in film criticism and the embracing of Marxist-influenced theories of structuralism and semiotics. This was signalled by the radical shift in editorial stance of journals such as *Cahiers du Cinéma* in France (from 1968) and *Screen* in Britain (from 1970), which now understood film less as an art form and more as an ideological tool where both content and form were determined by the economic structure of the industry that produced it. Accordingly, film theorists came generally around to the view that only those films produced outside the existing structures could be considered genuinely oppositional in terms of both their formal strategies and contexts of production. Hence the sort of films that were championed in intellectual film culture at this time were the experimental films of Jean-Luc Godard and the Dziga Vertov Group in France, the 'counter cinema' films of theorist-film-makers such as Peter Wollen and Laura Mulvey in Britain, and the radical political documentaries of the developing world such as Gillo Pontecorvo's *The Battle of Algiers* (1965) and Fernando Solanas and Octavio Getino's *Hour of the Furnaces* (1968), which came to be known as Third Cinema.[71] These films were oppositional not only in their content and form but also in institutional and ideological terms: they challenged the notion of cinema as a passive viewing experience and expected that audiences would be politically active and intellectually engaged. In this context the acts of film-making and even film criticism came to be seen as political statements. For theorists such as Jim Pines, the aim of a radical film culture was 'to develop a counter-cultural critique for, and a method of, revolutionising society, in which cinema functions as a weapon'.[72] Dave Douglass of Cinema Action also held to this view: 'You weren't trying to record history. You were trying to make history...The whole point of revolutionary film was to make the struggle.'[73]

While the film collectives and workshops were far from homogenous in their politics, they were all broadly aligned with the left. The workshop movement has sometimes been seen in relation to the political documentary tradition of the 1930s, whose 'rediscovery' was partly an outcome of the radicalization of intellectual film culture in the 1970s, though there are also very significant differences between the two periods. The political films of the 1930s were produced under the broad umbrella of the labour movement, whose constituent elements (political parties, trade unions, co-operative societies) were organizations with democratic but hierarchical structures and formal decision-making procedures. The workshop movement in contrast existed outside formal structures and was distinctly non-hierarchical. It brought together practitioners and academics radicalized by the events of the 1960s (especially the 'anti-colonialist' revolutionary struggles of the Third World such as the Algerian War and the Vietnam War) and influenced by the neo-Marxist analysis of culture and ideology expounded by theorists such as Louis Althusser, Walter Benjamin, R. D. Laing and Herbert Marcuse. There was a close association between the workshop movement and intellectual film culture. Paul Willemen and Claire Johnston, both closely associated with *Screen*, were involved in Cinema Action and the London Women's Film Group, respectively, while Alan Lovell, who resigned from the editorial board of *Screen* over its increasingly Marxist orientation in the 1970s, was a founding member of the Birmingham Film and Video Workshop.

Cinema Action exemplifies the combination of political activism and innovation in film practice that characterized the workshop movement. Its origins were in an initiative by German poet Gustav Schlacke and his British-born wife Ann Lamche to set up a mobile cinema for showing films in factories. Lamche had worked for the French state broadcaster ORTF and had acquired a print of a student-made film about the protests of May 1968. Other founding members included cameraman Humphrey Trevelyan and independent distributor Richard Mordaunt. Schlacke explained how the group emerged from screenings that brought together people interested in political film-making:

It was multiplying. For example, we showed the French film in Dagenham at Ford's and there were about four people looking and three of them were thinking about how to get to the pub – four workers looking at a French film in French and three of them not interested in the film! But one of the four was able to arrange a big showing at one of their main meetings. So, we had all of a sudden 2,000 people looking at that film, in French – unheard of in Britain![74]

The group progressed from showing films in factories to making short 'cine tracts' funded by subscriptions from workers and trade unions. One of its first films, *Fighting the Bill* (1970), was a campaign film against the controversial Industrial Relations Act of 1969. The make-up of the group was diverse and international, ranging from student activists such as David Adelstein, president of the Students' Union at the London School of Economics who had been suspended for his role in an occupation, to American anti-Vietnam war activists such as Daniel Schechter. Schlacke recalled 'a strong American contingent – people who had dodged the draft or were frightened they would be drafted'.[75]

Cinema Action saw the role of its films as being to 'record the social, political and community activities of contemporary life in Britain'.[76] Its early films were made in support of protest groups such as the campaigns by council tenants against rent increases by the Greater London Council (*Not a Penny on the Rent*, 1969) and to preserve the autonomy of student unions (*Hands Off Student Unions!*, 1972). It particularly associated with industrial communities and produced films supporting strikes by dockers (*Arise Ye Workers*, 1973) and miners (*The Miners' Film*, 1975). Cinema Action positioned itself as an oppositional group that identified with the socially marginalized and oppressed. *Squatters* (1970), for instance, was 'a film about the struggle of the homeless in opposition to the powerful and ruthless', while *The UCS Struggle* (1971) supporting the Clydeside shipyard strikers demonstrated 'the mobilisation to prevent the closure of the shipyards and to resist the destruction of the whole community'. *People of Ireland* (1972) was 'a film about what it means to belong to the Irish Working class and to support the people of Free Derry'.[77] Cinema Action's films document the industrial unrest of the 1970s and while they are highly partisan they nevertheless provide an important alternative to the reporting of those events in the national media.

Cinema Action was run as a collective and its ethos was one of inclusivity. It declared that 'the facilities and services provided by Cinema Action involve the participation of the community or working group who choose film to identify themselves, their lives and their problems as a means of developing awareness and support within the whole community' and that 'production of these "peoples [*sic*] films" is part of a discussion process in which all the elements, ideas and the dramatic composition of a particular project are decided according to the needs and wishes of the community'.[78] The films were black-and-white 16 millimetre, and were shown 'in such places as community halls, factory canteens, housing estates, youth clubs, schools, trade union meetings, building sites and pubs'.[79] There is some evidence to suggest that this strategy succeeded in promoting political awareness. Steve Sprung, who joined the group in 1970, did so as a result of attending one of its screenings:

I got involved with Cinema Action because I went to a showing of *Fighting the Bill* at a large political meeting...Seeing that film was revelatory. It wasn't that it was a great film as a film. But it was direct and talked to working-class people about things which were theirs.[80]

The films of Cinema Action are distinguished from contemporary television news and documentary accounts of industrial action through
their formal and ideological strategies. On a formal level they tend to
be shot with a hand-held camera and synchronous sound: they lack
the polished style of professional documentary and are often characterized by their shaky camerawork and fragmented *mise-en-scène*. They
eschew commentary altogether and instead allow their subjects to speak
with their own 'voice'. This voice may take the form of either prepared
statements by union activists (such as Jimmy Reid's 'Today Scotland
speaks' in *The UCS Stuggle*) or interviews with participants (excluding
the interviewer's questions so that the statements seem off-the-cuff).
On an ideological level the films associate unequivocally with their subjects. They depict organized working-class and trade union activism:
recurring images include shots of demonstrations, rallies, meetings and
pickets. However, they differ from the workers' newsreels of the 1930s in
the rhetoric of class war espoused by the activist interviews. Hence the
Clydeside shipyard workers 'put the working class on the offensive' (*The
UCS Struggle*) and the Troubles in Northern Ireland are understood as a
consequence of 'the crisis of capitalism' rather than sectarian divisions
(*People of Ireland*).

There is little evidence of the popular response to the films of Cinema
Action – their exhibition was largely confined to workers' groups and
trade union meetings, where it seems reasonable to assume they would
have been viewed favourably – but they did generate some degree of
academic criticism. However, the response of film theorists was conditioned more by formal concerns and focused on what they perceived
as the ideological limitations of the films. Claire Johnston and Paul
Willemen, for example, charged that 'Cinema Action has concentrated
on documenting workers' struggles (UCS, the dockers etc) from an essentially workerist perspective' – the authors do not suggest what other
perspective they believed films of this sort could take – and criticized
the films for 'their dependence on *cinéma-vérité* forms which purport to
capture the world as it "really is" '.[81] One of the dogmas of the intellectual film culture of which *Screen* was the vanguard in the 1970s was
to reject conventional ideas of realism and authenticity: realism was
itself an ideological-aesthetic construct determined by the formal properties and representational conventions of the film medium. David Glyn
and Paul Marris similarly found the 'theoretical position' of Cinema
Action 'inadequate ... because it makes demands of "agit-prop" cinema
which are derived from the aesthetic (as yet only partially formed) of
an anti-"classic realist" counter cinema, thus falling into the trap of

formalism'.[82] The charge of 'formalism' was a common feature of intellectual film theory in the 1970s: it tended to be applied to any films where aspects of film technique took precedence over the political content or message. It seems a particularly absurd criticism of Cinema Action's films where the political content is the whole point of the films.

The ideological critique of alternative film practice in the 1970s came to a head over the documentary *Nightcleaners* (1975). This was produced by the Berwick Street Collective, a breakaway group from Cinema Action set up in 1970 by Marc Karlin, Richard Mordaunt and Humphrey Trevelyan. According to Trevelyan:

> We felt that Cinema Action, because of their insistence on making campaign-led 'working-class films', were sort of perpetuating a socialist-realist mythology about the working class and all three of us, in different ways, felt that film could be much more than that. It had the capacity to express profound questions and ambiguities. Film could pretend to be black and white and could pretend to be definitive and didactic but actually it couldn't be, if you understood anything about how it actually works.[83]

The Berwick Street Collective's manifesto declared that its aim was 'to produce films that take politics as their subject both in terms of filmmaking and film content, i.e. to examine what constitutes the experience of politics, both on practical and theoretical levels'.[84] It was responsible for several films but the one that attracted most attention was the feature-length *Nightcleaners*. In one sense *Nightcleaners* can be seen in the tradition of the campaign films of Cinema Action: its subject was the campaign to improve conditions for female night-shift office-cleaners who had no union representation. However, it was shot over a longer period of time, with the film-makers following the campaign for two years between 1972 and 1974. And the style of *Nightcleaners* is very different from the Cinema Action films: it draws upon some of the techniques of 'counter-cinema' such as slowing the speed of the film, leaving the clapperboard in takes and including long continuous takes of non-action (for example, a long-held shot of one of the cleaners listening to a speech by a union official). This style emerged during the editing and was due largely to the influence of co-director James Scott, whose background was with the London Film-Makers' Co-operative.[85]

Claire Johnston believed that *Nightcleaners* 'is the most important political film ever to have been made in this country'. It differed from other examples of its kind because it 'contains within itself a reflection of its own involvement in the history of the events being filmed, an involvement which necessarily re-stated and re-defined the events themselves'.[86] In other words it adopted a self-reflexive style that acknowledged its own status as a 'text'. Quite how this is different from the 'formalism' that critics detected in the Cinema Action films is not explained. However, some of the workers who had allowed the film-makers to follow their campaign allegedly felt betrayed as they had expected a more didactic film rather than the avant-garde piece that resulted.[87] It is a moot point whether the political content of the film is undercut by its experimental qualities. Brian Winston, in a typically trenchant critique, avers that the effect of *Nightcleaners* is 'to reduce the deconstructionist agenda to a bathetic formalism . . . At best the film bored; at worst it got in the way of the nightcleaners' struggle'.[88] Even its co-director Marc Karlin conceded that '*Nightcleaners* has had more repercussions in film culture than in the labour movement.'[89]

How can we assess the achievements of the alternative film-makers of the 1970s? On the one hand there is evidence that the collectives and workshops had some influence on the wider film culture. This can be seen in the establishment of professional associations representing the interests of the independent sector, including the Independent Film-Makers' Association (IFA) in 1974 and the Association of Independent Producers (AIP) in 1976, and in events that aimed to raise the profile of alternative film practices beyond the academy, such as the Festival of Independent Film at the Arnolfini Gallery in Bristol in 1975 and the programme of screenings and seminars held at the Institute of Contemporary Arts in London under the banner 'Film and Community Action' in 1976. On the other hand, however, alternative films had limited distribution and exhibition and their impact seems to have been more in the arena of theoretical debate than direct political action. It was not a film such as *Fighting the Bill* that brought about the dilution of the Industrial Relations Act but a revolt by Labour MPs against their own government that removed the most controversial clauses. And films such as *The UCS Struggle* and its sequel *Class Struggle: Film from the Clyde* (1977) could not, in the end, prevent the closure of the Clydeside ship-yards. Moreover, the audiences for the campaign documentaries would seem by and large to have been activists rather than the general public: to this extent the films were preaching to those already converted.

Cinema Action remained active into the 1980s, when it was able to secure funding from the British Film Institute and Channel 4, though it gradually shifted from the agitprop campaign films to dramatized documentary such as the feature *Rocinante* (1987), which had a six-week run at the Renoir Cinema in London. The group ceased operating at the end of the 1980s when a computer contractor went bankrupt owing £10,000 and workshop funding from Channel 4 dried up.[90] However, the legacy of Cinema Action can be seen in other initiatives during the 1980s when a combination of ideological contexts (the political ascendancy of the New Right marked by the Conservative government of Margaret Thatcher) and technological developments (the advent of videotape recording as a cheaper and more flexible alternative to 16 millimetre film) created the conditions in which a second wave of workshops emerged, including Belfast Independent Video (founded in 1980), Platform Films (1982), Trade Films (1982) and the Derry Film and Video Collective (1984). The continuation of the tradition of workers' films is exemplified by the Miners' Campaign Tape Project of 1984. This project consisted of six video tapes produced to document the miners' strike from the perspective of the miners themselves. The project was supported by the National Union of Mineworkers and was intended specifically 'to draw attention to aspects of the dispute ignored or distorted by the mainstream media'.[91] The tapes were distributed free to miners on VHS cassettes: it is estimated that around 4,000 copies were in circulation during the strike.[92]

The Miners' Campaign Tape Project marks the coming together of various strands in oppositional documentary practice. The project was led by Platform Films – a London-based workshop whose members included Chris Reeves, Lin Solomon and Geoffrey Bell – which edited footage shot in different coalfields by several organizations, including Cinema Action, Amber Films, the Birmingham Film and Video Workshop and the Nottingham Video Project. The credits to supporters and sponsors include academics involved in the film and video workshop movement such as Sylvia Harvey and Sue Aspinall, and celebrities including the actress Julie Christie. A link to the political documentary tradition of the 1930s is also indicated by credits to Ralph Bond and Ivor Montagu and by the inclusion in the tapes of footage of miners and marches from the interwar period. The fact that the Miners' Campaign Tape Project won the BFI's John Grierson Award in 1985 further serves to reinforce its place in the history of British documentary film-making.

The tapes themselves are more interesting for their content than their formal qualities: they each ran for 10–15 minutes and consisted of a mixture of actuality video of strikes and pickets, focusing especially on confrontations with the police, interviews with union activists and the oral testimony of miners and their families, shot either individually or in groups. Within this format each film focuses on a specific theme, such as the role of miners' wives in forming support groups (*Not Just Tea & Sandwiches*), support for the strike from other trade unions (*Solidarity*), the apparent agenda of the National Coal Board to run down the mining industry (*The Coal Board's Butchery*), the biased representation of the strike in the press and broadcast media (*The Lie Machine*) and the confrontational tactics of the police (*Only Doing Their Job?*). The tapes are openly partisan but their value is that they express the voice of the miners themselves as well as supporters such as the left-wing Labour MP Dennis Skinner. The rhetoric is one of class war: the miners' strike is seen as 'the last chance for the British working class to defend itself against the blitz on jobs and on social conditions' (*Solidarity*), while the police are 'the private army of the ruling class which exists for the sole purpose of defending private property and profits' (*Only Doing Their Job?*). The inclusion of footage of the General Strike of 1926 and the Jarrow march of 1936 identifies the miners ideologically with the history of working-class industrial protest in Britain. The support of the National Union of Mineworkers (NUM) is evident in the prominence of NUM leader Arthur Scargill – extracts from his speeches feature in each of the tapes – and in references to the breakaway Union of Democratic Mineworkers as 'the Nottingham scabs' (*The Lie Machine*). While some of the views expressed are rhetorical hyperbole (for example Skinner's comparison of the miners to Jews during the Holocaust), there are nevertheless moments of insight. In *Only Doing Their Job?*, for example, miners arrested for their role in a picket discuss how they feel victimized by the police and compare themselves with Britain's black and Asian communities:

> I realize I was bloody ignorant – through the media – I was ignorant. I realize what them [*sic*] people have gone through for bloody years and what we've gone through for only sixteen or seventeen week [*sic*]. And we know that at the end ours'll finish. But theirs won't.

In this context the politics of the Miners' Campaign Tape Project may be aligned with the work of other organizations such as the Black Audio Film Collective.

Regional documentary practice: Amber Films

The emergence of regional documentary film groups in the 1970s was the outcome of several processes. The long-term structural decline of traditional heavy industries such as coal, steel and shipbuilding with their

bases in the Midlands and north of England was hastened by the economic depression of the 1970s, which in turn threw into sharp relief
the socio-economic inequality between those areas and the more prosperous southern England. It was only natural that more socially aware
and politically engaged film-makers would become interested in the
question of what was now widely being referred to as the 'north/south
divide'. At the same time there was a significant degree of subsidy for cultural activities through semi-public bodies such as the Arts Council and
regional arts boards. Regional documentary practice can also be seen as
another way in which alternative film-making asserted its independence
from the structures of the mainstream film and television industries,
which were predominantly London-centric. It is not clear whether John
Grierson ever saw any of the work of Amber Films but he was evidently
in sympathy with the project it represented. In his last interview before
his death in 1972 Grierson said: 'I don't think there's been any contribution by Britain to documentary in the last ten years of any sort. I see the
next chapter being making films really locally … the local film people
making films to state their case politically or otherwise.'[93]

Amber Films – founded in Newcastle-upon-Tyne in 1969 by a group of
film students from Regent Street Polytechnic in London – was the first
of the collectives outside London. It is also by some measure the most
enduring: it has continued its tradition of socially engaged regional documentary film-making for over four decades and several of the group's
founding members are still active film-makers. It was something of an
accident that the group came to be established in Newcastle. According
to Murray Martin, one of its founding members:

> At that time we opened ourselves up to anybody who was prepared to
> join the group and there were maybe six or seven people interested.
> We didn't decide at once to go to Newcastle, but we came to the
> conclusion that we were not going to stay in London. We looked at
> Bristol, Liverpool, Glasgow and Newcastle and I was the one probably
> most in favour of Newcastle. So I elected to go to Newcastle and about
> five other people came.[94]

Martin had lived for a while in Newcastle where he had studied fine
arts, but other founding members such as Finnish photographer Sirkka-
Liisa Konttinen had no particular connection with the north-east of
England. Others involved with the origins and early history of Amber
were cameraman Graham Denman and animator Peter Roberts. It has
become part of Amber folklore that its name was chosen after a local

ale, though a more mundane factor may have been that it 'would figure prominently early in any directory of film companies'.[95] The fact that Amber has survived so long when other collectives have disappeared would suggest that its political idealism has been tempered by a sharp business acumen.

Amber was representative of the workshop movement in that it worked as a collective and adopted a non-hierarchical structure. From the outset it was agreed that each member would be paid an equal wage. Martin explained the practice thus: 'I suppose I come from an egalitarian, socialist tradition which can't understand why a film director should get paid more than a dustbin man, and even more so, why the person directing the film should get paid more than the person doing the clapper loading.'[96] While individual members had their own specialisms, Amber's working practices were geared towards everyone undertaking a range of different roles, while the credits of its films usually assigned collective rather than individual authorship. This practice was only possible outside the structure of the mainstream film and television industries where the highly unionized organization prevented what was known as cross-grade working. Amber combined the activities of production and exhibition: in 1977 it opened its own cinema – the Side Gallery and Cinema – with funding from the Arts Council and Northern Arts. This was also an indication that Amber was interested in more than just film: indeed Kontinnen and other early members Graham Smith and Chris Killip were primarily still photographers rather than film-makers. From the outset Amber sought to forge links with other local arts groups. One of its early ventures was the 'River Project', which combined film, photography, painting, sculpture and writing. Amber also established relationships with local artists including sculptor Laurie Wheatley and actor-comedian Tim Healey, best known for the television comedy-drama series *Auf Wiedersehen, Pet.*

Amber saw its role as being to document working-class communities in north-east England. It identified particularly with workers in traditional heavy and manufacturing industries that were in decline by the 1970s. Many of its early film subjects were suggested by Tyneside local historian Stafford Lindsey, who pointed out working practices that should be recorded before they were lost to posterity. Its early films included documentaries about a high-valley small drift mine (*High Row*, 1974), the working of a pit railway from the 1820s (*Last Shift*, 1976) and a glass-blowing factory in Leamington (*Glass Works*, 1977). Amber's practice was to pay small groups of workers to re-enact their usual working patterns and film them 'on the job': the films are often therefore reconstructed rather than observational documentaries. Its aim was to provide a means through which the working classes could understand their own history. According to Martin: 'I felt there was a job to be done of recording working-class culture before it disappeared, and celebrating it.'[97]

Amber's documentary practice can be understood as both a continuation of and as a departure from the Griersonian tradition. On the one hand the subjects of its films often hark back to those of documentary in the 1930s: its early film *Launch* (1973) about the launching of an oil tanker in Wallsend from the perspective of the local community can be seen as part of a lineage of documentary film-making extending back to Rotha's *Shipyard*. And there are both visual and aural echoes of Jennings's *Spare Time* in Amber's *Wallsend 72* (1972), which accords prominence to a kazoo band (though actually described as a 'jazz band') known as the Rising Sun Legionnaires. Like the documentary movement of the 1930s, Amber's films can be seen as celebrations of the 'heroic' stature of the working classes – especially those in traditional industries. On the other hand, however, there are significant differences from the past. Amber was closer to its subjects than the GPO Film Unit had ever been: the miners of *High Row* are rather more individualized than those of *Industrial Britain* or *Coal Face*. A crucial difference was that Amber's funding through regional arts subsidies and later from Channel 4 meant that it was independent from both state and corporate sponsorship. It was therefore not tied to the ideological demands of sponsors and was free to make the sort of films it wanted. For Martin: 'The difference between that constituency and us was that in many ways the 1930s filmmakers worked for the state, were employed by it and censored by it. Hence there are no images of unemployment from the 1930s or at least very few.'[98]

The diversity of styles evident in the films of Amber suggest that there was no 'house' style: instead the representation seems to emerge from the nature of the subjects themselves. *Maybe* (1969) – Amber's first film and one of the few to include individual credits as 'a film by Graham Denman and Murray Martin' – sits within the 'poetic' documentary mode with its artful framing and use of close-ups in its representation of the thoughts of an engineer on the Tynemouth ferry. In contrast films such as *High Row* are notable for the absence of close-ups and seem to be more inclined to document working practices and conditions than to impose an interpretation upon them. *6 to Midnight* (1974) about a day at the Grainger Street market has a superficial similarity to *Every Day Except Christmas*, though on closer analysis it seems a much starker film: the absence of voice-over commentary (a feature of most Amber films) and the shots of empty, grey streets create a rather austere feel in comparison to the lyricism of Lindsay Anderson's film. And *Quayside* (1979) anticipates the work of artist film-maker Patrick Keiller in its representation of Newcastle's Quayside area that combines aspects of documentary and avant-garde practice. This film by Sirkka-Liisa Konttinen is best described as a slow montage in that it employs slow tracking shots and moving shots along roads (in a style reminiscent of the 'phantom rides' of early cinema) to showcase the architectural heritage of an industrial landscape earmarked for redevelopment.

Appropriately, given that its objective was to document the transformation of regional culture and identity, Amber's formal practices changed over time. *Byker* (1983) exemplifies a trend towards longer and more ambitious films in the 1980s. This film by Konttinen is an impressionistic description of a working-class area of Newcastle and its people that adopts a collage technique – including still photographs, film, songs and multiple commentaries – in its evocation of a community facing the inevitability of change. The film expresses mixed views about urban regeneration: on the one hand Byker was a poor area with an abundance of slum housing, while on the other hand the demolition of slums and the building of new housing estates is presented as breaking up traditional communities. The recollections of its older inhabitants contrast memories of privation ('I never had a pair of shoes when I was a kid') with nostalgia (it was 'a better time in many ways') and regret about how the area has changed ('It's a different class of people in Byker now – they're not content round here'). The sense of discomfort with the modern desire for material possessions expressed by one elderly lady might be seen as an implied critique of the materialist culture of Thatcherism in the 1980s.

The oppositional politics of Amber can be seen in its first feature-length film: *Seacoal* (1985). *Seacoal* has been unfairly neglected in the critical historiography of British social realist cinema of the 1980s, which has preferred fictional feature films such as *My Beautiful Laundrette* (1985) in constructing an ideology of cultural opposition to Thatcherism. *Seacoal* is a documentary drama in which the subject matter is an unusual local subsistence economy: the gathering of coal washed ashore on Lynemouth beach to sell at 'a pund a bag'. The film uses a mixture of actors (Ray Stubbs as Reg – an emasculated male protagonist who takes on a similar tragic stature to Bernard Hill's 'Yozzer' Hughes in *The Boys from the Blackstuff* – and Amber Styles as his long-suffering partner Betty) and real people who play versions of themselves (Trevor Critchlow as 'Critch', Gordon Tait as 'Taity'), and while the actors' lines were scripted the responses of the real people were not. *Seacoal* can be positioned within the formal development of Amber's films in the 1980s to explore 'the interface of documentary and fiction': to this extent it exemplifies the continuing evolution of the documentary-drama mode from television plays such as *Cathy Come Home*.[99] It is a film of austere visual beauty: the cinematography empha- sizes grey shades to represent the bleak landscapes of windswept beach and post-industrial urban decline. A closing caption informs us that common access to the beach – on which 'scavengers' such as Ray and Betty are dependent for their livelihood – has been closed: the beach and its 'public' coal supply have effectively been privatized. The mean- ing in the context of the Thatcher government's policy of privatization is clear.

The 1980s was a particularly productive period for Amber: *Byker* and *Seacoal* were among a number of films funded by Channel 4 under the terms of the ACTT (Association of Cinema and Television Technicians) Workshop Agreement, which recognized the practice of cross-grade working and so opened up the notoriously closed film and television industries to those working outside its institutional structures. It has always been something of an irony that a broadcaster whose origins were rooted in free-market principles – Channel 4 was the first televi- sion channel with a statutory requirement to commission programmes from outside contractors rather than producing its content in-house – became the principal supporter of alternative film-making practices dur- ing the 1980s, which adopted a defiantly oppositional stance towards the Thatcher government and its free-market ideology. 'A large chunk of our money since 1982 has come from television, almost exclusively from Channel Four', Martin testifies. 'Up to *Eden Valley* [1995] almost all our money was given under the Workshop Declaration to do as we wished.'[100] Amber received between £48,000 and £90,000 a year until the end of the agreement in 1994. It was advantageous for the group because if Channel 4 chose to broadcast any of the films it still had to pay separately for them.

The extent of television sales – also including to France, Germany, Scandinavia and Australia – meant that Amber's films reached a significantly larger audience than most other documentary films. It even exported behind the Iron Curtain when it collaborated with the East German state film organization DEFA (Deutsche Film- Aktiengesellschaft) in making a comparative study of Newcastle and Rostock entitled *From Marks and Spencer to Marx and Engels* (1988).[101]

The collaboration was not as incongruous as it might seem: both Amber and DEFA worked within a tradition of critical social realism, while the film met DEFA's ideological agenda as it seemed to suggest that those living in the communist state enjoyed a better quality of life than those in the north-east of England! The withdrawal of Channel 4 funding in the 1990s necessitated a retrenchment of Amber's production activities. It shifted away from longer films and turned instead to small-scale community engagement projects with series of ten-minute 'soaps' focusing on particular communities such as South Shields (*Shields Stories*) and County Durham (*Coalfield Stories*). Even during the heyday of television funding, however, Amber always remained true to its principles:

> We have talked on many occasions about making a film that has commercial potential, but the place where we start from doesn't allow us to do that. If you take a film like *Eden Valley*, which is about harness racing, we were offered the potential of a large budget from Channel 4 – £750,000 was mentioned – or we could have £50,000 and make it our way. The condition on the larger budget was that they would put in the writer. We took the £50,000 with not a lot of hesitation, because we knew we wanted to make a film which accurately reflected the community we represented.[102]

It is this continued commitment to the representation of regional working-class identity and social engagement with those communities that has made Amber's work stand out as one of the most unique and distinctive bodies of film in the history of British documentary.

The Black Audio Film Collective and *Handsworth Songs* (1986)

It is a curious fact that race seems to have had little impact on British independent film culture until the 1980s, despite the fact that black (mostly Afro-Caribbean) and Asian immigrants had been settled in Britain for several generations and race relations had been a theme of British feature films extending back to the 1950s (*Flame in the Streets*, *Sapphire*). The formation in London of several black film workshops in the mid-1980s – Ceddo, Sankofa and the Black Audio Film Collective – should be understood in several contexts. On one level it reflected an international trend in documentary towards the exploration of the experiences of ethnic minorities exemplified by the films of

African-American film-makers such as Marlon Riggs and St Clair Bourne. In a specifically British context the emergence of black documentary as a distinct category in its own right can also be understood as a response to the race riots in predominantly black inner-city areas such as Brixton in London, Toxteth in Liverpool and Moss Side in Manchester in the early 1980s, which threw into sharp relief not only the social and economic inequalities of working-class black Britons but also the culturally insensitive policing of those areas, which was deemed to have been a factor in triggering the disturbances. For the founding members of the Black Audio Film Collective there were different reasons for their interest in film-making. For Lina Gopaul it arose from '[a] deep sense of injustice from education. A deep sense of racism from things that have happened to me all my life.'[103] But for Ghanaian-born John Akomfrah it grew out of an intellectual interest in the politics of race: 'We'd fallen into this group of black students who were all interested in more or less the same stuff: the American political scene, African liberation theory, Jean-Paul Sartre.'[104]

The emergence of the black workshops has also been understood in the intellectual context of shifting discourses of race in Britain. Jim Pines argues that until the 1980s the dominant theoretical issue around ethnicity was the question of 'race relations' as explored in films with a broadly liberal agenda such as *Sapphire* and *To Sir With Love* or – to take a once popular but at the same time highly problematic example – the television situation comedy *Love Thy Neighbour*.[105] Two developments in the 1980s changed this. The first was that for the first time in Britain, cultural ownership of black representation was in the hands of black directors such as Menelik Shabazz (*Burning an Illusion*, 1981) and Isaac Julien (*Territories*, 1985). The other development was a shift away from race relations discourses to a critical engagement with the ways in which racial identity was constructed in the media. Stuart Hall explained the process thus:

What is at issue here is the recognition of the extraordinary diversity of subjective positions, social experiences and cultural identities which comprise the category 'black'; that is, the recognition that 'black' is essentially a politically and culturally constructed category, which cannot be grounded in a set of fixed trans-cultural or transcendental racial categories and which therefore has no guarantee in Nature. What this brings into play is the recognition of the immense diversity and differentiation of the historical and cultural experience of black subjects.[106]

From the outset the black film workshops were concerned with more than just the experience of being black and British: they looked to interrogate the cultural and ideological frameworks in which the idea of 'blackness' was itself constructed. Hence their work would adopt some of the techniques of avant-garde film in looking to deconstruct the formal properties of the medium – an approach that prompted some charges of cultural elitism.

Black Audio's *Handsworth Songs* (1986) was by some measure the most successful – and most controversial – of the films produced by the black film workshops. The film is best described as a discursive 'essay' on racial inequality in Britain that takes as its starting point the race riots in the Handsworth area of Birmingham in 1985 but extends beyond these events to explore the historical contexts of Caribbean immigration and the post-colonial experience. Evidence that the film was also informed to some extent by the intellectual agenda of film theory can be found in the language used by director John Akomfrah in explaining the formal construction of *Handsworth Songs*:

> Our task was to find a form and a structure which would allow us the space to deconstruct the hegemonic voices of British television newsreels. That was absolutely crucial if we were to succeed in articulating those spatial and temporal states of belonging and displacement differently. In order to bring emotions, uncertainties and anxieties alive we had to poeticise [*sic*] that which was captured through the lenses of the BBC and other newsreel units – by poeticising every image we were able to succeed in recasting the binary oppositions between myth and history, imagination and experiential states of occasional violence.[107]

This highlights a tension within the theoretical construction of *Handsworth Songs* as a documentary. On the one hand the imperative of providing an alternative to the coverage of the Handsworth riots on British television links the film to the work of Cinema Action and similar groups; elsewhere, Akomfrah mentions having seen 'some Cinema Action stuff'.[108] On the other hand the emphasis on the 'poeticization' of the raw material is suggestive of the Griersonian notion of 'the creative treatment of actuality'. Indeed members of Black Audio suggested that *Handsworth Songs* was made in 'the Griersonian spirit'. Akomfrah testified that we spent a lot of time watching a number of documentaries like *Industrial Britain*. One of the things which is important to acknowledge is that the mournful angelic quality of certain parts of *Handsworth Songs* has to do with that filmic history; it is to look at industrial Britain and say – 'that sort of confidence can't be spoken anymore in the 1980s'.[109]

Handsworth Songs is characterized by a high degree of formal complexity that draws upon a wide range of documentary practices. It combines archive footage of Afro-Caribbean immigrants arriving in Britain and their lives in Britain, television news footage of the 1985 riots (sometimes in slow motion), television footage of Prime Minister Margaret Thatcher speaking about immigration, on-camera interviews with people who witnessed the riots, and some actuality sequences shot specifically for the film, including a Rastafarian disco and a West Indian bus conductor in Birmingham. It also employs a wide range of both diegetic and non-diegetic sounds including voice-overs, reggae music and the 'songs' of the title: poetic commentaries by a female voice. The film's structure is non-linear – it alternates between past and present – and it includes scenes inserted for symbolic effect such as recurring shots of birds in the treetops and the face of a mechanical clown. The combination of non-linear narration and different formal devices has the effect of making *Handsworth Songs* a more 'open' text than most films: it seems to suggest that the reasons for the Handsworth riots are complex and cannot be reduced to a single cause. It shifts between modes and perspectives, raising profound questions but refusing to offer overly didactic answers.

Yet at the same time as drawing upon avant-garde practice, *Handsworth Songs* can also be seen to be rooted in the historical traditions of British documentary film. The most obvious influence is the 'poetic' style of Humphrey Jennings. *Handsworth Songs* might even be seen as a companion piece to a film such as *Listen to Britain* in that it employs both visual and aural montage in a discourse around the complex nature of identity. Of course there are also important differences: whereas the ideological objective of *Listen to Britain* had been to picture a nation united through its affection for culture, *Handsworth Songs* instead represents a society divided along class and racial lines. The consensual society represented by British documentary films of the 1930s and 1940s has now been transformed into a nation coming to terms with a new post-colonial identity and working through the social problems and tensions arising from that change. *Handsworth Songs* also echoes classic British documentary film in its representation of urban spaces; but in contrast to the films of the 1930s the iconography is one of industrial decline and a decaying infrastructure – exemplified in the melancholic final shot of a woman walking beside a derelict and overgrown railway viaduct.

Handsworth Songs was shown by Channel 4 and attracted much critical interest. It won a number of accolades, including the BFI John Grierson Award. But it also provoked a good deal of hostility and anger. This is perhaps not surprising given its formal complexity and challenging subject matter: *Handsworth Songs* was intended to spark debate and in that sense it succeeded. Some of the criticism focused on the old chestnut of authenticity: the use of library footage of the Brixton riots of 1981 seemingly passed off as Handsworth in 1985 was a liberty too far for some. However, this seems less problematic than in some other films, as *Handsworth Songs* does not make any claim to literal 'truth': indeed its formal structure is posited to a large extent on the use of images in a metaphorical or allegorical rather than a necessarily literal context. For Colin McCabe the issue was not the authenticity of the visual material but the film's 'outdated aesthetics' that were too reminiscent of the poetic realism of the 1930s.[110] The most contentious issue, however, was the film's representation of racial identities. The British-Indian author Salman Rushdie complained that *Handsworth Songs* was so preoccupied with representing black Britons as victims that the film-makers 'let us hear so little of the much richer language of their subjects'.[111] Akomfrah rebutted this charge in a characteristically erudite response: 'In the end, what Rushdie and other critics found really objectionable about the film ... is precisely that anti-ethnographic bias – that you can't use the film to construct other knowledges about Handsworth.'[112]

The impact of *Handsworth Songs* secured a contract for Black Audio from Channel 4 and all its subsequent films were produced under the Workshop Declaration until the contract ended in 1992. Although run as a collective, Black Audio had a different production ethos to groups like Amber Films. According to Avril Johnson: 'On the films people were paid according to grade ... Right from the word go, we had allocated roles in which we wanted to work in the television industry – producer, director, writer, whatever and we would then pay ourselves accordingly.'[113] Later Black Audio films included Reece Auguiste's *Twilight City* (1987) and Akomfrah's *Seven Songs for Malcolm X* (1993) – the latter adopting a more critical perspective than the Hollywood biopic directed by Spike Lee – though it would be fair to say that none of them matched the impact of *Handsworth Songs*. Akomfrah has also directed television documentaries on black subjects, including Martin Luther King (for the BBC's *Reputations* series in 1997) and Louis Armstrong (for the BBC's *Omnibus* in 1999). In 2013 he returned to theatrical documentary and revisited some of the themes of *Handsworth Songs* with the critically acclaimed *The Stuart Hall Project*.

This has been a necessarily selective overview of the history of alternative and oppositional documentary practice in Britain. There remain many avenues for further research, including (but not limited to) the role of independent distributors after the Second World War such as Stanley Forman's Plato Films and Charles Cooper's Contemporary Films, which provide a direct link between the political documentarists of the 1930s and the workshop movement, and the work of other groups in the early 1970s such as Liberation Films and the Newsreel Collective, which may have enjoyed lesser longevity than Cinema Action or Amber Films but demonstrate different organizational models and working practices. In particular there is a need to rescue alternative film practice from theoretical debates over ideology and form, and to research the contexts of production and distribution and the nature of the audiences for these films. In the meantime, however, two general points may be made. The first is that the history of alternative documentary practice should not be seen as linear but rather as one that has followed different trajectories and contours, alternating between periods of relative inactivity and others, sometimes quite short-lived, when it has emerged from the shadows and has been at the forefront of progressive film-making activities in Britain. While there are clearly continuities between the political documentaries of the 1930s and the 'people's films' of Cinema Action, there are also significant differences, and to trace a direct line of descent from the former to the latter is to construct a teleological narrative that does not sufficiently allow for the specific historical and ideological contexts in which each of those practices were formulated. The other general point is that alternative documentary should be seen as part of the broader history of documentary practice in Britain rather than being relegated to some sort of cultural ghetto. While many alternative forms have been marginal in the sense that their distribution and exhibition were extremely limited, it is evident that some of these films, including those presented under the Free Cinema banner, and *Handsworth Songs*, have enjoyed greater cultural visibility and have become the focus of cultural debates. In this sense the term 'oppositional' is itself perhaps somewhat misleading: these films exist alongside – indeed are often in dialogue with – the more mainstream traditions of documentary. Free Cinema positioned itself in opposition to the Griersonian tradition but was strongly influenced by the films of Humphrey Jennings. And Black Audio placed itself in what it termed the 'Griersonian spirit' even as it sought to deconstruct the formal conventions of documentary. There is no doubt that these films have enriched the history of British documentary: they should therefore be accorded their rightful place in that history rather than being set up as something apart from it.

Conclusion
British Documentary in Context

> As against the erosion of the movement in Britain, however, it must be remembered how in the years to come the documentary idea was, through its British exponents, to inspire growing points in many parts of the world – in Australia, India, Egypt, New Zealand and Malaysia among them.
>
> Paul Rotha[1]

The British documentary – both in film and in television – has undergone fluctuating critical fortunes. For many years documentary was claimed as 'Britain's outstanding contribution to the film' and this became the critical orthodoxy. This view persisted even in the wake of the decline (or as Rotha would have it 'erosion') of British documentary film after the Second World War. Later critiques of documentary focused on the perceived formal and ideological shortcomings of the films and highlighted the fact that documentary was a marginal mode of film practice. And in the 1980s the intellectual ascendancy of the 'documentary-realist tradition' in British film and television culture was itself challenged by the emergence of a revisionist historiography that sought to excavate those genres and traditions marginalized by realist aesthetics. The most persistent metaphor of recent British film historiography has been that of the 'lost continent' – a term coined by Julian Petley to describe the 'repressed side of British cinema, a dark, disdained thread weaving the length and breadth of that cinema, crossing authorial and generic boundaries, sometimes almost entirely invisible, sometimes erupting explosively, always received critically with fear and disapproval'.[2] A consequence of this revisionist historiography was the reclamation of popular but critically despised genres such as the Gainsborough costume melodramas and the Hammer horror

259

films, and individualistic *auteurs* such as Michael Powell and Ken Russell whose work did not fit conventional notions of quality cinema. Hence a new orthodoxy has emerged in the study of British cinema that posits a distinction between 'realism' and 'tinsel': between a realist cinema (including documentary) characterized by its social and moral purpose on the one hand, and a cinema of fantasy and visual excess on the other. An undercurrent in much of this work has been an intellectual reaction against the idea of a socially purposeful cinema in favour of a cinema of pure entertainment and escapism. As this is what the documentary movement set itself up in opposition to from the outset, it makes a useful starting point for an assessment of the historical significance of documentary in British cinema and television.

It would probably be fair to say that few today would accept uncritically the idea that documentary is 'almost the only British contribution to world cinema' worthy of note. British cinema is now recognized as the national cinema that produced popular genres and series such as the James Bond and 'Carry On . . . ' films as well as documentary and the new wave, and as the cinema that nurtured major directors including Alfred Hitchcock, Michael Powell and David Lean as well as Humphrey Jennings and Free Cinema. Similarly, the international success of *Doctor Who* and *Downton Abbey* demonstrates that there is much more to British television than the documentary-drama tradition of *Cathy Come Home*. To acknowledge the cultural and economic importance of other modes and forms, however, is not to suggest that the importance of documentary should be diminished. Rather, it is to suggest that it should be seen in the context of a wider film and television culture of which documentary has been just one – albeit at times privileged – component. So to what extent can documentary be adjudged to have been 'Britain's outstanding contribution to the film'?

Any assessment of the historical importance and achievement of British documentary must address three questions: the legacy of John Grierson; the extent to which documentary has ever been more than a marginal practice with limited popular appeal; and the charge that documentary lost its sense of progressive social purpose after the Second World War. The first of these questions – the legacy of Grierson – to some extent helps to answer the others. It is evident to even the most casual observer that Grierson's intellectual presence looms large over the history of British documentary. Grierson played a crucial role as both producer and theorist in the origins and early history of the British documentary film movement. It was Grierson who defined the terms in which documentary was (and to a large extent still is) understood and who did most to advocate its social purpose. It was Grierson who did most to persuade the state of the value of documentary as a medium of democratic communication and national projection. And it was Grierson whose commitment to a socially purposeful and aesthetically progressive cinema influenced several generations of documentarists in film and television. At the same time, however, it must be recognized that Grierson is not synonymous with British documentary. The tradition of non-fiction film-making in Britain may be traced back to the early years of cinema, and visionaries such as Charles Urban preceded Grierson in recognizing the social utility and educational value of cinema. Moreover, the Griersonian idea of documentary was formed within the historical and ideological contexts of the 1930s; and, as much as he recognized that documentary practice should adapt and evolve in response to changing circumstances, Grierson always referred back to what he saw as its first principles. As he wrote in a postscript to the revised edition of *Grierson on Documentary* in 1966:

> In developing the documentary approach to film-making it is now obvious that we served a useful purpose and, it may be, more purposes than we foresaw. A sense of purpose was certainly at the heart of the matter and, I think, still must be if the documentary film is to command wide and various public support and do justice to its æsthetic potential.[3]

Yet to what extent has documentary commanded wide public support? The limited theatrical distribution of documentary films in the 1930s and the difficulty of ascertaining the size of the non-theatrical audience has given rise to the perception that documentary was not popular with audiences. This view needs to be nuanced: distributors and exhibitors certainly were resistant to documentary but the evidence of popular reception is mixed. The cinemagoing audience was not homogenous and there were evidently some who were interested in documentary films. The experience of the Second World War when films such as *Target for Tonight* and *Desert Victory* were significant box-office successes suggests that documentary could find an appreciative audience in the commercial cinemas under particular ideological circumstances. Against this must be set the fact that post-war feature-length documentaries such as *Land of Promise* and *The World is Rich* did not succeed in reaching large audiences – though this may be explained in part by the attitude of renters who were reluctant to book the films. The success of the wartime films and other examples such as *North Sea* would suggest that audiences were not necessarily deterred by documentary per se.

It is when we turn to television that evidence of the public's interest in documentary becomes more apparent. Unlike cinema, where a documentary would usually be a supporting item on the programme, the act of watching a television documentary suggests a conscious choice on the part of the viewer. Of course this may be either a positive choice (in preference to, say, a soap opera or a quiz show) or a negative choice (in the absence of 'anything else') – though, even so, documentary has to be able to hold its own against other genres and leisure interests. Nevertheless, the reception of documentary dramas such as *Cathy Come Home* and historical-archival series such as *The World at War* suggests that the television audience is responsive to a range of documentary modes. Indeed the evidence is overwhelming that documentary has succeeded in reaching a significantly larger audience through television than it ever did in the cinemas. This is one reason for including television documentary as part of a wider history of documentary practice rather than regarding it as something entirely separate from film. And, while it is unlikely that, in the multi-channel era, a documentary series will ever achieve the impact of something like *The World at War*, the popularity of docusoaps indicates that the television audience is still receptive to documentary.

And so to the third question: whether or not documentary lost its progressive social purpose after the Second World War. This is a charge levelled against post-war documentary by some first-generation documentarists, including Rotha, as well as by academic critics such as Brian Winston. It is rooted in the view that the true purpose of documentary is the critical examination of social problems – in which respect, it must be said, both Rotha and Winston also find the films of the EMB and GPO Film Units wanting – and that it became impossible for documentarists to further this agenda under the different regimes of state or industrial sponsorship after 1945. However, it is a charge that does not stand up. Three points need to be made here. The first is that the ideological project of Griersonian (and 'Rotharian' for that matter) documentary was formed in response to the particular social and economic problems of the 1930s but that these had changed after the war: if there were fewer films like *Housing Problems* it was because the nature of social problems had changed. The second is that the social documentary did not in fact disappear – films such as *The Undefeated*, *David*, *Thursday's Children* and *I Think They Call Him John* demonstrate its persistence – but rather developed in different ways that preferred a more personal mode in favour of the dialectical agitprop style of Rotha. The films were no less effective for that. And the third point is that the Griersonian project of documentary as a vehicle for public information and education fed directly into television, where it was taken up by current affairs programmes such as *Panorama* and *World in Action*. Here again there is evidence of continuity between film and television documentary: indeed it can be argued that from the 1960s the mantle of social documentary passed from film to television, where it still persists today even if in a diluted form.

Further evidence that the social documentary remains alive and well is to be found in its recent re-emergence in British cinema. Ken Loach's *The Spirit of '45* (2012) and John Akomfrah's *The Stuart Hall Project* (2013) are both feature-length documentaries supported by the British Film Institute (and in the case of Loach's film also by Film 4) and afforded a theatrical cinema release in Britain. They each demonstrate, in their different ways, how contemporary documentary film is informed by and draws upon its own past. *The Spirit of '45* is Loach's hymn to the achievements of the post-war Labour government in Britain. It employs a mixture of archive footage (including documentaries such as *Housing Problems*), oral history transcripts and on-camera interviews to explore the context of Labour's landslide general election victory in 1945 – here understood as a response to the social and economic inequalities of the interwar period – and to assess its achievements in the establishment of the Welfare State and National Health Service. Loach mobilizes the documentary movement itself towards this end by including extracts from wartime films *Post 23* and *ABCA*, which feature people discussing their hopes and expectations for the post-war world. *The Spirit of '45* is a polemical though sincere argument in favour of state collectivism and common ownership of industries and public utilities. It concludes by contrasting the achievements of the Labour government with what it sees as the dismantling of the Welfare State, begun by the Thatcher government, and argues for the re-nationalization of major industries. Its assertively left-wing politics and advocacy of state collectivism position *The Spirit of '45* squarely in the tradition of films such as Rotha's *Land of Promise*: indeed it may be the most explicitly socialist film to emerge from the mainstream of British documentary since 1945.

In contrast *The Stuart Hall Project* illustrates the more personal and reflective mode characteristic of its director John Akomfrah. In his own words: 'I've been making projects on memory for a while now, but this one feels like the one I have been "preparing" for a very long time indeed, possibly all my working life.'[4] *The Stuart Hall Project* takes the form of an 'essay film' exploring the life and influence of Britain's most prominent black academic, compiled from archive footage of Hall's television and radio appearances. Like the director's *Handsworth Songs*, *The*

Stuart Hall Project belongs to a tradition of alternative documentary practice. This is evident in three ways: its interweaving of the personal biography of Stuart Hall with the wider social history of West Indian immigration in post-war Britain; its rejection of conventional linear narrative in favour of a more fragmented structure that reflects its subject's view (expressed in the film) that societies exist in 'a state of permanent revolution'; and the use of music (by jazz musician Miles Davis – a personal favourite of both Hall and Akomfrah) as more than just aural wallpaper but an integral part of the formal pattern of the film. While affectionate towards its subject, *The Stuart Hall Project* is no mere hagiography but a critical examination of the discourses of Britishness and racial identity. It shares stylistic similarities with *Handsworth Songs*, including its collage technique and a slightly melancholic tone (no doubt influenced by the fact that, at the time of its making, Stuart Hall was 81 and in poor health). The review of the film for *Sight and Sound* saw it as 'a successful crystallisation of Akomfrah's work to date; it is crafted in the style of, and intentionally haunted by, the ghosts of his previous films'.[5] This may be true; but at the same time *The Stuart Hall Project* also belongs to the tradition of socially informed documentary film exploring the issues of citizenship and identity in contemporary Britain. To this extent – and again like *Handsworth Songs* – it echoes the legacy of Griersonian documentary.

There is one final context in which British documentary may be placed. This book has explored the history of documentary production in British cinema and television: it has outlined the main contours of that history and has given some indication of how documentary has changed and adapted itself in response to changing ideological and institutional contexts. There remains another history to be written: to examine the influence of the British example on documentary practice across the world. Grierson, again, was instrumental in setting up the National Film Board of Canada – widely held up as an exemplar of progressive state support for documentary – while, as Rotha suggested, British documentary influenced developments elsewhere, including Australia (where the Commonwealth Film Unit was formed during the Second World War) and India (where an official state film unit was established shortly after independence in 1947: Basil Wright's role as an advisor to the Indian Films Division in the 1960s provides a direct link to the British documentary movement). It is both ironic and not a little piquant that just as the British government closed down its official documentary unit in the early 1950s other states – including British colonies such as Hong Kong and Singapore, as well as nations in the developing world – were setting up their own organizations that often took the EMB/GPO/Crown Film Unit as their model. And British documentarists were also closely involved in advising international bodies such as UNESCO (Grierson again) and the United Nations (Thorold Dickinson). Indeed the adoption of film by both national and international organizations in the later twentieth century was influenced to a very great extent by the British experience. In Britain, academic critics have too often focused on the perceived shortcomings of documentary or its deviation from what was assumed to be its true social purpose; but elsewhere British documentary has been held up as a model of enlightened state and corporate sponsorship of film for publicity and information purposes. It is for this reason – as well as for its commitment to a progressive idea of film and television as a social practice above and beyond the level of popular entertainment – that British documentary deserves to be afforded its rightful place in the sun.

Notes

Introduction: Critical and Historical Perspectives on British Documentary

1. Forsyth Hardy, 'The British Documentary Film', in Michael Balcon, Ernest Lindgren, Forsyth Hardy and Roger Manvell, *Twenty Years of British Film 1925–1945* (London, 1947), p.45.
2. Arts Enquiry, *The Factual Film: A Survey sponsored by the Dartington Hall Trustees* (London, 1947), p.11.
3. Paul Rotha, *Documentary Film* (London, 4th edn 1968 [1936]), p.97.
4. Roger Manvell, *Film* (Harmondsworth, rev. edn 1946 [1944]), p.133.
5. Paul Rotha, with Richard Griffith, *The Film Till Now: A Survey of World Cinema* (London, rev. edn 1967 [1930; 1949]), pp.555–6.
6. Michael Balcon, *Michael Balcon presents . . . A Lifetime of Films* (London, 1969), p.130.
7. André Bazin, *What Is Cinema? Volume II*, trans. Hugh Gray (Berkeley, 1971), pp.48–9.
8. Ephraim Katz, *The Macmillan International Film Encyclopedia* (London, 1994), p.374.
9. Kristin Thompson and David Bordwell, *Film History: An Introduction* (New York, 1994), p.352.
10. John Grierson, 'First Principles of Documentary', in Forsyth Hardy (ed.), *Grierson on Documentary* (London, 1946), pp.79–80.
11. Ibid., p.78.
12. Ibid., p.79.
13. This phrase – sometimes quoted as 'the creative interpretation of actuality' – is universally credited to Grierson but the source has proved elusive. It is sometimes misquoted with 'reality' substituted for 'actuality'. In the early 1940s, for example, the journal *Documentary News Letter*, published by Film Centre, which Grierson founded, carried the banner 'the creative interpretation of reality'.
14. Rudolf Arnheim, *Film as Art*, trans. L. M. Sieveking and Ian F. D. Morrow (London, 1958 [1932]), p.55.
15. See, for example, David Tucker (ed.), *British Social Realism in the Arts Since 1940* (Basingstoke, 2011). On British realist cinema, see especially John Hill, *Sex, Class and Realism: British Cinema 1956–1963* (London, 1986). For television drama, see John Caughie, *Television Drama: Realism, Modernism and British Culture* (Oxford, 2000).
16. Andrew Higson, ' "Britain's Outstanding Contribution to the Film": The Documentary-Realist Tradition', in Charles Barr (ed.), *All Our Yesterdays: 90 Years of British Cinema* (London, 1986), pp.72–97.
17. John Grierson, 'The Documentary Idea: 1942', *Grierson on Documentary*, p.113.

18. John Caughie, 'Progressive Television and Documentary Drama', *Screen*, 21: 3 (1980), p.34.
19. Peter Wollen, *Signs and Meaning in the Cinema* (London, 1969), p.115.
20. Lindsay Anderson, 'Alfred Hitchcock', *Sequence*, 9 (1949), p.113.
21. Alan Lovell, 'The British Cinema: The Unknown Cinema', paper presented to the British Film Institute Education Department Seminar, 13 March 1969, typescript held by the BFI Reuben Library, p.2. A slightly revised version of this paper was published as Alan Lovell, 'The Unknown Cinema of Britain', *Cinema Journal*, 11: 2 (1972), pp.1–9.
22. Paul Rotha, *Documentary Diary: An Informal History of the British Documentary Film, 1928–1939* (London, 1973); Forsyth Hardy, *John Grierson: A Documentary Biography* (London, 1979); Elizabeth Sussex, *The Rise and Fall of British Documentary: The Story of the Film Movement Founded by John Grierson* (Berkeley, 1975).
23. Harry Watt, *Don't Look at the Camera* (London, 1974), p.41.
24. Alan Lovell and Jim Hillier, *Studies in Documentary* (London, 1972), p.35.
25. Andrew Tudor, *Theories of Film* (London, 1974), p.75.
26. Lindsay Anderson, 'Only Connect: Some Aspects of the Work of Humphrey Jennings', *Sight and Sound*, 23: 4 (1954), p.181.
27. The critical literature on Jennings includes (but is not limited to): Keith Beattie, *Humphrey Jennings* (Manchester, 2010); Anthony W. Hodgkinson and Rodney E. Sheratsky, *Humphrey Jennings: More Than A Maker of Films* (Hanover, 1982); Mary-Lou Jennings (ed.), *Humphrey Jennings: Film-Maker, Painter, Poet* (London, 1982); Philip C. Logan, *Humphrey Jennings and British Documentary Film: A Re-assessment* (Farnham, 2011); Lovell and Hillier, *Studies in Documentary*, pp.62–120.
28. Quoted in Sussex, *The Rise and Fall of British Documentary*, p.110.
29. Paul Swann, *The British Documentary Film Movement, 1926–1946* (Cambridge, 1989), p.177.
30. Ian Aitken, *Film and Reform: John Grierson and the Documentary Film Movement* (London, 1990), p.14.
31. This point was raised by Andrew Higson in a review of Aitken's and Swann's books for *Screen*: 'It is almost as if Aitken wants to suggest that Grierson *is* the documentary movement...' *Screen*, 32: 3 (1991), p.354.
32. Aitken, *Film and Reform*, p.195.
33. Raymond Durgnat, *A Mirror for England: British Movies from Austerity to Affluence* (London, 1970), pp.118–9.
34. Stuart Hood, 'John Grierson and the Documentary Film Movement', in James Curran and Vincent Porter (eds), *British Cinema History* (London, 1983), p.102.
35. Robert Colls and Philip Dodd, 'Representing the Nation: British Documentary Film, 1930–45', *Screen*, 26: 1 (1985), p.24.
36. Hood, 'John Grierson and the Documentary Film Movement', p.102.
37. Roy Armes, *A Critical History of British Cinema* (London, 1978), p.264.
38. Kathryn Dodd and Philip Dodd, 'Engendering the Nation: British Documentary Film, 1930–1939', in Andrew Higson (ed.), *Dissolving Views: Key Writings on British Cinema* (London, 1996), p.47.

39. Jeffrey Richards and Anthony Aldgate, *Best of British: Cinema and Society 1930–1970* (Oxford, 1983), pp.3–4.
40. Bert Hogenkamp, *Deadly Parallels: Film and the Left in Britain 1929–39* (London, 1986), p.8.
41. Claire Johnston, ' "Independence" and the Thirties: Ideologies in History: An Introduction', in Don MacPherson (ed.), *Traditions of Independence: British Cinema in the Thirties* (London, 1980), p.9.
42. Brian Winston, *Claiming the Real: The Griersonian Documentary and its Legitimations* (London, 1995), p.7.
43. Ibid., p.11.
44. Ibid., p.46.
45. Ibid., p.42.
46. Ibid., p.53.
47. One of Winston's most curious claims is his assertion that 'almost no attention has been paid to documentary theory' (*Claiming the Real*, p.6). Yet this ignores a large body of such work – much of it listed in his own bibliography.
48. Brian Winston, *Fires Were Started* (London, 1999); Scott Anthony, *Night Mail* (London, 2007).
49. Scott Anthony and James G. Mansell (eds), *The Projection of Britain: A History of the GPO Film Unit* (London, 2011).
50. Alan Burton, *The British Consumer Co-operative Movement and film, 1980s–1960s* (Manchester, 2005).
51. Timothy Boon, *Films of Fact: A History of Science in Documentary Films and Television* (London, 2008).
52. Patrick Russell and James Piers Taylor (eds), *Shadows of Progress: Documentary Film in Post-War Britain* (London, 2010).
53. See the bibliography for specific articles. The journal special issues are *Journal of British Cinema and Television*, 10: 3 (2012), 'The Postwar British Documentary Movement – Decline or Transition?' edited by John Corner and Martin Stollery, and *Twentieth Century British History*, 23: 1 (2012), 'The Documentary Film Movement and the Spaces of British Identity', edited by Scott Anthony and James G. Mansell.
54. Brian Winston, 'The Griersonian Tradition Postwar: Decline or Transition?', *Journal of British Cinema and Television*, 11: 1 (2014), p.112.
55. John Ellis, *Visible Fictions: Cinema: Television: Video* (London, rev. edn 1992 [1982]), p.112.
56. Caughie, 'Progressive Television and Documentary Drama', p.23.
57. Higson, 'Britain's Outstanding Contribution to the Film', pp.94–5.
58. Derek Paget, *No Other Way To Tell It: Docudrama on Film and Television* (Manchester, 2nd edn 2011 [1998]), pp.151–6.
59. Ellis, *Visible Fictions*, p.146.
60. Quoted in ' "Death of a Princess" film criticised by ministers, peers and MPs', *Daily Telegraph*, 25 April 1980.

1   Documentary Before Grierson

1. Charles Urban, *A Yank in Britain: The Lost Memoirs of Charles Urban, Film Pioneer*, ed. Luke McKernan (Hastings, 1999), p.54.

2. See, for example, Kristin Thompson and David Bordwell, *Film History: An Introduction* (New York, 1994), pp.344–68. A good example of the standard international history of documentary is Erik Barnouw, *Documentary: A History of the Non-Fiction Film* (New York, 2nd rev. edn 1993 [1976]), which jumps straight from the early actuality films of the Lumières to Robert Flaherty.
3. Stephen Bottomore, 'Rediscovering Early Non-Fiction Film', *Film History*, 13: 2 (2001), pp.160–73.
4. A selection of this revisionist work is collected in Thomas Elsaesser (ed.), *Early Cinema: Space, Frame, Narrative* (London, 1990). On early British cinema history, see Michael Chanan, *The Dream That Kicks: The Prehistory and Early Years of Cinema in Britain* (London, 2nd edn 1996 [1980]), and Andrew Higson (ed.), *Young and Innocent?: The Cinema in Britain 1896–1930* (Exeter, 2000).
5. Tom Gunning, 'The Cinema of Attractions: Early Film, Its Spectator and the Avant-Garde', in Elsaesser (ed.), *Early Cinema: Space, Frame, Narrative*, p.58.
6. Quoted in John Barnes, *The Beginnings of the Cinema in England. Volume 1* (New York, 1976), p.64.
7. See Vanessa Toulmin, ' "We Take Them and Make Them": Mitchell and Kenyon and the Travelling Exhibition Showmen', in Vanessa Toulmin, Patrick Russell and Simon Popple (eds), *The Lost World of Mitchell and Kenyon: Edwardian Britain on Film* (London, 2004), pp.59–68.
8. See Richard Brown and Barry Anthony, *A Victorian Film Enterprise: The History of the British Mutoscope and Biograph Company, 1897–1915* (Trowbridge, 1999).
9. Cecil Hepworth, *Came the Dawn: Memories of a Film Pioneer* (London, 1951), p.56.
10. Boleslas Matuszewski, 'A New Source of History' [25 March 1898], trans. Laura Marks and Diana Koszarski, *Film History*, 7: 3 (1995), p.322.
11. Rachael Low and Roger Manvell, *The History of the British Film 1896–1906* (London, 1948), p.68.
12. Quoted in Luke McKernan, *Charles Urban: Pioneering the Non-Fiction Film in Britain and America, 1897–1925* (Exeter, 2013), p.50.
13. Ibid., p.19.
14. Ibid., p.66.
15. Ibid., p.67.
16. Charles Urban, *The Cinematograph in Science, Education, and Matters of State* (London, 1907), p.7.
17. Ibid., p.18.
18. Ibid., p.52.
19. Quoted in McKernan, *Charles Urban*, p.92.
20. *The Times*, 22 May 1911, p.12.
21. Paul Rotha, *Documentrary Diary: An Informal History of the British Documentary Film, 1928–1939* (New York, 1973), p.3; Ivor Montagu, *Film World: A Guide to Cinema* (Harmondsworth, 1964), pp.75–6.
22. Patrick Russell, *100 British Documentaries* (London, 2007), p.44.
23. McKernan, *Charles Urban*, p.4.
24. John Grierson, 'The Course of Realism', in Charles Davy (ed.), *Footnotes to the Film* (London, 1937), p.142.
25. Low and Manvell, *The History of the British Film 1896–1906*, p.23.

26. On the history of the collection and its discovery and restoration, see the introduction to Toulmin, Russell and Popple (eds), *The Lost World of Mitchell and Kenyon*, pp.3–5.

27. Leo Enticknap, ' "A Real Brake on Progress"? Moving Image Technology in the Time of Mitchell and Kenyon', in Toulmin *et al* (eds), *The Lost World of Mitchell and Kenyon*, p.27.

28. Tom Gunning, 'Pictures of Crowd Splendor: The Mitchell and Kenyon Factory Gate Films', in Toulmin *et al* (eds), *The Lost World of Mitchell and Kenyon*, p.53.

29. Andrew Prescott, ' "We Had Fine Banners": Street Processions in the Mitchell and Kenyon Films', in Toulmin *et al* (eds), *The Lost World of Mitchell and Kenyon*, pp.125–36.

30. Paul Dave, 'Tragedy, Ethics and History in Contemporary British Social Realist Film', in David Tucker (ed.), *British Social Realism in the Arts Since 1940* (Basingstoke, 2011), p.41.

31. John K. Walton, 'The Seaside and the Holiday Crowd', in Toulmin *et al* (eds), *The Lost World of Mitchell and Kenyon*, pp.158–68.

32. There are occasional examples to the contrary, such as the young male who makes a two-fingered gesture towards the camera in *Parkgate Ironworks* (1901), though this may simply be an irreverent expression prompted by the presence of the camera rather than an indication of underlying social dissent.

33. Rachael Low, *The History of the British Film 1914–1918* (London, 1950), p.16.

34. TNA INF 4/6: Department of Information memorandum to the War Cabinet, undated but from internal evidence c.1917.

35. *The Bioscope*, 18 March 1915, p.982.

36. *The Bioscope*, 21 January 1915, p.206.

37. *The Bioscope*, 28 January 1915, p.318.

38. *The Bioscope*, 20 January 1916, p.210.

39. The production and reception of the film is documented by S. D. Badsey, *'Battle of the Somme*: British War-Propaganda', *Historical Journal of Film, Radio and Television*, 3: 2 (1983), pp.99–115. A contemporary account of its making – albeit not a very reliable one – was provided by G. H. Malins, *How I Filmed the War* (London, 1920). The film's place in the context of propaganda policy is explored by Nicholas Reeves, *Official British Film Propaganda During the First World War* (London, 1986), pp.94–113.

40. Nicholas Reeves, 'Cinema, Spectatorship and Propaganda: *Battle of the Somme* and its Contemporary Audience', *Historical Journal of Film, Radio and Television*, 17: 1 (1997), pp.5–28.

41. Quoted in Badsey, *'Battle of the Somme'*, p.108.

42. *The Times*, 29 August 1916, p.5.

43. *The Manchester Guardian*, 16 August 1916, p.4.

44. *The Bioscope*, 24 August 1916, p.671.

45. Rowland Fielding, *War Letters to a Wife* (London, 1929), p.109.

46. *The Times*, 1 September 1916, p.7.

47. *The Times*, 5 September 1916, p.9.

48. D. S. Higgins (ed.), *The Private Diaries of Sir H. Rider Haggard, 1914–1925* (London, 1980), p.84.

49. Roger Smither, ' "A Wonderful Idea of the Fighting": The Question of Fakes in *The Battle of the Somme'*, *Imperial War Museum Review*, 3 (1988), p.15.
50. Ibid., p.5.
51. UNESCO Memory of the World Register Reference No. 2004–16: *The Battle of the Somme*: www.unesorg/nnew/fileadmin/MULTIMEDIA/HQ/OI/pdf/mow/nomination_forms_united_kingdom_battle_of_the_somme (accessed 18.04.2014).
52. Quoted in Smither, 'A Wonderful Idea of the Fighting', p.6.
53. TNA INF4/1B: 'First Report of the War Office Cinematograph Committee', September 1918. co.
54. Quoted in Reeves, *Official British Film Propaganda During the First World War*, p.152.
55. Quoted in Luke McKernan, *Topical Budget: The Great British News Film* (London, 1992), p.12.
56. Paul Rotha, with Richard Griffith, *The Film Till Now: A Survey of World Cinema* (London, rev. edn 1967 [1930]), p.322.
57. Rachael Low, *The History of the British Film 1918–1929* (London, 1971), p.130.
58. John Grierson, 'First Principles of Documentary', *Grierson on Documentary*, p.79.
59. Low, *The History of the British Film 1918–1929*, p.276.
60. *Picturegoer*, 13 January 1927, p.23.
61. Mark Connelly, 'Propaganda, Memory and Identity: The Battle of the Falkland Islands, December 1914', in David Welch (ed.), *Propaganda, Power and Persuasion: From World War I to Wikileaks* (London, 2014), p.25.
62. *Parliamentary Debates: House of Commons*, 5th Series, vol. 211, cols 953–4, 5 December 1927.
63. Michael Paris, 'Enduring Heroes: British Feature Films and the First World War, 1919–1997', in Michael Paris (ed.), *The First World War and Popular Cinema: 1914 to the Present* (Edinburgh, 1999), p.56.
64. Jay Winter, *Sites of Memory, Sites of Mourning: The Great War in European Cultural History* (Cambridge, 1995), *passim*.
65. Connelly, 'Memory, Propaganda and Identity', p.25.
66. *The Bioscope*, 23 September 1926, p.1041.
67. Quoted in Connelly, 'Memory, Propaganda and Identity', p.25–6.
68. *Close Up*, 1 (July 1927), p.19.
69. *The Observer*, 18 September 1927, p.21.
70. Low, *The History of the British Film 1918–1929*, p.181.
71. Ibid., p.132.
72. *The Times*, 7 May 1924, p.12.
73. For an account of Ponting's role as photographer for the expedition, see Dennis Lynch, 'The Worst Journey in the World: Herbert G. Ponting in the Antarctic, 1910–1912', *Film History*, 3: 4 (1989), pp.291–306.
74. 'Non-Fiction Films', *Sight and Sound*, 2: 7 (1933), p.101.

2   Documentary in the 1930s

1. John Grierson, 'The Course of Realism', in Charles Davy (ed.), *Footnotes to the Film* (London, 1937), p.153.

2. A. J. P. Taylor, *English History 1914–1945* (Oxford, 1965), p.313.
3. Simon Rowson, 'A Statistical Survey of the Cinema Industry in Great Britain in 1934', *Journal of the Royal Statistical Society*, 99 (1936), pp.67–129.
4. Paul Rotha, with Richard Griffith, *The Film Till Now: A Survey of World Cinema* (London, rev. edn 1967 [1930]), pp. 313, 316.
5. *BBFC Annual Report* (London, 1937). On the operation and policies of the BBFC, see Nicholas Pronay, 'The First Reality: Film Censorship in Liberal England', in K. R. M. Short (ed.), *Feature Films as History* (London, 1981), pp.113–37; Jeffrey Richards, 'The British Board of Film Censors and Content Control in the 1930s (1): Images of Britain', *Historical Journal of Film, Radio and Television*, 1: 2 (1981), pp.95–119; and James C. Robertson, *The British Board of Film Censors: Film Censorship in Britain 1996–1950* (London, 1950).
6. Jeffrey Richards, *The Age of the Dream Palace: Cinema and Society in Britain, 1930–1939* (London, 1984); Jeffrey Richards and Anthony Aldgate, *Best of British: Cinema and Society 1930–1970* (Oxford, 1983), pp.29–42; and Tony Aldgate, 'Ideological Consensus in British Feature Films, 1935–1947', Short (ed.), *Feature Films as History*, pp.94–112.
7. 'Hitchcock, Asquith and the English Cinema', in Forsyth Hardy (ed.), *Grierson on the Movies* (London, 1981), p.110.
8. Elizabeth Sussex, *The Rise and Fall of British Documentary: The Story of the Film Movement Founded by John Grierson* (Berkeley, 1975), pp.76–7.
9. Stuart Hood, 'John Grierson and the Documentary Film Movement', in James Curran and Vincent Porter (eds), *British Cinema History* (London, 1983), pp.99–112.
10. See Jamie Medhurst, *Alternative Film Culture in Interwar Britain* (Exeter, 2008). An interesting analysis of British documentary in comparison to international avant-garde practices is offered by Martin Stollery, *Alternative Empires: European Modernist Cinemas and Cultures of Imperialism* (Exeter, 2000).
11. Alan Lovell and Jim Hillier, *Studies in Documentary* (London, 1972), p.35.
12. Paul Swann, *The British Documentary Film Movement, 1926–1946* (Cambridge, 1989), pp.33–4.
13. *Cinema Quarterly*, which was published in Edinburgh, was edited by Forsyth Hardy, film critic of the *Scotsman* who was a close friend and future biographer of Grierson. *World Film News*, founded by Grierson himself following his departure from the GPO Film Unit in 1937, became in effect the house journal of the documentary movement. It ceased publication with Grierson's departure for Canada in 1939 and its place was taken from the beginning of 1940 by *Documentary News Letter*.
14. Paul Rotha, *Documentary Diary: An Informal History of the British Documentary Film, 1928–1939* (New York, 1973), p.31.
15. Jeffrey Richards and Dorothy Sheridan (eds), *Mass-Observation at the Movies* (London, 1987), p.2.
16. Philip C. Logan, *Humphrey Jennings and British Documentary Film: A Re-assessment* (Farnham, 2011), p.107.
17. Sussex, *The Rise and Fall of British Documentary*, p.77.
18. Leonard W. Doob, *Propaganda: Its Psychology and Technique* (New York, 1935), p.3.

19. For an overview of the subject, see Kevin Robins, Frank Webster and Michael Pickering, 'Propaganda, Information and Social Control', in Jeremy Hawthorn (ed.), *Propaganda, Persuasion and Polemic* (London, 1987), pp.1–17.
20. R. S. Lambert, *Propaganda* (London, 1938), p.102.
21. Amber Blanco White, *The New Propaganda* (London, 1939), p.305.
22. *The Times*, 13 April 1926, p.12.
23. T. J. Hollins, 'The Conservative Party and Film Propaganda Between the Wars', *English Historical Review*, 96: 379 (1981), p.366.
24. Philip M. Taylor, *British Propaganda in the Twentieth Century: Selling Democracy* (Edinburgh, 1999), p.95.
25. On Grierson's studies in the United States, see Ian Aitken, *Film and Reform: John Grierson and the Documentary Film Movement* (London, 1990), pp.48–89.
26. A representative sample of Grierson's writing from this period was collected together in Forsyth Hardy (ed.), *Grierson on Documentary* (London, 1946). Note that some minor editorial changes have been made from the originals and that the later paperback edition published by Faber and Faber (London, 1966) includes a slightly different selection of essays from the first edition published by Collins. An alternative sample of Grierson's work, including some previously unpublished papers, can be found in Ian Aitken (ed.), *The Documentary Film Movement: An Anthology* (Edinburgh, 1998). For a comprehensive list of Grierson's publications, see Jack C. Ellis, *John Grierson: A Guide to References and Resources* (Boston, 1986).
27. John Grierson, 'First Principles of Documentary', *Grierson on Documentary*, p.80.
28. Ibid., pp.81–6.
29. John Grierson, 'Films and the Community', *Grierson on Documentary*, p.127.
30. John Grierson, 'Summary and Survey: 1935', *Grierson on Documentary*, p.119.
31. John Grierson, 'The Documentary Idea: 1942', *Grierson on Documentary*, p.180.
32. John Grierson, 'Propaganda and Education', *Grierson on Documentary*, p.221.
33. Grierson, 'The Documentary Idea: 1942', p.181.
34. John Grierson, 'Education and the New Order', *Grierson on Documentary*, p.197.
35. John Grierson, 'The EMB Film Unit', *Grierson on Documentary*, p.101.
36. Nicholas Hiley, ' "No mixed bathing": The creation of the British Board of Film Censors in 1913', *Journal of Popular British Cinema*, 3 (2000), pp.5–19. See also Robertson, *The British Board of Film Censors*, pp.1–18.
37. Stephen Tallents, *The Projection of England* (London, 1932), p.39.
38. *Parliamentary Debates: House of Commons*, 5th Series, vol. 203, col. 2039, 16 March 1927, p. 2039.
39. Rachael Low, *The History of the British Film 1918–1929* (London, 1971), p.156.
40. The passage of the Cinematograph Films Act is documented in Margaret Dickinson and Sarah Street, *Cinema and State: The Film Industry and the British Government 1927–84* (London, 1985), pp.5–33.

41. *Parliamentary Debates: House of Commons*, 5th Series, vol. 204, col. 259, 22 March 1927, pp.257–9.
42. Andrew Higson, *Waving the Flag: Constructing a National Cinema in Britain* (Oxford, 1995), pp.26–97.
43. TNA CO 760/37: John Buchan to Walter Elliot, 26 May 1927.
44. Ibid.: Empire Marketing Board: Minutes of the First Meeting of the Film Conference, 1 February 1927.
45. Ibid.: John Grierson, 'Notes for English Producers Part II: English Cinema Production and the Naturalistic Tradition', 29 April 1927, p.17.
46. Quoted in Richards, *The Age of the Dream Palace*, p.246.
47. TNA CO 760/37: Grierson, 'Notes for English Producers Part II', pp.19–21.
48. Swann, *The British Documentary Film Movement*, pp.128–30.
49. Grierson, 'The Course of Realism', *Grierson on Documentary*, p.151.
50. *The Times*, 1 November 1938, p.12.
51. For an account of Tallents's career, see Scott Anthony, *Public Relations and the Making of Modern Britain: Stephen Tallents and the Birth of a Progressive Media Profession* (Manchester, 2012).
52. Swann, *The British Documentary Film Movement*, p.22.
53. Grierson, 'The EMB Film Unit', *Grierson on Documentary*, p.98.
54. Stephen Constantine, '"Bringing the Empire alive": The Empire Marketing Board and imperial propaganda, 1926–33', in John M. MacKenzie (ed.), *Imperialism and Popular Culture* (Manchester, 1986), pp.192–231.
55. TNA CO 760/37: 'The Cinema Activities of the Empire Marketing Board'.
56. Ibid.: EMB Film Committee: Minutes of the Sixth Meeting, 7 May 1928.
57. Ibid.: EMB Film Committee: Minutes of the Tenth Meeting, 28 October 1929.
58. Ibid.: EMB: Minutes of the Third Meeting of the Film Conference, 8 July 1927.
59. Ibid.: EMB Film Committee: Minutes of the Ninth Meeting, 23 July 1929.
60. Ibid.: EMB Film Committee: Minutes of the Seventh Meeting, 13 November 1928.
61. This story (which, incidentally, there is no reason to believe to be untrue) was told by Stephen Tallents. See, for example, the introduction to Hardy (ed.), *Grierson on Documentary*, pp.13–14.
62. TNA CO 760/37: EMB Film Committee: Minutes of the Eleventh Meeting, 30 January 1930.
63. Ibid.: 'The Cinema Activities of the Empire Marketing Board'.
64. *Kinematograph Weekly*, 14 December 1929, p.35.
65. John Grierson, 'Drifters', in Forsyth Hardy (ed.), *Grierson on Documentary* (London, rev. edn 1966), p.20.
66. Ibid.
67. TNA CO 760/37: E. Gordon Craig to Stephen Tallents, 18 February 1929.
68. Ibid.: EMB Film Committee: Minutes of the Eleventh Meeting, 30 January 1930.
69. *The Manchester Guardian*, 14 December 1929, p.7.
70. *Film Weekly*, 18 November 1929, p.5.
71. Rotha, *The Film Till Now*, p.318.

72. Jamie Sexton, 'Grierson's Machines: *Drifters*, the Documentary Film Movement and the Negotiation of Modernity', *Canadian Journal of Film Studies*, 11: 1 (2002), pp.40–59.
73. Grierson, 'Drifters', p.19.
74. TNA CO 760/33: EMB Film Committee: Minutes of the Tenth Meeting, 28 October 1929.
75. Ibid.: EMB Film Committee: Minutes of the Twelfth Meeting, 30 April 1930.
76. Ibid.: EMB Film Committee: Minutes of the Fourteenth Meeting, 28 July 1930.
77. Ibid.: EMB Film Committee: Minutes of the Sixteenth Meeting, 8 January 1931.
78. Ibid.: EMB Film Committee: Minutes of the Twelfth Meeting, 30 April 1930.
79. Ibid.: 'Creation of a Small Empire Marketing Board Producing and Editing Unit', 28 April 1930.
80. The 'Imperial Six' were *O'er Hill and Dale*, *The Country Comes to Town*, *Lumber*, *Upstream*, *Shadow on a Mountain* and *Industrial Britain*.
81. Sussex, *The Rise and Fall of British Documentary*, pp.26–7.
82. Michael Balcon, *Michael Balcon presents…A Lifetime of Films* (London, 1969), p.70.
83. Harry Watt, *Don't Look at the Camera* (London, 1974), p.72.
84. Balcon, *A Lifetime of Films*, pp.70–1.
85. Grierson, 'Summary and Survey: 1935', *Grierson on Documentary*, p.110.
86. Paul Rotha, with Sinclair Road and Richard Griffith, *Documentary Film* (New York, rev. edn 1952), pp.106–7.
87. André Bazin, *What is Cinema? Volume 1*, trans. Hugh Gray (Berkeley, 1967), p.162.
88. This figure is based on the filmography in Rachael Low, *The History of the British Film 1929–1939: Documentary and Educational Films of the 1930s* (London, 1979), pp.211–27.
89. Scott Anthony, *Night Mail* (London, 2007), p.7.
90. The first dedicated history of the GPO Film Unit is Scott Anthony and James G. Mansell (eds), *The Projection of Britain: A History of the GPO Film Unit* (London, 2011). Other accounts include: Aitken, *Film and Reform*, pp.127–49; Sussex, *The Rise and Fall of British Documentary*, pp.44–78; and Swann, *The British Documentary Film Movement*, pp.49–94.
91. Swann, *The British Documentary Film Movement*, p.53.
92. Leo Enticknap, 'Technology and the GPO Film Unit', in Anthony and Mansell (eds), *The Projection of Britain*, pp.188–98.
93. Quoted in Swann, *The British Documentary Film Movement*, p.56.
94. Ibid., pp.56–64.
95. Forsyth Hardy, 'The British Documentary Film', in Michael Balcon, Ernest Lindgren, Forsyth Hardy and Roger Manvell, *Twenty Years of British Film 1925–1945* (London, 1947), p.47.
96. BFI BW 1/1/4: 'Song of Ceylon', undated typescript by Wright chronicling the making of the film, p.2.
97. Harry Watt, *Don't Look at the Camera* (London, 1974), p.80. Rotha estimated the cost of *Night Mail* at 'around £1800'. *Documentary Diary*, p.132.

98. This group comprised *Weather Forecast, Cable Ship, 6.30 Collection, Granton Trawler, Spring on the Farm* and *Windmill in Barbados*.
99. BPMA POST 33/5089: Report of the Steward Committee, 12 April 1937.
100. Rotha, *Documentary Diary*, p.142.
101. Kevin Jackson, 'The Joy of Drooling: In Praise of Len Lye', in Anthony and Mansell (eds), *The Projection of Britain*, pp.89–97.
102. Quoted in Scott Anthony, 'The GPO Film Unit and "Britishness" in the 1930s', in Anthony and Mansell (eds), *The Projection of Britain*, p.11.
103. BPMA POST 109/91: 'The GPO Film Unit 1933–1940', unpublished manuscript by Forsyth Hardy, 1990, p.3.
104. Jeffrey Richards, 'John Grierson and the Lost World of the GPO Film Unit', in Anthony and Mansell (eds), *The Projection of Britain*, p.7.
105. BPMA POST 109/91: 'The GPO Film Unit 1933–1940', p.4.
106. Graham Greene, *The Pleasure-Dome: The Collected Film Criticism 1935–40* (London, 1972), p.25.
107. BFI BW 1/1/3: 'Song of Ceylon: Analysis' – handwritten lecture notes by Wright, n.d.
108. Arthur Vesselo, 'Documentary Films', *Sight and Sound*, 5: 17 (Spring 1936), pp.28–9.
109. Sussex, *The Rise and Fall of British Documentary*, p.80.
110. Watt, *Don't Look at the Camera*, p.104.
111. BPMA POST 33/5199: G. E. G. Forbes (deputy controller of GPO Publicity) to the Treasury, 14 June 1939.
112. Robert Flaherty, 'North Sea', *Sight and Sound*, 7: 26 (Summer 1938), p.62.
113. Sussex, *The Rise and Fall of British Documentary*, p.110.
114. Ibid., p.92.
115. *The Times*, 16 June 1938, p.12.
116. Alexander Wolcough, 'Memorandum: Aims of the Shell Film Programme' (February 1937). Quoted in Douglas Gordon, *Shell Films: The First Sixty Years* (London 1994), p.4.
117. Colin Burgess, 'Sixty Years of Shell Film Sponsorship, 1934–94', *Journal of British Cinema and Television*, 7: Z (2010), p.214.
118. Scott Anthony, 'The Future's in the Air: Imperial Airways and the British Documentary Film Movement', *Journal of British Cinema and Television*, 8: 3 (2011), pp.301–21; Nicholas Stanley-Price, 'Paul Rotha and the Making of Strand Films' *Air Outpost* (1937)', *Historical Journal of Film, Radio and Television*, 32: 1 (2012), pp.95–111.
119. John Grierson, 'A Scottish Experiment', *Grierson on Documentary*, pp.145–7.
120. Rotha, *Documentary Diary*, p.70.
121. Sussex, *The Rise and Fall of British Documentary*, p.101.
122. *The Times*, 1 July 1937, p.14.
123. Richard Griffith, 'Films at the New York World's Fair', *Documentary News Letter*, 1: 2 (February 1940), p.3.
124. *The Times*: 26 April 1935, p.6.
125. Geoffrey Crothall, 'Images of Regeneration: Film Propaganda and the British Slum Clearance Campaign, 1933–1938', *Historical Journal of Film, Radio and Television*, 19: 3 (1999), pp.339–58.
126. Brian Winston, *Claiming the Real: The Griersonian Documentary and its Legitimations* (London, 1995), p.60.

127. Rotha, *Documentary Diary*, pp.92–3.
128. TNA BT 55/3: John Grierson to Committee on Cinematograph Films, 17 June 1936.
129. Swann, *The British Documentary Film Movement*, p.118.
130. Dallas Bower, 'Film in the Social Scene', in Robert Herring (ed.), *Cinema Survey* (London, 1937), p.25.
131. TNA BT 55/4: Committee on Cinematograph Films: Evidence of Mr Paul Rotha on behalf of the Associated Realist Film Producers Ltd, 19 May 1936.
132. TNA BT 55/3: M. C. Pottinger to Board of Trade, 24 July 1936.
133. *The Cinema*, 22 January 1936, p.14.
134. TNA BT 55/3: Cinematograph Films Advisory Committee Paper FAC 183, 29 October 1935.
135. Ibid.: Memorandum on Documentary and Cultural Films and the Quota Regulations of the Cinematograph Films Act, 1927, submitted by the Associated Realist Film Producers Ltd, 12 May 1936.
136. Ibid.
137. TNA BT 55/3: Memorandum on short films, in particular documentary films, with suggestions for the improvement of the administration of the Cinematograph Film Act of 1927, submitted by the Strand Film Company Limited, n.d.
138. Ibid.: Memorandum of the observations of the Trades Union Congress General Council for submission to the Departmental Committee set up by the President of the Board of Trade to consider the position of British Films in view of the approaching expiry of the Cinematograph Films Act, 1927, n.d.
139. Ibid.: Pamphlet entitled: *Cinematograph Films Act, 1927. Evidence submitted on behalf of the Cinematograph Exhibitors' Association of Great Britain and Ireland by Theo H. Fligelstone (President)*, 26 May 1936.
140. Ibid.: Committee on Cinematograph Films: Draft Report (First Draft), n.d.
141. Swann, *The British Documentary Film Movement*, pp.180–1.
142. TNA INF 5/55: S. G. Fletcher to C. G. H. Ayres (MGM, London), 1 June 1938; Fletcher to Earl St John (Paramount Theatres, London), 9 August 1938.
143. Ibid.: Fletcher to 'Dear Bruce' (probably H. Bruce Woolfe), 2 February 1939.
144. Ibid.: Jean Benoit-Lévy to Fletcher, 13 January 1939.
145. Hector McCullie, 'Oh! London', *Sight and Sound*, 7: 26 (Summer 1938), p.73.
146. Leslie Halliwell, *Seats in All Parts: Half a Lifetime at the Movies* (London, 1985), p.48.
147. Richards and Sheridan (eds), *Mass-Observation at the Movies*, pp.32–136.
148. Ibid., pp.220–91.
149. Grierson, 'Summary and Survey: 1935', *Grierson on Documentary*, p.119.
150. TNA INF 17/37: Imperial Institute press release: 'The Empire Film Library: First thousand reels in circulation', 30 May 1936.
151. Ibid.: Imperial Institute press release: 'More acute than a year ago: Problem of the shortage of empire educational films', 27 September 1937.
152. J. B. Holmes, 'GPO Films', *Sight and Sound*, 6: 23 (Autumn 1937), p.17.
153. BPMA POST 33/5089: Steward Committee Report, 12 April 1937.
154. TNA T60/742: F. P. Robinson to Sir Stephen Tallents, 25 November 1936.
155. Rowson, 'A Statistical Survey of the Cinema Industry in Great Britain', p.85.
156. Arts Enquiry, *The Factual Film: A Survey Sponsored by the Dartington Hall Trustees* (London, 1947), p.59.

157. TNA T160/742: Sir Stephen Tallents to F. P. Robinson, 25 November 1935.
158. TNA INF 17/33: Letter from O. F. Croome, 23 January 1940. The file contains similar letters from R. A. Hindle of Oundle School, Northamptonshire (9 February 1940), E. A. Harrington of Burburry Street School, Birmingham (5 March 1940), G. J. Dennis of the Methodist School, Easingwold (14 March 1940), R. D. Hole of Monkton Combe School, Bath (15 March 1940), Robert Pattison of Burnley Municipal College (3 April 1940), and W. J. Walson of the Senior Boys School, St Albans (21 August 1940), and others.
159. Ibid.: Letter from Naomi Mitchim, n.d.

3   Documentary at War

1. *Documentary News Letter*, 2: 4 (April 1941), p.65.
2. See, for example, Anthony Aldgate and Jeffrey Richards, *Britain Can Take It: The British Cinema in the Second World War* (Oxford, 1986); Robert Murphy, *Realism and Tinsel: Cinema and Society in Britain 1939–48* (London, 1989); Neil Rattigan, *This Is England: British Film and the People's War, 1939–1945* (London, 2001): and Philip M. Taylor (ed.), *Britain and the Cinema in the Second World War* (London, 1988).
3. The first use of the term I have identified is by the documentarist John Shearman in his article 'Wartime Wedding', *Documentary News Letter*, 6: 54 (1946), p.53.
4. Frances Thorpe and Nicholas Pronay, with Clive Coultass, *British Official Films in the Second World War: A Descriptive Catalogue* (Oxford, 1980), p.ix.
5. A caveat should be lodged here in that *Documentary News Letter* was a small-circulation specialist publication: the extent of its influence is therefore difficult to judge. It probably had a smaller readership than *World Film News*, which had a wider scope covering the industry at large. Nevertheless there is anecdotal evidence to suggest that the MOI took notice of what it had to say. According to Basil Wright:

> It became a very, very influential journal throughout the war... This is no joking at all: many a time I went into a government office to see somebody and there would be a file marked 'priority', which would be a clipping from *Documentary News Letter* with a notice from the minister asking what was the answer to this question.

Elizabeth Sussex, *The Rise and Fall of British Documentary* (Berkeley, 1975), p.121.
6. The history of the MOI is documented in Ian McLaine, *Ministry of Morale: Home Front Morale and the Ministry of Information in World War II* (London, 1979). The role of the MOI Films Division is discussed in James Chapman, *The British at War: Cinema, State and Propaganda, 1939–1945* (London, 1998), pp.13–57.
7. TNA FO 371/22839: Addendum by Lord Halifax to a memorandum by Sir Robert Vansittart, 22 October 1939.
8. *Parliamentary Debates: House of Lords*, 5th Series, vol. 350, col. 1832, 26 September 1939.

9. Paul Rotha, *Rotha on the Film* (London, 1958), p.234.
10. Sussex, *The Rise and Fall of British Documentary*, p.119.
11. TNA INF 1/194: Sir Joseph Ball to Lord Macmillan, 10 October 1939.
12. TNA INF 1/628: Ball to Whyte, 23 October 1939.
13. Jo Fox, 'John Grierson, his "Documentary Boys" and the British Ministry of Information, 1939–1942', *Historical Journal of Film, Radio and Television*, 25: 3 (2005), pp.345–69.
14. Harry Watt, *Don't Look at the Camera* (London, 1978), p.128.
15. Ibid., p.129.
16. TNA BW 2/32: Minutes of the Joint Film Committee, 8 September 1939.
17. TNA INF 1/30: G. E. G. Forbes to Establishments Division, 1 November 1939.
18. Kenneth Clark, *The Other Half: A Self-Portrait* (London, 1986), p.10.
19. *Documentary News Letter*, 1 (January 1940), p.1.
20. TNA INF 1/867: Co-Ordinating Committee Paper No.1, 'Programme for Film Propaganda', 29 January 1940.
21. *Documentary News Letter*, 1: 6 (June 1940), p.1.
22. *Documentary News Letter*, 1: 5 (May 1940), p.1.
23. Thorpe and Pronay, *British Official Films*, p.36.
24. TNA BW 4/62: M. Neville Kearney to Stuart, 25 April 1941.
25. TNA BW 63/2: Neville Kearney to A. E. Haigh, 2 December 1940.
26. Sussex, *The Rise and Fall of British Documentary*, p.122.
27. These figures are based on the listings in Thorpe and Pronay, *British Official Films in the Second World War*, pp.61–184. They do not include films commissioned directly by other government agencies than the MOI (such as the British Council) or by private companies. Nor do they include the short 'trailers' such as 'food flashes', which were shown without credits during most cinema programmes.
28. Sussex, *The Rise and Fall of British Documentary*, p.137.
29. TNA INF 1/206: Dorothy G. Keeling to Dr Stephen Taylor, 7 August 1940.
30. *Documentary News Letter*, 1: 8 (August 1940), p.2.
31. Sussex, *The Rise and Fall of British Documentary*, p.141.
32. *Daily Film Renter*, 27 June 1940, p.2.
33. Jeffrey Richards and Dorothy Sheridan (eds), *Mass-Observation at the Movies* (London, 1987), p.457.
34. *Thirteenth Report from the Select Committee on National Expenditure*, 21 August 1940, Cmd 573, para 26, p.10.
35. *The Factual Film*, p.78.
36. Paul Swann, *The British Documentary Film Movement, 1926–1946* (Cambridge, 1989), p.169.
37. Helen Forman, 'The Non-Theatrical Distribution of Films by the Ministry of Information', in Nicholas Pronay and D. W. Spring (eds), *Propaganda, Politics and Film, 1918–45* (London, 1982), p.224.
38. Paul Marris (ed.), *BFI Dossier Number 16: Paul Rotha* (London, 1982), p.25.
39. *Documentary News Letter*, 2: 9 (September 1941), p.170.
40. TNA BT 64/117: 'Competition from Official Film Units', n.d.
41. For a fuller history of the Crown Film Unit during the war, see Chapman, *The British at War*, pp.114–37.
42. TNA INF 1/56: E. St John Bamford to Sir Kenneth Clark, 21 February 1940.

43. Ibid.: 'Notes of a meeting held at the Ministry of Information on Tuesday, 27 February 1940 at 11 a.m. to discuss taking over of GPO Film Unit'.
44. *Daily Film Renter*, 24 April 1940, p.1.
45. Elizabeth Sussex, 'Cavalcanti in England', *Sight and Sound*, 44: 4 (1975), p.208.
46. TNA INF 1/56: Bamford to Jack Beddington, 13 July 1940.
47. TNA INF 1/57: Memorandum by Stanley Fletcher, 26 July 1940.
48. 1/57 Ibid.: Michael Balcon to Beddington, 1 August 1940.
49. Ibid.: Beddington to Balcon, 2 August 1940.
50. Ibid.: Balcon to Beddington, 6 August 1940.
51. *Kinematograph Weekly*, 12 December 1940, p.1.
52. Ian Dalrymple, 'The Crown Film Unit, 1940–43', in Pronay Spring (eds), *Propaganda, Politics and Film, 1918–45*, p.212.
53. Watt, *Don't Look at the Camera*, p.183.
54. TNA INF 1/57: Stanley Fletcher to Jack Beddington, 5 August 1940.
55. TNA INF 5/66: Alberto Cavalcanti to David Macdonald, 1 March 1940.
56. Ibid.: Notes of a meeting held at the Air Ministry, 8 March 1940.
57. Watt, *Don't Look at the Camera*, p.134.
58. TNA INF 6/328: COI record sheet for *London/Britain Can Take It*.
59. Watt, *Don't Look at the Camera*, pp.137–8.
60. *The Spectator*, 25 October 1940, p.415.
61. Richards and Sheridan, *Mass-Observation at the Movies*, p.443.
62. TNA INF 5/75: Notes on 'Xmas Film' by Harry Watt, undated.
63. The critical literature on Jennings is extensive. On his wartime films see in particular: Aldgate and Richards, *Britain Can Take It*, pp.218–45; Philip C. Logan, *Humphrey Jennings and British Documentary Film: A Re-Assessment* (Farnham, 2011), pp.121–282; Malcolm Smith, 'Narrative and Ideology in *Listen to Britain*', in Jeremy Hawthorn (ed.), *Narrative: From Malory to Motion Pictures* (London, 1985), pp.145–57; Jeffrey Richards, 'Humphrey Jennings: The Poet as Propagandist', in Mark Connelly and David Welch (eds), *War and the Media: Reportage and Propaganda, 1900–2003* (London, 2005), pp.127–38; and Wendy Webster, '*The Silent Village*: The GPO Film Unit Goes to War', in Scott Anthony and James G. Mansell (eds), *The Projection of Britain: A History of the GPO Film Unit* (London, 2011), pp.263–71.
64. Basil Wright, *The Long View: A Personal Perspective on World Cinema* (London, 1974), p.200.
65. BFI Humphrey Jennings Collection 13: 'Royal Marines' film treatment c. September 1943.
66. Quoted in Mary-Lou Jennings (ed.), *Humphrey Jennings: Film-Maker, Painter, Poet* (London, 1982), p.33.
67. Sussex, *The Rise and Fall of British Documentary*, p.144.
68. *The Spectator*, 13 March 1942, p.282.
69. *Documentary News Letter*, 2: 5 (May 1941), p.89.
70. *Documentary News Letter*, 4: 6 (June 1943), p.232.
71. *Documentary News Letter*, 4: 4 (April 1943), p.200.
72. *Documentary News Letter*, 4: 6 (June 1943), p.232.
73. Roger Manvell, *Films and the Second World War* (London, 1974), p.149.
74. Forman, 'The Non-Theatrical Distribution of Films by the Ministry of Information', p.230.

75. Roy Armes, *A Critical History of British Cinema* (London, 1978), p.154.
76. The film's production is documented in Aldgate and Richards, *Britain Can Take It*, pp.219–45.
77. Richards and Sheridan, *Mass-Observation at the Movies*, p.249.
78. Ibid., p.225.
79. K. R. M. Short, 'RAF Bomber Command's *Target for Tonight'*, *Historical Journal of Film, Radio and Television*, 17: 2 (1997), pp.181–218.
80. TNA INF 1/210: Undated memorandum entitled 'Bomber Command film'.
81. TNA INF 5/78: Harry Watt to Wing-Commander Williams, 7 February 1941.
82. TNA INF 1/867: Co-Ordinating Committee Paper No.1, 'Programme for Film Propaganda', 29 January 1940.
83. Watt, *Don't Look at the Camera*, p.149.
84. TNA INF 6/335: COI record sheet.
85. TNA INF 1/199: 'Receipts from commercial distribution of films', May 1944.
86. TNA INF 1/210: Lord Beaverbrook to Sidney Bernstein, 31 July 1941.
87. Eric Rhode, *A History of the Cinema from its Origins to 1970* (London, 1978), p.372.
88. Dai Vaughan, *Portrait of an Invisible Man: The Working Life of Stewart McAllister, Film Editor* (London, 1983), p.78.
89. Jeffrey Richards, 'Wartime Cinema Audiences and the Class System: The case of *Ships With Wings* (1941)', *Historical Journal of Film, Radio and Television*, 7: 2 (1987), pp.129–41.
90. J. R. Williams, 'Status of British Documentary', *Documentary News Letter*, 5: 6 (1944), p.66.
91. *The New York Times*, 21 September 1941, p.1.
92. TNA INF 1/120: Paul [Illegible] to Sidney Bernstein, 24 July 1941.
93. TNA INF 1/210: *Ferry Pilot* is listed as a five-minute film in a production schedule dated 8 November 1940.
94. TNA INF 1/199: 'Receipts from commercial distribution of films', May 1944.
95. Sussex, *The Rise and Fall of British Documentary*, p.137.
96. TNA INF BT 64/116: Undated memorandum 'Competition from Official Film Units'.
97. Ibid.
98. TNA INF 1/212: Jack Beddington to Ian Dalrymple, 26 November 1942.
99. Aldgate and Richards, *Britain Can Take It*, pp.238–40. Pat Jackson's account of the film is in his autobiography, *A Retake Please! 'Night Mail' to 'Western Approaches'* (Liverpool, 1999), pp.178–256.
100. TNA INF 1/213: E. St John Bamford to S. G. Gates, 7 September 1942.
101. Ibid.: Lord Beaverbrook to Jack Beddington, 6 November 1944.
102. Shearman, 'Wartime Wedding', p.53.
103. TNA INF 1/56: Ralph Nunn May to Jack Beddington, 24 April 1945.
104. Ibid.: Cyril Radcliffe to Brendan Bracken, 9 April 1945.
105. Some of these feature films were directed by documentarists, including Harry Watt (*Nine Men*, 1943; *The Overlanders*, 1946) and Pat Jackson (*White Corridors*, 1951).
106. Ian Grant, *Cameramen at War* (Cambridge, 1980), p.191.
107. *Documentary News Letter*, 2: 4 (April 1941), p.62.
108. *Daily Sketch*, 5 November 1941, p.3.
109. TNA INF 1/627: Ralph Nunn May to Jack Beddington, 27 February 1942.

110. TNA INF 6/342: COI record sheet for *Wavell's 30,000*.
111. TNA PREM 4 12/2: T. L. Rowan to Winston Churchill, 16 March 1943.
112. TNA INF 1/199: 'Receipts from commercial distribution of films', May 1944.
113. *The Times*, 4 March 1943, p.6.
114. Tony Aldgate, 'Mr Capra Goes to War: Frank Capra, the British Army Film Unit, and Anglo-American Travails in the Production of *Tunisian Victory*', *Historical Journal of Film, Radio and Television*, 11: 1 (1991), pp.21–39.
115. James Chapman, ' "The Yanks are Shown to Such Advantage": Anglo-American Rivalry in the Production of *The True Glory* (1945)', *Historical Journal of Film, Radio and Television*, 16: 4 (1996), pp.533–54.
116. Ian Jarvie, 'The Burma Campaign on Film: *Objective Burma* (1945), *The Stillwell Road* (1945) and *Burma Victory* (1945)', *Historical Journal of Film, Radio and Television*, 8: 1 (1988), pp.55–73.
117. Sussex, *The Rise and Fall of British Documentary*, p.175.
118. Rotha, *Rotha on the Film*, pp.228–9.
119. *Documentary News Letter*, 1 (January 1940), p.1.
120. *Documentary News Letter*, 2: 2 (February 1941), p.28.
121. J. B. Priestley, *Postscripts* (London, 1940), pp.35–6.
122. Paul Addison, *The Road to 1945: British Politics and the Second World War* (London, 1975), p.17.
123. Ibid., p.146.
124. Nicholas Pronay, ' "The Land of Promise": The Projection of Peace Aims on Britain', in K. R. M. Short (ed.), *Film and Radio Propaganda in World War II* (London, 1983), p.55.
125. George Orwell, 'Poetry and the Microphone' [1943] in Sonia Orwell and Ian Angus (eds), *The Collected Essays, Journalism and Letters of George Orwell Volume 2: My Country Right or Left, 1940–1943* (Harmondsworth, 1970), p.381.
126. Forman, 'The Non-Theatrical Distribution of Films by the Ministry of Information', p.221.
127. Information from transcript of an interview with John Taylor by Charles Barr (24 November 1988).
128. *Documentary News Letter*, 3: 5 (May 1942), p.68.
129. John Ellis, 'Victory of the Voice?', *Screen*, 22: 2 (1981), p.72.
130. Alan Burton, *The British Consumer Co-operative Movement and film, 1890s–1960s* (Manchester, 2005), p.157.
131. *Documentary News Letter*, 2: 7 (July 1941), p.129.
132. *Documentary News Letter*, 2: 9 (September 1941), p.161.
133. Sussex, *The Rise and Fall of British Documentary*, p.161.
134. Pronay, 'The Land of Promise', p.53.
135. Toby Haggith, 'Post-War Reconstruction as Depicted in Official British Films of the Second World War', *Imperial War Museum Review*, 7 (1992), p.44.
136. TNA INF 1/214: Paul Rotha to Arthur Elton, 15 October 1941.
137. Ibid.: A. Manktelow to Arthur Calder Marshall, 11 April 1942.
138. Ibid.: Sidney Bernstein to Jack Beddington, 26 August 1942.
139. David Pearson, 'Speaking for the Common Man: Multi-Voice Commentary in *World of Plenty* and *Land of Promise*', in Marris (ed.), *BFI Dossier No.18: Paul Rotha*, pp.64–85.

140. *The New Statesman and Nation*, 12 June 1943.
141. *Documentary News Letter*, 5: 49 (1945), p.2.
142. Pronay, 'The Land of Promise', p.72.

4   Post-War Documentary

1. 'Turning It Over', *Documentary Film News*, 7: 67 (July 1948), p.1.
2. Elizabeth Sussex, *The Rise and Fall of British Documentary* (Berkeley, 1975). Chapter 7 is entitled 'The Post-War Decline' – a verdict endorsed by most of the interviewees. See also Jack C. Ellis, 'The Final Years of British Documentary as the Grierson Movement', *Journal of Film and Video*, 36: 4 (1984), pp.43–4.
3. Sussex, *The Rise and Fall of British Documentary*, pp.176–7.
4. TNA INF 12/564: 'Draft Memorandum on Production Prospects', unsigned and undated but from internal evidence written by R. E. Tritton before July 1947.
5. Jennings was scouting locations for a film on the Greek island of Poros in September 1950 when he fell off a cliff and struck his head: he never regained consciousness.
6. Martin Stollery and John Corner, 'The Postwar British Documentary Movement – Decline or Transition?', *Journal of British Cinema and Television*, 10: 3 (2012), pp.387–94.
7. Free Cinema is discussed in chapter six in the context of alternative documentary practices.
8. Michael Balcon, 'The British Film During the War', *The Penguin Film Review*, 1 (1946), p.69.
9. John Ellis, 'The Quality Film Adventure: British Critics and the Cinema 1942–1948', in Andrew Higson (ed.), *Dissolving Views: Key Writings on British Cinema* (London, 1996), pp.66–93.
10. 'Sponsorship – or Films Don't Grow on Trees', *Documentary News Letter*, 56 (April–May 1947), p.83.
11. The growth of the Rank empire is outlined in Geoffrey Macnab, *J. Arthur Rank and the British Film Industry* (London, 1993), pp.17–50.
12. BFI BW 3/25: Paul Rotha, 'The Government and the Film Industry', 12 December 1945. This paper is published in Duncan Petrie and Robert Kruger (eds), *A Paul Rotha Reader* (Exeter, 1999), pp.208–20.
13. TNA COAL 32/2: Donald Alexander to L. J. H. Hayes, 26 January 1953. Alexander was films officer for the National Coal Board and was using *This Modern Age* as a comparison to illustrate the economical production of the NCB's *Mining Review*.
14. Leo Enticknap, '*This Modern Age* and the British Non-Fiction Film', in Justine Ashby and Andrew Higson (eds), *British Cinema, Past and Present* (London, 2000), pp.217–9.
15. TNA INF 12/564: Ronald Tritton to Miss Malherbe, 2 December 1947.
16. TNA INF 12/565: 'The Future of the Government Information Services in Relation to Films', memorandum by the Federation of Documentary Film Units, 25 May 1948.

17. On the 'crisis' in the film industry in the late 1940s, see Margaret Dickinson and Sarah Street, *Cinema and State: The Film Industry and the British Government 1927–84* (London, 1985), pp.170–226.
18. Political and Economic Planning, *The British Film Industry: A report on its history and present organisation, with special reference to the economic problems of British feature film production* (London, 1952), p.98.
19. TNA INF 12/564: Harold Wilson to Herbert Morrison, 25 November 1947.
20. *Today's Cinema*, 6 February 1948, p.14.
21. TNA INF 12/564: R. E. Tritton to B. C. Sendall, 4 December 1947.
22. Ibid.: Sir Robert Fraser to Kingsley Martin, 5 January 1948. Fraser was writing to Martin, editor of the *New Statesman*, in response to a review of the film *A Trip to Cyprus* by its film critic William Whitebait.
23. BFI Robert Angell Collection 1: 'Out Takes: Experiences of an Independent Documentary Producer', unpublished manuscript, 1992, p.58b.
24. Quoted in Elizabeth Sussex, *Lindsay Anderson* (London, 1969), p.23.
25. BFI Angell 1: 'Out Takes', p.58d.
26. Sussex, *The Rise and Fall of British Documentary*, p.161.
27. Mariel Grant, 'Towards a Central Office of Information: Continuity and Change in British Government Information Policy, 1939–51', *Journal of Contemporary History*, 34: 1 (1999), pp.49–67.
28. 'Grierson Asks for a Common Plan', *Documentary News Letter*, 46 (1945), p.50.
29. TNA INF 12/564: John Grierson: 'UK Documentary Film Problems 1947'.
30. Ibid.: B. C. Sendall to Sir Robert Fraser, 28 August 1947. Sendall continued: 'Even under Socialism there is a wide field of human life in which the Public Service has little part to play. The Documentarists seem to have failed conspicuously to enter into it.'
31. *Parliamentary Debates: House of Commons*, 13 May 1948, vol. 450, col. 2340.
32. *Parliamentary Debates: House of Commons*, 18 October 1950, vol. 478, col. 2079.
33. BFI BW 3/25: Paul Rotha, 'Government Information Services and the Documentary Film Companies', 2 August 1947.
34. TNA INF 12/564: Sendall to Sir Robert Fraser, 28 August 1947.
35. Ibid.: John Grierson to Fraser, 14 August 1947.
36. Ibid.: 'Draft Memorandum on Production Prospects'.
37. Ibid.: R. E. Tritton to Sendall, 28 October 1947.
38. 'Off With Their Heads!', *Documentary Film News*, 7: 67 (July 1948), p.77.
39. See Sue Harper and Vincent Porter, *British Cinema of the 1950s: The Decline of Deference* (Oxford, 2003), pp.185–8.
40. TNA INF 12/564: 'Draft Memorandum on Production Prospects'.
41. TNA INF 5/1: Alexander Shaw to Sendall, 11 April 1946.
42. Ibid.: Shaw to Sendall, 10 May 1946.
43. Ibid.: Sendall to Shaw, 16 April 1946.
44. Ibid.: Sendall to Sir Robert Fraser, 3 June 1946.
45. TNA INF 5/51: Alexander Shaw: 'A note on the state of the Crown Film Unit at the end of February, 1947', 28 February 1947.
46. TNA INF 5/52: Central Office of Information: Crown Film Unit Committee minutes, special meeting, 1 January 1948.
47. Ibid.: Crown Film Unit Committee minutes, 4 May 1948.

48. Ibid.: Transcript entitled 'Meeting on Crown Film Unit', 29 July 1948.
49. Philip C. Logan, *Humphrey Jennings and British Documentary: A Re-Assessment* (Farnham, 2011), pp.283–7.
50. TNA INF 12/564: Ronald Tritton to Miss Malherbe, 2 December 1947.
51. BFI Humphrey Jennings Collection 1: Press clipping, *News Chronicle*, 7 February 1948.
52. TNA INF 5/51: John Taylor to Sendall, 8 December 1947.
53. TNA T219/120: Sam Harris to R. A. Butler, 1 February 1952. Harris was managing editor of the trade paper *The Cinema* and prepared a memorandum of evidence for Butler (the Chancellor of the Exchequer) in advance of a parliamentary debate on the proposed cuts to government information services.
54. A. J. Harding, 'The Closure of the Crown Film Unit in 1952: Artistic Decline or Political Machinations?', *Contemporary British History*, 18: 4 (2004), pp.22–51.
55. TNA T219/120: John Boyd-Carpenter to George Lambert, 11 March 1952.
56. Ibid.: 'Crown Film Unit – Film Distribution Service'.
57. Ibid.: 'Crown Film Unit: Adjournment Debate', signed 'D. J.', 10 March 1952.
58. Ibid.: The file includes letters protesting against the closure from the National Association of Theatrical and Kine Employees (7 February 1952), the Association of Cinematograph and Allied Technicians (27 February 1952), the National Union of Journalists (8 March 1952) and the Trades Union Congress.
59. *The Times*, 4 February 1952, p.5.
60. TNA T219/120: Ralph Nunn May to J. A. Boyd-Carpenter, 14 January 1952.
61. Ibid.: 'D. J' to Jenkyns, 17 January 1952.
62. Ibid.: J. A. Boyd-Carpenter to E. B. Wakefield, 14 February 1952.
63. Ibid.: 'Note for record', initialled 'J. S', 5 February 1952.
64. TNA INF 1/634: 'Government Film Production and Distribution', 1 November 1945.
65. TNA INF 6/592: COI summary record sheet for *Britain Can Make It*.
66. Toby Haggith, 'Post-War Reconstruction as Depicted in Official British Films of the Second World War', *Imperial War Museum*, 17 (1992), pp.34–45.
67. Charlotte Wildman, '*A City Speaks*: The Projection of Civic Identity in Manchester', *Twentieth Century British History*, 23: 1 (2012), pp.80–99.
68. Timothy Boon, *Films of Fact: A History of Science in Documentary Films and Television* (London, 2008), pp.145–6.
69. 'Interview: Rotha on Rotha', in Paul Marris (ed.), *BFI Dossier Number 16: Paul Rotha* (London, 1982), p.27.
70. Roger Manvell, 'Land of Promise', *British Films*, publicity sheet issued by the British Council's Overseas Press Department, 5 June 1946, in the digitized microfiche for *Land of Promise* held by the BFI Reuben Library.
71. *Sunday Times*, 28 April 1948.
72. BFI Library microfiche: *Daily Mirror*, 25 April 1946; *Sunday Express*, 28 April 1948; *News Chronicle*, 27 April 1946; *Tribune*, 30 April 1946; *Daily Worker*, 26 April 1946; *Daily Herald*, 27 April 1946; *Daily Telegraph*, 29 April 1946.
73. Boon, *Films of Fact*, p.159.
74. BFI BW 3/25: Paul Rotha, 'Government Information Services and the Documentary Film Companies', 2 August 1947.

75. TNA INF 12/564: Tritton to Miss Malherbe, 2 December 1947.
76. Boon, *Films of Fact*, p.165.
77. TNA INF 12/564: Tritton to Sendall, 28 October 1947.
78. Quoted in Logan, *Humphrey Jennings and British Documentary Film*, p.311.
79. Kevin Jackson, *Humphrey Jennings* (Oxford, 2004), p.338.
80. Kenneth O. Morgan, *The People's Peace: British History* (Oxford, 1990), p.110.
81. Ben Jones and Rebecca Searle, 'Humphrey Jennings, the Left and the Experience of Modernity in Mid Twentieth-Century Britain', *History Workshop Journal*, 75 (2013), pp.190–212.
82. BFI BW 1/11/1: Letter from Stuart Legg to the *New Statesman*, 21 October 1950.
83. *Monthly Film Bulletin*, 18: 214 (November 1951), p.222.
84. BFI BW 1/11/1: Letter from Gavin Lambert to the *New Statesman*, 7 October 1950.
85. Lindsay Anderson, 'Postscript (1982): Only Connect: Some Aspects of the Work of Humphrey Jennings', in Mary-Lou Jennings (ed.), *Humphrey Jennings: Film-Maker, Painter and Poet* (London, 1982), p.59.
86. Keith Beattie, *Humphrey Jennings* (Manchester, 2010), p.127.
87. Sarah Easen, 'Film and Festival of Britain', in Ian MacKillop and Neil Sinyard (eds), *British Cinema of the 1950s: A Celebration* (Manchester, 2003), pp.51–63.
88. Leo Enticknap, ' "I Don't Think He Did Anything After That": Paul Dickson', in Patrick Russell and James Piers Taylor (eds), *Shadows of Progress: Documentary Film in Post-War Britain*, (London, 2010), p.160.
89. *Kinematograph Weekly*, 17 December 1953, p.10.
90. Leslie Halliwell, *Seats in All Parts: Half a Lifetime at the Movies* (London, 1985), p.178.
91. On the film's critical reception, see James Chapman, 'Cinema, Monarchy and the Making of Heritage: *A Queen Is Crowned* (1953)', in Claire Monk and Amy Sargeant (eds), *British Historical Cinema* (London, 2002), pp.82–91.
92. The John O'Gaunt speech provided the titles of no fewer than three wartime feature films: *This England* (1941), *The Demi-Paradise* (1943) and *This Happy Breed* (1944).
93. David Cannadine, 'James Bond and the Decline of England', *Encounter*, 53: 3 (1979), p.46.
94. TNA BW 4/64: 'Four British Council Films', n.d. The MOI also criticized a film on Kew Gardens for not reflecting wartime conditions: this was somewhat disingenuous as the film in question (*Kew Gardens* by Philip Leacock) had been made in 1937!
95. Ibid.: Sir Malcolm Robertson to Brendan Bracken, 8 December 1941.
96. *Report of the Independent Committee of Enquiry into the Overseas Information Services* (Cmnd. 9138).
97. Karel Reisz, 'A Use for Documentary', *Universities and New Left Review* (Winter 1958), p.24.
98. Brian Winston, 'The Griersonian Tradition Postwar: Decline or Transition?', *Journal of British Cinema and Television*, 11: 1 (2014), p.110.
99. TNA INF 12/564: Hartford to Herbert Morrison, 11 December 1947.
100. Ibid.: Sendall to White, 24 December 1947.

101. Rotha averred that 'Cripps had always believed in documentary, in British documentary, that is.' Quoted in Sussex, *The Rise and Fall of British Documentary*, p.161.
102. TNA INF COAL 32/2: Donald Alexander to L. J. H. Noyes, 26 January 1953.
103. Ibid.: Terrick FitzHugh to Sir Guy Nott Power, 6 February 1952.
104. Ibid.: Noel Gee to J. M. Pumphrey, 29 July 1957.
105. Ibid.: NCB General Purposes Committee: ' "Mining Review" Film-Magazine', memorandum by Noel Gee, 4 February 1958.
106. TNA COAL 32/6: Donald Alexander to Sir Guy Nott Bower: 'Film Proposals for 1952', n.d.
107. TNA COAL 32/2: Noel Gee to J. M. Pumphrey, 29 July 1957.
108. TNA COAL 32/6: Alexander to Bower: 'Film Proposals for 1952'.
109. Ibid.: Donald Alexander: 'NCB Film Programme for 1952'.
110. Ibid.: 'National Coal Board: General Purposes Committee: Instruction and Technical Films', 14 June 1955.
111. TNA COAL 32/2: Geoffrey Kirk to A. F. Hancock, 27 January 1961.
112. 'Production', in Russell and Taylor (eds), *Shadows of Progress*, p.35.
113. TNA COAL 32/16: 'Working Group on Film Policy: Proposals for 1962'.
114. TNA COAL 32/6: Donald Alexander: 'NCB Film programme for 1952'.
115. Sussex, *The Rise and Fall of British Documentary*, p.178.
116. Schlesinger became an acclaimed feature film director whose CV included *A Kind of Loving* (1962), *Billy Liar* (1963), *Darling* (1965), *Far From the Madding Crowd* (1967) and, in America, *Midnight Cowboy* (1969). Watkin was a distinguished cinematographer whose credits included *The Knack* (1967), *The Charge of the Light Brigade* (1968), *Chariots of Fire* (1981) and *Out of Africa* (1985).
117. 'Sponsorship', in Russell and Taylor (eds), *Shadows of Progress*, p.75.
118. Ibid., p.77.
119. Patrick Russell, 'Shooting the Message: John Krish', in Russell and Taylor (eds), *Shadows of Progress*, p.249.
120. TNA BR 111/144A: *BTC Outline Plan: Public Relations*, 10 April 1962.
121. BFI Ken Gay Collection 34: *Visual Aids*, June 1956, p.7.
122. John Burder, *The Work of the Industrial Film Maker* (London, 1973), p.12.
123. Quoted in Douglas Gordon, *Shell Films: The First Sixty Years* (London, 1994), n.p.
124. John Roberts, 'The Aims of Films on Industry', *The Guardian*, 20 April 1964, p.27.
125. TNA COAL 32/6: Donald Alexander: 'NCB Film Programme for 1952'.
126. TNA T219/120: Edward Cook to J. A. Boyd-Carpenter, 8 December 1951.
127. Edgar Anstey, 'Called to account', *The Times*, 2 November 1964, p.ii.
128. BFI Robert Angell Collection 1: 'Out Takes: Experiences of an Independent Documentary Producer', unpublished autobiography, 1992, pp.49–50.
129. Winston, 'The Griersonian Tradition Postwar: Decline or Transition?', p.110.
130. Ibid., p.107.
131. Quoted in Colin Burgess, 'Sixty Years of Shell Film Sponsorship, 1934–94', *Journal of British Cinema and Television*, 7: Z (2010), p.222.
132. 'Can We See Our Feet?', *Documentary News Letter*, 6: 53 (1946), p.33.

133. Sue Harper, *Women in British Cinema: Mad, Bad and Dangerous to Know* (London, 2000), pp.192–3.
134. BFI BECTU Oral History Project: Interview with Paul Dickson, 25 August 2004.
135. *The Times*, 9 August 1951, p.21.
136. Enticknap, ' "I Don't Think He Did Anything After That": Paul Dickson', pp.158–9.
137. Erik Hedling, 'Meet the Pioneers: Early Lindsay Anderson', in Russell and Taylor (eds), *Shadows of Progress*, p.327.
138. Paul Sutton (ed.), *Lindsay Anderson: The Diaries* (London, 2004), p.59.
139. Ros Cranston, 'A Person Apart: Guy Brenton', in Russell and Taylor (eds), *Shadows of Progress*, p.328.
140. Russell, 'Shooting the Message: John Krish', p.253.
141. André Bazin, *What Is Cinema? Volume II*, trans. Hugh Gray (Berkeley, 1971), p.81.
142. Kate McGahan, 'I Think They Call Him John', in *A Day in the Life: Four Portraits of Post-War Britain by John Krish*, booklet accompanying BFI DVD9.
143. BFI Angell 1: 'Out Takes: Experiences of an Independent Documentary Producer', p.44.

5   Television and Documentary

1. Duncan Ross, 'The Documentary in Television', *BBC Quarterly*, 5: 1 (1950), p.19.
2. For an overview, see Andrew Crisell, *An Introductory History of British Broadcasting* (London, 1997). The standard institutional histories are Asa Briggs, *The History of Broadcasting in the United Kingdom Volume IV: Sound and Vision 1945–1954* (Oxford, 1995) and *The History of Broadcasting in the United Kingdom Volume V: Competition 1955–1974* (Oxford, 1995). On the public service ideology in British television, see Paddy Scannell, 'Public Service Broadcasting: The History of a Concept', in Andrew Goodwin and Garry Whannel (eds), *Understanding Television* (London, 1990), pp.11–29.
3. Susan Sydney-Smith, *Beyond Dixon of Dock Green: Early British Police Series* (London, 2002), p.25.
4. Briggs, *The History of Broadcasting in the United Kingdom Volume V*, p.1005.
5. Linda Wood (ed.), *British Film Industry: A BFI Refererence Guide* (London, 1980), p.3A.
6. Robert Dillon, *History on British Television: Constructing Nation, Nationality and Collective Memory* (Manchester, 2010), p.36.
7. TNA PREM 11/408: Basil Nicolls (Acting Director-General of the BBC) to J. R. Colville (Churchill's Private Secretary), 28 October 1952.
8. Ross, 'The Documentary in Television', p.20.
9. Elaine Bell, 'The Origins of British Television Documentary: The BBC 1946–1955', in John Corner (ed.), *Documentary and the Mass Media* (London, 1986), p.77.
10. Ibid., p.69.
11. Quoted in Jo Fox, 'From Documentary Film to Television Documentaries: John Grierson and *This Wonderful World*', *Journal of British Cinema and Television*, 10: 3 (2013), p.502.

12. Paul Rotha, *Rotha on the Film: A Selection of Writings About the Cinema* (London, 1958), p.154.
13. Quoted in Bell, 'The Origins of British Television Documentary', pp.72–3.
14. Elizabeth Sussex, *The Rise and Fall of British Documentary* (Berkeley, 1975), p.205.
15. Quoted in Tim Boon, *Films of Fact: A History of Science in Documentary Films and Television* (London, 2008), p.207.
16. Quoted in Bernard Sendall, *Independent Television in Britain Volume 1: Origin and Foundation* (London, 1982), p.208.
17. Forsyth Hardy, *John Grierson: A Documentary Biography* (London, 1979), pp.204–14.
18. Fox, 'John Grierson and *This Wonderful World*', pp.500–1.
19. Jonathan Conlin, *Civilisation* (London, 2009), p.6.
20. Peter Waymark, 'Television and the Cultural Revolution: The BBC under Hugh Carleton Greene', PhD thesis (The Open University, 2005), p.207.
21. Dai Vaughan, *For Documentary: Twelve Essays* (Berkeley, 1999), pp.13–14.
22. Derek Paget, *No Other Way To Tell It: Docudrama on Film and Television* (Manchester, 2nd edn 2011), p.186.
23. Quoted in Arthur Swinson, *Writing for Television* (London, 1955), pp.81–2.
24. BBC WAC T16: Robert Barr, 'TV Documentary', 3 August 1951.
25. Quoted in Swinson, *Writing for Television*, p.82.
26. Quoted in Bell, 'The Origins of British Television Documentary', p.70.
27. Quoted in Paget, *No Other Way To Tell It*, p.193.
28. Michael Barry, *From the Palace to the Grove* (London, 1992), p.71.
29. Brian Winston, *Claiming the Real: The Griersonian Documentary and its Legitimations* (London, 1995), pp.181–8.
30. Quoted in Vaughan, *For Documentary*, p.11.
31. On *Monitor*, see Mary M. Irwin, '*Monitor*: The Creation of the Television Arts Documentary', *Journal of British Cinema and Television*, 8: 3 (2011), pp.322–36.
32. Quoted in Waymark, 'Television and the Cultural Revolution', p.86.
33. *Radio Times*, 13 May 1965, p.31.
34. BBC WAC T32/1095/2: Audience Research Report: *The Debussy Film*, 4 June 1965.
35. BFI Robert Angell Collection 1 'Out Takes: Experiences of an Independent Documentary Producer', unpublished memoir, 1992.
36. Peter Goddard, John Corner and Kay Richardson, *Public Issue Television: 'World in Action', 1963–99* (Manchester, 2007), p.8.
37. Waymark, 'Television and the Cultural Revolution', p.25.
38. Robert Rowland, '*Panorama* in the Sixties', in Anthony Aldgate, James Chapman and Arthur Marwick (eds), *Windows on the Sixties: Exploring Key Texts of Media and Culture* (London, 2000), p.158.
39. *Report of the Committee on Broadcasting 1960. Chairman: Sir Henry Pilkington*, Cmnd. 1953 (London, 1962), p.67. For the background to the Pilkington Report, see Briggs, *The History of Broadcasting in the United Kingdom Volume V*, pp.257–308.
40. Quoted in Patricia Holland, *The Angry Buzz: 'This Week' and Current Affairs Television* (London, 2006), p.1.
41. Ibid., p.47.

42. Quoted in Goddard *et al*, *Public Issue Television*, p.25.
43. Ibid.
44. Ibid., p.27.
45. Rowland, *'Panorama* in the Sixties', p.158.
46. Holland, *The Angry Buzz*, p.113.
47. Rowland, *'Panorama* in the Sixties', p.178.
48. Quoted in Holland, *The Angry Buzz*, p.126.
49. Quoted in Philip Schlesinger, Graham Murdock and Philip Elliot, *Televising Terrorism* (London, 1983), p.122.
50. Quoted in Liz Curtis, *Ireland: The Propaganda War – The British Media and the Battle for Hearts and Minds* (London, 1984), p.150.
51. Holland, *The Angry Buzz*, pp.204–5.
52. Ibid., p.198.
53. The critical literature includes (but is not limited to): John Corner, *The Art of Record: A Critical Introduction to Documentary* (Manchester, 1996), pp.90–107; John Hill, *Ken Loach: The Politics of Film and Television* (London, 2011), pp.52–68; and Derek Paget, ' "Cathy Come Home" and "Accuracy" in British Television Drama', *New Theatre Quarterly*, 15: 1 (1999), pp.75–90. The fullest account of the production and reception is Stephen Lacey's monograph *Cathy Come Home* (London, 2011) for the BFI 'Television Classics' series.
54. M. K. MacMurraugh-Kavanagh, 'The BBC and the Birth of *The Wednesday Play*, 1962–66: Institutional Containment Versus "Agitational Contemporaneity" ', *Historical Journal of Film, Radio and Television*, 17: 3 (1997), pp.367–81.
55. BBC WAC T48/513/1: Alan Cooke to Jeremy Sandford, 8 July 1964.
56. Ibid.: David Benedictus to Jonathan Clowes (Sandford's agent), 19 November 1965.
57. Graham Fuller (ed.), *Loach on Loach* (London, 1998), p.23.
58. *The War Game* is discussed in Chapter 6.
59. Fuller (ed.), *Loach on Loach*, p.23.
60. BBC WAC T48/513/1: Audience Research Report VR/66/629: *Cathy Come Home*.
61. *Morning Star*, 14 January 1967.
62. *Daily Mail*, 17 November 1966.
63. *Sunday Telegraph*, 20 November 1966.
64. Hill, *Ken Loach*, p.61.
65. Fuller (ed.), *Loach on Loach*, p.24.
66. *Daily Telegraph*, 17 November 1966.
67. *Sunday Times*, 20 November 1966.
68. *Sunday Telegraph*, 8 January 1967.
69. Paget, *No Other Way To Tell It*, p.209.
70. Lacey, *Cathy Come Home*, p.7.
71. Dillon, *History on British Television*, p.72.
72. Noble Frankland, *History at War: The Campaigns of an Historian* (London, 1998), p.183.
73. Ibid., pp.183–4.
74. BBC WAC T32/1139/1: Tony Essex to Gordon Watkins, 23 April 1964.

75. For a fuller account of the falling-out, see Mark Connelly, 'The Devil is Coming', *Historical Journal of Film, Radio and Television*, 22: 1 (2002), pp.21–7.
76. BBC WAC T32/827/1: Audience Research Department: VR1/64/461: *The Great War* – 'Kitchener's Army', 11 September 1964.
77. The reception of the series is discussed by Emma Hanna, *The Great War on the Small Screen: Representing the First World War in Contemporary Britain* (Edinburgh, 2009), pp.36–52.
78. Jeremy Isaacs, 'All Our Yesterdays', in David Cannadine (ed.), *History and the Media* (London, 2004), p.37.
79. Frankland, *History at War*, p.188.
80. Jeremy Potter, *Independent Television in Britain Volume 2: Politics and Control, 1968–80* (Basingstoke, 1989), p.28.
81. Quoted in Greg Neale, 'One Man Went to War', *BBC History Magazine*, 4: 2 (2001), p.22. Christopher Chataway, the former middle-distance runner, was Postmaster General in the Conservative government.
82. Frankland, *History at War*, p.189.
83. 'Jeremy Isaacs, Producer of "The World at War", Defines his Objectives', *Journal of the Society of Film and Television Arts*, 2: 9–10 (1974), p.1.
84. 'Raye Farr, Film Researcher' [interview], *Cineaste*, 9: 2 (1978–9), p.18.
85. IWM/Thames Television Archive for *The World at War*: Jeremy Isaacs to 'All Second World War Personnel', 4 October 1972.
86. Arthur Marwick, *The Nature of History* (London, 3rd edn 1989), p.315.
87. James Chapman, 'Television and History: *The World at War*', *Historical Journal of Film, Radio and Television*, 31: 2 (2011), pp.247–75.
88. 'Susan McConachy, Researcher-Interviewer', *Cineaste*, 9: 2 (1978–9), p.23.
89. Taylor Downing, *The World at War* (London, 2012), p.152.
90. Quoted in Joe Seider, 'The Family (1974)', *Screenonline*: http://www.screenonline.org.uk/tv/id/ 444743 (accessed 09.05.2014).
91. 'The Family's Margaret Wilkins, "first lady" of reality TV, is dead', *MailOnline*, 19 August 2008: http://www.dailymail.co.uk/news/article_1047125 (accessed 09.05.2014).
92. *The Guardian*, 19 January 1982, p.9.
93. Paget, *No Other Way to Tell It*, p.222.
94. Ibid., p.223.
95. Quoted in Elizabeth Sussex, 'Getting It Right', *Sight and Sound*, 51: 1 (1981–2), p.11.
96. Quoted in Anthony Goodwin, Paul Kerr and Ian Macdonald (eds), *BFI Dossier No.19: Drama-Documentary* (London, 1983), p.29.
97. Sussex, 'Getting It Right', p.14.
98. Ibid., p.14.
99. Quoted in ' "Death of a Princess" film criticised by ministers, peers and MPs', *Daily Telegraph*, 25 April 1980.
100. Paget, *No Other Way To Tell It*, p.218.
101. Ibid., p.231.
102. Ibid., p.233.
103. Ibid., p.243.
104. Ibid., pp.262–96.

105. *Dunkirk* and *D-Day to Berlin* were each series of three 50-minute episodes: the others were all one-off feature-length films. See James Chapman, 'Re-Presenting War: British Television Drama-Documentary and the Second World War', *European Journal of Cultural Studies*, 10: 1 (2007), pp.13–33.
106. *Broadcast*, 30 January 2004, p.22.
107. Toby Haggith, 'D-Day Filming – For Real: A Comparison of "Truth" and "Reality" in *Saving Private Ryan* and Combat Film by the British Army's Film and Photographic Unit', *Film History*, 14: 3–4 (2002), pp.332–55.
108. Andrew Crissell, *An Introductory History of British Broadcasting* (London, 1997), pp.227–9.
109. Holland, *The Angry Buzz*, p.214.
110. Caroline Dover, ' "Crisis" in British Television Documentary: The End of a Genre?', *Journal of British Cinema and Television*, 1: 2 (2004), pp.242–59.
111. Corner, *The Art of Record*, p.181.
112. Ibid., p.182.
113. Mandy Rose, 'Through the Eyes of the *Video Nation*', in John Izod and Richard Kilborn, with Matthew Hibberd (eds), *From Grierson to the Docu-Soap: Breaking the Boundaries* (Luton, 2000), p.161.
114. Dafydd Sills-Jones, '*The Second World War in Colour*: The UK History Documentary Boom and Colour Archive', *Journal of British Cinema and Television*, 7: 1 (2010), pp.115–130.
115. Richard Kilborn, 'The Docu-Soap: A Critical Assessment', in Izod *et al* (eds), *From Grierson to the Docu-Soap*, pp.111–19.
116. Betsy A. McLane, *A New History of Documentary* (London, 2nd edn 2012), p.322.
117. 'Seven Up! Now we are 56', *The Telegraph*, 16 April 2012: www.telegraph.co.uk/culture /tvandradio/9206960/Seven-Up-Now-we-are-56.html (accessed 28.04.2014).
118. 'Channel 4's "50 Greatest Documentaries" ', *The Internet Movie Database*, 18 April 2011: http://www.imdb.com/list/Pixb1R4U0t4/ (accessed 28.04.2014).

6   Alternative and Oppositional Documentary

1. Lindsay Anderson, John Fletcher, Walter Lassally, Karel Reisz, 'Free Cinema Six: The Last Free Cinema', National Film Theatre programme notes, March 1959.
2. The term is borrowed from Don MacPherson (ed.), *Traditions of Independence: British Cinema in the Thirties* (London, 1980).
3. See the excellent study by Stephen G. Jones, *The British Labour Movement and Film, 1918–1939* (London, 1987).
4. Paul Rotha, 'Films and the Labour Party' (1936), in Ian Aitken (ed.), *The Documentary Film Movement: An Anthology* (Edinburgh, 1998), p.178.
5. For example Rachael Low, *The History of the British Film 1929–1939: Films of Comment and Persuasion of the 1930s* (London, 1979), p.166.
6. 'The New Road to Progress' (*Kino News* 1, December 1935), reprinted in MacPherson (ed.), *Traditions of Independence*, p.148.
7. Quoted in Anthony Aldgate, *Cinema and History: British Newsreels and the Spanish Civil War* (London, 1979), p.24.

8. See Nicholas Pronay, 'British Newsreels in the 1930s: 1. Audiences and Producers', *History*, 56 (1971), pp.411–18; Pronay, 'British Newsreels in the 1930s: 2. Their Policies and Impact', *History*, 57 (1972), pp.63–72.

9. See Bert Hogenkamp, *Deadly Parallels: Film and the Left in Britain 1929–39* (London, 1986).

10. Paul Rotha, *Documentary Diary: An Informal History of the British Documentary Film, 1928–1939* (New York, 1973), p.164.

11. James Robertson, *The Hidden Cinema: British Film Censorship in Action, 1913–1975* (London, 1989), p.3.

12. Quoted in 'Politics on the Screen', *Sight and Sound*, 5: 18 (1936), p.20.

13. Rotha, *Documentary Diary*, p.168.

14. 'Politics on the Screen', p.21.

15. Alan Burton, *The British Consumer Co-operative Movement and Film 1860s–1960s* (Manchester, 2005), p.156.

16. BFI Thorold Dickinson Collection Box 2 f.2: *Spanish ABC* – List of scenes shot, typed sheet, undated.

17. Thorold Dickinson, 'Experiences in the Spanish Civil War', *Historical Journal of Film, Radio and Television*, 4: 2 (1984), p.190.

18. BFI Dickinson Box 2 f.4: Film Society Programme: 105th Performance, 14th Season, New Gallery Cinema, 8 January 1939.

19. BFI Dickinson Box 2 f.3: Press clippings from the *Glasgow Herald* (12 August 1938), *Nottingham Journal* (6 January 1939) and *Kentish Mercury* (17 March 1939).

20. BFI Dickinson Box 49 f.1: Typed transcript of an interview for *Film Dope* c.1976. This is an unedited text of David Badder and Bob Baker, 'Interview with Thorold Dickinson', *Film Dope*, 11 (1977), pp.1–21.

21. *The Manchester Guardian*, 24 June 1938, p.10.

22. Hogenkamp, *Deadly Parallels*, p.204.

23. Low, *Films of Comment and Persuasion of the 1930s*, p.196.

24. *The Times*, 15 June 1939, p.8.

25. Hogenkamp, *Deadly Parallels*, p.209.

26. Andrew Spicer, *Sydney Box* (Manchester, 2006), p.28.

27. Free Cinema 1 (February 1956) consisted of Linday Anderson's *O Dreamland* (1953), Karel Reisz and Tony Richardson's *Momma Don't Allow* (1956) and Lorenza Mazetti's *Together* (1956). Free Cinema 3 (May 1957) included Claude Goretta and Alain Turner's *Nice Time* (1957), the Norton Park Film Unit's *The Singing Street* (1952) and Anderson's *Every Day Except Christmas* (1957). Free Cinema 6 (March 1959) comprised Robert Vas's *Refuge England* (1959), Michael Grigsby's *Enginemen* (1959), Reisz's *We Are the Lambeth Boys* (1959) and Elizabeth Russell's *Food for a Blush* (1959).

28. Quoted in Alexander Walker, *Hollywood, England: The British Film Industry in the Sixties* (London, 1974), p.27.

29. Lorenza Mazzetti, Lindsay Anderson, Karel Reisz, Tony Richardson, 'Free Cinema', National Theatre programme note February 1956.

30. 'Look at Britain! Free Cinema 3', National Film Theatre programme notes, May 1957.

31. BFI Special Collections: British Film Institute Production Board, PC6 Paper No.2, Budget – 'Jazz' – Picture Only, November 1954, authorized £250; PC8

Paper No.4., Budget – 'Jazz', 30 June 1955, authorized another £175 'for the addition of sound and completion of the picture'.

32. Arthur Marwick, '*Room at the Top, Saturday Night and Sunday Morning*, and the "Cultural Revolution" in Britain', *Journal of Contemporary History*, 19: 1 (1984), pp.127–52.
33. Quoted in Stuart Hall, 'The "First" New Left: Life and Times', in Robin Archer *et al* (ed.), *Out of Apathy: Voices of the New Left Thirty Years On* (London, 1989), p.33.
34. Quoted in Colin Gardner, *Karel Reisz* (Manchester, 2006), p.85.
35. See M. Ali Issari and Doris A. Paul, *What is Cinéma Vérité?* (Metuchen, 1979), pp.52–7; Erik Barnouw, *Documentary: A History of the Non-Fiction Film* (New York, 2nd rev. edn 1993), pp.231–3; and Kristin Thompson and David Bordwell, *Film History: An Introduction* (New York, 1994), pp.559–73.
36. 'Look at Britain! Free Cinema 3'.
37. Mazzetti *et al*, 'Free Cinema'.
38. See John Gibbs, '*Sequence* and the Archaeology of British Film Criticism', *Journal of Popular British Cinema*, 4 (2001), pp.14–29; and Erik Hedling, 'Lindsay Anderson: *Sequence* and the Rise of Auteurism in 1950s Britain', in Ian MacKillop and Neil Sinyard (eds), *British Cinema of the 1950s: A Celebration* (Manchester, 2003), pp.23–31.
39. Lindsay Anderson, 'Only Connect: Some Aspects of the Work of Humphrey Jennings', *Sight and Sound*, 23: 4 (1954), p.182.
40. *The Times*, 18 March 1959, p.13.
41. Quoted in Erik Hedling, *Lindsay Anderson: Maverick Film-Maker* (London, 1998), p.34.
42. Gavin Lambert, 'Free Cinema', *Sight and Sound*, 25: 4 (1956), p.177.
43. Penelope Houston, *The Contemporary Cinema* (Harmondsworth, 1963), pp.114–5.
44. Alan Lovell and Jim Hillier, *Studies in Documentary* (London, 1972), pp.139–40.
45. Ibid., p.142.
46. Raymond Durgnat, *A Mirror for England: British Movies from Austerity to Affluence* (London, 1970), pp.127–8.
47. Roy Armes, *A Critical History of British Cinema* (London, 1978), pp.264–5.
48. Ibid., p.267.
49. BBC WAC S251 Box 8: 'The Story of *The War Game*', pp.4–5. This was an internal dossier compiled at the BBC's request by Guy Phelps to document the production of *The War Game* when it became apparent that the film would be controversial.
50. BBC WAC T32/515/3: Peter Watkins to Huw Wheldon, 24 February 1964.
51. Ibid.
52. Nicholas J. Cull, 'Peter Watkins' *Culloden* and the Alternative Form in Historical Filmmaking', *Film International*, 1 (2003), p.49.
53. BBC WAC T32/515/3: Watkins to Wheldon, 17 March 1964. *Spotlight* was the directory of professional actors.
54. BBC WAC T32/515/2: Watkins to John Prebble, 10 July 1964.
55. Robert A. Rosenstone, 'Introduction', in Rosenstone (ed.), *Revisioning History: Film and the Construction of a New Past* (Princeton, 1995), p.8.
56. Cull, 'Peter Watkins' *Culloden*', p.51.

57. *New York Times*, 3 April 1966, S2, p.19.
58. BBC WAC T56/263/2: Peter Watkins to Alan Shuttleworth, 14 July 1963.
59. Ibid.: Watkins to Richard Cawston, 1 February 1966.
60. See Michael Tracey, 'Censored: *The War Game* Story', in Crispin Aubrey *et al* (eds), *Nukespeak: The Media and the Bomb* (London, 1982), pp.38–54; Patrick Murphy, '*The War Game* – The Controversy', *Film International*, 3 (2003), pp.25–8; James Chapman, 'The BBC and the Censorship of *The War Game* (1965)', *Journal of Contemporary British History*, 41: 1 (2006), pp.75–94.
61. TNA CAB 21/5808: Lord Normanbrook to Sir Burke Trend, 7 September 1965.
62. TNA PREM 13/139: Mitchell to Sir Burke Trend, 12 October 1965.
63. BBC WAC T16/679/1: Normanbrook to Trend, 24 November 1965.
64. BBC WAC R44/1334: 'The War Game', internal circular, undated.
65. John R. Cook and Patrick Murphy, 'After the Bomb Dropped: The Cinema Half-Life of *The War Game*', *Journal of Popular British Cinema*, 3 (2000), pp.129–32.
66. The response to the 1938 broadcast is analysed in a contemporary academic study by Hadley Cantril, with Hazel Gaudet and Herta Herzog, *The Invasion from Mars: A Study in the Psychology of Panic* (Princeton, 1940).
67. BBC WAC T16/682/1: John Boorman to Controller West Region, 15 February 1966.
68. BBC WAC T16/679/1: Robert Lusty to Normanbrook, 28 September 1965.
69. Ibid.: O. J. Whitley to Normanbrook, 27 September 1965.
70. See Arthur Marwick, *The Sixties: Cultural Revolution in Britain, France, Italy and the United States, c.1958–c.1974* (Oxford, 1998), *passim*.
71. On Third Cinema, see Jonathan Buchsbaum, 'A Closer Look at Third Cinema', *Historical Journal of Film, Radio and Television*, 21: 2 (2001), pp.153–66; and Jim Pines and Paul Willemen (eds), *Questions of Third Cinema* (London, 1989).
72. Jim Pines, 'Notes on Political Cinema', *Cinema Rising*, 1 (1972), p.17.
73. Quoted in Margaret Dickinson (ed.), *Rogue Reels: Oppositional Film in Britain, 1945–90* (London, 1999), p.1.
74. Ibid., pp.265–6.
75. Ibid., p.269.
76. 'Cinema Action' information sheet 1975, reprinted in Petra Bauer and Dan Kidner (eds), *Working Together: Notes on British Film Collectives in the 1970s* (Southend, 2013), p.112.
77. Ibid.
78. Ibid.
79. Claire Johnston and Paul Willemen, 'Brecht in Britain: The Independent Political Film (on *The Nightcleaners*)', *Screen*, 16: 4 (1975–6), p.103.
80. Dickinson (ed.), *Rogue Reels*, pp.269–70.
81. Johnston and Willemen, p.64.
82. Glyn and Marris, p.68.
83. 'Humphrey Trevelyan in Conversation with Petra Bauer and Dan Kidner', in Bauer and Kidner (eds), *Working Together*, p.47.
84. Berwick Street Collective: programme note for the 'First Festival of British Independent Cinema' [1975], reprinted in Bauer and Kidner (eds), *Working Together*, p.117.

85. 'Humphrey Trevelyan in Conversation', p.50.
86. Claire Johnston, 'The Nightcleaners Part 1', in Dickinson (ed.), *Rogue Reels*, pp.150–1.
87. Johnston and Willemen, 'Brecht in Britain', pp.113–4.
88. Brian Winston, *Claiming the Real: The Griersonian Documentary and its Legitimations* (London, 1995), p.199.
89. Marc Karlin, Claire Johnston, Mark Nash and Paul Willemen, 'Problems of Independent Cinema', *Screen*, 21: 4 (1980–1), p.22.
90. Dickinson (ed.), *Rogue Reels*, p.284.
91. Julian Petley, 'Doing Without the Broadcast Media', *Broadcast*, 28 June 1985, p.7.
92. Chris Reeves, 'Redressing the Balance: Making the Miners' Campaign Tapes', in booklet accompanying the DVD of *The Miners' Campaign Tapes* (BFIVD 847), p.9.
93. Elizabeth Sussex, 'Grierson on Documentary: The Last Interview', *Film Quarterly*, 26: 1 (1972), p.30.
94. 'Amber: interview recorded in 1995 with Murray Martin, founder member of Amber', in Dickinson (ed.), *Rogue Reels*, p.249.
95. Anon., *Amber: A Short History* (Newcastle, 2005): booklet included in the DVD of *The Tyne Documentaries*, p.3.
96. 'Amber', *Rogue Reels*, p.250.
97. Darren Newbury, 'Documentary Practices and Working-class Culture: An Interview with Murray Martin', *Visual Studies*, 17: 2 (2002), p.119.
98. Quoted in Huw Beynon, 'Documentary Poet: Murray Martin', in Sheila Rowbotham and Huw Beynon Beynon (eds), *Looking at Class: Film, Television and the Working Class in Britain* (London, 2001), p.162.
99. Jack Newsinger, 'The Interface of Documentary and Fiction: The Amber Film Workshop and Regional Documentary Practice', *Journal of British Cinema and Television*, 6: 3 (2009), p.921.
100. Dickinson (ed.), *Rogue Reels*, p.255.
101. James Leggott and Tobias Hochscherf, 'From Marks and Spencer to Marx and Engels: A Transnational DEFA and Amber Film Documentary Project across the Iron Curtain', *Studies in Documentary Film*, 2: 2 (2008), pp.123–35.
102. Neil Young, 'Forever Amber: An Interview with Ellin Hare and Murray Martin of the Amber Film Collective', *Critical Quarterly*, 43: 4 (2001), p.69.
103. 'Black Audio Film Collective', in Dickinson (ed.), *Rogue Reels*, p.307.
104. Ibid.
105. Jim Pines, 'British Cinema and Black Representation', in Robert Murphy (ed.), *The British Cinema Book* (London, 1997), p.213.
106. Stuart Hall, 'New Ethnicities', in Kobena Mercer (ed.), *Black Film/British Cinema* (London, 1988), p.28.
107. Paul Gilroy and Jim Pines, 'Handsworth Songs: Interview with the Black Audio Film Collective', *Framework*, 35 (1988), p.7.
108. 'Black Audio Film Collective', p.308.
109. Gilroy and Pines, 'Handsworth Songs', p.13.
110. Colin McCabe, 'Black Film in 80s Britain', in Mercer (ed.), *Black Film/British Cinema*, p.32.
111. *The Guardian*, 2 January 1987.
112. Gilroy and Pines, 'Handsworth Songs', p.14.
113. 'Black Audio Film Collective', p.313.

Conclusion: British Documentary in Context

1. Paul Rotha, *Documentary Diary: An Informal History of the British Documentary Film, 1928–1939* (New York, 1973), p.286.
2. Julian Petley, 'The Lost Continent', in Charles Barr (ed.), *All Our Yesterdays: 90 Years of British Cinema* (London, 1986), p.98.
3. John Grierson, 'Postscript to the New Edition', in Forsyth Hardy (ed.), *Grierson on Documentary* (London, rev. edn 1966), p.222.
4. John Akomfrah, 'Director's Statement', in *The Stuart Hall Project: Revolution, Politics, Culture and the New Left Experience*, p.5, booklet accompanying DVD of *The Stuart Hall Project* (BFIVD998).
5. Ashley Clark, 'The Stuart Hall Project', *Sight and Sound*, New Series 23: 10 (October 2013), p.67.

Bibliography

Archival sources

BBC Written Archives Centre, Caversham, Reading (BBC WAC):
R9: Audience Research Department: Viewing and Listening Barometers.
S251 Box 8: 'The Story of *The War Game*' (aka the Phelps dossier).
T16: BBC policy files, including material relating to *The War Game*.
T32: Television documentary programme files, including *Culloden*, *The Great War* and *The Debussy Film*.
T65: Television drama programme files, including *Cathy Come Home*.

British Film Institute Special Collections Unit, London (BFI):
Robert Angell Collection
Film Centre Collection
Thorold Dickinson Collection
Humphrey Jennings Collection
Basil Wright Collection

British Postal Museum and Archive, London (BPMA):
POST 33: Records of the GPO Film Unit, including contracts, finance, distribution and an unpublished manuscript documenting the history of the unit.

John Grierson Archive, University of Stirling (JGA)
G2: Papers and correspondence relating to the EMB Film Unit.
G3: Papers and correspondence relating to the GPO Film Unit.

Imperial War Museum, London (IWM):
IWM/Thames Television *World at War* Collection: Production memos and correspondence relating to *The World at War*.

The National Archives, Kew, London (TNA):
BT: Board of Trade – including representations by documentary film-makers regarding the Cinematograph Films Act.
BW: British Council – including commissioning of documentary films and their distribution overseas.
CAB: Cabinet Office – including correspondence regarding *The War Game*.
COAL: National Coal Board – including production and distribution of films and records of the NCB Film Unit.
CO: Colonial Office – including records of the EMB Film Unit.
COI: Central Office of Information – including policy towards documentary film.
INF: Ministry of Information – including policy papers, production records for documentary films and records of the Crown Film Unit.

PREM: Prime Minister's Office – including Winston Churchill's correspondence regarding *Desert Victory* and *Victory at Sea*.

T: Treasury – including material on the film-making activities of government departments.

Published reports

Parliamentary Debates: House of Commons (Hansard).

Report of the Independent Committee of Enquiry Into the Overseas Information Services. Chairman: Lord Drogheda, Cmd 1938 (London: HMSO, 1954).

Report of the Committee on Broadcasting 1960. Chairman: Sir Henry Pilkington, Cmd 1953 (London: HMSO, 1962).

Thirteenth Report from the Select Committee on National Expenditure, Cmd 573 (London: HMSO, 1940).

Newspapers and periodicals

The Guardian/ The Manchester Guardian
Daily Telegraph
The New Statesman and Nation
The Observer
The Spectator
The Times

Film/television journals and trade papers

The Bioscope
Broadcast
Cinema Quarterly
Close Up
Daily Cinema
Documentary Film News
Documentary News Letter
Film Weekly
Kinematograph Weekly
Monthly Film Bulletin
Radio Times
Sight and Sound
Today's Cinema

Biographies, autobiographies and diaries

Attenborough, David, *A Life on Air* (London: BBC Books, 2002)

Balcon, Michael, *Michael Balcon presents ... A Lifetime of Films* (London: Hutchinson, 1969)

Barry, Michael, *From the Palace to the Grove* (London: Royal Television Society, 1992)

Clark, Kenneth, *The Other Half: A Self Portrait* (London: Hamish Hamilton, 1986 [1977])

Frankland, Noble, *History at War: The Campaigns of an Historian* (London: Giles de la Mare, 1998)

Halliwell, Leslie, *Seats in All Parts: Half a Lifetime at the Movies* (London: Granada, 1985)

Hardy, Forsyth, *John Grierson: A Documentary Biography* (London: Faber and Faber, 1979)

Hepworth, Cecil, *Came the Dawn: Memories of a Film Pioneer* (London: Pheonix House, 1951)

Jackson, Kevin, *Humphrey Jennings* (London: Picador, 2004)

Jackson, Pat, *A Retake Please! 'Night Mail' to 'Western Approaches'* (Liverpool: Liverpool University Press/Royal Naval Museum Publications, 1999)

Sussex, Elizabeth, *Lindsay Anderson* (London: Studio Vista, 1969)

Sutton, Paul (ed.), *Lindsay Anderson: The Diaries* (London: Methuen, 2004)

Watt, Harry, *Don't Look at the Camera* (London: Paul Elek, 1974)

Anthologies of film criticism

Aitken, Ian (ed.), *The Documentary Film Movement: An Anthology* (Edinburgh: Edinburgh University Press, 1998)

Bazin, André, *What Is Cinema? Volume I*, trans. Hugh Gray (Berkeley: University of California Press, 1967)

Bazin, André, *What Is Cinema? Volume II*, trans. Hugh Gray (Berkeley: University of California Press, 1971)

Cook, Christopher (ed.), *The Dilys Powell Film Reader* (Manchester: Carcanet Press, 1991)

Donald, James, Anne Friedberg, and Laura Marcus (eds), *Close Up 1927–1933: Cinema and Modernism* (London: Cassell, 1998)

Hardy, Forsyth (ed.), *Grierson on Documentary* (London: Collins, 1946)

Hardy, Forsyth (ed.), *Grierson on the Movies* (London: Faber and Faber, 1981)

Jackson, Kevin (ed.), *The Humphrey Jennings Film Reader* (Manchester: Carcanet Press, 1993)

Lejeune, Anthony (ed.), *The C. A. Lejeune Film Reader* (Manchester: Carcanet Press, 1991)

Orwell, Sonia, and Ian Angus (eds), *The Collected Essays, Journalism and Letters of George Orwell Volume 2: My Country Right or Left, 1940–1943* (Harmondsworth: Penguin, 1970)

Parkinson, David (ed.), *Mornings in the Dark: The Graham Greene Film Reader* (Manchester: Carcanet Press, 1993)

Petrie, Duncan, and Robert Kruger (eds), *A Paul Rotha Reader* (Exeter: University of Exeter Press, 1999)

Rotha, Paul, *Rotha on the Film* (London: Faber and Faber, 1958)

Books and monographs

Addison, Paul, *The Road to 1945: British Politics and the Second World War* (London: Jonathan Cape, 1975)

Aitken, Ian, *Film and Reform: John Grierson and the Documentary Film Movement* (London: Routledge, 1990)

Aitken, Ian, *Alberto Cavalcanti: Realism, Surrealism and National Cinemas* (Trowbridge: Flicks Books, 2000)

Aldgate, Anthony, *Cinema and History: British Newsreels and the Spanish Civil War* (London: Scolar Press, 1979)

Aldgate, Anthony, and Jeffrey Richards, *Britain Can Take It: The British Cinema in the Second World War* (Oxford: Basil Blackwell, 1986)

Andrew, J. Dudley, *The Major Film Theories: An Introduction* (Oxford: Oxford University Press, 1976)

Anthony, Scott, *Night Mail* (London: British Film Institute, 2007)

Anthony, Scott, *Public Relations and the Making of Modern Britain: Stephen Tallents and the Birth of a Progressive Media Profession* (Manchester: Manchester University Press, 2012)

Anthony, Scott, and James G. Mansell (eds), *The Projection of Britain: A History of the GPO Film Unit* (London: Palgrave Macmillan/British Film Institute, 2011)

Armes, Roy, *A Critical History of the British Cinema* (London: Secker & Warburg, 1978)

Arnheim, Rudolf, *Film as Art*, trans. L. M. Sieveking and Ian F. D. Morrow (London: Faber and Faber, 1958 [1932])

Arts Enquiry, *The Factual Film: A Survey Sponsored by the Dartington Hall Trustees* (London: Geoffrey Cumberlege/Oxford University Press, 1947)

Austin, Thomas, *Watching the World: Screen Documentary and Audiences* (Manchester: Manchester University Press, 2007)

Barnouw, Erik, *Documentary: A History of the Non-Fiction Film* (New York: Oxford University Press, 2nd rev. edn 1993 [1976])

Bauer, Petra, and Dan Kidner (eds), *Working Together: Notes on British Film Collectives in the 1970s* (Southend: Focal Point Gallery, 2013)

Beattie, Keith, *Humphrey Jennings* (Manchester: Manchester University Press, 2010)

Boon, Timothy, *Films of Fact: A History of Science in Documentary Films and Television* (London: Wallflower Press, 2008)

Briggs, Asa, *The History of Broadcasting in the United Kingdom. Volume IV: Sound and Vision 1945–1955* (Oxford: Oxford University Press, 1995)

Briggs, Asa, *The History of Broadcasting in the United Kingdom. Volume V: Competition 1955–1974* (Oxford: Oxford University Press, 1995)

Brown, Richard, and Barry Anthony, *A Victorian Film Enterprise: The History of the British Mutoscope and Biograph Company, 1897–1915* (Trowbridge: Flicks Books, 1999)

Burton, Alan, *The People's Cinema: Film and the Co-operative Movement* (London: British Film Institute, 1994)

Burton, Alan, *The British Co-operative Movement Film Catalogue* (Trowbridge: Flicks Books, 1997)

Burton, Alan, *The British Consumer Co-operative Movement and Film, 1890s–1960s* (Manchester: Manchester University Press, 2005)

Calder, Angus, *The People's War: Britain 1939–1945* (London: Jonathan Cape, 1969)

Cantril, Hadley, with Hazel Gaudet and Herta Herzog, *The Invasion from Mars: A Study in the Psychology of Panic* (Princeton: Princeton University Press, 1940)

Chanan, Michael, *The Dream That Kicks: The Prehistory and Early Years of Cinema in Britain* (London: Routledge, 2nd edn 1996 [1980])

Chapman, James, *The British at War: Cinema, State and Propaganda, 1939–1945* (London: I.B. Tauris, 1998)

Chibnall, Steve, and Brian McFarlane, *The British 'B' Film* (London: Palgrave Macmillan/ British Film Institute, 2009)

Conlin, Jonathan, *Civilisation* (London: Palgrave Macmillan/British Film Institute, 2009)

Corner, John, *The Art of Record: A Critical Introduction to Documentary* (Manchester: Manchester University Press, 1996)

Crisell, Andrew, *An Introductory History of British Broadcasting* (London: Routledge, 1997)

Curtis, Liz, *Ireland: The Propaganda War – The British Media and the Battle for Hearts and Minds* (London: Pluto Press, 1984)

Davy, Charles (ed.), *Footnotes to the Film* (London: Lovat Dickson, 1937)

Dickinson, Margaret, and Sarah Street, *Cinema and State: The Film Industry and the British Government 1927–84* (London: British Film Institute, 1985)

Dickinson, Margaret (ed.), *Rogue Reels: Oppositional Film in Britain, 1945–90* (London: British Film Institute, 1999)

Dillon, Robert, *History on British Television: Constructing nation, nationality and collective memory* (Manchester: Manchester University Press, 2010)

Doob, L. W., *Propaganda: Its Psychology and Technique* (New York: Henry Holt, 1935)

Downing, Taylor, *The World at War* (London: Palgrave Macmillan/British Film Institute, 2012)

Durgnat, Raymond, *A Mirror for England: British Movies from Austerity to Affluence* (London: Faber and Faber, 1970)

Ellis, Jack C., *John Grierson: A Guide to References and Resources* (Boston: G. K. Hall, 1986)

Ellis, John, *Visible Fictions: Cinema: Television: Video* (London: Routledge, 2nd edn 1992 [1982]).

Ellis, John, *Documentary: Witness and Self-revelation* (London: Routledge, 2012)

Elsaesser, Thomas (ed.), *Early Cinema: Space, Frame, Narrative* (London: British Film Institute, 1990)

Fuller, Graham (ed.), *Loach on Loach* (London: Faber and Faber, 1998)

Gardner, Colin, *Karel Reisz* (Manchester: Manchester University Press, 2006)

Goddard, Peter, John Corner and Kay Richardson, *Public Issue Television: World in Action, 1963–98* (Manchester: Manchester University Press, 2007)

Goodwin, Anthony, Paul Kerr and Ian Macdonald (eds), *BFI Dossier No. 19: Drama-Documentary* (London: British Film Institute, 1983)

Goodwin, Anthony, and Garry Whannel (eds), *Understanding Television* (London: Routledge, 1990)

Grieveson, Lee, and Colin MacCabe (eds), *Empire and Film* (London: British Film Institute/Palgrave Macmillan, 2011)

Grieveson, Lee, and Colin MacCabe (eds), *Film and the End of Empire* (London: British Film Institute/Palgrave Macmillan, 2011)

Hanna, Emma, *The Great War on the Small Screen: Representing the First World War in Contemporary Britain* (Edinburgh: Edinburgh University Press, 2009)

Harper, Sue, *Women in British Cinema: Mad, Bad and Dangerous to Know* (London: Continuum, 2000)

Harper, Sue, and Vincent Porter, *British Cinema of the 1950s: The Decline of Deference* (Oxford: Oxford University Press, 2003)

Hawthorn, Jeremy (ed.), *Propaganda, Persuasion and Polemic* (London: Edward Arnold, 1987)

Hedling, Erik, *Lindsay Anderson: Maverick Film-Maker* (London: Cassell, 1998)

Higson, Andrew, *Waving the Flag: Constructing a National Cinema in Britain* (Oxford: Clarendon Press, 1995)

Higson, Andrew (ed.), *Dissolving Views: Key Writings on British Cinema* (London: Cassell, 1996)

Higson, Andrew (ed.), *Young and Innocent?: The Cinema in Britain 1896–1900* (Exeter: University of Exeter Press, 2000)

Hill, John, *Sex, Clas and Realism: British Cinema 1956–1963* (London: British Film Institute, 1986)

Hill, John, *Ken Loach: The Politics of Film and Television* (London: British Film Institute/ Palgrave Macmillan, 2011)

Hodgkinson, Anthony W., and Rodney E. Sheratsky, *Humphrey Jennings: More Than a Maker of Films* (Hanover: University of New England Press, 1982)

Hogenkamp, Bert, *Deadly Parallels: Film and the Left in Britain 1929–39* (London: Lawrence and Wishart, 1986)

Hogenkamp, Bert, *Workers' Newsreels in the 1920s and 1930s: Our History Pamphlet 68* (London: History Group of the Communist Party, n.d.)

Holland, Patricia, *The Angry Buzz: 'This Week' and Current Affairs Television* (London: I. B. Tauris, 2006)

Horne, Philip, and Peter Swaab (eds), *Thorold Dickinson: A World of Film* (Manchester: Manchester University Press, 2008)

Houston, Penelope, *The Contemporary Cinema* (Harmondsworth: Penguin, 1963)

Issari, M. Ali, and Doris A. Paul, *What is Cinéma Vérité?* (Metuchen, NJ: Scarecrow Press, 1979)

Izod, John, and Richard Kilborn with Matthew Hibberd (eds), *From Grierson to the Docu- Soap: Breaking the Boundaries* (Luton: University of Luton Press, 2000)

Jennings, Mary-Lou (ed.), *Humphrey Jennings: Film-Maker, Painter, Poet* (London: British Film Institute/Riverside Studios, 1982)

Jones, Stephen G., *The British Labour Movement and Film, 1918–1939* (London: Routledge & Kegan Paul, 1987)

Katz, Ephraim, *The Macmillan International Film Encyclopedia* (London: Macmillan, 1996)

Lacey, Stephen, *Cathy Come Home* (London: Palgrave Macmillan/British Film Institute, 2011)

Lambert, R. S., *Propaganda* (London: Nelson and Sons, 1938)

Logan, Philip C., *Humphrey Jennings and British Documentary Film: A Re-Assessment* (Farnham: Ashgate, 2011)

Lovell, Alan, and Jim Hillier, *Studies in Documentary* (London: Secker & Warburg/British Film Institute, 1972)

Low, Rachael, and Roger Manvell, *The History of the British Film 1896–1906* (London: George Allen & Unwin, 1948)

Low, Rachael, *The History of the British Film 1914–1918* (London: George Allen & Unwin, 1950)

Low, Rachael, *The History of the British Film 1918–1929* (London: George Allen & Unwin, 1971)

Low, Rachael, *The History of the British Film 1929–1939: Documentary and Educational Films of the 1930s* (London: George Allen & Unwin, 1979)

Low, Rachael, *The History of the British Film 1929–1939: Films of Comment and Persuasion in the 1930s* (London: George Allen & Unwin, 1979)

Low, Rachael, *The History of the British Film: Film Making in 1930s Britain* (London: George Allen & Unwin, 1985)

MacPherson, Don (ed.), *Traditions of Independence: British Cinema in the Thirties* (London: British Film Institute, 1980)

McKernan, Luke, *Topical Budget: The Great British News Film* (London: British Film Institute, 1992)

McKernan, Luke, *Charles Urban: Pioneering the Non-Fiction Film in Britain and America, 1897–1925* (University of Exeter Press, 2013)

McLaine, Ian, *Ministry of Morale: Home Front Morale and the Ministry of Information in World War II* (London: George Allen & Unwin, 1979)

McLane, Betsy A., *A New History of Documentary* (New York: Continuum, 2nd edn 2012)

Macnab, Geoffrey, *J. Arthur Rank and the British Film Industry* (London: Routledge, 1993)

Manvell, Roger, *Film* (Harmondsworth: Penguin, rev. edn 1946 [1944])

Manvell, Roger, *The Film and the Public* (Harmondsworth: Penguin, 1955)

Manvell, Roger, *Films and the Second World War* (London: J. M. Dent, 1974)

Marris, Paul (ed.), *BFI Dossier No. 16: Paul Rotha* (London: British Film Institute, 1982)

Marwick, Arthur, *The Nature of History* (London: Macmillan, 3rd edn 1989 [1968])

Marwick, Arthur, *The Sixties: Cultural Revolution in Britain, France, Italy and the United States, c.1958–c.1974* (Oxford: Oxford University Press, 1998)

Montagu, Ivor, *Film World: A Guide to Cinema* (Harmondsworth: Penguin, 1964)

Morgan, Kenneth O., *The People's Peace: British History 1945–1990* (Oxford: Oxford University Press, 1990)

Murphy, Robert, *Realism and Tinsel: Cinema and Society in Britain, 1939–48* (London: Routledge, 1989)

Murphy, Robert (ed.), *The British Cinema Book* (London: British Film Institute, 1997)

Murphy, Robert (ed.), *Directors in British and Irish Cinema: A Reference Companion* (London: British Film Institute, 2006)

Newton, Darrell M., *Paving the Empire Road: BBC Television and Black Britons* (Manchester: Manchester University Press, 2011)

Paget, Derek, *True Stories: Documentary Drama on Radio, Stage and Television* (Manchester: Manchester University Press, 1990)

Paget, Derek, *No Other Way to Tell It: Docudrama on Film and Television* (Manchester: Manchester University Press, 2nd edn 2011)

Pines, Jim, and Paul Willemen (eds), *Questions of Third Cinema* (London: British Film Institute, 1989).

Political and Economic Planning, *The British Film Industry: A report on its history and present organisation, with special reference to the economic problems of British feature film production* (London: Political and Economic Planning, 1952)

Potter, Jeremy, *Independent Television in Britain. Volume 2: Politics and Control, 1968–80* (London: Macmillan, 1989)

Potter, Jeremy, *Independent Television in Britain. Volume III: Companies and Pro-grammes 1968–80* (London: Macmillan, 1990)

Priestley, J. B., *Postscripts* (London: William Heinemann, 1940)

Pronay, Nicholas, and D. W. Spring (eds), *Propaganda, Politics and Film, 1918–45* (London: Macmillan, 1982)

Rattigan, Neil, *This Is England: British Cinema and the People's War, 1939–1945* (London: Associated University Presses, 2001)

Reeves, Nicholas, *Official British Film Propaganda During the First World War* (London: Croom Helm, 1986)

Richards, Jeffrey, *The Age of the Dream Palace: Cinema and Society in Britain 1930–1939* (London: Routledge & Kegan Paul, 1984)

Richards, Jeffrey, *Thorold Dickinson: The Man and His Films* (London: Croom Helm, 1986)

Richards, Jeffrey, and Anthony Aldgate, *Best of British: Cinema and Society 1930–1970* (Oxford: Basil Blackwell, 1983)

Richards, Jeffrey, and Dorothy Sheridan (eds), *Mass-Observation at the Movies* (London: Routledge & Kegan Paul, 1987)

Robertson, James. C., *The British Board of Film Censors: Film Censorship in Britain, 1986–1950* (London: Croom Helm, 1985)

Robertson, James C., *The Hidden Cinema: British Film Censorship in Action, 1913–1975* (London: Routledge, 1989)

Rosenthal, Alan (ed.), *New Challenges for Documentary* (Berkeley: University of California Press, 1988)

Rotha, Paul, *Documentary Diary: An Informal History of the British Documentary Film, 1928–1939* (New York: Hill and Wang, 1973)

Rotha, Paul, with Richard Griffith, *The Film Till Now: A Survey of World Cinema* (London: Spring Books, rev. edn 1967 [1930])

Rotha, Paul, with Sinclair Road and Richard Griffith, *Documentary Film* (New York: Hastings, 3rd edn 1952 [1936])

Russell, Patrick, *100 British Documentaries* (London: British Film Institute, 2007)

Russell, Patrick, and James Piers Taylor (eds), *Shadows of Progress: Documentary Film in Post-War Britain* (Basingstoke: Palgrave Macmillan/British Film Institute, 2010)

Ryall, Tom, *Alfred Hitchcock and the British Cinema* (London: Croom Helm, 1986)

Schlesinger, Philip, Graham Murdock and Philip Elliot, *Televising Terrorism* (London: Comedia, 1983)

Sexton, Jamie, *Alternative Film Culture in Interwar Britain* (Exeter: University of Exeter Press, 2008)

Spicer, Andrew, *Sydney Box* (Manchester: Manchester University Press, 2006)

Stollery, Martin, *Alternative Empires: European Modernist Cinemas and Cultures of Imperialism* (Exeter: University of Exeter Press, 2000)

Sussex, Elizabeth, *The Rise and Fall of British Documentary: The Story of the Film Movement Founded by John Grierson* (Berkeley: University of California Press, 1975)

Swann, Paul, *The British Documentary Film Movement, 1926–1946* (Cambridge: Cambridge University Press, 1989)

Sydney-Smith, Susan, *Beyond Dixon of Dock Green: Early British Police Series* (London: I.B. Tauris, 2002)

Tallents, Stephen, *The Projection of England* (London: 1932)

Taylor, A. J. P., *English History 1914–1945* (Oxford: Oxford University Press, 1965)

Taylor, Philip M., *The Projection of Britain: British Overseas Publicity and Propaganda 1919–1939* (Cambridge: Cambridge University Press, 1981)

Taylor, Philip M. (ed.), *Britain and the Cinema in the Second World War* (London: Macmillan, 1982)

Thompson, Kristin, *Exporting Entertainment: America in the World Film Market 1907–1934* (London: British Film Institute, 1985)

Thompson, Kristin, and David Bordwell, *Film History: An Introduction* (New York: McGraw-Hill, 1994)

Thorpe, Frances, and Nicholas Pronay, with Clive Coultass, *British Official Films in the Second World War* (Oxford: Clio Press, 1980)

Toulmin, Vanessa, Simon Popple, and Patrick Russell (eds), *The Lost World of Mitchell and Kenyon: Edwardian Britain on Film* (London: British Film Institute, 2004)

Tucker, David (ed.), *British Social Realism in the Arts since 1940* (Basingstoke: Palgrave Macmillan, 2011)

Tudor, Andrew, *Theories of Film* (London: Secker & Warburg/British Film Institute, 1974)

Urban, Charles, *The Cinematograph in Science, Education, and Matters of State* (London: Charles Urban Trading Company, 1907)

Vaughan, Dai, *Portrait of an Invisible Man: The Working Life of Stewart McAllister, Film Editor* (London: British Film Institute, 1983)

Vaughan, Dai, *For Documentary: Twelve Essays* (Berkeley: University of California Press, 1999)

Walker, Alexander, *Hollywood, England: The British Film Industry in the Sixties* (London: Michael Joseph, 1974)

Welch, David (ed.), *Propaganda, Power and Persuasion: From World War I to Wikileaks* (London: I. B. Tauris, 2014)

White, Amber Blanco, *The New Propaganda* (London: Victor Gollancz, 1939)

White, Basil, *The Lobe View: A Personal Perspective on World Cinema* (London: Secker & Warburg, 1974)

Winston, Brian, *Claiming the Real: The Griersonian Documentary and its Legitimations* (London: British Film Institute, 1995)

Winston, Brian, *'Fires Were Started-'* (London: British Film Institute, 1999)

Winter, Jay, *Sites of Memory, Sites of Mourning: The Great War in European Cultural History* (Cambridge: Cambridge University Press, 1995)

Wollen, Peter, *Signs and Meaning in the Cinema* (London: Secker & Warburg/British Film Institute, 1969)

Wood, Linda (ed.), *British Film Industry: A BFI Reference Guide* (London: British Film Institute, 1980)

Articles and book chapters

Aldgate, Tony, 'Mr Capra Goes to War: Frank Capra, the British Army Film Unit, and Anglo- American travails in the production of *Tunisian Victory*', *Historical Journal of Film, Radio and Television*, 11: 1 (1991), pp.21–39.

Anderson, Lindsay, 'Alfred Hitchcock', *Sequence*, 9 (1948), pp.113–23.

Anderson, Lindsay, 'Only Connect: Some Aspects of the Work of Humphrey Jennings', *Sight and Sound*, 23: 4 (1954), pp.181–6.

Anthony, Scott, 'The Future's in the Air: Imperial Airways and the British Documentary Film Movement', *Journal of British Cinema and Television*, 8: 3 (2011), pp.301–21.

Auguiste, Reece, '*Handsworth Songs*: Some Background Notes', *Framework*, 35 (1988), pp.4–8.

Aitken, Ian, 'The British Documentary Film Movement', in Robert Murphy (ed.), *The British Cinema Book* (London: British Film Institute, 1997), pp.58–67.

Badsey, S. C., '*Battle of the Somme*: British war-propaganda', *Historical Journal of Film, Radio and Television*, 3: 2 (1983), pp.99–115.

Baird, Thomas, 'Films and the Public Services in Great Britain', *Public Opinion Quarterly*, 2: 1 (1938), pp.96–9.

Bell, Elaine, 'The Origins of British Television Documentary: The BBC 1946–55', in John Corner (ed.), *Documentary and the Mass Media* (London: Edward Arnold, 1986), pp.65–80.

Bottomore, Stephen, 'Rediscovering Early Non-Fiction Film', *Film History*, 13: X (2001), pp.160–73.

Burgess, Colin, 'Sixty Years of Shell Film Sponsorship, 1934–94', *Journal of British Cinema and Television*, 7: 2 (2010), pp.213–31.

Caughie, John, 'Progressive Television and Documentary Drama', *Screen*, 21: 3 (1980), pp.9–34.

Chapman, James, ' "The Yanks are Shown to Such Advantage": Anglo-American rivalry in the production of *The True Glory* (1945)', *Historical Journal of Film, Radio and Television*, 16: 4 (1996), pp.533–54.

Chapman, James, 'Cinema, monarchy and the making of heritage: *A Queen is Crowned*', in Claire Monk and Amy Sargeant (eds), *British Historical Cinema* (London: Routledge, 2002), pp.82–91.

Chapman, James, 'The BBC and the Censorship of *The War Game* (1965)', *Journal of Contemporary History*, 41: 1 (2006), pp.75–94.

Chapman, James, 'Re-presenting War: British television drama-documentary and the Second World War', *European Journal of Cultural Studies*, 10: 1 (2007), pp.13–33.

Chapman, James, 'Television and History: *The World at War*', *Historical Journal of Film, Radio and Television*, 31: 2 (2011), pp.247–75.

Colls, Robert, and Philip Dodd, 'Representing the Nation: British Documentary Film, 1930–45', *Screen*, 26: 1 (1985), pp.21–33.

Connelly, M. L., '*The Great War*, Part 13: The Devil is Coming', *Historical Journal of Film, Radio and Television*, 22: 1 (2002), pp.21–8.

Constantine, Stephen, ' "Bringing the Empire alive": the Empire Marketing Board and imperial propaganda, 1926–33', in John M. Mackenzie (ed.), *Imperialism and Popular Culture* (Manchester: Manchester University Press, 1986), pp.192–231.

Cook, John R., ' "Don't forget to look *into* the camera!": Peter Watkins' approach to acting with facts', *Studies in Documentary Film*, 4: 3 (2010), pp.227–39.

Cook, John R., and Patrick Murphy, 'After the Bomb Dropped: The Cinema Half-Life of *The War Game*', *Journal of Popular British Cinema*, 3 (2000), pp.129–32.

Coultass, Clive, 'The Ministry of Information and Documentary Film, 1939–45', *Imperial War Museum Review*, 4 (1989), pp.103–11.

Crothall, Geoffrey, 'Images of Regeneration: film propaganda and the British slum clearance campaign, 1933–1938', *Historical Journal of Film, Radio and Television*, 19: 3 (1999), pp.339–58.

Cull, Nicholas J., 'Peter Watkins' *Culloden* and the Alternative Form in Historical Filmmaking', *Film International*, 1 (2003), pp.48–53.

Dover, Caroline, ' "Crisis" in British Documentary Television: the End of a Genre?', *Journal of British Cinema and Television*, 1: 2 (2004), pp.242–59.

Easen, Sarah, 'Film and the Festival of Britain', in Ian MacKillop and Neil Sinyard (eds), *British Cinema of the 1950s: A Celebration* (Manchester: Manchester University Press, 2000), pp.51–63.

Ellis, Jack C., 'The Final Years of British Documentary as the Grierson Movement', *Journal of Film and Video*, 36: 4 (1984), pp.41–9.

Ellis, John, 'Art, Culture, Quality: Terms for a Cinema in the Forties and Seventies', *Screen*, 19: 3 (1978), pp.9–49.

Ellis, John, 'Victory of the Voice?', *Screen*, 22: 2 (1981), pp.69–72.

Enticknap, Leo, '*This Modern Age* and the British Non-Fiction Film', in Justine Ashby and Andrew Higson (eds), *British Cinema, Past and Present* (London: Routledge, 2000), pp.207–20.

Fox, Jo, 'John Grierson, His "Documentary Boys" and the British Ministry of Information, 1939–1942', *Historical Journal of Film, Radio and Television*, 25: 3 (2005), pp.245–69.

Fox, Jo, 'From Documentary Film to Documentary Television: John Grierson and *This Wonderful World*', *Journal of British Cinema and Television*, 10: 3 (2013), pp.498–523.

Fox, Jo, ' "To Be a Woman": Female Labour and Memory in Documentary Film Production, 1929–50', *Journal of British Cinema and Television*, 10: 3 (2013), pp.584–602.

Garnham, Nicholas, 'TV Documentary and Ideology', *Screen*, 13: 2 (1972), pp.109–15.

Gilroy, Paul, and Jim Pines, '*Handsworth Songs*: Audiences/Aesthetics/Independence. Interview with the Black Audio Collective', *Framework*, 35 (1988), pp.9–17.

Grant, Mariel, 'Towards a Central Office of Information: Continuity and change in British government information policy, 1939–51', *Journal of Contemporary History*, 34: 1 (1999), pp.49–67.

Haggith, Toby, 'Post-War Reconstruction as Depicted in Official British Films of the Second World War', *Imperial War Museum*, 17 (1992), pp.34–45.

Haggith, Toby, 'D-Day Filming – For Real: A Comparison of "Truth" and "Reality" in *Saving Private Ryan* and Combat Film by the British Army's Film and Photographic Film Unit', *Film History*, 14: 304 (2002), pp.332–55.

Hardy, Forsyth, 'The British Documentary Film', in Michael Balcon, Ernest Lindgren, Forsyth Hardy and Roger Manvell, *Twenty Years of British Film 1925–1945* (London: Falcon Press, 1947), pp.45–60.

Hiley, Nicholas, ' "No mixed bathing": The creation of the British Board of Film Censors in 1913', *Journal of Popular British Cinema*, 3 (2000), pp.5–19.

Higson, Andrew, ' "Britain's outstanding contribution to the film": the documentary-realist tradition', in Charles Barr (ed.), *All Our Yesterdays: 90 Years of British Cinema* (London: British Film Institute, 1986), pp.72–97.

Hodgkins, John, 'Hearts and Minds and Bodies: Reconsidering the Cinematic Language of *The Battle of the Somme*', *Film and History*, 38: 1 (2008), pp.9–19.

Hollins, T. J., 'The Conservative Party and Film Propaganda Between the Wars', *English Historical Review*, 96: 379 (1981), pp.359–69.

Hood, Stuart, 'John Grierson and the Documentary Film Movement', in James Curran and Vincent Porter (eds), *British Cinema History* (London: Weidenfeld and Nicolson, 1983), pp.99–112.

Irwin, Mary M., '*Monitor*: The Creation of the Television Arts Documentary', *Journal of British Cinema and Television*, 8: 3 (2011), pp.322–36.

Isaacs, Jeremy, 'All Our Yesterdays', in David Cannadine (ed.), *History and the Media* (London: Palgrave Macmillan, 2004).

Jones, Ben, and Rebecca Searle, 'Humphrey Jennings, the Left and the Experience of Modernity in mid twentieth-century Britain', *History Workshop Journal*, 75 (2013), pp.190–212.

Kuhn, Annette, '*Desert Victory* and the People's War', *Screen*, 22: 2 (1981), pp.45–68.

Leggott, James, and Tobias Hochscherf, ' "From Marks and Spencer to Marx and Engels": A transnational DEFA and Ambr Film documentary project across the Iron Curtain', *Studies in Documentary Film*, 2: 2 (2008), pp.123–35.

Long, Paul, Yasmeen Baig-Clifford, and Roger Shannon, ' "What We're Trying to Do is Make Popular Politics": The Birmingham Film and Video Workshop', *Historical Journal of Film, Radio and Television*, 33: 3 (2013), pp. 377–95.

Lovell, Alan, 'The Unknown Cinema of Britain', *Cinema Journal*, 11: 2 (1972), pp.1–9.

Lovell, Alan, 'Notes on British Film Culture', *Screen*, 13: 2 (1972), pp.5–16.

Lynch, Dennis, 'The Worst Journey in the World: Herbert G. Ponting in the Antarctic, 1910–1912', *Film History*, 3: 4 (1989), pp.291–306.

MacMurraugh-Kavanagh, M. K., 'The BBC and the Birth of *The Wednesday Play*, 1962–66: institutional containment versus "agitational contemporaneity" ', *Historical Journal of Film, Radio and Television*, 17: 3 (1997), pp.367–81.

Matuszewski, Boleslaw, 'A New Source of History' [1898], trans. Laura Marks and Diana Koszarski, *Film History*, 7: 3 (1995), pp.322–5.

Newsinger, Jack, 'The Interface of Documentary and Fiction: The Amber Film Workshop and Regional Documentary Practice', *Journal of British Cinema and Television*, 6: 3 (2009), pp.387–406.

Paget, Derek, '*Cathy Come Home* and "Accuracy" in British Television Drama', *Theatre Quarterly*, 15: 1 (1999), pp.75–90.

Paris, Michael, 'Enduring Heroes: British Feature Films and the First World War', in Michael Paris (ed.), *The First World War and Popular Cinema: 1914 to the Present* (Edinburgh: Edinburgh University Press, 1999), pp.51–73.

Pötzsch, Holger, 'Renegotiating difficult pasts: Two documentary dramas on Bloody Sunday, Derry 1972', *Memory Studies*, 5: 2 (2012), pp.206–22.

Pronay, Nicholas, 'British Newsreels in the 1930s: 1. Audience and Producers', *History*, 56 (1971), pp.411–18.

Pronay, Nicholas, 'British Newsreels in the 1930s: 2: Their Policies and Impact', *History*, 57 (1972), pp.63–72.

Pronay, Nicholas, 'The First Reality: Film Censorship in Liberal England', in K. R. M. Short (ed.), *Feature Films as History* (London: Croom Helm, 1981), pp.113–37.

Pronay, Nicholas, ' "The Land of Promise": The Projection of Peace Aims in Britain', in K. R. M. Short (ed.), *Film and Radio Propaganda in World War II* (London: Croom Helm, 1983), pp.51–77.

Ramsden, J. A., '*The Great War*: The making of the series', *Historical Journal of Film, Radio and Television*, 22: 1 (2002), pp.7–19.

Reeves, Nicholas, 'Cinema, spectatorship and propaganda: *Battle of the Somme* (1916) and its contemporary audience', *Historical Journal of Film, Radio and Television*, 17: 1 (1997), pp.5–28.

Richards, Jeffrey, 'The British Board of Film Censors and Content Control in the 1930s (1): Images of Britain', *Historical Journal of Film, Radio and Television*, 2: 1 (1981), pp.97–116.

Richards, Jeffrey, 'Humphrey Jennings: The Poet as Propagandist', in Mark Connelly and David Welch (eds), *War and the Media: Reportage and Propaganda 1900–2003* (London: I. B. Tauris, 2005), pp.127–38.

Robins, Kevin, Frank Webster, and Michael Pickering, 'Propaganda, Information and Social Control', in Jeremy Hawthorn (ed.), *Propaganda, Persuasion and Polemic* (London: Edward Arnold, 1987), pp.1–17.

Rowland, Robert, '*Panorama* in the Sixties', in Anthony Aldgate, James Chapman and Arthur Marwick (eds), *Windows on the Sixties: Exploring Key Texts of Media and Culture* (London: I. B. Tauris, 2000), pp.154–82.

Rowson, Simon, 'A Statistical Survey of the Cinema Industry in Great Britain in 1934', *Journal of the Royal Statistical Society*, 7: 2 (1987), pp.129–41.

Sexton, Jamie, 'Grierson's Machines: *Drifters*, the Documentary Film Movement and the Negotiation of Modernity', *Canadian Journal of Film Studies*, 11: 1 (2002), pp.40–59.

Short, K. R. M., 'RAF Bomber Command's *Target for Tonight*', *Historical Journal of Film, Radio and Television*, 17: 2 (1997), pp.181–218.

Shaw, Tony, 'The BBC, the State and Cold War Culture: The case of television's *The War Game* (1965)', *Past & Present*, 494 (2006), pp.1351–84.

Sills-Jones, Dafydd, '*The Second World War in Colour*: The UK History Documentary Boom and Colour Archive', *Journal of British Cinema and Television*, 7: 1 (2010), pp.115–130.

Smith, Malcolm, 'Narrative and Ideology in *Listen to Britain*', in Jeremy Hawthorn (ed.), *Narrative: From Malory to Motion Pictures* (London: Edward Arnold, 1987), pp.143–57.

Smither, Roger, ' "A Wonderful Idea of the Fighting": The Question of Fakes in *The Battle of the Somme*', *Imperial War Museum Review*, 3 (1988), pp.4–16.

Stanley-Price, Nicholas, 'Paul Rotha and the making of Strand Films' *Air Outpost* (1937)', *Historical Journal of Film, Radio and Television*, 32: 1 (2012), pp.95–111.

Stollery, Martin, and John Corner, 'The Postwar British Documentary Movement – Decline or Transition?', *Journal of British Cinema and Television*, 10: 3 (2012), pp.387–94.

Sussex, Elizabeth, 'Grierson on Documentary: The Last Interview', *Film Quarterly*, 26: 1 (1972), pp. 24–30.

Sussex, Elizabeth, 'Cavalcanti in England', *Sight and Sound*, 44: 4 (1975), pp.206–9.

Sussex, Elizabeth, 'Getting It Right', *Sight and Sound*, 51: 1 (1981–2), pp.10–15.

Sussex, Elizabeth, 'The Fate of Film F3080', *Sight and Sound*, 53: 2 (1984), pp.92–7.

Swann, Paul, 'John Grierson and the GPO Film Unit, 1933–1939', *Historical Journal of Film, Radio and Television*, 3: 1 (1983), pp.17–34.

Vail, John, and Robert G. Hollands, 'Cultural Work and Transformative Arts: The dilemmas of the Amber Collective', *Journal of Cultural Economy*, 5: 3 (2012), pp.337–53.

Ward, Kenneth, 'British Documentaries in the 1930s', *History*, 62 (1977), pp.426–31.

Wildman, Charlotte, '*A City Speaks*: The Projection of Civic Identity in Manchester', *Twentieth Century British History*, 23: 1 (2012), pp.80–99.

Winston, Brian, 'The Griersonian Tradition Postwar: Decline or Transition?', *Journal of British Cinema and Television*, 11: 1 (2014), pp.101–15.

Young, Neil, 'Forever Amber: An Interview with Ellin Hare and Murray Martin of the Amber Film Collective', *Critical Quarterly*, 43: 4 (2001), pp.61–80.

Unpublished papers and theses

Enticknap, Leo, 'The Non-Fiction Film in Britain, 1945–51', PhD thesis, University of Exeter, 1999.

Lovell, Alan, 'The British Cinema: The Unknown Cinema', British Film Institute Education Seminar, 13 March 1969, typescript held by the BFI Reuben Library.

Waymark, Peter Astley Grosvenor, 'Television and the Cultural Revolution: The BBC under Hugh Carleton Greene', PhD thesis, The Open University, 2005.

Index

Printed and bound by CPI Group (UK) Ltd, Croydon, CR0 4YY

009673646